CARIBBEAN

D0316232

James Hamlyn

 Publishing

Page 3: *Sunset off the coast of Jamaica*
Page 4: *Cruise liner at Ocho Rios, Jamaica*
Page 5: *Bar worker, Jamaica*
Page 6: *Bougainvillea and coconut palm, Bequia*
Page 7 (b): *Local art work from Martinque*
Page 8: *Aerial view of Saint-Martin*
Page 67: *Darkwood Beach, Antigua*
Page 105: *A pelican, Saint-Martin*
Page 239: *Policeman, Jamaica*
Page 269: *Food stall, Jamaica*

Written by James Hamlyn
Original photography by Peter Baker
Revisions by Emma Stanford
Reprinted 2002. Information verified and updated
Revised fourth edition 2000
Reprinted with new cover 1999
Reprinted Oct 1998
Revised second edition 1998
First published 1994

Edited, designed, produced and distributed by AA Publishing.
Maps © The Automobile Association 1994, 1998, 2000, 2002

The contents of this publication are believed correct at the time of printing. Nevertheless, the publishers cannot be held responsible for any errors or omissions or for changes in the details given in this guide or for the consequences of any reliance on the information provided by the same. Assessments of attractions, hotels, restaurants and so forth are based upon the author's own personal experience and, therefore, descriptions given in this guide necessarily contain an element of subjective opinion which may not reflect the publishers' opinion or dictate a reader's own experiences on another occasion. We have tried to ensure accuracy in this guide, but things do change and we would be grateful if readers would advise us of any inaccuracies they may encounter.

A CIP catalogue record for this book is available from the British Library.

ISBN 0 7495 2279 8

Published by AA Publishing (a trading name of Automobile Association Developments Limited, whose registered office is Millstream, Maidenhead Road, Windsor, Berkshire, SL4 5GD. Registered number 1878835).

Colour separation by LC Repro, Aldermaston
Printed and bound in Italy by Printer Trento srl

AA World Travel Guides publish over 300 guidebooks to a full range of cities, countries and regions across the world. Find out more about AA Publishing and the wide range of services the AA provides by visiting our website at www.theAA.com

How to use this book

ORGANISATION

The Caribbean Is,
The Caribbean Was
Discusses aspects of life and culture
in the contemporary Caribbean
and explores significant periods in
its history.

A–Z
Breaks down the islands into regional
chapters, and covers places to visit,
including walks and drives. Within
this section fall the Focus On articles,
which consider a variety of subjects in
greater detail.

Travel Facts
Contains the strictly practical
information vital for a successful trip.

Hotels and Restaurants
Lists recommended establishments
throughout the Caribbean, giving a
brief summary of their attractions.

KEY TO ADMISSION CHARGES
Standard admission charges are
categorised in this book as following:

Inexpensive: under US$5
Moderate: US$5–US$10
Expensive: over US$10

ABOUT THE RATINGS
Most places described in this book
have been given a separate rating.
These are as follows:

► ► ►   Do not miss

► ►   Highly recommended

►   Worth seeing

MAPS
Some of the maps in this book use
internationally agreed symbols to
denote nation states:

BS   Bahamas
C   Cuba
CO   Colombia
CR   Costa Rica
DOM   Dominican Republic
HN   Honduras
NIC   Nicaragua
RH   Haiti
YV   Venezuela

Contents

How to use this book 4

Contents pages 5–7

My Caribbean 8

THE CARIBBEAN IS 9–24
Landscapes 10–11
People 12–13
Farming and fishing 14–15
Religion 16–17
Politics 18–19
Tourism 20–21
Food and drink 22–24

THE CARIBBEAN WAS 25–37
Arawaks and Caribs 26–27
Christopher Columbus 28–29
Conquest and trade 30–31
Settlers and slaves 32–33
Sugar 34–35
Emancipation 36–37

A–Z

The Windward Islands 38–65
Dominica 41–45
Grenada 46–52
The Grenadines 53–55
St Lucia 56–63
St Vincent 64–65
Focus On
The Carib people 43
River bathing 45
Spices 48
Markets 50
When the boat comes in 54
Bananas 58

Folklore 61
Winds and eruptions 62–63

The Leeward Islands 66–87
Anguilla 70–71
Antigua and Barbuda 72–77
Montserrat 78–81
Nevis 82–3
St Kitts (St Christopher) 84–87
Focus On
Marine life 74–75
Nelson's Dockyard 77
Caribbean music 80–81
Forts 87

The Virgin Islands 88–103
Tortola 92
Virgin Gorda 93–95
Smaller British Virgin Islands 96
Sir Francis Drake Channel 97
St Croix 98
St John 99–101
St Thomas 102–103
Focus On
Sailing and watersports 94
Scuba-diving 95
Pirates 100–101

Walk
Charlotte Amalie 103

The French Antilles 104–123
Guadeloupe 108–113
Martinique 114–119
Saint-Barthélemy 120–121
Saint-Martin 122–123
Focus On
Walking and rain forests 111
Caribbean fauna 116–117

The Netherlands Antilles
124–143
Aruba 128–129
Bonaire 130–131
Curaçao 132–135
Saba 136–137
Sint Eustatius 138–139
Sint Maarten 140–143
Focus On
Caribbean architecture 141
Tropical fruits 143

Other Caribbean States 144–238
Jamaica 146–161
The Cayman Islands 162–165
Cuba 166–175
Haiti 176–179
The Dominican Republic 182–193
Puerto Rico 194–211
Barbados 212–223
Trinidad and Tobago 224–238
Focus On
Port Royal 151
Jamaican music 152
Bob Marley 156

Rastas 161
Cigars 172
Voodoo 180–181
Palm trees 189
Sugar 191
Coral and karst 200
Fishing 202
Caribbean flora 206–207
Gambling and games 209
Cricket and baseball 219
Rum 221
Turtles 230
Carnival 234–235
Calypso 238
Walk
Old San Juan 205

TRAVEL FACTS 239–268

HOTELS AND RESTAURANTS
269–283

Index 284–288

Acknowledgements 288

Maps and plans
Western Caribbean IFC
The Windward Islands 39
Dominica 41
Grenada 46
The Grenadines 53
St Lucia 56
St Vincent 64
The Leeward Islands 66
Anguilla 70
Antigua 72

Barbuda 76
Montserrat 78
Nevis 82
St Kitts (St Christopher) 84
The Virgin Islands 88–89
Charlotte Amalie walk 103
The French Antilles 104
Guadeloupe 108
Martinique 114
Saint-Barthélemy 120
Saint-Martin 122
Aruba, Bonaire and Curaçao 124
Saba, Sint Eustatius
  and Sint Maarten 125
Aruba 128
Bonaire 130

Curaçao 132
Saba 136
Sint Eustatius 138
Sint Maarten 140
Jamaica 146–147
Grand Cayman 164
Little Cayman and Cayman
  Brac 165
Cuba 166–167
Haiti 176–177
The Dominican Republic 182–183
Puerto Rico 194–195
Old San Juan walk 205
Barbados 212–213
Trinidad and Tobago 224–225
Eastern Caribbean IBC

James Hamlyn's childhood was spent on the move around the world – a habit that has stuck, particularly since he discovered the Caribbean islands more than a decade ago. His time now is spent island-hopping, checking out the bars and restaurants, and perfecting his skills with Caribbean dances such as the merengue. He has written several guidebooks to the Caribbean as well as many articles for American and British newspapers and magazines.

My Caribbean

Carnival. A sea of satin costumes shimmers and sparkles in the tropical sun; masqueraders strut and thrust, swaying at the hip, midriffs clamped in a conga-line like a massive sequinned snake. The noise is deafening – close at hand the raucous clanging of steel bands, elsewhere the thunder of amplified soca drumbeats. Carnival typifies the exuberance of the Caribbean – the colour, the high spirits and the irresistible dancing rhythms. To be part of it is an amazing experience.

After the week's nonstop dancing at Carnival, you will actually need a vacation, but then that's the Caribbean's speciality. Somewhere quiet, perhaps, on a deserted beach, a place to rest and let the ringing in your ears subside with a cocktail and an uninterrupted view over the sea to the sunset. An easygoing life among the charming West Indian people, in a setting of startling tropical beauty and gentle reggae music – this is the other side to the islands.

The Caribbean islands are ideal for a little laziness, but after a while I begin to get the itch for activity. An ideal day would be spent scuba-diving or windsurfing in the morning, enjoying lunch in the elegance of an old plantation house, with the afternoon spent walking in the rain forest or exploring a colonial city. As ever, though, the day ends with dancing in the warm tropical night, to rhythms of salsa, merengue and zouk.

Every Caribbean traveller has their favourite island, a charmed isle where they feel they belong. You may fall in love with it the moment your feet touch the sand on coming ashore, or it may grow on you gradually, within the heady mix of tropical smells, music and rum, but you'll know it when you find it.

My favourite island? Well, it's a tough choice and I love them all. There are about 50 islands, ranging from tiny coral outcrops to large and lively industrialised nations, and they each have their own distinct charm and appeal. Read on and you'll find out more...
James Hamlyn

The Caribbean Is

Swimmers off the south coast of Barbados

With its endless beaches, swaying palm trees and a warm turquoise sea, the Caribbean does, surprisingly, live up to its idyllic image. But the landscapes extend far beyond the travel agent's clichés – from sheer volcanic mountains and lush rain forests to inhospitable deserts; and Caribbean life has been changed beyond recognition within a relatively short space of time.

Top: St Vincent. Above: Shaw Park Gardens, Ocho Rios, Jamaica

THE ARCHIPELAGO Stretching in an arc from the bottom of Florida to the top of South America, the Caribbean archipelago is as varied as it is beautiful. Islands range in size from Cuba (110,860sq km) to tiny Saba (8sq km); mountains soar to over 3,175m high in the Dominican Republic and flat sand-spits barely reach sea level. There are extensive rain forests in Puerto Rico and Dominica and barren cactus-filled wildernesses in Haiti and Aruba. The landscape may change around each corner, as mangrove swamp gives way to pasture land and pine forests replace palm trees. Intensive agriculture and tourist development are gradually altering the Caribbean's contours and climate. Blessed with warm weather all the year round and cooled by the Trade Winds, the region is also occasionally cursed by violent rainstorms and hurricanes.

Known for its coral reefs and its beaches (every island claims the best), the Caribbean also boasts waterfalls, hot springs and caves. Two bizarre geological attractions are Trinidad's Pitch Lake, a seemingly inexhaustible pool of hot black tar (see page 232) and Jamaica's Cockpit Country, an inhospitable area of limestone hills and hollows, still populated by descendants of runaway slaves (see page 149).

CHANGING NATURE Humans have left an indelible impression on the Caribbean landscape. Many of the islands that were once covered in virgin rain forest are now scarred by deforestation and erosion. In Haiti, the island described by Columbus as the most beautiful he had ever seen, tree-felling and over-farming have created virtual deserts in some areas, where drought and famine are constant threats.

Strangely, little of the flora and fauna that make up the typical Caribbean landscape is indigenous to the region. Sugar cane, which still flourishes on many islands, was introduced from the Mediterranean by Spanish colonists. Other crops (bananas, citrus fruits, coffee beans) and animals (cattle, dogs, horses) came from Asia and Europe.

DIFFERENT WORLDS The past has shaped the look of the Caribbean through a variety of influences. Cities, towns and villages bear the unmistakable imprint of former colonial powers. Spanish-built Havana, with its colonnades and plazas, seems a different world from British-built Bridgetown, with its handsome yet pompous Victorian architecture and "tropical Anglican" cathedral.

Differing histories have also moulded the countryside itself. In the formerly Spanish colonies of Cuba, Puerto Rico and the Dominican

❏ The Caribbean is one of the last bastions of colonialism. Martinique, Guadeloupe, St Barts and St Martin are technically French *régions*; the six islands of the Netherlands Antilles remain allied to Holland; Britain still maintains Montserrat, Anguilla, the Cayman Islands and the BVI as crown colonies or dependent territories. Puerto Rico is a "free and associated state" of the USA, but may one day become the 51st state. ❏

Republic, sugar plantations stretch to the horizon as they have for 500 years. In Haiti, however, where a slave revolution expelled the French at the beginning of the 19th century, precarious smallholdings have replaced the hated plantations.

Despite the proximity of the USA, European influence is still keenly felt. In the French *départements d'outre-mer* of Martinique and Guadeloupe you can buy baguettes, drink *pastis* and see policemen in *képis*. There is no mistaking the Dutch style of Curaçao or Aruba, where gabled pastel warehouses lining the canal and port conjure up a tropical Amsterdam. And Britain has left the paraphernalia of colonial rule in its former possessions: red postboxes, English place names and cricket fields.

11

A dramatic Caribbean sunset over the shores of Tobago

"Out of many one people" is Jamaica's national motto and it applies just as well to the rest of the Caribbean. The region's population is a rich mixture of African, European, American, Asian and East Indian influences, its legacy a fusion of slavery, colonialism and migration. This has created a unique culture, developed from centuries of interaction.

STRANGERS IN PARADISE

The original indigenous population of the Caribbean all but disappeared within half a century of European conquest. Since then, people have come, willingly or not, from every corner of the earth. This process included one of history's biggest forced migrations – the importation of some five million African people into the Caribbean's plantation economy.

ARAWAKS AND CARIBS

Little remains of the people who pre-dated the Caribbean's "discovery" 500 years ago. However, some of their words have entered the vocabulary – barbecue and hammock, for instance – but none of the placid Arawak people survived the cultural devastation of the conquest. Today, only a handful of Carib descendants are still found in areas of Dominica and St Vincent, scraping a living by selling their handicrafts.

EUROPEANS

Europe conquered, colonised and re-created the Caribbean in its own image. The first Europeans to settle in the Caribbean named cities, villages and rivers after more familiar places at home. But with few exceptions, the physical legacy of European colonisation has all but disappeared save in Spanish-speaking areas of Cuba, the Dominican Republic and Puerto Rico, which received influxes of European immigration well into the present century. Europeans make up a tiny minority in most Caribbean societies though they tend to be well-connected and play a somewhat paternalistic role outside government circles. The exceptions to the rule are the "poor

Top: children in Montego Bay, Jamaica
Right: a flower-seller in Jamaica balances her load with care

12

whites" of Barbados, a community descended from indentured British labourers that has so far refused to intermix at all with any of the other Bajan communities.

AFRICANS The great majority of Caribbean people are at least in part descended from the millions of Africans who crossed the notorious "middle passage". Africa is alive in all dimensions of local life: music, language, religion and cooking. "Jamaica Talk", for instance, the island's patois, is largely based on West African Ashanti dialect, while African speech and customs are commonplace in Haiti and around the eastern tip of Cuba.

INDIANS Around 40 per cent of the population of Trinidad is East Indian in origin. The shops and restaurants of Port of Spain, the island capital, are filled with the sounds, sights and scents of the Indian subcontinent – from sari shops to street traders. Meanwhile Hindu prayer flags surround many countryside homes. In Guyana, slightly more than half the population is Indian, descended from the indentured labourers of the 19th century.

INEQUALITIES This rich diversity of race and colour conceals massive inequalities, within and between individual countries. Some Caribbean nations, most notably Haiti and the Dominican Republic, are among the world's poorest, while others, including Puerto Rico, Trinidad and the Virgin Islands, enjoy relative prosperity. Economic hardship has prompted many to leave the Caribbean's poorer countries to live and work in North America and Europe: perhaps one in seven Dominicans lives in the US. In the 1950s, nearly 10 per cent of all Jamaicans emigrated to Britain. These exile communities provide Caribbean islanders with a vital financial lifeline.

13

LANGUAGE A region of many tongues, the language of each island is dictated by its chief colonial influence. Though English is widely spoken, visitors will find a few words of French a distinct advantage in the French Antilles and Spanish invaluable, even essential, outside tourist areas in the Dominican Republic.

A Trinidad palm-weaver

Mangoes, pineapples, papaya, breadfruit, callaloo…the list of Caribbean fruit and vegetables is never-ending. Drop a seed in the soil and you'll have a tree inside a week, say local farmers. But despite extraordinary fertility, Caribbean agriculture faces critical problems: what to do with crops that nobody wants and what to put in their place.

MARKETS The market is the traditional centre of Caribbean social and economic life. By bus or on foot, the marketwomen arrive before dawn to set up their displays of fresh fruit and vegetables. Whether in the town square or simply at a rural crossroads, the market and its mostly female workforce display the vibrancy of the region's tropical agriculture. Vast piles of mysterious tubers (widely known as "ground provisions") sit side by side with bunches of green bananas and plantains, the Caribbean's starchy staples. Red-hot peppers, tangy limes and enormous avocados are some of the other offerings. Beyond the market, most people seem to have a small piece of land, if only enough to grow a few fruit trees. While there is widespread poverty in the Caribbean, few actually go hungry.

The Caribbean is still a largely agricultural region, but important changes are taking place in what crops are grown and where they go. From the earliest colonial days, the region was an exporter of agricultural commodities, most importantly sugar. In its 18th-century heyday, Saint-Domingue (now Haiti) exported more raw sugar and created more wealth than the whole of the British empire. Sugar, the fabled "white gold", made fortunes, caused wars and brought millions of Africans across the Atlantic in slave-ships.

❏ In 1975 a pound of sugar fetched 76 cents on the world market; by 1982 it was worth only 5 cents. ❏

The discovery of European sugar-beet, global overproduction and changing diets have long since undermined the Caribbean sugar industry. Only Cuba is still heavily dependent on sugar exports, while other islands have moved away into other agro-industries. The next boom crop to feel the pinch was bananas, especially in Dominica and St Lucia, where it represented up to 70 per cent of export earnings. Bananas grow everywhere in these small volcanic islands: up steep slopes, around houses, by the roadside. They are mostly cultivated on smallholdings by individual farmers, who pack them into boxes and drive them down to the port. After a long period of special access into the British market, Caribbean bananas are now under fire from the big plantation-based producers of Latin America who grow cheaper, if not better, fruit.

FRAGILE FRUIT Worries about the future of the banana industry reveal the vulnerability of Caribbean agriculture. Worse even than hurricanes are unstable world commodity markets, over which small producers have no control. Every crop – sugar, coffee, cocoa, tobacco – has seen its ups and downs and an uncertain future awaits the new "exotic nontraditionals", which farmers are now trying to export to Europe and the USA. The current generation of export crops includes ginger, mangoes, passion fruit and cut flowers, much of it destined for supermarkets and gourmet food shops in US cities. However, visitors will find no shortage of local delicacies such as golden apples, soursops and tamarinds.

14

FISHING Lobster, red snapper and flying fish are found on menus throughout the region. But despite extensive coastlines, most islands have to import fish. The lack of a fishing industry, in part a legacy of slavery and colonialism, has also resulted from inadequate marine nutrients, storage and marketing, as well as a risk of ciguaterra (a neuro-toxin found in tropical reef fish). Consequently, the islands depend on salted and canned fish from Canada and fresh fish flown in from the USA. Attempts to upgrade the fishing industry have been made, but experts warn that the Caribbean Sea cannot withstand intensive fishing.

Fish for sale on Aruba

15

High in the hills of Haiti, animal sacrifices, rhythmic drumbeats and entranced dancers swirling around a crackling bonfire are all part of the island's most famous and mysterious religion: voodoo. It is just one of many faiths in a region that claims more churches per capita than anywhere else in the world.

A Baptist worshipper on Tobago. The Caribbean islands accommodate a vast range of religious denominations, imported from all corners of the globe

RELIGION From continuous radio and TV broadcasts to tiny ramshackle churches on every street corner, religion is part and parcel of the Caribbean. There are mosques in Trinidad, Hindu temples in Guyana and pilgrimage sites in the Dominican Republic. With significant communities of Jews, Muslims and Hindus, the region is influenced by most major faiths, as well as US-based evangelical groups.

CHRISTIANS Most Caribbean people would describe themselves as Christians. European colonisers brought differing Christian beliefs, a fact reflected in the islands' many churches. Catholicism, officially the main faith of Haiti and the Dominican Republic, is widely practiced in the eastern Caribbean and is now tolerated in Cuba. Anglicanism holds sway in the former British colonies of Jamaica and Barbados. The influence of US Protestant groups is increasingly powerful throughout the Caribbean and these have joined the myriad existing churches. In Barbados, for example, it is estimated that no fewer than 140 different denominations are active, one for every 2,000 Bajans.

AFRICAN RELIGIONS Christianity was the religion of the masters; the slaves had their own faiths, brought with them from Africa. Religious beliefs and practices survived the horrors of slavery, preserving the slaves' identity and memories of their homelands. Over time, these beliefs merged with Christian religion to create new forms of faith and ceremony. These have different names on different islands (*santería* in Cuba, *pocomania* in Jamaica), but the best known is voodoo in Haiti, where religious activity is evident in all walks of life. Each tiny village has its quota of churches – Catholic, Methodist, Baptist and hundreds more – and every church has its faithful congregation. But there are no open signs of Haiti's other religious phenomenon. As an old joke has it, Haitians are 99 per cent Christian and 100 per cent voodooist. Even so, voodoo remains largely invisible to foreigners, although visitors have ample opportunity to see suitably arranged versions of the authentic ceremonies (see pages 180–181).

RASTAFARIANISM Popularised in the 1970s and 1980s by reggae stars, Rastafarianism has its roots in Jamaica and its followers on many other islands. Rastafarianism expresses many people's longing for an African identity by invoking Ethiopia as the holy land and the late Emperor Haile Selassie as a god and promotes the smoking of marijuana (ganja) as a sacrament (see page 161).

RADICALS IN RELIGION Many priests in the Caribbean have long since left the pulpit to become involved in social and political issues. The churches have traditionally been active in health and education and since "liberation theology" spread from Latin America during the 1970s, they have become increasingly politically outspoken. In Haiti, a radical Roman Catholic priest, Jean-Bertrand Aristide, was elected president in 1991, only to be overthrown by the army nine months later. He was restored to power in 1994 by means of US-led intervention.

17

Caribbean politics are anything but dull. Most people love a political argument and insults can often fly thick and fast. Elections are usually a pretext for a party, while parliamentary procedure is guaranteed to be good entertainment. The Caribbean has had – and still has – its share of unrest, but most islands enjoy healthy democracies and lively debate.

18

POLITICAL SYSTEMS The region's differing regimes are an integral part of its mixed cultural heritage. The British bequeathed the "Westminster model" of parliamentary democracy and all English-speaking islands hold regular elections. The British Queen is still nominally head of state in most Commonwealth countries, represented in each by a Governor General. The Spanish islands, meanwhile, have tended to adopt a presidential system, with a greater tradition of "strong man" leadership.

PARTY GAMES Most independent Caribbean territories have a multi-party electoral system of government. Elections are fiercely contested events and can spill over into violence. On small islands, personalities are often as important as policies, especially when most electors know the candidates personally! Problems have been greatest in Jamaica, where "political tribalism" caused around 800 deaths in the 1980 election campaign. But political violence is not common and most states are proud of their constitutional credentials.

HOT SPOTS Of all the Caribbean territories, only two are generally agreed to have undemocratic governments. Cuba has been dominated by Fidel Castro and the Communist Party since the 1959 revolution and has ever since alienated the USA by refusing to hold free elections. Once the scene of a near-nuclear confrontation between the USA and the former USSR in 1962, Cuba has become increasingly isolated. Economically strangled by the US embargo, the island suffers intermittent shortages of basic goods, but has become a popular tourist destination for Europeans, Canadians and Latin Americans, who bring hard currency into the economy. Meanwhile, the Cuban community in Miami keeps a close watch on developments.

Haiti has had the most turbulent political history of all the Caribbean nations. Wracked by instability and dictatorship since a slave revolution won independence from France in 1804, the country was ruled by the ruthless Duvaliers until 1986. When "Baby Doc", son of the infamous "Papa Doc", was finally forced to flee the country, a movement for democracy evolved, culminating in the overwhelming election triumph of Jean-Bertrand Aristide, in 1991 (see page 17). In the years since, American efforts to keep a lid on Haiti's bloody factionalism have not always been a success. At present, a tenuous peace is in place, although who knows how long it will last?

BACKYARD POLITICS The US invasion of Grenada in October 1983 was an indication of how seriously the White House viewed the rise of radicalism in its "backyard", but with the end of the Cold War, the Caribbean has lost much of its geo-political importance in the eyes of US policy-makers. Since then, support for left-wing movements has dwindled and conservatives hold power on most English-speaking islands.

TRADING PLACES Current political controversy influences the region's position in the world economy. With the coming of the North American Free Trade Agreement between the

USA, Canada and Mexico, the islanders' fear of marginalisation in trade and influence has led to more talk of integration and co-operation in the hope that a united front will help them weather economic storms.

Government House, St Thomas

They come in their millions every year. Migrating south to the tropics in search of the sun, tourists are the lifeblood of the Caribbean, bringing vital dollars and jobs into the region. Although the locals may laugh at the poolside limbo lessons, they know that, for better or worse, tourism represents their economic survival.

PACKAGE HOLIDAYS With the advent of charter flights and affordable hotels, Caribbean tourism is no longer the preserve of the wealthy. In the 1950s only the rich could afford to go to the Caribbean, normally island-hopping by yacht. Now a few hundred dollars or pounds will buy an all-inclusive package deal to Antigua, Barbados or Jamaica. All the islands are chasing the tourist jackpot; the fastest-growing holiday destination of the Caribbean is Cuba.

A modern-day "pirate ship" caters for tourists

Tourism injects billions of dollars into the Caribbean economies and, in many cases, tourist earnings far outweigh exports even in larger and more prosperous islands such as Jamaica and Barbados. Overall, economists believe that it has created hundreds of thousands of direct jobs throughout the region. Add to this the thousands of people who sell agricultural produce to hotels, who make handcrafted goods and who act as "guides", and the figure may be nearer millions.

CRUISING Several times a week, the sleepy port of St George's, Grenada, springs into frenetic action as the cruise ship arrives. As the tourists gingerly step onto *terra firma*, they are greeted by a horde of taxi-drivers, guides, vendors and scalpers. Few of the hopeful locals will make a fortune. On average, each tourist spends a paltry $20–30 before returning to the safety of the cruise ship. A cruise tour may cost thousands, but little of that money reaches the islands themselves.

SPENDING Understandably, governments and businesses prefer tourists who stay in hotels, holiday flats and guesthouses on the islands and spend time and money in their destinations. The multitude of restaurants, shopping complexes and souvenir stands that line the tourist resorts are proof of this single-minded pursuit of foreign currency. But foreign ownership of airlines and hotels often means that bills are paid outside the Caribbean, reducing the hoped-for "trickle-down" effect.

More worrying still is the growing popularity of all-inclusive club holidays, where one price covers every drink or surfboard lesson. This, as the local restauranteurs and taxi drivers will tell you, is not a major incentive for going out and spreading the wealth.

20

The Golden Lemon Hotel on St Kitts, in the Leeward Islands

BLESSING OR CURSE? Tourism has brought welcome employment and investment to otherwise stagnant economies. For many young locals, work as a waiter or cleaner is a much better prospect than traditional farming. But tourism's impact is not all positive. Many older people complain that hustling, drugs and petty crime have become a way of life for the young. Others feel that jealousy and resentment are inevitable consequences of the divide between developed and developing countries. More seriously, tourism is a shaky bet for sustainable development, as it is notoriously vulnerable to economic instability in the sender countries. Recession in North America and Europe can send Caribbean tourism revenues plummeting.

BEYOND THE BEACH Eco-tourism is the new buzzword in the local industry. Realising that people can become bored with sand and sea, operators are now offering holidays which appeal to the adventurous and environmentally aware. You can dive among coral reefs in Bonaire, explore rain forests in Dominica or hike through mountains in Jamaica. Advocates of eco-tourism praise it as an intelligent use of natural resources; critics point out that in some instances it can harm the very nature that it sets out to market.

Caribbean food can be as bland or as exciting as you choose it to be. McDonalds, Kentucky Fried Chicken and all the other familiar names are in evidence. But step outside the tourist circuit and there is food to daunt the most adventurous gastronome. Some iguana, perhaps? Or goat's offal? And don't forget the rum – the world's best.

REGIONAL FOOD Real Caribbean food reflects the many diverse influences, historical and cultural, which have shaped the region. The hearty breakfast lives on in Jamaica, but you may be offered mackerel and banana along with your bacon and eggs. In Trinidad, the spicy *roti*, a generous chapati pancake often filled with curry, is an unmistakable taste of India. Meanwhile, the French territories of Martinique and Guadeloupe claim the Caribbean's most sophisticated cuisine. A classic dish is red snapper in white wine, garlic and limes. The hamburger may have made serious inroads into regional tastes, but the imprints of Europe, Africa and India are still very much in evidence. Supermarkets are inevitably stocked with American brands, but don't be surprised to see Camembert in Martinique, Gouda in Curaçao or Yorkshire pudding mix in Barbados.

VARIETY Most of the Caribbean islands share a few basic dishes. Rice 'n' peas (or red beans) is a staple everywhere and especially good when cooked in coconut water. Root vegetables are a cheap filler, boiled or fried, and go by literally hundreds of different names across the region. Bananas and plantains are ubiquitous, as are the common fruits such as guava, pineapple and mango. But on top of these staples, each island has developed its own, often idiosyncratic, recipes. In Jamaica the national favourites are curry goat (often beef) and saltfish and ackees. The latter dish harks back to the era of slavery when salted fish was imported from Canada to feed the island's slave population. The small island of Dominica specialises in "mountain chicken", which is actually a local frog. In the Dominican Republic, *mondongo*, a tripe stew, is considered a miracle cure for a hangover.

RUM There is, of course, ample opportunity to acquire a hangover. Every island produces rum, ranging from mass-market brands to local firewater. Some of the so-called overproof rum (140 proof) is a serious risk to health, especially when mixed into apparently innocuous cocktails. Perhaps the best way to sample the better rums is with ice and lime juice, the basis of the classic Planter's Punch cocktail. Although each island predictably claims to make the best, the better quality rums are generally those from Cuba, Haiti, Jamaica, Martinique (especially *rhums vieux*) and Barbados.

Colourful Caribbean cocktails can be strong when mixed into overproof rum

BEER The Caribbean is not a wine-producing area, but every island, however small, has its own brewery. Some international brands such as Budweiser and Guinness are widely available, but locals swear – often correctly – that their beer is better. Perhaps the best known is Jamaica's Red Stripe, but other superior brews are Barbados' Banks, Trinidad's Carib and St Vincent's Hairoun. Less known and arguably the best is Presidente from the Dominican Republic, which often comes served in iced glasses.

HUNGER For the tourist, hunger is less of a risk than a gradually expanding waistline. Nor are many people in the main tourist islands likely to go hungry. Hardship is largely restricted to Cuba, where rationing and embargo have drastically reduced dietary intakes for the locals, and Haiti, the hemisphere's poorest nation. Also worrying is the growing dependency of Caribbean countries on importing basic foods in order to feed their own populations. While most countries are now desperate to export their "exotic non-traditionals", they are forced to import basic ingredients such as rice, beans and sugar for local consumption. This means that the Caribbean is increasingly consuming what it does not produce and producing what it does not consume.

One of the Caribbean's distinctive dishes: ackees

Recommended specialities

Antigua Goat water (hot goat stew) and fungi (similar to polenta).

Barbados Flying fish, dolphin (dorado or mahi mahi, not the mammal), pickled breadfruit and blood sausage.

Cuba *Moros y cristianos* – the local name for rice 'n' peas.

Curaçao *Rijsttafel* ("rice table", with up to 40 different meat and vegetable dishes, originally from Indonesia).

Dominica "Mountain chicken" (a large local frog) and *agouti* (a small rodent, usually stewed or smoked).

Dominican Republic *Mondongo*, *sancocho* (a stew made of six different meats and vegetables), *casabe* (cassava bread).

Grenada *Souse* (pig's feet stew), armadillo, iguana. Also famous for its spices, nutmeg and mace.

Haiti *Griot* (deep-fried pork) and most French-influenced sauces.

Jamaica Saltfish and ackees, curry goat and jerk chicken, barbecued and sold from roadside stalls. Also known for producing Blue Mountain coffee.

Martinique and Guadaloupe *Ti-boudin* (spicy sausage), *poulet au coco* (chicken with coconut).

Puerto Rico *Pastillas* (pork, chickpeas and raisins stuffed in dough, wrapped in plantain leaves and steamed), the paella-like *asopao*. (Puerto Rico also has fast food services).

Trinidad *Roti*, *pelau* (rice and curry).

Cooling drinks are a treat and often a necessity in the Caribbean heat

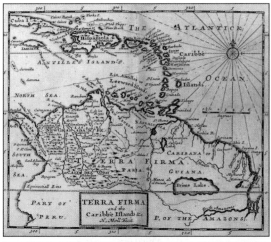

The Caribbean Was

Long before Columbus "discovered" the Caribbean islands, Native Americans had started clearing the ground to build villages and plant their crops. Tribes of Arawaks and Caribs had been living on the Caribbean shores of South America since about 5000 BC, but by 1000 BC the Arawaks were fleeing their aggressive neighbours and driving out Jamaica's earliest settlers, the Ciboneys.

26

FIRST SETTLERS Three groups of Arawak settlers established villages on the islands: the Tainos, on Jamaica, Cuba and Haiti; the Lucayanos, in the Bahamas; and the Borequinos, on Puerto Rico. For a few hundred years they led a peaceful life, left alone by Carib warriors. But the Caribs finally caught up and by the late 15th century, when Columbus arrived, their canoe raids and violent attacks were a constant threat.

NATIVE AMERICAN LIFE While the Arawaks practised skills such as basket-weaving and traded their crops – cassava, maize, sweet potatoes, cotton and pepper – from island to island, the Caribs sent raiding parties to loot villages for slaves and supplies. Their expertise in making and using weapons was formidable; Caribs were fast and accurate bowmen, shooting fire- or poison-tipped arrows and they used a variety of clubs and spears with gruesome added extras. Nevertheless, they did develop some talents other than maiming and killing. Caribs were fine potters; each settlement had its own "trademark", often in the form of an animal, which was carved onto its pots and, as an essentially belligerent, nomadic tribe, the Caribs excelled at canoe building.

Arawak communities were based on the family, with a *cacique* (clan chief) ruling each group of villages, helped by a committee of elders or *nitayanos*. They were also religious leaders, in touch with the ancestral and natural spirits and sometimes acting as their mouthpiece, inhaling tobacco fumes to induce a trance and

Native Americans sowing maize

conveying advice or predictions from the spirit world. *Zemis*, wood, stone or bone figures representing the gods of nature, were housed in special huts, set apart from the ordinary round, thatched homes of the villagers. Religious worship involved dancing, games and tobacco-smoking; the powdered leaf was lit inside a forked tube (*tabaco*), which was wedged up the nostrils. Caves were used as burial sites by some clans (bones, canoe paddles and *zemis* have been excavated); carvings of symbols and mask-like faces can still be seen covering cave walls and rocks on several Caribbean islands.

Fighters and killers were the most respected members of Carib society. Chief warriors were elected on the basis of their performance in battle and religious activities revolved

❏ Gold was one of the commodities traded by Arawaks, but it was prized only as an ornament. Carib warriors decorated their bodies with paint, petals, coral bracelets and anklets and shells or bones were worn in pierced ears, lips and noses. Arawaks used dyed clay and grease to cover their bodies and would bind their babies' heads to give them long, tough skulls. ❏

ceremonial; fat from the body of a brave enemy would be rubbed over Carib boys to give them courage. Even so, Carib society was undeniably brutal and prisoners were starved and tortured, as a test of their endurance, before eventually being killed and served up.

around appeasing a vengeful god. When European settlers arrived in the Caribbean they painted a grim picture of the Caribs as vicious cannibals who were liable to make a meal out of anyone straying onto their territory. In fact, any cannibalism that did take place is likely to have been

Both tribes relied to a great extent on the Caribbean's abundant marine life for much of their food, but any edible creature was regarded as fair game. Lizards, snails and turtle eggs were all snapped up; birds were caught in nets strung between branches and fish were hooked, speared, or even stunned by poison bark thrown into the water. Each day's catch would be added to a pepperpot, a seasoned stew left to simmer for weeks. Pepperpots (now with different ingredients) can still be sampled on Grenada (see page 52).

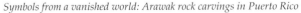

Symbols from a vanished world: Arawak rock carvings in Puerto Rico

After five weeks of sailing the uncharted Atlantic, Christopher Columbus and his crew were within hours of giving up their voyage of exploration when land was sighted on 12 October, 1492. The sailors – who believed they had found Japan – were actually heading for the Bahamas and about to begin an unprecedented era of wealth, war and oppression.

THE GREAT EXPLORER Columbus was born in Genoa in the late 1440s, becaming an avid sea-voyager and a collector of maps and charts. By the 1480s, convinced that Japan and the riches of the "East Indies" could be reached by sailing west, he set about searching for the finances to back an expedition. Portugal and Britain turned him down – they had their own ideas for finding new trade routes. The Spanish monarchs, Ferdinand and Isabella, made Columbus wait five years while they drove the Moors from the country; then they agreed to his plan, eager to spread the influence of Spain and of the Catholic church and to break the long-established Arab monopoly of trading routes to the Indies.

Columbus set out with his fleet of three ships – the *Niña*, the *Pinta* and his flagship, the *Santa Maria* – on 3 August, 1492. By the time land was sighted he was having trouble preventing mutiny; the worried crew was threatening to throw Columbus overboard and head back home. After naming his first "discovery" San Salvador, the explorer persuaded some of its Arawak inhabitants – who welcomed the newcomers as protection against the Caribs – to come aboard and direct him towards Hispaniola. Here, the *Santa Maria* ran aground, leaving 40 Spaniards to build the first European fort in the Caribbean. Columbus was disappointed at the scarcity of gold and spices on the islands, but returned to

Columbus is greeted by Arawak islanders on San Salvador

Spain with a few "Indians", plants and tobacco leaves as promise of wonders yet to emerge.

Explorer and treasure-seeker: a 16th-century Spanish portrayal of Christopher Columbus

THE NEW COLONIES

A second voyage followed in 1493, with a much larger fleet bringing builders and farmers to create new settlements and priests to convert the natives. Many of the settlers were convicted criminals, pardoned on condition that they join the fleet. Before long the colonists – who had no prospect of returning home – started to abuse the Arawaks, demanding food and taxes of gold and cotton, stealing the women and forcing the men into slavery. War broke out and within three years, most of the 200,000 Native Americans were dead, overwhelmed by Spanish guns and swords or by the smallpox that the settlers had brought with them. The Europeans established a capital in Santo Domingo and a row of forts to protect their new colony.

Columbus himself returned to Spain after charting a course to Jamaica and Cuba; five years later he was back again, determined to find the mainland – which he did, after visiting Trinidad and quelling a rebellion among the Hispaniola colonists. The ambitious admiral was intensely disliked, however, and a commissioner sent by Queen Isabella to investigate complaints promptly had him arrested and shipped back to Spain. A fourth voyage also ended in disaster; after sailing along the Central American coast, Columbus's ships were wrecked off the shores of Jamaica and the explorer and his stranded sailors had to wait for a year before a ship could be sent to rescue them.

Columbus died in 1506, having failed to supply the unlimited riches that had been promised. But a new world was now opened to Spain, with gold reserves to be mined, crops to be farmed and souls to be saved – at the expense of many hundreds of thousands of lives.

29

❏ Columbus was eager to exploit the native Americans as free labour and many were set to work mining for gold. The Spanish monarchy, however, disapproved of enslaving potential converts to Christianity and would only sanction slavery for criminals or captured warriors. European accounts of native American atrocities and cannibalism were often invented to justify the taking of slaves. ❏

Anxious to reap the benefits of Columbus's voyages, Ferdinand and Isabella persuaded Pope Alexander VI to give them legal possession of the Americas. Under the Treaty of Tordesillas (1494), a boundary was drawn up dividing the "New World" between Spain and Portugal and excluding the rest of Europe from claims to these territories.

LAYING DOWN THE LAW The Caribbean was to be a stepping stone for further exploration and Spain was to have a strict monopoly over trade with the new colonies; but naturally developments did not go according to plan. In the years after Columbus's

Pirates attack a Spanish ship

last voyage, thousands of settlers arrived from Spain, eager to find gold, to own land and to be given power over a workforce of native Americans under the royal grants known as *encomiendas*. Their vicious treatment of the Arawaks was bitterly condemned by Antonio de Montesinos, a Dominican friar, and by an ex-*encomendero*, Bartolomé de las Casas. Eventually their outspoken attacks led to two sets of laws, passed by two successive kings. In 1512 Ferdinand assented to the Laws of Burgos, dictating limited working hours and the provision of food rations for Arawak labourers; and in 1542 Charles V put an end to new grants of *encomiendas* under the New Laws. But Spain had little control over the actions of its Caribbean colonists and by the 1520s so many native Americans had been killed off, especially by "European" diseases to which they had no immunity, that the settlers were already beginning to ship in African slaves to take their place.

CONQUISTADORES In the meantime, the search continued for richer lands and groups of armed *conquistadores* set out to stake new claims. Juan Ponce de Léon led a party of men to conquer Puerto Rico, massacring the Borequino inhabitants and clearing the land for plantations and ranches. Diego Velázquez took three years to wipe out the native Americans on Cuba and by 1520 the *conquistadores* had reached Mexico and the rich prizes of the Aztec Empire. When word got out that the Spanish had struck gold on the mainland, hordes of settlers made for wider, wealthier territories. At the same time, sailors from other European countries saw an opportunity for easy money. Spanish claims to exclusive rights over the spoils of their settlements were ignored, as pirates attacked their ships and ports.

30

PIRATES Spanish cargoes were also looted by privateers, sea captains who were authorised by their governments to plunder enemy ships in time of war – and the European powers were in an almost constant state of warfare during the 17th and 18th centuries. Spain's monopoly on trade with the colonies could not be maintained. Aside from pirate attacks, the system was unwieldy and inefficient.

A buccaneer pictured in 1905

Caribbean settlers would be kept waiting for months on end, while fleets of Spanish ships loaded up with goods underwent rigorous checks at the Customs Office in Seville. Impatient with restrictions imposed by a distant state, colonists were soon doing a brisk illegal trade with ships from Britain, France and the Netherlands and there was little that Spain could do to stop them. Unofficial trade has continued to be part of Caribbean life ever since.

Looting Spanish ships was risky business and by the early years of the 17th century the rival European powers were considering ways of earning long-term profits from Caribbean lands. While Spanish island colonies dwindled, forgotten by their home country, British and French adventurers were trying their luck at building settlements of their own.

TOBACCO Early experiments in tobacco-growing on the Guyana coast had been dismal failures; the small groups of British and French planters were soon defeated by fever and Carib attacks. In 1622 one of the Guyana colonists, Thomas Warner, decided to try the fresher climate and fertile soil of the Lesser Antilles and

their own plots of land. In the meantime, France was turning its attention to the Caribbean and in 1635 Cardinal Richelieu formed a company to colonise Guadeloupe, Martinique, St Lucia and Grenada. For the following few years or so, settlers made the best living they could, fending off Carib or Spanish

Slaves being shipped from Africa were forced to dance to keep "fit"

attacks and sending home their harvests of tobacco and cotton.

set up a plantation on St Christopher (St Kitts). Britain, at war with Spain, was quick to see the advantages of a foothold in the "New World" and within three years the Earl of Carlisle was charged with colonising St Kitts, Nevis, Barbados and Montserrat. To cultivate the land, indentured labourers were shipped from Britain and bonded to work for five years, after which they were free to take up

TENSION Relations between the colonies and their mother countries were uneasy: British settlers resented the imposition of rents and taxes; the French state neglected its Caribbean territories when their profits failed to live up to expectations. Colonists relied heavily on Dutch ships for their supplies and, in turn, the Dutch took every opportunity to extend their own empire, colonising Aruba,

32

Curaçao and Bonaire, which lay near Spanish mainland ports and Saba, Sint Eustatius and Sint Maarten, conveniently placed on their trade routes with Spain's island colonies.

SUGAR AND SLAVERY In the course of war against Spain and Portugal, the Dutch had captured several sugar plantations in Brazil and their ships brought news of the vast profits to be made from the crop. They also seized Portugal's West African slavery centres and established a monopoly of slave provision for the labour-intensive plantations. African men, women and children, kidnapped from their villages during midnight raids or captured and sold by rival chiefs, were shackled to each other by their necks and marched to coastal slave markets, where dealers picked the healthiest and branded them with irons. Eager for the biggest possible profit margins, captains would fill every available space on their ships, forcing the chained captives to lie shoulder to shoulder beneath the decks for their eight-week voyage. When the ships docked, the surviving slaves were auctioned off to planters, having been oiled and rubbed to cover the effects of their terrible journey.

CONFLICT In an attempt to break the Dutch hold on the slave trade, Britain attacked Dutch strongholds, triggering one of many conflicts between the colonial empires. France, Holland, Britain and Spain were all anxious to strengthen their economies and expand their influence so colonised islands switched hands several times, being stormed by one

I would not have a Slave to till my ground
To carry me, to fan me while I sleep,
And tremble when I wake, for all the wealth
That sinews bought and sold, have ever earn'd.
We have no Slaves at home—why then abroad?
COWPER.

An 1827 condemnation of slavery

navy after another. British Lord Protector Oliver Cromwell sent a small army to Jamaica in the 1650s; in 1664 the French Minister of Finance, Jean-Baptiste Colbert, bought back Martinique, Guadeloupe and other colonies from the private companies that had taken them over 20 years earlier. By 1678 Holland was forced to use ships registered in neutral Denmark to break through trade barriers, encouraging Danish settlement on the Virgin Islands of St John and St Thomas. By the end of the 17th century most of the Caribbean islands were divided between the French and British empires, which proceeded to exploit the new-found wealth of their sugar industry and the thousands of slaves who produced it.

33

During the early years of conquest and settlement, Europeans had hoped to find unlimited supplies of gold in the West Indies. In the 18th century their dreams of immense wealth were realised as the demand for "white gold" soared and the sugar islands became the Caribbean's richest exporters, supplying over 160,000 tonnes during the late 1760s.

Slaves working on a treadmill in Jamaica, 1830

RIGHTS OF SLAVES The rewards of this trade were restricted to a very few plantation owners – many of whom lived in Europe and left the management of their estates to agents. Even those who lived in the Caribbean tended to build their great houses at a considerable distance from the plantation fields, partly for comfort but also for security: by the 1770s slaves outnumbered whites by about 10 to one on the main sugar islands and their harsh conditions had already prompted several revolts. Strict laws were passed controlling the movements and rights of slaves: they were forbidden from gathering in large groups, from owning land and from giving evidence in court; slaves from the same areas of Africa or with similar cultures were parted in an attempt to destroy feelings of solidarity and close relationships. Nevertheless, African culture did survive in the traditions of story-telling (see page 61), dance and music (see pages 80–81) and spirit-worship (see pages 178–179). Many slaves risked imprisonment and whipping by running away and over the years runaways established strong communities in more inaccessible parts of several islands.

For most slaves, however, life was a constant grind for 16 to 18 hours every day, digging the fields, gathering the sugar cane, feeding it into the crushing mills or pouring boiling sugar extract into coppers. Freedom was a rare reward, granted to long-serving slaves or to the offspring of white men and slave women. Even freemen had to carry passes guaranteeing their status for seven years and were often forbidden from owning property above a certain value.

BOOM AND DECLINE For 100 years the white minority managed to suppress slave rebellions while they kept up a steady flow of raw sugar (trade laws allowed the refining industry to operate only in the home countries). Wars continued to break out at regular intervals between the European powers, each one ending in the inevitable shuffling around of territories. By 1763, when the Seven Years War between the British and French came to an end, Britain owned five of the 10 most profitable sugar islands – Jamaica alone produced over 30,000 tonnes a year – and their planters had become some of the empire's most prosperous and influential men.

The rot soon set in. Plantations cost a lot of money to run and by the late 18th century many had been overused, exhausting the soil. At the same time the French planters, who paid lower export duties, were selling cheaper sugar to more European

markets and Saint-Domingue, the French-owned part of Hispaniola, claimed to be the Caribbean's biggest sugar producer.

When the colonies in North America rebelled against "taxation without representation", sparking off the Revolutionary War, Britain forbade the Caribbean planters from trading with the mainland, cutting off a valuable source of income. The Americans turned to French and Spanish sugar islands instead and British islands were forced to find ways to cut costs and provide their own supplies. New crops were planted, such as mangoes and breadfruit trees (brought by Captain Bligh of *Bounty* fame in 1793), and botanical gardens were opened to cultivate new species; coffee, cotton and spices were grown to supplement the main sugar crop. But, by the end of the 18th century, most of the sugar islands were in decline and the West Indies were on the verge of radical social and economic change.

A Caribbean sugar mill, 1816

Anti-slavery movements were gathering force in late 18th-century Europe. In France the issue was brought to a head with the Revolution in 1789. The National Assembly resisted the demands of abolitionists such as the Paris-based Société des Amis des Noirs and in Saint-Domingue the free "coloureds", angered by government failure to grant them full legal rights, armed their own slaves.

SLAVES' REVOLT Thousands of whites were killed in the ensuing uprising and 300 plantations were set alight. A French army sent to restore order promised emancipation; the new Jacobin Assembly fulfilled this promise and freed slaves on Guadeloupe in 1794. British and Spanish troops, sent to support Saint-Domingue's planters, were driven out by ex-slave Toussaint l'Ouverture and his army. In 1802 Napoleon had l'Ouverture imprisoned and restored slavery on Guadeloupe; in response, 55,000 blacks took up arms and declared Saint-Domingue the independent state of Haiti.

In Britain, the "West India interest" was losing ground with the decline of sugar profits and slavery was abolished in 1834. Ex-slaves were obliged to serve four years of unpaid "apprenticeship", but many fled from the cane fields and set up their own plots of land; on Jamaica sugar production slumped by 50 per cent. To make up the labour shortage planters took on immigrants as indentured labourers; by 1917 about 280,000 indentured workers from the Indian subcontinent had moved to Jamaica and Trinidad. On islands with little spare land, ex-slaves lacked the option of cultivating their own plots and Barbados, Antigua and St Kitts continued to prosper as sugar islands for many years.

Emancipation alarmed the old plantocracy, who feared the loss of political dominance. In 1865, after an episode of violent racial conflict in Morant Bay, Jamaica's assembly asked to be replaced with direct rule and by 1898 Britain had imposed the status of Crown Colony on almost all of its Caribbean Islands.

The French finally abolished slavery on its remaining islands in 1848. As on

Emancipation portrayed by François Auguste Biard, 1848

Edmund Burke speaks out against slavery in the British Parliament

the British islands, sugar production plummeted and the planters encouraged thousands of Indian labourers to take up indentures. France pursued a policy of integrating its colonies, allowing each island to send three representatives to the National Assembly and granting the vote to all adult men in 1871.

CUBA Prosperity was late coming to the Spanish islands of Puerto Rico and Cuba, and only when trade restrictions had been lifted in the late 18th century did Cuba's sugar industry flourish. As a result, slavery was not abolished until 1886. Resentment against Spanish rule and taxes led to

fierce civil war in the 1860s and 1870s and again in the 1890s, by which time a separatist movement had won strong US support. In 1898 US warships destroyed two Spanish fleets off Cuba and under the Treaty of Paris in that year the island gained independence, while Puerto Rico was ceded to America. By 1917, when Denmark sold its Virgin Islands to the Americans, the US was the Caribbean's main political and economic power, funding successful sugar, banana and coffee industries. To defend this commerce, the USA intervened in the political life of Cuba, Haiti and the Dominican Republic (western Hispaniola) during the 20th century.

The Caribbean suffered badly during the 1930s Depression. Corrupt and repressive governments exacerbated the harsh conditions on Haiti and on Cuba, where Fidel Castro's revolutionary forces took control in 1959. On the British islands economic hardship gave rise to powerful labour movements, riots and strikes. An attempt to form a federation of British Caribbean islands in the late 1950s failed and in the 1960s Jamaica and Trinidad were the first to gain independence, followed by nearly all the other British islands.

The new millennium has been a time of re-evaluation in the Caribbean. Some islands have found new roles as luxury tourist destinations; many are struggling with severe economic problems and with political instability. This region is still coming to terms with its complex historical legacy of conflict and conquest.

Dancers in traditional costume

WINDWARD TRAVEL
The quickest way to travel between the islands is on one of the island-hopping planes that run up and down the island chain at least twice a day. Alternatively you can try travelling by boat. This takes time; you may have to wait several days.

THE WINDWARD ISLANDS Crowned by sheer volcanic peaks and fringed with beautiful beaches, the islands of Grenada, St Lucia, Dominica and St Vincent are among the loveliest in the Caribbean region. The advent of eco-tourism has added another, adventurous dimension to the more traditional appeal of beaches, river swimming and yachting. With the necklace of the Grenadine Islands strung between Grenada and St Vincent offering some of the Caribbean's best sailing, each of the Windwards has its enthusiasts, and each has a range of guesthouses and hotels to suit all tastes and budgets.

The four Windward Islands lie facing the Trade Winds head on, in a line of jagged, volcanic protrusions, some still active and liable to erupt about once every 100 years.

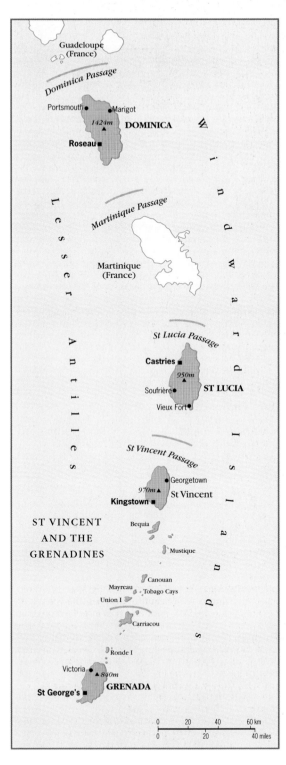

The Windward Islands

The Windward Islands

▶ ▶ ▶ REGION HIGHLIGHTS

Bequia *page 53*

Carriacou *page 52*

Morne Trois Pitons National Park *page 42*

Papillote Wilderness Retreat *page 42*

The Pitons *page 60*

St George's Carenage Market Square *page 49*

The Tobago Cays *page 55*

Marigot Bay *page 60*

St Vincent Botanic Gardens *page 65*

40

Calabash Hotel, L'Anse aux Epines Bay, Grenada

Regularly spaced on the tectonic fault-line between the Atlantic and Caribbean oceans, these protrusions are similar to each other in appearance and are all very small (not more than 46km by 25km), but they are nonetheless physically dramatic, with clouds hanging over the mountain peaks, and thick rain forest and bamboo covering the fertile land.

The islands no longer grow sugar, but their fertility is still the source of some wealth; fruit and vegetables are shipped as far as Trinidad and Anguilla, and the banana is an important export to Europe.

HISTORY Peaceful Arawak islanders were decimated by invading Caribs in about AD 1000; five centuries later the Caribs were defending themselves against European colonists. As late as 1748, Dominica was left to the Caribs in the Treaty of Aix-la-Chapelle. After passing between the European powers several times in the 18th century, the Windward Islands finally came into British hands and was made a Crown Colony in 1874, administered from Grenada. The islands all gained their independence from Britain in the 1970s, although they remain within the Commonwealth and still use the British judicial system.

ISLAND LIFE At one time during the to-and-fro of colonial control, all the Windwards were owned by France and the French heritage is still strong. Names such as Beausejour Bay and Snug Corner can be seen side by side in Grenada, and French patois is spoken by the country people in Dominica, St Lucia and Grenada. The strongest influence, however, is African; most islanders are the descendants of African slaves, freed in 1834 and able to survive by working their own plots of land.

These are relaxed yet lively islands, both as tourist destinations – with all the sun, sea, sand, dancing and rum punches that implies – and in the local life.

The Windwards have a remarkable breadth of tourism, from secluded mountain retreats to busy yachting marinas, and from fun-packed, all-inclusive hotels to the most sophisticated elegance. St Lucia is the most developed island and is becoming increasingly crowded with tourists attracted to its good restaurants and hotels; Grenada is also developing a reputation for stylish hotels and diving. St Vincent is still practically untouched, but the Grenadines offer easy island life and island-hopping by yacht (or mail-boat). Dominica, which joined in 1939, is not so developed, but have nature tourism and scuba-diving.

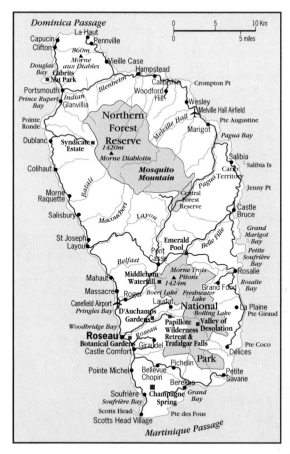

Dominica Passage

0   5   10 Km
0   5 miles

Capucin
La Haut
Clifton   Pennville
860m
Morne
aux Diables   Vieille Case
Douglas   Cabrits   Hampstead
Bay   Nat Park
Blenheim   Calibishie
Portsmouth   Woodford   Crompton Pt
Prince Rupert   Indian   Hill
Bay   Glanvillia   Wesley
Pointe   Melville Hall Airfield
Ronde   Northern   Pte Augustine
Dublanc   Forest   Marigot
Syndicate   Reserve   Pagua Bay
Estate
1420m
Colihaut   Morne Diablotin   Salibia
Mosquito   Carib   Salibia Is
Mountain   Territory   Jenny Pt
Morne
Raquette   Central   Castle
Salisbury   Macoucheri   Layou   Forest   Bruce
Reserve
St Joseph   Grand
Layou   Emerald   Marigot
Pont   Pool   Bay
Belfast   Casse   Belle Fille   Petite
Soufrière
Mahaut   Middleham   Morne Trois   Bay
Waterfall   Pitons   Rosalie
Massacre   Roger   1424m   Rosalie
Canefield Airport   Boeri Lake   Freshwater   Bay
Pringles Bay   Laudat   Lake
D'Auchamps   National   La Plaine
Woodbridge Bay   Gardens   Boiling Lake   Pte Giraud
Roseau   Papillote   Valley of
Botanical Gardens   Wilderness   Desolation
Castle Comfort   Giraudel   Retreat &   Pte Coco
Trafalgar Falls   Délices
Pichelin   Park
Pointe Michel   Bellevue   Petite
Chopin   Savane
Berekua
Soufrière   Champagne   Grand
Soufrière Bay   Spring   Bay
Scotts Head   Pte des Fous
Scotts Head Village
Martinique Passage

Dominica

Dominica claims to have a river for every day of the year and it's probably true. A lush, green, volcanic island, it is full of spectacular scenery and pretty coastal villages. Not an obvious choice for beach-lovers, this is a must for naturalists and those who want to experience the simple, small-island rural life.

At 46km by 25km, Dominica is the largest of the Windwards – but it is also the poorest and least developed. Many islanders scrape a living on the land or by fishing, and access to much of the country is difficult, despite a number of new roads. For hundreds of years this was a Carib stronghold; the descendants of those who survived French invasion in the 18th century still live here. Developed as a free port, Dominica made its money from coffee, sugar and slaves – many of whom escaped into the jungle to live as maroons, occasionally taking up arms against the authorities. British and French colonies were established here in turn; positioned between the French islands of Martinique and Guadeloupe, Dominica had strategic value for France and it has retained a strong French heritage. Many of the 71,000 Dominicans are Roman Catholics and Créole-speakers.

JEAN RHYS
The novelist Jean Rhys was born on Dominica in 1894 and lived there until 1907, when she left to continue her education in the UK. After travelling to Paris in the 1920s, Rhys began her long writing career and set her most famous work, *Wide Sargasso Sea* (1966), in the Caribbean. This book describes the degenerate and stultifying atmosphere of colonial Caribbean life, as seen through the eyes of a Créole heiress, destined to become Rochester's mad wife in *Jane Eyre*.

41

Castle Bruce Bay, on the rough Atlantic coast of Dominica

LIME JUICE
Dominica was at one time the biggest producer of limes in the world. One of the major buyers was Rose's, the company that supplied the British Navy with fruit juice. British sailors took a daily ration of lime in order to prevent scurvy – hence their nickname "Limeys".

MORNE TROIS PITONS NATIONAL PARK
UNESCO has declared Dominica's Morne Trois Pitons National Park a World Heritage Site, thereby both celebrating and preserving its natural beauty. Guides are recommended for several of the more difficult hikes such as the Boiling Lake and the Valley of Desolation. (For information on this and the island's other magnificent parks, tel: 448 2401. *Admission: inexpensive*.)

42

The Catholic cathedral at Roseau, completed in 1848

Dominica's capital, **Roseau▶▶**, lies in the southwest of the island; it's a small, working town of about 20,000 people, with a mixture of modern buildings and pretty stone and wooden Victorian townhouses. In the oldest part is Dawbiney Market Square, now the site of a craft market, tourist information centre and the Dominica Museum (tel: 448 8923; call for hours. *Admission: inexpensive*), which has informative descriptions of island life from colonial times to the present in pictures and exhibits, and includes volcanic geology. The new market is at the other end of the Bay Front. The Catholic cathedral, north of the old market site, was built under cover of darkness, after the government refused to support its construction. Not far from here is Fort Young, now a hotel.

The real beauty of Dominica becomes apparent on the outskirts of town. Beneath the huge white crucifix on Morne Bruce are the **Botanical Gardens▶▶**, now more like a park since the devastation from hurricanes, but still good for a walk to see the 150 species of plants and the endemic Dominica parrots (tel: 448 2401. *Open* daily. *Admission free*). The best place to see plants is directly inland in the Roseau Valley, a fantastically fertile gorge with tiny Dominican houses clinging to the slopes. At its head are the **Papillote Wilderness Retreat▶▶** and three waterfalls called the **Trafalgar Falls▶▶** (see panel on page 44). The excellent D'Auchamps Gardens are halfway up the valley.

Reached along another fork in the road, the village of Laudat is an entry point to the scenic **Morne Trois Pitons National Park▶▶▶** (see panel), which takes its name from a mountain peak. The park has the best view of Dominica's forests, and walks to the Freshwater Lake (sadly the site of hydroelectric work) and the Boeri Lake. The adventurous might consider walking to the Valley of Desolation, an area of bubbling pools and mudponds and the Boiling Lake, a crater of steaming water that can boil an egg in three minutes and the second largest of its kind in the world.

South of the capital, the road passes a small strip of hotels in Castle Comfort, crossing lime country (see panel) to reach Soufrière, named for the nearby sulphur spring. The best sites for scuba-diving are in this area. Near the pinnacles, caves and drop-offs, a freshwater hot spring called Champagne fizzes at scalding temperatures.

Some of the last survivors of the Carib race, which gave its name to the Caribbean, live on the east coast of Dominica. Once these proud and warlike people held sway over the Eastern Caribbean, but by the late 18th century, after a war of attrition with the expansionist Europeans, the few hundred remaining had been forced to the remotest part of Dominica and were forgotten. Only in 1903 were they officially granted their own territory.

The Caribs first appeared on the Caribbean islands around AD 1000. They came from South America (where there are still distantly related tribes) and island-hopped their way north along the chain, supplanting the peaceful Arawak tribe. Although they grew a few crops, the Caribs were mainly hunters and fishermen, who would stun parrots (for their feathers) by burning pepper beneath them and fire arrows with amazing speed and accuracy.

Caribs were said to be cannibals, but this may well have been a lie circulated by Europeans to justify their acts of genocide. One early traveller tells of being presented with a pickled human arm, but there is little archeological evidence of systematic cannibalism.

On the beach at Castle Bruce you can watch canoes being made by traditional Carib methods (see panel). Just over 9km north of Castle Bruce lies the 1,497-hectare Carib Territory, which was established in 1903. (Don't expect much in the way of ancient culture and costume; the people who gave the Caribbean its name live pretty much as other West Indians.) Although there are no "pure" Caribs left and their language has died out, their descendants still have characteristic silky blue-black hair. In addition to canoe-building, they have maintained their woodcarving and basket-weaving skills. Carib wares are displayed and can be purchased in little thatched huts along the road. Of interest on the reservation are the Roman Catholic church, whose altar was once a canoe, and L'Escalier Tête Chien ("trail of the snake staircase"), a hardened lava flow that juts down to the ocean.

CANOES
Caribs still build their canoes in the traditional way, hollowing them out from gommier trees. In the past, a large Carib canoe could carry over 100 people. Builders would select a suitable tree and fell it, then hollow it out with tools made from conch shells. Rocks and fire were used to widen the sides, which were then built up with planks before the canoe was finally launched. A war canoe could be paddled at the same speed as a European warship in full sail.

43

Spaniards get a hostile reception from Caribs in 1525

Try your hand at bargaining with the ladies of the Roseau market

WILDERNESS AND WATERFALLS

At the head of the Roseau Valley, a half-hour's journey from the capital, are the Papillote Wilderness Retreat and the Trafalgar Falls (tel: 448 2401. *Admission: inexpensive*). It is possible to climb into the waterfalls, which are harnessed for hydro power as they crash onto sulphur-dyed black and orange rocks. The Papillote Wilderness Retreat (tel: 448 2287) is a small hotel set in a 5-hectare garden fed by a small stream from a 30m waterfall. Paths wind among bamboo trees, begonias, bromeliads and orchids, and visitors can bathe in warm springs.

The road inland from Canefield climbs into the rain forest and mountains, touching the northern limits of the National Park and giving access to **Middleham Falls**▶▶ and the **Emerald Pool**▶ and waterfall (pleasant but tame). From here the road descends to Castle Bruce on the coast and turns north to **Carib Territory** ▶▶ (see page 43).

Back on the calmer Caribbean coast, the Layou River Gorge has good spots for swimming; beyond it, the road passes beneath Morne Diablotin (the island's tallest peak) in the Northern Forest Reserve. Here you can arrange to walk through the rain forest to a hideout, where there is a chance you might see one of Dominica's two indigenous parrots, the Sisserou and the Jacquot.

Portsmouth, set on a huge bay in the northwest, is the island's second town and is even quieter than Roseau. Canoe trips arranged here take passengers through the Indian River mangroves; the area's malarial swamps drove British settlers to Roseau, ruining Portsmouth's chances of becoming the capital. The excellently restored **Cabrits National Park**▶▶ (tel: 448 2401. *Open* daily. *Admission: inexpensive*) is an old military garrison set on the nearby promontory (cruise ships dock on the peninsula itself). Many of the barrack buildings have been repaired and there is a museum in Fort Shirley. The Park also includes a marine section, with scuba-diving sites. Portsmouth's black sand beaches are passable, but Dominica's best beaches are to the east, in the hidden north coast coves; try Hampstead or Calibishie – swimmers should beware the fierce Atlantic swells.

Caribbean islands are best known for their picture-postcard beaches, where silken sands are lapped by gentle waves. But there are other treats for waterlovers; the mountainous interiors of many islands are laced with rivers, where cool freshwater cascades crash and tumble through thick forests, and waterfalls pour into clear rockpools, making ideal spots for secluded and refreshing dips after hiking through the rain forest.

Rivers were once gathering places on the Caribbean islands. Before piped water was introduced, the population would go there to collect water and do the Monday washing, and washerwomen (*blanchisseuses* in the French Caribbean) can still occasionally be seen sudsing the clothes up at the riverside and then laying them out on the rocks to dry. Another long-standing practice was (and remains) taking a bath in the river. Although West Indians never go nude on their beaches, they do often take off their clothes in order to wash in fresh water.

Rivers play an important part in Caribbean folklore and legend; many islands share the legend of a beautiful girl sitting by a rockpool, combing her hair with a golden comb and perhaps granting a wish. The story goes that anyone who manages to steal her comb and take it down to the sea can keep it. The rockpools of Trinidad are said to be the home of the unpleasant Mama Dlo, the spirit of the water, who is half woman and half anaconda.

The Windward Islands are so well watered that they actually sell water to some of the drier islands. The best islands for river bathing are the Eastern Caribbean islands from Guadeloupe down to Trinidad. There are also large rivers in the Greater Antilles. Many of the rockpools and rivers are off the beaten track and so bathers should be careful of their personal security. Rivers of slow-moving water might best be avoided – cases of bilharzia (caused by a parasitic flat-worm that enters the blood and bladder), though rare, have been known to occur.

RIVER HUNTS
On Dominica, hunting parties search the rivers by night for frogs and crabs. Hunters once used flaming torches (they are more likely to be electric flashlights nowadays) to attract the animals, which are so startled by the light that they do not even attempt to hide and can be simply picked up.

RIVERS IN RELIGION
In Haiti waterfalls have religious significance. On saints' days the Catholic and voodoo faithful gather at the riverside for ceremonies that include baptism in the waters of the cascades.

Swimmers can enjoy the pools at Dunn's River Falls in Ocho Rios, Jamaica

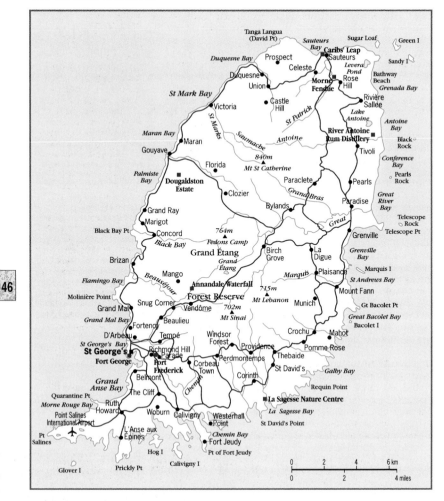

FÉDON'S CAMP

High up in Grenada's rain forest, Fédon's Camp takes its name from French Créole planter Julien Fédon, leader of a rebellion against British authorities in 1795. Supplied by French revolutionaries in Guadeloupe, he led a brutal insurrection and set himself up in his estate at Belvidere with 50 prisoners, all of whom were killed. The British eventually regained the island, but Fédon is thought to have escaped to Trinidad or Cuba.

Grenada

Long recovered from the political traumas of the 1980s, Grenada has relaxed into a sleepy island with the Caribbean's most picturesque port, St George's. A warm, friendly place of small villages and mountain walks, it is ideal for either an active or a completely lazy break.

It was on Grenada that the Caribbean rum punch was perfected. In his book, *Touch the Happy Isles*, Quentin Crewe retells the story of a planter who sprinkled a mystery ingredient into his guests' glasses at a party in 1813. The addition was nutmeg and it was such a success that West Indians have used it in their recipes for rum punch ever since. The nutmeg fruit, which now appears on the Grenadian flag, was for a while one of the country's largest exports; nutmeg trees still grow all over the island. This and the many other spices grown in the hills – cinnamon, cocoa, cloves, pimento and bay leaves to name a few – have given Grenada its title of the Caribbean's Spice Island.

Grenada is the most southerly in the chain of the Windward Islands and is not as mountainous as the others. Of the Grenadines, its string of offshore islets surrounded by coral reefs, only two are inhabited: Carriacou and Petit Martinique. Grenada itself is developing slowly but steadily; package tourism is confined to the southwestern corner of the island, around Grand Anse and L'Anse aux Epines, where the best hotels, restaurants and bars can be found. Elsewhere on the island you will see Grenadians living a pastoral, country life, often fishing or farming for a living.

Nowadays Grenada's atmosphere is calm and relaxed, but the island has a history of conflict and violence, aggravated by its strenghthening ties to Communist Cuba. In the recent past, the 1983 "intervention" by the USA and its Caribbean allies provoked strong reactions, of both outrage and approval. The troops moved in after Maurice Bishop, leader of the increasingly repressive People's Revolutionary Government, had been killed by a rival faction, along with nine of his colleagues. A return to the 1974 constitution, established when Grenada gained independence from Britain, paved the way for parliamentary elections and the island returned to a state of comparative stability. Some Grenadians still remember Maurice Bishop favourably – he had taken power in a bloodless coup, replacing the corrupt administration of Premier Eric Gairy in 1979 – but only the occasional piece of graffiti remains as a reminder of turbulent times.

ST GEORGE'S Grenada's capital, **St George's▶ ▶ ▶**, is a very pretty town on a natural harbour. Its Georgian stone houses and more recent concrete homes are neatly ranged in curved lines on the crumbled slopes of a long-inactive volcanic crater, their red tiled and tin roofs offset by the tropical greens of the surrounding forest. On the heights above stands a protective ring of churches and fortresses.

BEFORE THE REVOLUTION
When Eric Gairy was elected Grenada's first leader after Independence, he had already built up a large following as a member of the colonial administration, promoting the cause of the workers. However, Gairy's government grew increasingly corrupt and repressive, its policies enforced by the secret Mongoose Gang and soon an underground anti-government movement gathered strength. The New Jewel Movement united Gairy's socialist opponents; in March 1979 it took advantage of the leader's absence from Grenada to stage a coup, and, with Cuban support, Maurice Bishop's new administration began to implement its socialist policies.

47

"Mango, banana and tangerine", *as sung in the film* Dr No. *St George's Market has them all*

A century ago, the cocoa estates of Grenada would ring to the sound of fiddlers, who played for the workers as they "danced" the cocoa beans. The beans were laid out on boucans, or drying trays, and the workers would shuffle through them, turning them so that they dried evenly. Spices grow throughout the Caribbean, but Grenada's mild climate and fertile soil have earned it the title of "Spice Isle".

COCOA WALKS

Cocoa trees need to be shaded from the tropical sun if they are to flourish, so planters imported the tall and bushy *bois immortelle* or *madre de cacao* trees for that purpose. Shaded by their leaves, the "cocoa walks" are cool even in the middle of the day. In January and February the *bois immortelle* flowers bright orange and whole hillsides in Grenada, Trinidad and Tobago are patched with flaming orange blooms.

Spice Isle produce

Nutmeg and mace The nutmeg tree (*myristica fragrans*) actually yields two spices: nutmeg and mace. This bushy tree grows to 20m and produces a yellow fruit like an apricot, which splits open when ripe. Its flesh, used to make preserves, protects the nut itself, which is covered with a scarlet waxy netting. This is stripped off and sold as mace, for use as a food flavouring and in cosmetics. The kernel of the nutmeg is extracted from the shell and used to flavour foods (and to treat rheumatism).

Cocoa The Aztecs used cocoa beans for barter and made their national drink, *chocolada*, with them. The cocoa tree (*theobroma*, "food of the gods") grows to about 15m and sprouts yellow, brown and purple oval-shaped pods, in which the beans lie in a sweet, white, sticky pulp. These must be fermented, to strip the pulp, and then dried in the sun for several days.

Allspice "Jamaica pepper" and "pimento", as allspice is also known, is native to the Caribbean and tastes like a combination of clove, cinnamon and nutmeg. Used mainly as a flavouring for foods, it is an essential ingredient in jerk seasoning.

Other herbs and spices Oil extracted from the leaves and twigs of the bayberry tree (not to be confused with the Mediterranean bay) is used in perfumes and is distilled to make aromatic and medicinal bay rum. Ginger was brought to the Americas from the Far East by the Spaniards. Oil of ginger is used as a pain-reliever in the Windward Islands. The sweet-smelling bark of the cinnamon tree is used in confectionery and in cooking.

48

Flags hang in the streets of St George's in preparation for Carnival in August

The heart of town is the **Carenage▶▶▶**, the inner harbour, where the traditional island sloops and visiting cruise ships tie up. Waterfront warehouses now house restaurants and bars, and water-taxis pick up passengers for the bay crossing or the return to Grand Anse.

On Young Street, the **Grenada National Museum▶** (*Open* Mon–Fri 9–4:30, Sat 10:30–2. *Admission: inexpensive*) is set in a French stone barrack building and shows memorabilia including Josephine Bonaparte's childhood bathtub from Martinique, Arawak rock carvings and artefacts of the plantation era. Dominating the harbour is Fort George, also the island police headquarters, where Maurice Bishop and his supporters were killed.

Over the hill (or through the Sendall Tunnel) the other half of St George's, the Esplanade, is on the Caribbean seafront. Once the site of the public executions, the **Market Square▶▶▶** was not easy to reach before the tunnel was built between the town's two halves in the late 19th century. Today it also serves as the bus station for the west coast, and Saturday mornings are renowned for particular chaos, as vendors and busmen exchange shouts and jokes. Vendors hardly ever use the market buildings; they prefer to lay out their wares on tables under golfing umbrellas on the square. Near by is the Minor Spices Society, where Grenada's home-grown spices are on sale; and the **Yellow Poui Art Gallery▶▶** on Cross Street exhibits work by Caribbean artists.

St George's botanical gardens, on the Lagoon, are a little run down; the Bay Gardens on Richmond Hill are a better bet, showing a range of flora from forest walkways.

GRAND ANSE Not far along the coast to the south of St George's is **Grand Anse▶▶**, Grenada's best beach. There are several hotels on the beach itself (others are ranged behind it) and beach bars on the sand. Grand Anse is also the best area for watersports. Other good, secluded beaches, including **Morne Rouge Bay▶▶**, nestle in the coves towards the southwestern tip of the island.

The daily market is one of the liveliest and most accessible features of Caribbean life. Whether it be the overwhelming press of a large city market or a series of small stalls under a tree, the market is a vital focus of community and business. An amazing variety of goods is sold, from tropical fruit and vegetables to pots and pans, from candy and soap to human hair for braiding – all to the accompaniment of the shouts and patter of the marketeers.

THE FLOATING MARKET

Curaçao's floating market is made up of 15 or so moored boats. Vendors store their goods on board overnight and lay them out on the quayside stalls during market hours, shading them with flysheets (which are attached to the masts and rise and fall with the movement of the boats). The vendors are resupplied every few days with produce from Venezuela.

Crowds at St George's market

CASSAVA

Cassava is a familiar item on most Caribbean vegetable stalls. Most of its 160 species contain a poisonous, cyanide-like juice that must be extracted before the vegetable can be consumed. Carib methods included grating the tuber on a sea fan coral and then squeezing the pulp in a woven bag that tightened as it was stretched. Dried cassava can be used like flour to make cassava bread and cakes (called "bammy" in Jamaica).

Caribbean markets have always been more than just a place for buying and selling. In the days before emancipation in the 19th century, slaves would be allowed to make a little money by selling the fruit and vegetables they had grown. After slavery had been abolished, markets became gathering places where people would meet and swap stories. Colonial market buildings are usually made of red corrugated tin (the finest and the busiest is the Marché de Fer in Port-au-Prince in Haiti, which covers about half a hectare), but vendors often spread their goods out on blankets on the ground outside, rather than on the tables provided. Most stallholders are women, who sit on low boxes or benches with their skirts rolled up over their knees, shaded by two-tone golfing umbrellas. They arrive from the country in the early morning, often leaving by mid-afternoon, when the goods are sold.

Tropical vegetables are an essential feature of most Caribbean markets and include cassava (see panel); sweet potato, which can be oval or pointed with white, purple or orange flesh; eddoe, also called dasheen, whose spherical tubers have slender stems and heart-shaped leaves; and yam, which is long, thin and hairy.

On Grenada's south coast, L'Anse aux Epines has a number of hotels and bars, as well as a sailing marina, and further east, beyond the offshore island of Calivigny (where Grenadians often go for picnics), there is a charming dark sand beach with a hotel-restaurant at La Sagesse Bay. The **La Sagesse Nature Centre**▶▶ (tel: 444 6458) is set in a 40-hectare plantation, where guided trails offer interesting glimpses of plant and birdlife.

Ribbons and hair braids for the children of Grand Anse Roman Catholic School

A visit to the **Grand Etang National Park and Forest Reserve**▶▶ (tel: 440 6160) is worth the tortuous drive into the mountains. The rain forest can be fully appreciated from the trails, which afford good views of ferns spreading in the upper branches of the taller trees. The Grand Etang Visitor's Centre (*Open* Mon–Fri 8–4, Sat–Sun 9–5. *Admission: inexpensive)* contains a museum and an easy walking trail circles the Grand Etang crater lake (about 1.5 hours). Longer and more strenuous trails lead to Mount Qua Qua, Concord Falls and beyond.

From here the road descends into Grenada's most fertile valleys. In Grenville, which is not much more than a fishing village, one of Grenada's two large **nutmeg processing stations**▶▶ is based. The **River Antoine Rum Distillery**▶▶ (tel: 442 7109. *Open* Mon–Fri 8–5, Sat 10–4. *Admission: inexpensive)* shows a water-driven canecrusher in action as well as the process of boiling and distilling in order to make rum; visitors can taste the extremely strong result. The cane-crusher is one of the last of its kind operating in the Caribbean region.

The road north from St George's follows the switchbacks of the western coastline to Molinière Point, where there is good snorkelling. At the **Dougaldston Estate**▶▶ (tel: 444 8213. *Open* Mon–Fri 8–3, Sat–Sun 8–1. *Admission free)*, just south of Gouyave, Grenadian spices are prepared for sale. In Gouyave itself there is a **nutmeg co-operative**▶▶ where nutmeg and mace are prepared and visitors are welcome during the working week (nominal tip required).

NUTMEG PROCESSING PLANTS
It is well worth visiting either of Grenada's two main nutmeg co-operatives; one is in Gouyave, north of St George's and the other in Grenville on the Atlantic coast. Each factory is filled with groaning hessian sacks waiting for export and the pungent aroma of the spice itself. Once the mace has been stripped and graded (according to colour), the nut of the nutmeg is put through a crusher and the kernel is extracted from the shells. It is then put through a water test: the finest nutmegs sink and are used in food flavouring; those that float are used by the pharmaceutical industry.

MR CANUTE CALISTE

Mr Canute Caliste is Carriacou's resident artist. He has been painting for many years in his own unique, naïve style, using the bright colours of the Carriacou sea and island folklore to express his charming vision of island life. If you are on the island it is well worth visiting his studio in L'Esterre, where his works are on sale. Another Carriacouan, Frankie Franks, exhibits in the Carriacou Museum in Hillsborough.

52

Maurice Bishop, leader of Grenada's People's Revolutionary Government in the 1980s

The village of Sauteurs, on the northern coast, serves as a reminder of the last Carib people in Grenada, who jumped to their deaths off a cliff here (Caribs' Leap) rather than be taken prisoner by French colonists in 1651. Inland, to the southwest of Sauteurs in the hills, is the delightful **Morne Fendue**▶▶▶ (tel: 442 9330. *Open* daily for lunch), a modest plantation house, where rum punch is served on the veranda and the famous lunch consists of pepperpot, a dish that can last for 60 years if replenished and boiled daily. The last pepperpot had to be abandoned during the revolution, when there was a curfew; the current pot is approaching its twentieth anniversary. Beaches in the northern area include Bathway, where there is a protective reef against the Atlantic waves.

Carriacou and Petit Martinique Carriacou▶▶▶ is the biggest of the two inhabited islands politically attached to Grenada. Attractive, welcoming and extremely laid-back, it measures only 8km by 13km and has 7,000 inhabitants, who earn their living by selling vegetables and livestock in Grenada and pursuing "unofficial" trade with other islands. Boat-building is a major island tradition and the colourful sloops constructed by hand in Windward, on the eastern coast, and Tyrrel Bay are launched with great pomp and circumstance. The festive Carriacou Regatta is held every August. Ferries to Carriacou sail from the Carenage, St George's, daily and take 30 mins to 4 hours (they also come from Union Island further north), and flights land at Lauriston airport. The island is graced with some magnificent beaches and its southern shore has a view stretching 40km to Grenada and taking in a number of uninhabited islands and cays. Beaches well worth visiting include the one at Anse la Roche, Windward Beach and Paradise Beach. Tyrrel Bay is a superb place to watch the sunset.

Petite Martinique▶ is situated 5km to the east of Carriacou and has a population of around 900 islanders. As there is only one place to stay, this figure does not often increase: it is untouched by tourism.

Map

ST VINCENT
Kingstown
Young I
Bequia Channel
Bequia
Admiralty Bay • Port Elizabeth
Battowia
Isle à Quatre
Baliceaux
Mustique
Petit Mustique
Petit Canouan
Savan I
Canouan
Mayreau
Tobago Cays
Sail Rock
Union Island
Clifton
Palm I
Petit St Vincent
ST VINCENT & THE GRENADINES
GRENADA
Carriacou
Petite Martinique
Tyrrel Bay
Hillsborough
Saline I
Large I
Frigate I
Diamond
Les Tantes
Ronde I
Caille
GRENADA

0 5 10 15 20 km
0 5 10 miles

FAIR EXCHANGE
Young Island is said to have been swapped for a horse. Governor Young had brought a black charger with him to St Vincent from Britain and it was greatly admired by the local Carib chief, so he presented the creature to him as a gift. Some time later the two men were together on the veranda of St Vincent's Government House, looking out towards the idyllic, forested islet just offshore. When Governor Young admired the island, the Carib chief returned the favour and made him a present of the land.

Admiralty Bay, used by the British Navy and then abandoned for lack of water, is now a favourite anchorage for yachts

The Grenadines

Administered by St Vincent (see page 64), the Grenadines appeal to adventurous singles and couples who prefer sailing, seclusion and sports to glitz, gambling or designer shopping. Hotels are small, the food is simple and the residents' hospitality provides a peaceful, laid-back atmosphere. The 32 islands and cays that make up the lush and mountainous Grenadines offer numerous unspoiled white sand bays and coves, and superb snorkelling, hiking, sailing and swimming. Island-hopping by ferry is a practical alternative to flying.

Just off St Vincent, **Young Island▶** (tel: 458 4826) is a private resort with only about 20 cottages. **Bequia▶▶▶** lies 14km south of St Vincent. This is an island of fishermen, seafarers, boat-builders and whalers, where tourists rub shoulders with the locals in an excellent string of waterfront bars in Port Elizabeth, the main settlement and ferry harbour. The best places to stay include Frangipani, overlooking the harbour, and the Friendship Bay Hotel on the south coast. You can reach the excellent beaches of Princess Margaret Beach and Lower Bay by water taxi, or walk over to the secluded sand at Industry Bay in the east.

The graceful profiles of locally built boats are a familiar sight in the Grenadines. Brightly painted sloops still ply their trade from island to island as they have for centuries. Life in the Caribbean has always been dependent on shipping and even now the smaller islands only really seem to come alive when crowds gather to greet the weekly mail boat.

Before island-hopping planes, Caribbean communities were linked by frequent boat services. Unfortunately, the use of small boats has died off on the larger islands, but part of the fun of visiting the Grenadines, the Virgin Islands and the French islands off Guadeloupe is to hop from one island to the next by mailboat, ferry or traditional schooner.

There is a long history of boat-building and sea-faring around the Caribbean islands. Caymanians and Sabans were particularly renowned as sailors and they crewed and captained vessels all over the world for the big shipping lines. Closer to home, inter-island trading was established as a necessary way of life – Anguillans would sail west to Jamaica and south to Trinidad to sell their products. Captains would fund the boat-building by travelling abroad to earn money first for the hull, then for the planking and the deck, then finally for the mast and fittings. Nowadays Grenadine sloops travel regularly to Trinidad, taking fruit and vegetables for sale and returning with goods such as crisps and canned food. They also go as far north as Sint Maarten in the Leeward Islands, to buy supplies including export alcohol and goods from Europe.

Today's master boat-builders are the Bequians and Carriacouans; although their trade is now dying, it is still possible to see hulls taking shape on the beach and being painted bright red and orange – essential for clear visibility against a turquoise sea.

Smuggling has always been part of Caribbean life. Although drugs do pass through the islands *en route* elsewhere, inter-island smuggling is usually confined to alcohol, cigarettes and large appliances, primarily for the avoidance of island duty. Buyers are told in advance when a boat will be putting in at a particular cove – usually in the dead of night.

54   *Making sure everything is shipshape*

BOAT-LAUNCHING
A boat-launch is an excuse for a big party. The boat is christened and blessed by a priest with holy water (and sometimes with the blood of a goat). It is even given godparents, whose duty it is to raise it if it sinks. As the boat is launched, as many people clamber on board as possible, all dressed in their Sunday best, before returning to shore to eat and drink.

A scrubby outcrop 40 years ago, **Mustique**▶▶ now has 75 of the Caribbean's most luxurious villas, 50 of which are for rent, for a price (gardener, maids, cooks and moped, or donkey, thrown in). Just 2.4km by 5km, Mustique has two hotels; the Cotton House is set in the restored plantation house. Celebrities such as Mick Jagger and Princess Margaret have been known to emerge from the seclusion of their villas on Wednesdays, jump-up night at Basil's beach bar on stilts (tel: 457 2713). The Caribbean seems as incidental to Mustique as it is essential to Bequia.

On **Canouan**▶▶, around 1,000 people eke out a quiet living recently boosted by the arrival of the Suish Carenage Bay Beach Golf Club resort (tel: 458 8000). This small island (5km by 1.6km) of gentle green peaks is rimmed with white sand. Offshore reefs protect the windward bays and Grand Bay, on the leeward side, is a favourite yacht anchorage.

Mayreau▶▶, smaller and quieter, does not even have a jetty. Loading and unloading passengers can be a precarious business when the occasional cruise ships do put in. There are only 150 inhabitants and a couple of cars, but the beaches are wonderful.

Although its towering mountains make **Union Island**▶ the most beautiful of the Grenadines, this is a working island; its marina and airstrip are used by a constant stream of people travelling to the quieter islands near by. Most of the 2,000 islanders are employed in the resorts or fish and trade by sea.

The five **Tobago Cays**▶▶▶, Petit Rameau, Petit Bateau, Barabal, Jamesby and Petit Tobac, rise gently from the water, protected by a reef 1km offshore. They are uninhabited and maintained as a marine park and offer excellent sailing and snorkelling.

Close by are two tiny cays, each entirely devoted to a single luxurious hotel. **Palm Island**▶▶ (tel: 458 8824) has 24 villas set on the beach or scattered among hundreds of palms. **Petit St Vincent**▶▶▶ (tel: 458 8801), known as PSV, specialises in low-key super-luxury, where residents communicate with room service by raising a yellow flag.

BEACHES

Beaches with bright white sand can be found throughout the Grenadines, many of them sheltered in coves formed by the irregularly shaped, mountainous islands. On the northern shore of Admiralty Bay on Bequia are the golden sands of Princess Margaret Beach and Lower Bay; Endeavour Bay is the best beach on Mustique, although the whole island is rimmed with ankle-deep, soft sand. Canouan has a number of pretty beaches and isolated coves, including Maho, Corbay and Rameau Bay. On Mayreau the best beaches are Salt Whistle Bay and Saline Bay. One of the finest beaches in the West Indies is on Carriacou, at Anse la Roche. None of the beaches has formal facilities, but if there is a restaurant, the staff will normally let you change there.

55

Named after a governor in the 1700s, Young Island lies about 200m off St Vincent's southern shore

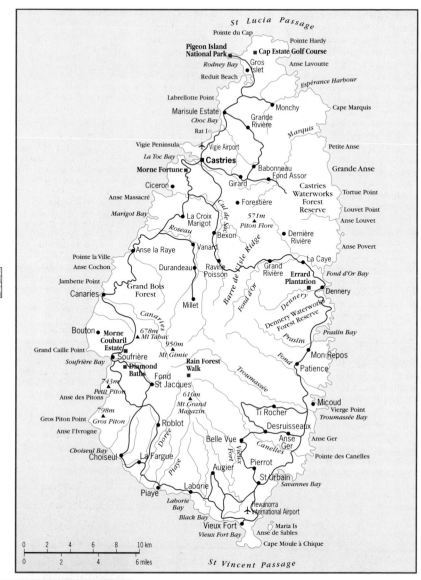

St Lucia Passage
Pointe du Cap
Pointe Hardy
Pigeon Island Cap Estate Golf Course
National Park
Rodney Bay Gros Anse Lavoutte
Islet
Reduit Beach Espérance Harbour
Labrellotte Point
Marisule Estate Monchy Cape Marquis
Choc Bay Grande
Rivière
Rat I○ *Marquis*
Vigie Peninsula Petite Anse
La Toc Bay Vigie Airport
Castries Grande Anse
Morne Fortune Babonneau
Fond Assor
Ciceron Girard Castries Tortue Point
Waterworks
Anse Massacré Forestière Forest Louvet Point
Marigot Bay Reserve Anse Louvet
La Croix 571m
Marigot *Piton Flore*
Roseau Bexon Dernière
Vanard Rivière Anse Povert
Anse la Raye
Pointe la Ville Durandeau Ravine Grand La Caye
Anse Cochon Poisson Rivière **Errard** Fond d'Or Bay
Jambette Point **Plantation**
Canaries **Grand Bois** Dennery
Forest
Canaries Millet *Dennery*
Dennery Waterworks
Forest Reserve
Bouton **Morne** 678m *Praslin* Praslin Bay
Coubaril Mt Tabac
Grand Caille Point **Estate** 950m Mon Repos
Soufrière Bay Soufrière Mt Gimie Patience
Diamond Rain Forest
Baths Walk *Troumassée*
743m Fond
Petit Piton St Jacques
Anse des Pitons 616m
Mt Grand Micoud
798m Magazin Vierge Point
Gros Piton Point *Gros Piton* Ti Rocher *Troumassée Bay*
Anse l'Ivrogne Desruisseaux
Roblot Anse
Choiseul Bay Belle Vue Ger Anse Ger
Choiseul La Fargue *Canelles*
Pierrot Pointe des Canelles
Augier
St Urbain
Laborie *Savannes Bay*
Piaye
Laborie Hewanorra
Bay International Airport
Black Bay
Vieux Fort Maria Is
Vieux Fort Bay Anse de Sables
Cape Moule à Chique
St Vincent Passage

0 2 4 6 8 10 km
0 2 4 6 miles

St Lucia

On Friday nights crowds gather at Gros Islet, a village on St Lucia's Rodney Bay, in the north. This Caribbean jump-up transforms the settlement of wooden houses into one big street party: the thumping pulse of local soca, Martiniquan zouk and Jamaican reggae can be heard from afar and dancers spill onto the road, winding and grinding beneath the banks of flashing lights and the stacks of speakers, while vendors sell grilled fish and chilled beer. The mix of people at Gros Islet is typical of St Lucia, where tourists and locals rub shoulders easily in the towns and on the beach. Lying between the French island of Martinique and St Vincent to the south, this is one of the most welcoming of the Caribbean islands and has become an increasingly popular tourist destination in recent years. The rapid development of a tourist industry, with beach hotels and restaurants sprouting all over the island, threatens to swamp the quiet agricultural life that has characterised St Lucia for many years, but as yet tourism is concentrated in the northwest, between the capital, Castries, and the northern tip of the island, where the best beaches are to be found. Venture into the city and beyond and there is still a beautiful island to explore, boasting inland rain forests harbouring indigenous parrots, and secluded coves accessible only by boat.

ISLAND LIFE Most St Lucians are chatty and forthcoming, as will soon become apparent to anyone taking a walk on the streets of Castries or in the country villages. Most speak patois, a Créole language derived mainly from French, but English is the official language.

This was a British colony for one-and-a-half centuries, until Independence on 22 December, 1979, but before that the island had a history of struggle and conquest. St Lucia's strategic importance sparked off several battles for its possession between the British and French until Britain finally took control in 1814. However, the French legacy remains, in the names of many towns, the predominant religion (Catholicism) and the Créole food, which includes such delights as *soupe germou* (pumpkin soup with garlic) and *pouile dudon* (a chicken dish that is cooked in coconut and sugar).

St Lucia is the most populous (there are around 150,000 islanders) and the most developed of the Windward Islands. Besides tourism, there is some light manufacturing and an extensive agricultural sector that, until recently, depended mainly on bananas grown for export to Britain under special trade arrangements, but is now coming under threat from cheaper producers in Central America (see page 58).

CASTRIES St Lucia's capital, **Castries▶▶**, was named after a French Minister of the Marine, the Maréchal de Castries, and laid out beside a natural harbour in the 1760s. It soon crept over the heights that surround the bay. Now a sprawling town of 70,000, Castries has burned down many times (most recently in 1948) and only a few colonial buildings remain. However, traditional Caribbean architecture survives on the hills around town, on Vigie Point and Morne Fortune.

The main square in the centre of town has been renamed after one of St Lucia's Nobel Prize winners, Derek Walcott. It is dominated by a huge saman tree and the brick Cathedral of the Immaculate Conception, built in 1897. On the south side are a number of old Créole timber-frame houses.

PRIZE WINNERS
The island of St Lucia can claim two Nobel Prize winners: in 1979 Sir Arthur Lewis won a Nobel Prize for Economic Sciences, and in 1992 Derek Walcott was awarded a Nobel Prize for Literature. Walcott, born in St Lucia in 1930, was educated at the University of the West Indies and has taught in a number of American universities. He is best known for his poetry collections, including *The Fortunate Traveller* (1982), *Midsummer* (1984) and *Omeros* (1990). The last, arguably his masterwork, is an ambitious retelling of *The Odyssey* set in the islands Walcott knows so well.

Opposite: harbour view from Castries

The edible banana's botanical name is **Musa sapientum**, *or "muse of the wise man". It is said that Southeast Asian sages would sit in the shade of banana trees, enjoy the fruit and have wise thoughts. Since the banana made its way to the Caribbean, this pastime has been readily adopted by islanders.*

THE "BANANA BOAT SONG"

Harry Belafonte's "Banana Boat Song" was originally a Jamaican working song, sung by female banana packers as they raced up and down the gangplanks, loading bunches of bananas onto the United Fruit Company ships. After working through the night, they would sing "Day-oh, day-oh" as day was dawning; the "tally-man" referred to in the song would give the workers tokens each time they came past with a load of bananas, tallying up the tokens at the end of the night and paying the women accordingly.

CLAIMS TO FAME

Bananas are highly valued by sportsmen and women, particularly tennis players and marathon runners, because they have a wide and complex range of sugars. These are digested at different rates, thereby releasing energy over a longer period than other sugary foods, such as chocolate. The fruit has a rather less creditable reputation in Sri Lanka, where the story of Adam and Eve has the serpent tempting Eve not with an apple but with a banana.

Banana plants grow singly and in groves all over the Caribbean, their leaves exploding in graceful, green curves to heights of up to 6m. Each plant gives fruit only once before it dies: then another plant sprouts from the same root system. As they grow, they throw off drooping stems, on which the 150 or so individual bananas sprout, coming to maturity over nine months. The plants are protected from insects by blue plastic bags and some are tied in a cat's cradle of string to prevent them from falling over. Bananas grow in clusters, or "hands", of about 12; a group of 10 or so hands on a single stem is known as a "bunch". Names and species vary. The yellow cavendish is the type of banana seen most in Europe and America, because it travels well, but Caribbean markets sell smaller, fatter, sweeter canary bananas (about 12cm long) and green vegetable-bananas called plantains. In the Windward Islands bananas range from big yellow *gros michels* to small "rock figs", and plantains called "green fig", "bluggo" and "buggoman".

Since the 1950s the export of bananas has improved life dramatically for many small farmers in Jamaica, the French Caribbean and the Windward Islands. Instead of seasonal work in the cane fields, they now have a year-round income. In the late 1990s, bananas accounted for three-quarters of the Windward Islands' export earnings. But free market agreements such as GATT and NAFTA have brought Caribbean bananas under threat, especially from "dollar bananas", grown more cheaply in Central America. The loss of traditional markets is hitting the Caribbean growers hard and farmers will have to diversify to survive.

A West Indian woman carrying her cargo on her head

A short walk away, Castries life is at its most ebullient in the market all along the waterfront in the new tin-roofed vegetable market and in the craft market.

Cruise ships dock on the north side of Castries harbour and passengers head straight into the shopping complex at Pointe Seraphine, where the St Lucia Tourist Board provides current information on hotels and events.

OUTSIDE CASTRIES Many of the island's hotels are set in coves north of the capital, an easy taxi or bus ride from Castries. The most popular area is **Rodney Bay▶ ▶**, with a marina, restaurants, hotels and the island's liveliest beach. Reduit Beach is a long strip of white coral sand with watersports facilities, it is particularly busy at weekends in late May when "Aqua Action" takes place, a programme of serious and fun watersports. Across the lagoon entrance is Gros Islet, the place to be on Friday nights.

Rodney Bay has long been a centre for sailing craft and beach bars, popular with locals at weekends. Before the gin-joints came Carib canoes, Spanish galleons, pirate sloops and naval ships. Two centuries ago Admiral Rodney himself fortified **Pigeon Island National Park▶** (tel: 450 8167. *Open* daily 8:30–6. *Admission: inexpensive*),

ROADSIDE REFRESHMENT
In the hot weather it is essential to have a ready supply of liquid and among Windward islanders there is a tradition of selling soft drinks at the roadside. A cup of crushed ice, topped with water, sweet fruit concentrate and a straw, is a great way to keep cool. Sometimes the vendor offers a topping of condensed milk or crushed nuts. Street snacks include locally grown peanuts, plantain chips or coconut chips cut from the dried copra in the centre of the coconut.

59

across the bay from Reduit Beach. It was designated a National Park in 1979 and its walkways pass barrack rooms and gun-pits, with a museum and restaurant at the end of the trail. There is one nine-hole golf course among the chic villas of the Cap Estate further north; and another at La Toc, south of Castries.

Different kinds of bananas and plantains are on sale in Castries market

The Windwards

*The two Pitons,
volcanic plugs
covered by rain forest,
rise dramatically from
the sea in the south-
west of St Lucia*

SPA FIT FOR SOLDIERS
King Louis XVI of France
provided the funds to
build the Diamond Baths
in the 1780s after
hearing of the volcanic
water's healing powers,
as described by the
Governor, Baron de
Laborie. According to
reports at the time, the
water was believed to
cure rheumatism, among
other ailments, and Louis
was eager for his troops
to feel the benefit. Water
flows from the volcano at
temperatures of about
40.5 degrees Centigrade.

HOT WATER
The volcanic Windward
Islands are active beneath
the surface of the water
as well as above it, and in
the sea off the Pitons you
will find patches of warm
water let out by the
Soufrière. In Dominica, for
instance, the bubbles
released make scuba-
diving feel like swimming
in champagne.

South of Castries, over Morne Fortune (pronounced "Fortunay"), there is a less feverish, less developed St Lucia of valleys and coastal villages, where banana farmers and fishermen are unaffected by tourism. Beyond Cul de Sac on the west coast is **Marigot Bay►►►**, a steep-sided inlet lined with palm trees, which was once a hideout for pirates and navvies. A couple of cafés are set on the road down to the bay and there are bars on the beach. At Canaries the coast road turns inland and climbs into rain forest beneath Morne Gimie (950m), the highest peak on the island. The descent into the town of Soufrière offers fine views of the **Pitons►►►**, two pyramid-shaped volcanic mountains that soar from the sea to heights of 744m and 800m.

Soufrière, the first settlement to be built on the island but rejected in favour of Castries and its better harbour, is a town of clapboard houses with overhanging balconies. Its name comes from the nearby **Soufrière►**, the world's only drive-in volcano, a simmering cauldron of mud, which can be tracked down by its foul smell. This is a solfatara – a volcanic vent that steams steadily rather than blowing cataclysmically like others in the area. Inland from Soufrière, at the **Diamond Baths►** (tel: 459 7565. *Open* Mon–Sat 10–5, Sun 10–3. *Admission: inexpensive*) it is possible to bathe in the naturally heated pools. Botanical gardens nearby give a good introduction to tropical flora. At the **Morne Coubaril Estate►►** you can see cocoa-making, go hiking and horse-riding (tel: 459 7340). The **Rain Forest Reserve►►** is a protected area with walking trails and is also home to St Lucia's own species of parrot, now near extinction. Contact the National Trust (tel: 452 5005) before using the trails; guides are also available.

The road from Castries down the east coast is an easier run, as it is used to meet flights into Hewanorra international airport, near the southern tip. After passing over the rainforested Barre de l'Isle mountain range, it descends into banana plantations at Dennery before reaching the more remote villages strung out along the coast. You can visit working cocoa, coconut and coffee plantations at the Marquis Estate at **Errard Plantation** near Dennery.

Before the age of television, whole villages would gather under a tree to enjoy an evening of storytelling. Many of the tales, often with song, centred around Anancy the Rogue and a cast of other characters – Dog, Goat, Jackass, Kisander the Cat and Tiger – all of whom had human characteristics. All over the Caribbean, Islanders still tell stories about them.

Anancy is the best-loved character in Caribbean folklore. Sometimes a man, sometimes a spider, he is a sweet-talking trickster who, as a man, is considered rather laughable because he speaks with a lisp, but who can turn into a spider and hide when the need arises. Anancy is lazy and greedy and far happier tricking a slow neighbour out of his meal than working honestly. But he is also fully capable of outwitting his opponents – particularly Tiger, his traditional enemy. Even in his greed, Anancy wins the listener's sympathy and is often used to deliver home truths – though storytellers may dissociate themselves from his actions by ending their tales with the words: "Jack Mantora me no choose any".

Above all, Anancy is good entertainment. When he wants a meal of crabs he dresses up as a priest and persuades them to be baptised (promptly throwing them into boiling water); having taken a bet that he cannot catch Snake, he taunts him into bragging about his length and while measuring him against a log, ties Snake to it and captures him.

The island of Trinidad has a strong tradition of folklore, illustrated in Port of Spain's National Museum. Papa Bois, the guardian of the forest, warns animals of the hunter's presence (see panel). La Diablesse, the devil woman, appears as an old crone whose petticoats clank with chains or as an attractive girl who can drive men mad with desire, and the soucouyant is an old woman who turns into a ball of fire at night and goes round sucking human blood.

Mama Dlo, the mother of the water, is half woman, half anaconda and sometimes sings at the water's edge, but vanishes immediately if she is disturbed.

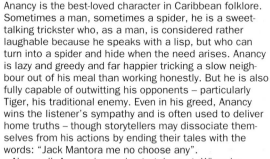

PAPA BOIS

Papa Bois will usually let hunters keep their kills from the forest, but if any become too greedy he will appear as a deer and lure them deep into the forest before turning back into an old man and issuing a stern warning, sometimes sentencing the offending hunter to be married to Mama Dlo.

DUENNES

Never shout the name of your child in the Trinidadian forest; he or she will be stolen by the Duennes. These infant tricksters, who reputedly roam among the trees, are the ghosts of children who died before they were christened and if they hear a child's name, they will call and lead the child away into mischief.

Top: the soucouyant
Below: Mama Dlo
Left: Papa Bois

61

The Caribbean climate is virtually ideal. Surrounded by sea, the islands enjoy an almost constantly warm temperature, even at night, and during the day the sun is tempered by the Trade Winds, cooling breezes that rise on the Atlantic. But at times, the benevolent ocean will deliver disaster in the form of a hurricane. These whirlwinds, accompanied by torrential rain, are immensely destructive. Land movement can cause chaos in the Eastern Caribbean, an area of tectonic activity where volcanoes occasionally blow and earthquakes strike.

HURRICANE SEASON
A traditional rhyme serves as a reminder of when hurricanes are most likely to strike: "June, too soon; July, stand by; September, remember; October, all over". Most hurricanes do, in fact, occur in the middle of September.

TRADE BY NAME
Although they were useful to merchant ships and used by sailors from the very first days of transatlantic travel, the Trade Winds are not named for their commercial value. The term was coined in the 16th century as "tread winds" – meaning directional winds.

The calm after the storm, but a wrecked boat sits offshore after a hurricane

Trade Winds These equatorial winds flow from a high pressure area in the mid-Atlantic to low pressure regions nearer the equator. They hit the Caribbean islands from the northeast, at an angle that varies through the year because of the earth's tilting. The Trade Winds reduce humidity, while bringing plenty of rain to the more mountainous islands. Known as *Les Alizes* on the French islands, the *Passaatwinden* on Dutch land and *Brisas Aliseas* in the Spanish territories, the so-called "Christmas winds" blow most strongly in the winter months, bringing with them the balmiest temperatures.

Hurricanes Terrible damage can be inflicted by hurricanes, whose name is derived from the Carib language. They rise in the Atlantic, at the meeting point of the Trade Winds from both hemispheres (north of the equator in the summer). In a phenomenon known as the "coriolis effect", the warm, moist air rises and then condenses, releasing heat, falls and then rises again, strengthening the updraft until it begins to spiral. Immature hurricanes set off west-northwest, moving at around 20kph and steadily building up size and power. The winds spiral inwards around a vortex known as the "eye" (about 20km across) and can reach sustained speeds of up to 170kph, with bursts of around 300kph. Extending up to 800km across, hurricanes are immensely

powerful; their effect is measured in atom bombs per second. They are identified by a sequence of alternately male and female names.

All the Caribbean islands from Grenada northwards lie in the hurricane zone and in recent years some have been very badly hit. Hurricane Gilbert swept through Jamaica and the Cayman Islands in 1988 and in 1989 Hurricane Hugo, the worst in the 20th century, laid waste to Guadeloupe, St Croix and Montserrat (where over 90 per cent of the houses were destroyed). 1995 brought Marilyn on the heels of Luis, both causing terrible destruction in St Maarten, Anguilla and St Thomas in the USVI. 1998's Georges wreaked havoc in the Dominican Republic and tore up Nevis, St Kitts, Antigua, Puerto Rico and Haiti.

Volcanoes The Eastern Caribbean is also an area of active volcanoes. This line of islands stretches in a curve from Saba to Grenada in the south, on the meeting point of the Atlantic and Caribbean tectonic plates. As the plates move slowly against each other, the magma (hot molton rock) contained beneath them occasionally escapes in the form of volcanic eruptions.

Volcanoes in the Eastern Caribbean all go by the name Soufrière, taken from the French word for sulphur because of the foul smell that they give out. The most active volcanoes are on St Vincent, Guadeloupe and Martinique; these erupt about once every 100 years with lava flows and plumes of smoke 6,000m high.

St Lucia and Dominica experience less devastating "fumaroles", where the pressure is let off constantly and more steadily – though the heat and pressure in Dominica is enough to make a lake boil. There is also an active volcano in the Grenadines: Kick 'em Jenny is underwater at the moment, but is expected to reach the surface in the future. Galway's Soufrière in Montserrat became active in 1995, showering the south of the island with ash and lava and rendering large areas uninhabitable.

Earthquakes Another effect of living on the bridge of two tectonic plates are earthquakes, which may accompany major volcanic eruptions and cause land slippages.

The Soufrière "drive-in" volcano, St Lucia

63

HOME SAFE HOME
Traditional Caribbean architecture was designed to cope with rare but severe climatic problems. Stone foundations gave a solid base during earthquakes, while a wooden upper storey could wobble but survive in the windblasts of a hurricane. St John's Cathedral in Antigua has been lined with wood to preserve it from the effects of hurricanes and earthquakes.

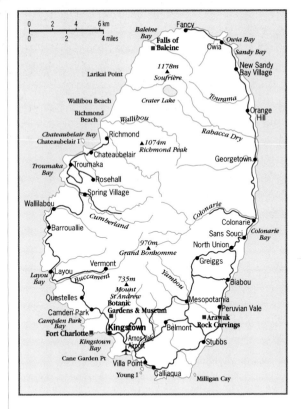

CAPTAIN BLIGH
The 18th-century mutiny on the *Bounty* has become a popular subject for films and books, but less well known is the reason for Captain Bligh's eventful voyage. He had been commissioned by the Society of West Indian Merchants to bring bread-fruit plants to the West Indies from the South Pacific. Bligh's second attempt to transport the plants, in 1793 in the ship *Providence*, was more successful and he delivered the plants to botanical gardens around the Caribbean. Trees grown from cuttings of the original plants can still be seen in the St Vincent Botanic Gardens. The ackee tree – *Blighia sapida* – is named after the captain, who brought it to the region from West Africa.

St Vincent

St Vincent is a fertile and beautiful island, from its cultivated valleys to the rain-forested slopes of its active volcano, Soufrière. Linked to Grenada by the 120km string of the Grenadines, it is usually considered as a starting point for yachting trips; however, its rugged east coast and fascinating Arawak settlement are worth seeing. There is also first-rate diving and snorkelling and hiking on trails as verdant as any in Hawaii.

The 110,000 Vincentians are mainly of African origin, the descendants of plantation slaves, but this was not always a plantation island. Like Dominica, St Vincent was one of the last strongholds of the Carib people. Here, the local tribe, known as the Yellow Caribs, and escaped African slaves produced a race of Black Caribs, who held out against the colonists. In 1797 they were eventually defeated and their survivors were deported to Roatan, an island off Honduras. The British took over St Vincent and

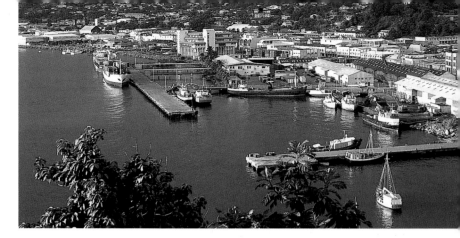

built up a trade of sugar, cotton and arrowroot. Independence was gained in 1979, though St Vincent remains within the British Commonwealth.

Agriculture still provides much of the island's living; exports include arrowroot starch, bananas and coconuts. St Vincent is relatively undeveloped, with a small area of hotels in the southeast and a few other isolated spots.

The capital of St Vincent and the Grenadines is **Kingstown**▶▶, a few streets of Georgian townhouses with cobbled, arched walkways set on a wide south-western bay. The town is fairly quiet, except around the Grenadines pier when ships come in and at the market on Halifax Street, the centre of island gossip. Nearby are the Law Courts, where the St Vincent Parliament sits and the unusual Gothic and Romanesque Roman Catholic church, which was built in 1823. There are plans to relocate the National Museum (which is currently closed) and its collections of Amerindian relics to the Old Public Library building.

Away from the waterfront, the ground rises through outlying suburbs to the range of hills surrounding the town. In the northwest are the 8ha of the **St Vincent Botanic Gardens**▶▶▶ (*Open* daily), dating back to 1763. Here, species include the sealing wax palm, red hot cat tail and roucou, used as body-paint by the Carib tribes. On the heights to the southwest lies Fort Charlotte where, on a clear day, the view extends south to Grenada.

Past the airport in the southeast nestles Villa Point, where restaurants and bars are set among the pretty tin-roofed villas on the waterfront, looking across a small stretch of water to Young Island. Inland are the fertile valleys where St Vincent's market produce is grown and at Yambou, off the road to the town of Mesopotamia, Arawak **rock carvings**▶▶ date from before AD 1000.

A journey up the west coast on the Leeward Highway reveals the West Indies at its most natural: small and simple villages filled with hordes of shouting school-children. There are rain forest walking trails in the **Buccament Valley**▶▶ and the hike up the Soufrière (1,180m) is a day's trip, best started from the Rabacca Dry River, north of Georgetown, or Richmond, north of Chateaubelair. Boats sail from Kingstown to the Falls of Baleine, a 18m cascade into a rockpool at the island's northern tip, past the villages of the leeward shore.

The port at Kingstown is a picturesque place

UNDER SHELTER
It rains so regularly in the Windward Islands that the old streets were built with colonnades so that the market vendors could sell their wares under cover and people would be sheltered as they walked around the town. Where other islands had wooden houses (now often burned down), Kingstown has some particularly attractive stone arches and cobbles. Most modern buildings are made of concrete and topped with tin roofs.

FORT DUVERNETTE
Young Island is the nearest of the Grenadines to St Vincent's shore and, beyond it, perched on its 60m overgrown rock, is the defensive bastion that once protected the larger island's southern waters. Cannons dating from the 18th century are still at the ready, but these days only tourists are likely to invade the fort (via steps in the rockface), to enjoy the impressive views.

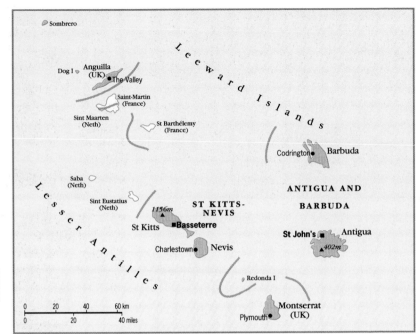

One of the Leeward islanders: a resident of Antigua

The Leeward Islands

THE LEEWARD ISLANDS The English-speaking Leewards have maintained much of their small-island charm in the face of growing tourism. With a vast choice of beaches, friendly small towns and varied local customs, they stand in refreshing contrast to the bigger tourist destinations. Antigua is the most developed holiday island; Anguilla has developed quite quickly over the past few years and St Kitts and Nevis have followed a policy of sustainable development. Poor Montserrat, which was developing its tourism slowly, has been stopped in its tracks by the eruption of its volcano. Two centuries ago the islands were isolated outposts and fast communications were essential. Now their remoteness is a selling point, and many visitors pay a lot of money to enjoy it, particularly on Anguilla and St Kitts.

The six Leeward Islands (they were to the lee side of ships arriving from Europe) lie in two lines. To the west, Montserrat, Nevis and St Kitts are the rain-forested peaks of a relatively young volcano chain (about 15 million years old). To their east are the protrusions of a much older range: Antigua, Barbuda and – beyond the French islands of St Barts and Saint-Martin – Anguilla, the most northerly of the Lesser Antilles. Capped with coral limestone, the Lesser Antilles have some of the finest sand in the Caribbean.

▶▶▶ **REGION HIGHLIGHTS**

Anguilla beaches
page 71

Brimstone Hill Fortress
pages 86–87

Friar's Bay *page 86*

The frigatebird sanctuary *page 76*

Nelson's Dockyard *page 76*

The Nelson Museum *page 83*

Pinney's Beach *page 82*

68

HISTORY The islands are connected by a common history, having been British colonies for many years, but most have now gone their own way. The islands of Antigua and Barbuda negotiated their full independence in the early 1980s and were soon followed by St Kitts and Nevis, but they remain in the British Commonwealth. Montserrat and Anguilla are still Crown Colonies of Britain.

British settlers first arrived at St Kitts in 1623, but continual disputes over the island's possession took place between Britain and France right up until 1783. Using an army of slave labourers, the colonisers planted sugar cane frantically and became immensely wealthy. But when slavery was abolished in the British Empire in 1834, the Leeward Islands quickly went into decline. The freed slaves took to the land, dividing it into small individual plots and scraping a poor living from

subsistence farming. Today you will still see subsistence farmers living on the Leeward Islands; their lifestyle is only gradually changing now after 150 years.

Coconut palm silhouettes in the calm of an Antiguan sunset

ISLAND LIFE Unfortunately, the Leeward Islands' economies are precarious and, despite the success of a few small industries, all depend to some extent on tourism. This has developed steadily over the past 20 years and in places it seems to have swamped local Caribbean life and traditions, which have all but disappeared in some parts. The more developed islands, Antigua and Anguilla, tend to have better restaurants, but a stroll around Nevis, or a visit to one of its rum stores, is more likely to give a taste of local life. Each island has its special points, whether it is rum-soaked rumbustiousness during Sailing Week (usually the last week of April) on Antigua, a glimpse of the planters' leisurely way of life amid historic surroundings on St Kitts and Nevis, the marine reserve and wildlife of Barbuda, or the deserted beaches of Anguilla. There are also good opportunities for hopping by boat and plane to other islands nearby.

The islanders are English-speakers (as they are on the nearby Dutch Windward Islands), but accents vary from island to island, as do the characteristics of their people. Distinct traces of Irish can be heard in the inflections and pronunciations of Anguillan and Montserratian islanders, which are not present in the accents of St Kitts, Nevis and Antigua. While there is a certain reserve and politeness on Montserrat and Nevis, the people of Anguilla and Barbuda have a reputation for a proud and independent outlook. Nevertheless, all Leeward Islanders are known for their easy-going attitude, which is well expressed in the favourite Caribbean expression "no problem".

REMISSIONS
The economies of the Leeward Islands have traditionally depended on "remissions" from abroad. Since the sugar industry foundered, people have either cultivated small plots of land or travelled in search of work, sending some of their earnings home to their families. Many islanders worked on the digging of the "Ditch" – the Panama Canal – and in the Dominican Republic's cane fields at the turn of the century. Later there was a rush to the oil refineries of Aruba and Curaçao and in the 1950s and 1960s there were widespread emigration to Britain. Most emigration is now to the USA or Canada.

Anguilla

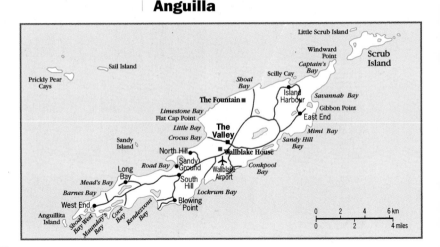

REBEL MARINE
You will soon come to know the sleek contours of boats made by Rebel Marine, an Anguillan boat-yard. The gull-winged ferries that make the run from Blowing Point to Saint-Martin are made by them (as is the North Sound Express boat in the British Virgin Islands) and many others lie at anchor in Sandy Ground and around the island. The designs take traditional Anguillan lines (from a long tradition of boat-building) and adapt them to modern materials.

Only 20 minutes by ferry from Saint-Martin/Sint Maarten, Anguilla offers some of the Caribbean's best restaurants and beaches. There are about 30 tiny, secluded coves, snorkelling beaches and walking strands, all with fine sand washed by a clean turquoise sea. Anguilla has a string of luxurious hotels, though it is possible to find cheaper options: the Anguilla Tourist Office, The Valley (tel: 497 2759) can offer useful advice. There are no buses on the island, but taxis can be picked up at the airport, from the Blowing Point ferry dock, or from hotels. Just 26km long, the island is made up of coral limestone. Its flat land is covered in thick scrub, which is steadily being cleared for building. Anguilla is a rapidly developing island, but it is still a quiet place with little visual history and comparatively few "sights". Its chic and expensive hotels are a second home to film stars and executives seeking a retreat from the humdrum. (Those who are wanting nightlife and shopping can always sneak over to Sint Maarten.)

It may come as something of a surprise to learn that this peaceful island once had a revolution (albeit bloodless). In the 1960s Anguilla became part of the Associated State

Lobsters: a speciality on the island

of St Kitts-Nevis-Anguilla, but its inhabitants objected to St Kitts' prominent role (see panel). Anguilla was separated from the three-island state in 1971 and regained its status as a UK-dependent territory. The island suffered badly in the hurricanes of 1995, but its buildings and beaches have now completely recovered.

In the middle of the island, close to the airport, is the small capital, The Valley, where the administrative offices, banks, shops and the only hospital are all based. The other main settlements are Sandy Ground, the main port and Island Harbour, a fishing village in the northeast. Near by is the Fountain, a cave used by the indigenous Arawak Indians, where carved faces are arranged to be lit by the sun in turn.

Beaches ring the island and most hotels have watersports facilities. On the north coast, near the western tip, **Barnes Bay**▶▶ is a strip of sand backed with rocks and broad-leaved sea grape trees. Heading east, **Mead's Bay**▶, a curve of deep sand, has a lovely sunset view from the Malliouhana end. Calm and protected **Road Bay**▶▶ harbours local boats and some larger ships and has a string of restaurants and bars. Just beyond Crocus Bay is **Little Bay**▶▶▶, access to which is by boat or by climbing down the cliff, and **Limestone Bay**▶▶. **Shoal Bay**▶▶▶ has fine sand, a modest string of beach bars, watersports concessions and snorkelling offshore. On the north coast lies **Captain's Bay**▶▶, a half-moon of secluded sand (ask for directions and follow the coastline). On the south coast, past Blowing Point, is **Rendezvous Bay**▶▶, a mangrove and dune-backed walking strand with a clear view of Saint-Martin and an excellent bar like a shipwrecked galleon, *The Dune*. The moorish domes of the Cap Juluca Hotel (tel: 497 6666) dominate crescent-shaped **Maunday's Bay**▶▶; beyond here, **Shoal Bay West**▶▶▶ is overlooked by the tall, white curves of the Cove Castles hotel villas (tel: 497 6801). Sandy Island and Prickly Pear Cays have fine beaches and are good for a day's sailing trip: one departs from Island Harbour for the spit of land called Scilly Cay, famed for its grilled lobster and beach party atmosphere.

THE REVOLUTION
As Britain divested itself of Caribbean colonies in the 1960s, Anguilla was faced with independence and a marriage of convenience to St Kitts and Nevis. The Anguillans rebelled. A few shots were fired and St Kitts policemen were expelled from the island. As tension grew, the British sent a detachment of paratroopers in 1969 – an "invasion" (welcomed by the Anguillans) that was later dubbed the "Bay of Piglets". Anguilla's rebels got their way and the link with St Kitts was cut forever, but a satisfactory political solution was found only in 1982, when the island was eventually granted its own constitution, headed by a Council of Ministers and a House of Assembly.

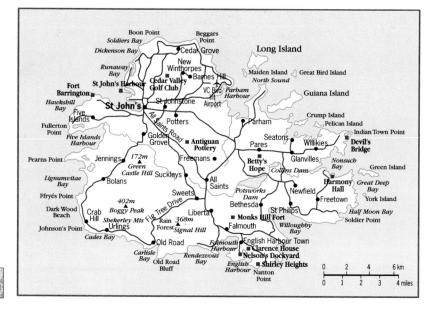

Boon Point
Soldiers Bay
Dickenson Bay
Beggars Point
Cedar Grove
Long Island
New Winthorpes
Runaway Bay
St John's Harbour
Cedar Valley Golf Club
Barnes Hill
Maiden Island
Great Bird Island
North Sound
Fort Barrington
VC Bird Intl
Parham Harbour
Guiana Island
Hawksbill Bay
St Johnstone
Airport
St John's
Crump Island
Pelican Island
Fullerton Point
Five Islands
Potters
Parham
Indian Town Point
Five Islands Harbour
Golden Grove
Antiguan Pottery
Seatons
Pares
Willikies
Devil's Bridge
Pearns Point
Jennings
172m
Green Castle Hill
Freemans
Betty's Hope
Collins Dam
Glanvilles
Nonsuch Bay
Green Island
Lignumvitae Bay
Bolans
Suckleys
All Saints
Potsworks Dam
Newfield
Harmony Hall
Great Deep Bay
Ffryes Point
402m
Sweets
Bethesda
Freetown
York Island
Dark Wood Beach
Boggy Peak
Liberta
St Philips
Half Moon Bay
Crab Hill
Shekerley Mts
Rain Forest
368m
Signal Hill
Monks Hill Fort
Willoughby Bay
Soldier Point
Johnson's Point
Urlings
Falmouth
Cades Bay
Old Road
Falmouth Harbour
English Harbour Town
Carlisle Bay
Old Road Bluff
Rendezvous Bay
Clarence House
Nelson's Dockyard
English Harbour
Shirley Heights
Nanton Point

0   2   4   6 km
0   1   2   3   4 miles

Antigua and Barbuda

Contentment on an island cruise

The territory of Antigua and Barbuda actually consists of three islands: Antigua, the main island at 280sq km with excellent beaches and most of the 66,000 population; Barbuda, a smaller, wooded island to the north with a population of 1,100 and excellent, undeveloped beaches; and Redonda, a small, uninhabited rocky islet lying 40km southwest of Antigua, which has no beaches at all.

Pirate ships were once feared and avoided in the Caribbean's waters; now "pirate cruises" are popular tourist attractions

ANTIGUA The largest, the most popular and the most developed of the Leewards, Antigua has a mostly dry and flat landscape. Its foremost attractions are the superb beaches, the restored English Harbour historic area of Nelson's Dockyard, and Falmouth Harbour and its sailing facilities. English Harbour is also a hive of sailing activity during Race Week at the end of April every year.

Antigua is made of limestone coral, covered in grassy flatlands that rise steadily to the southwest. Two centuries ago the island was blanketed with sugar cane and ruins of the windmills in which the cane was crushed are dotted all over the island. The two main centres are the capital, St John's, in the northwest, and English Harbour.

St John's is a busy harbour town, particularly when a cruise ship is in dock. Founded in the early 18th century, it has attractive 19th-century buildings, with wooden gingerbread balconies. Some of the finest are in **Redcliffe Quay**▶▶ where restored warehouses and townhouses are now occupied by shops and cafés. Near the Tourist Information Office (Thames Street) is the Old Court House, where the **Antigua and Barbuda Museum**▶▶ (tel: 462 1469. *Open* Mon–Fri 8:30–4:30, Sat 10–2. *Admission: donation*) has displays on Amerindian Antigua and the colonial past. **St John's Cathedral**▶▶ is a towering building from 1848, close to the Recreation Ground where international cricket matches have been hosted here since Antigua and Barbuda became independent on 1 November, 1981. **St John's Public Market**▶, south of town, is liveliest on Saturday mornings.

Antigua's main tourist areas are to the west of the capital on the beaches of Five Islands Peninsula and to the north on **Runaway** and **Dickenson Bays**▶▶. From here, the road follows the coastline north through chic residential areas and past secluded coves to VC Bird International Airport and the Cedar Valley Golf Club. In the eastern area of the island the coastline and sea are spectacular (but not suitable for bathing except in well-protected bays) and at Indian Town you can see the Devil's Bridge, an archway of rock carved out by the waves. The 200-year-old plantation estate of **Betty's Hope**▶ (see panel), to the west, has been restored, with a visitor centre and a renovated windmill. In another windmill on the southeast coast is **Harmony Hall**▶▶ gallery (tel: 460 4120), selling good quality Caribbean arts and crafts.

PLANTATION ESTATE
At Betty's Hope (tel: 462 4930. *Open* Tue–Sat 10–4. *Admission: donation*) you can see the layout of a typical Caribbean plantation estate. The windmill was placed high up not only to catch the wind, but also so that the cane juice could run downhill in a sluice to the boiling house. The estate house had the best position – for the view and so that the owners could watch the activity on the estate. There is a huge cistern because, on a dry island like Antigua, water collection was vital.

73

VIV RICHARDS
Antigua's greatest hero was, for most of the 1980s, captain of perhaps the strongest West Indies cricket team ever. Considered to be the world's finest batsman, he regularly destroyed the bowling of English, Australian, Indian and Pakistani teams. Born in 1952, Richards played for Antigua and Leeward Islands teams soon after leaving school. He moved to Britain in 1974 to play for Somerset and in the same year played for the West Indies for the first time, becoming captain in 1984. Richards retired from international cricket in 1991.

An extraordinarily fertile and colourful marine life exists beneath the Caribbean waves. Corals grow like forests on the reefs and slopes, and hiding among them are weird and wonderful shellfish and crabs, while schools of tropical fish with exotic names and colours cruise by.

Corals, sponges and shellfish Corals are animals that grow in salt water shallow enough to be within the range of the sunlight. Of the 75 or so species in the Caribbean Sea, about 10 account for nine-tenths of the growth. Perhaps the most familiar is the white brain coral, with a surface that resembles a human brain; other hard corals include staghorn, which grows like crusty deer antlers; elkhorn, with huge sloping branches; starlet coral, with polyps like teeth; and orange clump coral, which has a mass of tentacles. Gorgonians consist of sea fans, which face the tidal flow to sift nutrients and sea whips, which blow like feathers in the tide.

Sponges and anemones add their own colour and variety to the marine world. Tube sponges can grow to 2m, in shades of pink, orange, purple and yellow and the white cryptic sponge hides in the crevices of the reef.

Anemones look like intricate flowers, with many only open at night; those that emerge during the day will often snap back into the rock if the water around them is disturbed. Shrimps (visible in daylight) often live in conjunction with anemones – the banded coral shrimp has a striking red-and-white striped body.

Night-diving reveals another, self-contained submarine society. Crabs and spiny lobsters come out for food, and starfish, some of which look like underwater plants, open up to feed in the dark. An octopus, squid, or a tiny seahorse might be spotted – though their camouflage is

74

AQUARIUMS
For non-divers several aquariums in the Caribbean provide alternatives to viewing from glass-bottom boats. The Guadeloupe Aquarium is between Bas du Fort and Gosier and has well-marked displays of tropical fish from the Caribbean and elsewhere. On Curaçao the Sea Aquarium is in the Underwater Park, east of Willemstad. A spiral-shaped aquarium operates in the Parque Lenin, south of Havana, in Cuba, but perhaps the most interesting display is at the small but fascinating St Croix Aquarium in Christiansted, where the underwater world is explained in fascinating detail by a guide. All aquariums charge an entry fee; prices vary, but they can be expensive.

excellent; the sea cucumber, by contrast, is easy to make out, resembling a mobile underwater hot dog. The biggest and best known of the molluscs (shell animals), which are also best seen at night, is the conch, known as the *lambi* in the French-speaking Caribbean. Lobsters migrate in their hundreds, like a herd of galloping horses.

There are a number of species to avoid when underwater: a touch from the fire coral can give a nasty sting, as can some jellyfish. Avoid the spiny black sea urchin at all costs – its spines cause agonising wounds if they break off in your flesh.

Fish Around a thousand species of fish live in the Caribbean, many of them on the reefs, where there is plenty of food.

Schools of angel fish and butterfly fish can be seen waving in the current; the four-eye butterfly fish has an imitation pair of eyes on its tail to confuse predators. Other species are dazzlingly beautiful – such as the queen angel fish, which is a luxurious shade of velvet-like blue and gold; and the yellow and black rock beauty. Many fish have names that describe their forms and habits. Damsel fish hide and lay their eggs in the reefs, grazing on algae, and striped sergeant majors defend their eggs aggressively. Grunts are named after the noise they make when alarmed, and surgeon fish have scalpel-sharp fins in their tails. Wrasses are scavengers that school in a harem, with a single male. If the male is eaten, the biggest female simply switches sex and takes over his job. Parrotfish eat off the reef, biting the polyps and their rocky coral base and spitting out crunched-up coral.

Predatory fish include groupers (who have been known to use scuba divers as a smokescreen in the hope of a meal – other fish are also attracted by them and come out of their crevices) as well as snappers, one of the most numerous species. They school facing into the current, all moving in time and snapping at any food that passes by. Barracuda patrol in small groups or singly, often around a chosen rock. Larger fish such as blue marlin tend to live in deep water drop-offs, where they are pursued by big-game fishing boats (see page 202).

Top: orange clown fish

EATING HABITS
The dentist or cleaner shrimp cleans the teeth of other, larger fish, thereby getting food for itself. The sponge crab takes small lumps of sponge to use as camouflage and when it fails to find food, it takes the sponge off its back and eats it. The remora, or sucker fish, is a long, thin fish that attaches itself to a larger fish, such as a shark, and feeds off the remains of its meal.

75

CORAL CLAIMS
In 1726 the French naturalist Jean André Peyssonnel declared to the Paris Academy of Sciences that coral reefs were made up of living animals, not marine shrubs, as was generally thought. He was ridiculed and had to live out his life as a scientist in exile in Guadeloupe – and though he was proved right during his lifetime, Peyssonnel received no credit.

Above left: the angel fish is one of the prettiest in the Caribbean waters

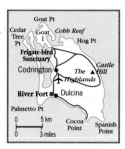

Barbuda

THE FRIGATEBIRD COLONY

The crooked wingspan and forked tail of the huge, black frigatebird is easy to recognise. Its most surprising feature is the male's gullet, a bright red balloon blown to the size of a basketball during display. Although it can be seen on Barbuda, it also flies to the other islands to feed, travelling at up to 150kph. It even attacks other birds on the wing for food, swooping in from above, grabbing a tail or leg and shaking the victim until it drops its meal. Barbuda's frigatebird sanctuary is well worth a visit; the birds soar high above it, returning to the mangroves to nest in large colonies. Located on the north end of the Codrington Lagoon, the sanctuary is only accessible by boat and so can only be visited during daylight hours; you'll have to hire a local person to take you there.

The hilly southwest of Antigua has excellent beaches, fine views from Green Castle Hill and a ring of stones thought by some to be ancient megaliths. Beneath Boggy Peak (at 402m the highest point of the island), Old Road, now a small village, was the site of Antigua's first European settlement in 1632. Nearby Fig Tree Hill is a lush valley covered with large, shiny "elephant ear" leaves and bananas, an example of vegetation more usual on the larger Windward Islands to the south.

In the southeast are the fortifications erected by British colonists when Antigua was at the height of its strategic and economic importance. Opposite Falmouth Harbour towers Monks Hill Fort, a refuge for women, children and animals in case of attack. Beyond it are the tourist and sailing areas of English Harbour and **Nelson's Dockyard►►►** (see opposite) which faces Clarence House, built in 1787 for the future King William IV, who was posted to Antigua by the Royal Navy. The dockyard is the centrepiece of the Nelson's Dockyard National Park (tel: 460 1146. *Open* daily 8–6. *Admission: moderate*), which extends above the harbour to **Shirley Heights►►**, a series of Georgian barrack buildings and gun emplacements constructed in the 1780s as a defence against the French. Here the **Dow's Hill Interpretation Centre►►** has a multimedia show of Antiguan history, from Indian settlement through Columbus and the colonial era, to the present day.

BARBUDA Lying 48km to the north of Antigua, Barbuda is one of the few truly undeveloped Caribbean islands. Like Antigua, with which it was politically merged in 1860, it is all coral limestone and has glorious beaches. Otherwise, its 155sq km are covered in scrub, where goats, donkeys and wild boar roam. The only town is Codrington, named after the family who owned the island and used it as a private ranch for 200 years before its incorporation into Antiguan territory. (When Antigua began negotiations for independence from Britain, it was the proud Barbudans who objected, calling for more governing powers of their own.) Sights on Barbuda include caves in the northeast, where Indian rock carvings have survived, the **frigatebird sanctuary►►►** (see panel; tel: 460 0604. *Open* daily. *Admission: inexpensive*) and River Fort, a Martello tower on the south coast.

Inventive headgear on one of the streets in Codrington, Barbuda's only town

Nelson's Dockyard is as active today as it was 200 years ago, when English Harbour was the most important naval base in the area. But in place of whistles and cannon blasts, there is now a peaceful atmosphere. Preparations may occasionally be as feverish as they were during the 18th-century wars, but today's sailors are more likely to be doing battle in yacht races.

The pillars of the old Boat House and Sail Loft, where the sails were laid out for repair

Nelson's Dockyard is the best-preserved colonial shipyard in the Caribbean, restored and rejuvenated into one of its top sailing destinations. Covered in bougainvillaea and hibiscus, the beautiful old stone warehouses contain hotels, bars, galleries and a museum; but life still centres on the harbour, where boats line the wharves.

Tucked into the recesses of a deep and sinuous bay, the dockyard was first developed in 1725 as a victualling and repair station. Ships sheltered here during hurricanes and could be careened (beached on their sides) to clean their bottoms of barnacles and weeds. Eventually the dockyard became one of the most important stations in the British Caribbean and the massive fortifications of Shirley Heights were built in order to defend it.

The dockyard's first building is the old Pitch and Tar Store (pitch from Trinidad was used to waterproof ships' hulls), now housing the Admiral's Inn, a small hotel whose restaurant and bar is *the* spot for the yachting set. Next door are the pillars of the old Boat House and Sail Loft (the building has lost its upper storey), where ships' sails were laid out for repair. A museum in the Naval Officer's House, across the way, has been restored and has excellent hands-on exhibits, maps and model ships from the dockyard's heyday. Next door is the Old Copper and Lumber Store, where sheet metal and wood were kept and able seamen slept in upstairs dormitories; today the old store houses a comfortable hotel. In September 1998, Hurricane Georges seriously damaged the Dockyard seawall and the old officers' quarters building. The restoration of the seawall in 1999, costing $3 million, has enabled the officers' quarters (previously converted to stores and galleries) to reopen.

NELSON
It is unlikely that Horatio Nelson would ever have consented to give his name to the dockyard. The famous British admiral served here between 1784 and 1787 while he was captain of *HMS Boreas* – and he hated it, considering the dockyard itself a "vile spot". He was lonely and had the unpleasant job of putting a stop to unofficial trading between the Leeward Islanders and ships from the young American nation. At one point Nelson was confined to ship for eight weeks, knowing that if he set foot ashore he would be arrested by the resentful planters. He returned to the Caribbean only once, for 24 hours in 1805, when he was searching for the French Admiral Villeneuve in the chase that culminated in the Battle of Trafalgar.

Hibiscus in bloom

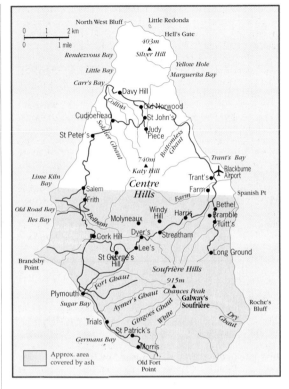

Montserrat

The Caribbean's very own self-styled Emerald Isle, Montserrat's lush green hills and fertile valleys, volcanic sand beaches and tranquil bays once offered discerning visitors one of the gentlest and most charming retreats in the region until the Soufrière Hills volcano rumbled into action in 1995. Since then, volcanic eruptions and lava flows have transformed about two-thirds of the 100-sq km island into an uninhabitable danger zone. However, this activity has quietened down considerably, and the Montserratians are now trying to rebuild their low-key tourist industry by attracting day trippers from Antigua and visitors who fancy a close-up look at a live volcano.

Sighted in 1493 by Christopher Columbus and named by him after an abbey in the mountains of Spain, Montserrat is the most southerly of the Leeward Islands. It was originally settled, in the 17th century, by the descendants of Irish catholics, refugees from Protestant persecution of St Kitts. Although Montserrat remains a British colony, the Irish gave it its nickname and also contributed elements of Irish style: St Patrick's Day is celebrated and the island's stamps feature an Irish harp.

Tragically, much of Montserrat's emerald green has been replaced by ash grey. In the summer of 1995, after over 350 years of dormancy, Soufrière Hills began erupting on the southern half of the island. A major fall of ash landed on the capital town of Plymouth, on the southwest

The Montserratian smile

coast, in August of that year and the town was evacuated. By October 1995, a dome of flowing lava could be seen protruding from the crater. There was erratic volcanic activity until June 1997, when the dome collapsed, causing a high-speed pyroclastic flow that levelled seven villages, destroying over 200 homes and killing 19 people. This lava flow also forced the closure of the airport runway and emitted so much ash that people were forced to wear ash masks. Two months later, a shower of red-hot rocks landed on Plymouth, which caught fire. The once pretty little town is now an ash-covered ruin.

As well as destroying Plymouth and many other smaller towns and villages, the volcano has ruined or rendered inaccessible several of the island's main tourist attractions, including the Great Alps Waterfall and Galway's Soufrière. However, it has created a new attraction in the form of the **Montserrat Volcano Observatory**▶▶ (tel: 491 5647), which houses scientists monitoring the island's volcanic activity. Visitors can tour the observatory with a guide and watch videos of volcanic action. Other activities include boat rides with views of Plymouth and other ruined settlements; sport fishing; and even hiking and birdwatching in the Silver and Centre Hills with the Montserrat Forest Rangers (contact the tourist board – see panel).

At present Montserrat's entire population (dramatically reduced from 11,000 prior to the 1995 eruptions down to 4,000) is confined to the northern portion of the island and this is where visitors will find the handful of hotels, restaurants and other businesses ready and willing to serve them. (Two rather optimistic hotels even have conference facilities.) Although Montserrat is in no position to offer the classic sun and sand Caribbean vacation experience, it is by no means inaccessible and it might even be argued that those still living there deserve as many visitors – and dollars – as they can handle.

HELICOPTER FLIGHTS
There are regular helicopter flights from Antigua departing Mon–Tue, Thu–Fri 8 AM, 10 AM, 5 PM; Sat 8 AM and 5 PM; flights depart from Montserrat 30 minutes later. The journey takes about 20 minutes. A ferry service also operates between the two islands. The trip takes about an hour, departing Antigua at 6:30 AM and 4 PM daily except Sun. Return trips are scheduled for about 90 minutes after arrival on Montserrat.

For more information, contact Montserrat Aviation Services (tel: 491 2362/2533, fax: 491 2362); in Antigua, contact Carib World Travel (tel: 460 6101, fax: 480 2995) or Carib Aviation at VC Bird International Airport (tel: 462 3147). For updates on volcanic activity and listing of available accommodation, the Montserrat Tourist Board can be reached on 491 2230/8730.

Lush vegetation typical of Montserrat

79

Music is played everywhere in the Caribbean: on buses, on vast personal stereos, in bars and clubs and at Carnival, when whole islands stop work to dance in the streets. West Indians will tune almost anything to make music: wheel hubs, bamboo poles and even cheese graters, but the most famous instrument of all is the steel drum, or "pan", invented in Trinidad about 60 years ago.

Almost every Caribbean island has its own unique musical style; all of them have a strong rhythm that irresistibly inspires dancing. Particular styles of dancing vary from island to island, but the movement always centres around the hips and pelvis.

Caribbean music also incorporates a tradition of social comment. The Calypsonians of Trinidad are the most famous satirists and many other styles have carried messages of protest: ska was a shout from the poor ghettos of Kingston in Jamaica in the 1950s and even in Cuba, where dissent is not traditionally tolerated, *trova* songs have been known to question the integrity of party members and government officials.

Reggae and soca The British Caribbean has two main rhythms: the best known is, of course, reggae from Jamaica. This has developed full circle since Bob Marley popularised it in the 1970s, becoming dancehall in the 1980s and recently softening again to culture reggae in the mid-1990s. Soca, which originated in Trinidad, is played in the southeastern Caribbean. Soca (a contraction of "soul-calypso") consists of a fast and hard rhythm with a double beat.

Salsa and merengue Salsa comes from Puerto Rico and Cuba (other Cuban rhythms include the rumba and the cha-cha-cha). This is a bustling, Latin rhythm; dancing partners face one another as if they were waltzing, but

FESTIVALS
A biennial World Steel Band Music Festival takes place in Trinidad in October and Pan Jazz, a mix of steel band music and jazz, is held in November. Other music festivals include Cuba's December Jazz Festival, St Lucia's Jazz Festival in May, Jamaica's Reggae Sunsplash in February and, in July, the Merengue Festival in Santo Domingo, in the Dominican Republic. The Barbados Jazz Festival takes place in January.

Transforming a steel drum into a musical instrument

their legs move elastically in a subtly sensual movement. Merengue is another hip-swinging Latin rhythm from the Dominican Republic.

Zouk and compas The French islands of Martinique and Guadeloupe have produced their own rhythm with a double beat and a very quick tempo, zouk, whose songs have French Créole lyrics. In Haiti, compas is another French-inspired, raw rhythm.

Steel pans The steel band, whose sound has come to represent the whole Caribbean, was invented in Trinidad during World War II. It started in the back streets of Port of Spain, where the discarded oil drums of Trinidad's oil industry were beaten, tuned and turned into musical instruments. Initially pan was regarded suspiciously by the authorities, partly because the yards where the music developed were the hangouts of ghetto gangs. But its popularity grew and soon pan replaced "tamboo bamboo" (musical bamboo poles) as the music of Carnival.

Steel pan lids are bashed out in a bowl and given a number of flat surfaces to produce different notes. There are five different ranges in the pan orchestra. Bass pan players have nine full-size drums (each one can only give three or four notes). Cello pan players have three pans which are cut down to three-quarter size, each having seven notes. Guitar pans and double second pans both come in pairs, playing notes in the middle range (the guitar pan plays chords, while the double second takes the melody). Tenor pans, or "ping pongs", are the lead instruments in the orchestra and the highest in the range. They have 30 notes, covering a two-and-a-half octave range and are about 30cm deep.

A steel band has as many as 120 players and it is well worth visiting a "pan yard" to see them. Not only is the noise impressive (a symphony of pings, clangs and bongs that combine into a coherent sound) but the energetic drummers are also a form of sheer entertainment in themselves.

Pan yards play all year round, though the best time to see them at work is during the run-up to Carnival at the beginning of the year. Steel bands with colourful names – "Desperadoes", "Renegades" and "Invaders" – have nowadays been superseded by soca as the main music of Carnival, but they still play at Jouvert, the parade which takes place on the Monday morning of Carnival week.

A musician from the Dominican Republic

INDEPENDENCE

Ever since St Kitts and Nevis joined forces to achieve independence from Britain, the Nevisians have in turn contemplated independence from St Kitts. In 1998, a referendum narrowly failed to return the two-thirds majority required to sever the twin-island nations' individual parts. However, many Nevisians still believe they should go it alone, though it is unlikely St Kitts will want them to do so.

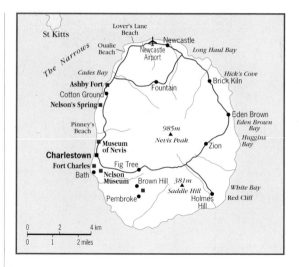

ALEXANDER HAMILTON

Nevis's most famous son is Alexander Hamilton, who is commemorated in the museum set in his former home in Charlestown. Born in 1755, he lived here for the first five years of his life, until his mother moved to St Croix (now one of the US Virgin Islands). Impressed by the wealth of merchants on St Thomas, he described them as "wheeling their gold through the streets in wheelbarrows". Hamilton moved to North America, where he fought in the Revolutionary War as George Washington's aide and was instrumental in establishing the American Constitution, becoming the first Secretary of the Treasury. Known as the Little Lion, because he was a short man with a fierce temper, Hamilton died in a duel in 1804.

Nevis

The small volcanic island of Nevis lies between St Kitts, across a strait called the Narrows, and Montserrat. It is almost circular – just 9km by 13km – and rises to a central peak of 985m. A semi-permanent wreath of clouds on the summit reminded early travellers of snow and inspired the name Nuestra Señora de la Nieves – Our Lady of the Snows. Nowadays, life for the 10,000 Nevisians is pretty gentle and the grandeur of the island's prosperous past – when it was known as the "Queen of the Caribbees" – has pretty well disappeared into the undergrowth; but the island is proud of its beautifully restored plantation houses, which is where many visitors stay. The atmosphere of the island has changed with the arrival of a large beach hotel – but it still has a certain regal calm and an evening stroll along its lit walkways, while the air rings to the singing of tree frogs and flashes with fireflies, is an unforgettable experience.

Nevis is politically attached to St Kitts (see panel) but its personality is very different. Visitors to Nevis enjoy the peace and quiet, the hammocks for snoozing and lobster-bakes on palm-fringed beaches. The island's capital is **Charlestown▶▶**, a small collection of stone and timber-frame houses laid out irregularly on the leeward coast. Except on market days (Thursday and Saturday morning) and when the ferry arrives from St Kitts, the town is pretty quiet. Inland from the waterfront is Memorial Square, a triangular park overlooked by banks and shops. Nearby are the Court House and Library and a small tourist office. At the northern end of the town is the **Museum of Nevis History▶▶** (tel: 469 5786. *Open* Mon–Fri 8–4, Sat 9–12. *Admission: inexpensive*), set in a stone townhouse (see panel), in which the Nevis Assembly conducts its business four times a year.

North of Charlestown, **Pinney's Beach▶▶▶** is the island's best beach: a 5km strip of golden sand backed with tall palms, with views across the Narrows to St Kitts. The island's first settlement of 80 planters, who arrived

Beach bar with palm-thatched parasols

from St Kitts in 1628, was situated here, until it was tipped into the sea by an earthquake. It is now the site of the Four Seasons Hotel, with its 18-hole golf course. The circular island road passes other good beaches *en route* to Nevis's airport (Oualie Beach is lovely, as is Lover's Lane Beach) and the only other town, Newcastle.

To the south of Charlestown are the ruins of **Fort Charles▶**, the island's primary defence in colonial times; nearby are the old **Bath Hotel and Spring▶**, built in 1778 and now used by the Nevis police force. In its heyday as a spa hotel, the Bath welcomed thousands of aristocratic visitors, who came to take the curative waters.

A little further down the road, the **Nelson Museum▶** (tel: 469 0408. *Open* Mon–Fri 8–4, Sat 9–12. *Admission: inexpensive*), displays assorted mementoes and artefacts from the Admiral's life, including letters and pictures. At **Fig Tree Church▶**, on the road east of Charlestown, you can see a copy of the official register of Horatio Nelson's marriage to Nevisian Fanny Nisbet on 11, March 1787, during a moment off from his lonely duties around the Leeward Islands. Look for the right turn to the Montpelier Estate, where Nelson and Fanny were married. Down the lane, the lovely **Botanical Garden of Nevis▶ ▶** (tel: 469 3680. *Open* Mon–Sat 8:30–4:30. *Admission: moderate*) covers seven beautifully landscaped acres. From here you pass into the less populous eastern parts of the island, where abandoned plantations, once the focus of the island's wealth, are now only mouldering ruins. However, several gracious plantation house hotels survive, such as the Montpelier Plantation Inn (tel: 469 3462) and the Hermitage Plantation (tel: 469 3477) both serving lunch and dinner to non-residents. The tourist office in Charlestown will be able to supply details of other plantation houses, as will the Tourist Boards (see **Travel Facts**).

A deserted windmill stands as a reminder of colonial wealth

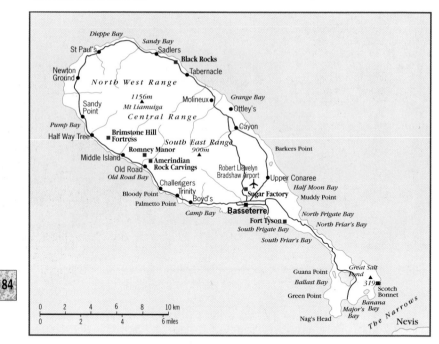

Looking towards Nevis from Timothy Hill, St Kitts

St Kitts (St Christopher)

Two centuries ago, most of the West Indies looked like St Kitts, with vast tracts of bright green sugar cane swaying in the breeze and estate houses standing aloof in colonial elegance. Many of these houses have been preserved, along with an atmosphere so English that it seems natural to play croquet and take afternoon tea. But the modern age has caught up with St Kitts, in the form of beach tourism. The island's southeastern peninsula, which has the best golden sand beaches, has been set aside for development and the tourist race is on – although it remains relatively low-key for the time being.

St Kitts is larger and livelier than its sister Nevis, appealing to a more active crowd. Nevis is just a few kilometres to the south and the Dutch island of St Eustatius 8km to the north. Measuring around 176sq km, St Kitts is shaped vaguely like a paddle, with forest-clad mountains and an old volcanic crater occupying its blade. In the northwest the highest peak, the impressive 1,156m Mount Liamuiga, is believed to take its name from the indigenous Indian name for the island.

St Kitts is an informal version of the island's original European name, St Christopher, given by Columbus on his second voyage in 1493. Historically, this was the "Mother Colony" of the West Indies – the first island in the Eastern Caribbean to be settled successfully by Europeans, in 1623. British and French colonists helped each other to establish a foothold in hostile Indian and Spanish territory, before sending colonisers to other islands. Using indentured workers and slaves, they turned St Kitts into a rich plantation island. They also began to fight over it, as they were to do for centuries afterwards. For proof of the bitterness of their battle, you need only visit Brimstone Hill, one of the biggest forts in the Caribbean (see page 87). An early French Governor of the island was de Poincy, whose name is remembered in the poinciana, a tree that grows all over the Caribbean islands. Together with Nevis, St Kitts became independent in September 1983. There are 35,000 Kittitians, many working in agriculture or tourism.

Basseterre▶▶, the island's capital, was built on the protected Caribbean coast. Its name is one of the few remaining vestiges of the island's French heritage – unfortunately, its French buildings were all destroyed in fires. However, there are attractive British colonial timber-frame and stone buildings around the town centre, some of which house cafés and restaurants. The Port Zante waterfront complex has been developed with shops, a marina and a new cruise ship terminal. Just behind here is the original town centre, the **Circus▶▶**, an open traffic circle overlooked by stone buildings that have elegant upper-storey balconies, with a colonial clock-tower, and the Berkeley Memorial at its centre. Nearby is **Independence Square▶▶**, an open park with a fountain, poincianas and palm trees.

The square is surrounded by elegant townhouses, one of which contains the splendid **Spencer Cameron Art Gallery▶▶**, displaying local and expatriate Caribbean works of art, and the Catholic Cathedral of the Immaculate Conception, with its twin spires and a magnificent rose window. On Cayon Street stands the Anglican St George's Church, built of brown stone in traditional English parish church style. The St Kitts Tourist Board has its office in Pelican Mall, just down from the new waterfront buildings.

Rawlins Plantation: one of a number of hotels in St Kitts that are set in former sugar estate houses

The Black Rocks make an ideal spot for fishing

INTRIGUING TREES

The poinciana is sometimes jokingly referred to as the "tourist tree" because it turns a startlingly bright shade of red in July and August. Its pods, which look like long wooden string beans, are used by children to create music – as they make a "shack-a-shack-a-shack" noise when shaken. Another brightly flowering tree is the African tulip tree, which has red blooms all year round. It is also known as the "flame of the forest" or the "fountain tree" because its unopened buds squirt water when they are squeezed.

The main tourist area on St Kitts is southeast of Basseterre. There are hotels, villas, a golf course and a popular beach in **Frigate Bay▶▶**, while **Friar's Bay▶▶▶**, over the next hill, has a marvellous beach of soft golden sand, which gets busy as soon as cruise ships arrive. The rollercoaster peninsular road leads up and down hill and past the salt ponds, which used to form common ground in the days of joint English and French occupation, to the southern beaches, where there is a beach bar and superb views across the narrows to Nevis.

Northwest of the capital, the road emerges into sugar cane country, which is planted on the coastal flats beneath the central mountain range. A circular road (accompanied by a railway to transport harvested cane) follows the coast, touching all the small Kittitian villages; it can be driven comfortably in a day. A walk into the rain forest on the mountain can be arranged by tour operators.

Old Road Bay▶ marks the site of the first British settlement and was the capital until 1727. Amerindian **rock carvings▶▶** can be seen on the Wingfield Estate, nearby. Romney Manor, a 17th-century great house set in tropical gardens, is the home of **Caribelle Batik▶▶**, a shop selling silk-screened prints and clothes, where you can watch local women practising the art of batik. At Middle Island is the **grave of Thomas Warner▶**, who led the successful settlement in 1623. From here the road soon passes under the huge defenses of **Brimstone Hill▶▶▶** (tel: 465 2609. *Open* Mon–Sat 8–5:30. *Admission: moderate*. See opposite).

Around the northern tip of the island the **Black Rocks▶▶** are a curious formation of volcanic lava; from here the road leads south along the wild Atlantic coast, passing through quiet villages and returning to Basseterre via the airport and the **sugar cane factory▶▶**, which is open to visitors between January and June.

Huge forts still tower over many Caribbean settlements as monuments to an era when imperial fleets and armies were sent to defend their valuable territories. Two centuries ago the Caribbean was a hardship posting, beset by disease, and these massive bastions recall a time of violence and instability, when loud drum rolls and frantic whistle blasts would herald urgent preparations for war.

Building and maintaining a fort the size of Brimstone Hill, on St Kitts, which could hold over 1,000 troops, involved a complex operation. Every stone had to be dragged up to the summit to create the huge structure's bastions and ramparts, inner stronghold, parade ground, barracks, cookhouses and hospital.

Brimstone Hill (named for the satanic whiffs of sulphur from a nearby volcanic vent) took 100 years to build and was occupied by both British and French during the long 18th-century wars. In 1782 it faced its severest test when it was attacked by 8,000 French troops. The defenders, who held out for a month, were bombarded so heavily that only two rooms in the fort were left undamaged. When they eventually surrendered, the soldiers were allowed to march out with colours flying as a tribute to their bravery. A museum in Fort George, the central bastion, has exhibits explaining the history of St Kitts and the fortress, and the shop has a video presentation.

Other forts On Antigua, the hills around English Harbour, an important link in the chain of British defences, are cluttered with ramparts and barracks, described at the Dow's Hill Interpretation Centre.

Puerto Rico's two bastions overlook the approaches to San Juan, itself surrounded by walls 10m thick. On the point stands San Felipe del Morro, with its 30m ramparts and a maze of tunnels; at the other end of Old San Juan is Fuerte San Cristobal, built so each of the outer bastions had to be captured before the citadel could be taken.

The most impressive Caribbean fort is Haiti's Citadelle, where 10,000 men could hold out for a year without resupply; its walls are over 30m high and 9m thick. Thousands died building it (see page 181).

CANNONS
Cannons litter the Caribbean islands, some abandoned in the forts, others put to good use, buried upright in the ground at the corners of buildings to protect them from passing truck wheels. On the British islands many cannons are printed with the cypher of King George III, a crown superimposed over the letters GR (George Rex). A small arrow can often be seen, stamped into the metal – the symbol used by naval stores.

A cannon at Brimstone Hill fortress covers the northern approaches from St Eustatius

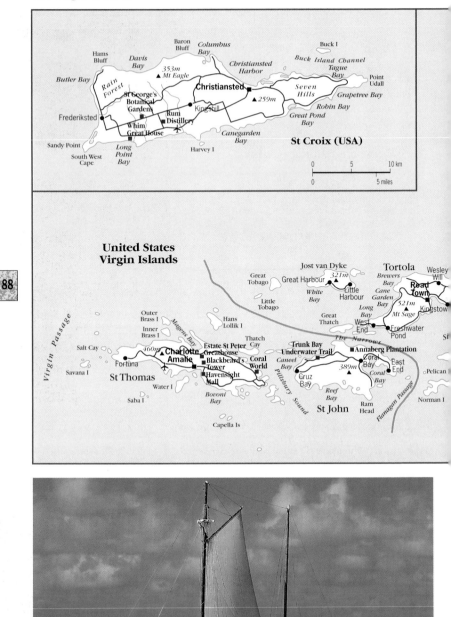

Tranquil touring among the Virgin Islands by yacht

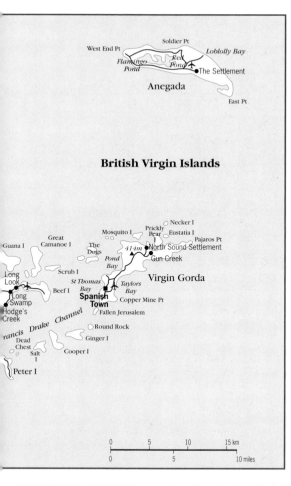

British Virgin Islands

Anegada

West End Pt — Soldier Pt — Loblolly Bay
Flamingo Pond — Red Pond — The Settlement
East Pt

Necker I
Mosquito I — Prickly Pear — Eustatia I
Great Camanoe I — Pajaros Pt
Guana I — The Dogs — North Sound Settlement
414m — Pond Bay — Gun Creek
Scrub I
Long Look — St Thomas Bay — **Virgin Gorda**
Beef I — Taylors Bay
Spanish Town — Copper Mine Pt
Long Swamp — Fallen Jerusalem
Hodge's Creek — Francis Drake Channel — Round Rock
Dead Chest — Ginger I
Salt I — Cooper I
Peter I

| 0 | 5 | 10 | 15 km |
| 0 | | 5 | 10 miles |

THE VIRGIN ISLANDS In mood and style, the US and British Virgin Islands (BVI) are worlds apart. The British islands are quieter and less developed, with secluded and isolated bays, and beaches and scattered cays ideal for sailing – islanders have an old-world reserve and courtesy. The US islands of St Thomas and St Croix have more in the way of attractions and entertainment. With sailing and watersports almost a way of life, these prosperous and sophisticated islands are ideal for those who don't intend to stray too far from the beach. For something more laid back, visitors gravitate to St John, or the BVI, where Tortola is less crowded and largely caters to yachts.

Scattered over an expanse of incomparably blue sea, the Virgin Islands are, with the exception of Anegada, steep and green, being the peaks of a submerged chain of volcanoes. Just under half the 90 or so islands are a British Crown Colony; the rest are "an unincorporated territory of the USA". In the west are the three main United States Virgin Islands (USVI): St Thomas and St John with St Croix lying 64km to the south. Sprinkled to the east, the British Virgin Islands are smaller and more numerous: the largest are Tortola and Virgin Gorda.

The Virgin Islands

A deserted sugar mill

▶▶▶ **REGION HIGHLIGHTS**

The Baths *page 93*

Cane Garden Bay
page 92

Charlotte Amalie
page 102

Christiansted *page 98*

Cooper Island *page 97*

Jost van Dyke *page 96*

Necker Island *page 96*

St Croix Aquarium
page 98

Smuggler's Cove
page 92

**THE DANISH IN THE
CARIBBEAN**
The Danes settled
St Thomas in 1665,
encouraging its use as a
trading base by declaring
it a free port. They moved
on to St John in 1717 and
St Croix in 1733 and
planted them entirely with
sugar cane, bringing in
slaves to work the fields.
The Danes were the first
to ban the slave trade,
in 1792, but slavery itself
continued on the islands
until 1848, when the
Governor went against
his King's orders and
declared emancipation.

In the USVI, where people work at resorts on land once owned by their forebears, there is great disparity between rich and poor, and some resentment towards American immigrants and tourists. In the BVI, people tend to own the land. There is virtually no shopping or nightlife here; on Tortola and Virgin Gorda no hotels are taller than a palm tree and most are owned by locals or expatriates. The USVI are for visitors who want a bustling environment; the BVI are for sailors and those who want to escape the crowds.

HISTORY The Virgin Islands were given their name by Columbus when he sailed among them on his second voyage of exploration. He compared the islands to the 11,000 beautiful followers of St Ursula, who according to legend were killed by Huns on a pilgrimage to Cologne. For many years, pirates roamed the islands' shores, waiting for ships to plunder and refitting their vessels in hidden coves. Charlotte Amalie, on St Thomas, became a busy market-place for the pirates' captured goods.

The USVI were owned for centuries by Denmark, but not much remains of Danish influence except in street and town names such as Charlotte Amalie, Christiansted and Dronningens Gade (Charlotte Amalie's main street); the Dutch influence can be seen in the islands' many red-roofed buildings. The islands were bought by the US in 1917 for $25 million.

Meanwhile the BVI remained barren backwaters, planted while the going was good, but soon falling back into obscurity. At one point the British Government considered selling these islands to America as well. It never happened, but the pull to the US is still strong. The BVI have adopted the US dollar as their currency and many islanders move to find work on St Thomas.

ISLAND LIFE Today, the USVI offer all the expected American comforts and conveniences, but with a tropical setting and lilting Caribbean accent. The banks are American, as are the fast food joints, the currency, the supermarkets and the baseball. St Thomas and St John are geographically close, but in character they could not be further apart. St Thomas is overdeveloped and crowded (particularly when cruise ships dock), but has great shopping in Charlotte Amalie, as well as good bars and restaurants. St John, just a 20-minute ferry ride away, is quiet and undeveloped. About two-thirds of it is undisturbed jungle, protected by its National Park status. There are, nevertheless, a number of places to stay in Cruz Bay and at Coral Bay in the East End. The third island, and the largest of the Virgin Islands, St Croix offers a good variety of beach hotels, restaurants and interesting town buildings in Christiansted and Frederiksted. St Croix's first casino opened late in 1998, signalling a determination to jazz up the local nightlife.

By comparison, the pace of life on the British islands is slow and peaceful. For every 15 people who travel to the USVI on holiday, the BVI get one. Of the BVI's 150,000 or so visitors a year, three-quarters come from the US – and most come to sail, without even booking into a hotel. The BVI are not about discos, high-rise hotels, fast food and casinos. They are about superb beaches, many only accessible from the sea, and excellent bars. While the USVI have gone for numbers, the BVI target bank rolls, so the islands are expensive. Tortola is the hub of BVI yachting and from here there is access by ferry to many other islands, including tranquil Jost van Dyke or Virgin Gorda, with its top-rank hotels, secluded beaches and offshore cays. Like the pirates of yore, you can sail among the Virgins by day and anchor in a cove for the night; but nowadays you can order dinner over the radio and have a barbecue waiting when you arrive.

A British touch on Virgin Gorda

91

Bomba's Surf Side Shack is famous for its full-moon parties

New marina developments are springing up in Tortola; this one is at Frenchman's Cay near West End

GUANA ISLAND
Guana Island is a wildlife sanctuary off the northeastern tip of Tortola. Its 343 hectares are said to harbour the richest fauna seen on any island of its size in the world – from flamingos to hawks, from bats to cats, and from wild donkeys to sea turtles.

A bar sign at Frenchman's Cay, western Tortola

Tortola

A century ago, when even St Thomas was a backwater, Tortola was written off as "forsaken". Today the island is enjoying something of a boom, which has led to growing development, as the 16,000 islanders and expatriates build on the island's towering hillsides. A dock for cruise ships has been constructed and the island is developing steadily, but there are still plenty of charming, isolated spots to be found.

Tortola is only 19km by 5km and has a scrubby and meandering spine of steep mountains, rising to 520m at Mount Sage. The main settlement is Road Town, a modern, sprawling capital made up of a few streets collected around a deep bay in the southern coastline. Features include yachting marinas, a small museum, a botanical garden, bars and restaurants, and a number of shops. Tortolans themselves live in small settlements around the coast; transport around the island is customarily by taxi or hired car.

The best bays and beaches are on the island's north side. At the West End, where most of the hotels are, you will find waterside pubs and shops at the Soper's Hole marina complex and the main ferry terminal; to the north is a perfect, isolated curve of sand called **Smuggler's Cove►►►**. Heading east you come to Long Bay, a superb run of white sand, and Apple Bay, where surfers enjoy the big waves (look for Bomba's Surfside Shack, a beach bar made of driftwood). The long and lovely **Cane Garden Bay►►►** has small places to stay and a string of excellent beach bars; Quito's Gazebo has live music most nights in season. From here, there is an almost impossibly steep climb to the mountain's spine, which eventually descends into Road Town.

East of Road Town, the road follows the coastline to Long Look, where there is a small town. A toll bridge leads to Beef Island, the site of Tortola's airport. There are good beaches here, including Josiah's Bay and **Long Bay►►** on Beef Island. The Last Resort is a lively restaurant and bar on an island in Trellis Bay and you can also spend the day on Marina Cay, which has good watersports; there is a free ferry.

Virgin Gorda

Virgin Gorda is even quieter than Tortola, but it has some chic resorts hidden in its coves and offshore cays. Lying east of Tortola (and reached by ferry), it was patronised, like St John in the USVI, by Laurance Rockefeller, who built the Little Dix Bay hotel here. Virgin Gorda means "the fat Virgin" – the island supposedly looks like a reclining woman. Its 21-sq km area is divided into three mounds and covered in scrub and cactus, rising to a 414m peak in the north. The most distinctive scenery is in the south, where massive granite boulders form The Baths, a maze of water-filled caves.

Boats from Tortola dock at the southern settlement of The Valley, where many of the 3,000 or so islanders live. The town is really little more than its marina, with bars and an easy-going atmosphere. Virgin Gorda's best beaches – including The Baths – are south of The Valley. In the southeast of the island are the ruins of an old copper mine which was active during the last century.

The road to the north of the island passes isolated coves such as Savannah Bay and Pond Bay before reaching Virgin Gorda's second town, Gun Creek. This overlooks the North Sound, a stretch of water surrounded by tall peaks, cays and small islands with fine beaches. Two splendid hotels lie at this end of the island, accessible only by boat from Gun Creek. Biras Creek (tel: 494 3555) is a place of understated wealth overlooking a calm sound, a bay (with the main beach) and wild Atlantic surf. The Bitter End Yacht Club (tel: 494 2475) prints a newspaper showing the wide range of watersports on offer. Gathering places on the islands around the sound include the Lighthouse (tel: 495 7154) in Leverick Bay; an elegant restaurant, Drake's Anchorage (tel: 494 2254), on Mosquito Island; a beach bar on Prickly Pear Cay and the tiny Saba Rock, a bar that wakes up in the evenings.

The Baths, where waves wash through tunnels and caverns made from jumbled rocks

THE BATHS
The Baths form a series of coves to the south of The Valley. Best approached by sea, the boulders are stacked in jumbled piles and backed by coconut palms. From the land you can reach them through the scrub from the Top of the Baths restaurant. Made of granite, a stone that does not normally appear in the Caribbean, they may have been carried here by glacial movement during the Ice Ages.

Watersports are an integral part of a Caribbean holiday. The warm seas and constant Trade Winds make its islands excellent places for windsurfers, scuba-divers, jet-skiers and para-sailors. But there is nothing to beat the freedom of sailing and the calmer stretches of sea are flecked with white as yachts of all shapes and sizes ride the ocean breezes, with dolphins dipping and darting alongside their prows.

94

REGATTAS
The biggest annual sailing event in the Caribbean is Race Week in Antigua, which includes five days of races. A major regatta is held in the British Virgin Islands every April and in June and July Martin-iquans race the *yoles rondes*, with distinctive square sails and crews of 12 leaning out over the water on booms. In August Anguilla's race week pitches locally built boats against each other; and Carriacou, in the Grenadines, stages its own small regatta. The Caribbean Ocean Triangle Series (CORT) sets sail in March and April and includes the Heineken International Cup in Puerto Rico, BVI's Spring Regatta and St Thomas' International Rolex Cup Regatta.

With such a variety of islands lying within easy reach of one another, island-hopping by yacht is an enjoyable way of seeing the Caribbean. Yachts are readily available for four to eight people or more and can be rented as bare-boats (no crew) or crewed (with captain and hands to order the supplies and do the sailing and cooking). All yachts have fridges, kitchenware and bedding, most pro-vide masks and snorkels and some carry windsurfing and diving equipment. Day sails are available from all the islands and many beachfront hotels have small sailing boats which can be enjoyed near the shore. For a bird's-eye view, have a go at parasailing.

The best sailing destinations are the Virgin Islands and the Grenadines. Both regions are spectacularly beautiful, with convenient sailing distances separating their islands. The Virgins have good marina facilities, but this means crowds during the high season. The Grenadines have a wilder beauty, but restaurants and bars have found their way even to many of the quieter bays.

Reliable year-round winds make windsurfing a popular Caribbean sport. The best windsurfing areas are: the Dominican Republic, particularly around Cabarete on the northern shore, where World Championships are occasion-ally held; Barbados's southern shore around Maxwell and Silver Sands; and Aruba. The sport is catered for in the French Caribbean around St François and Le Moule on Guadaloupe and in the southeast of Martinique.

Divers acknowledge the Caribbean as an ideal setting for one of the world's most exotic sports, with its vast areas of colourful coral and its strange and beautiful tropical fish. Snorkellers, too, can enjoy access to offshore reefs from most islands; and glass-bottom boat trips provide views of underwater wonders without even the need to get wet.

Although it does not have the abundance of the Indo-Pacific area, the Caribbean can boast around 75 species of corals, which include brain corals, sea fans and whips, hydra-headed anemones, gorgonians and sponges. More mobile sea creatures include crabs, spiny lobsters, starfish, rays, eels and even turtles or sharks. Diving at night reveals a completely different world, as some corals close and others open, while fish emerge to feed on them, crunching away at the polyps, or sleep tucked away in sleeping bags of mucus so that their scent cannot be picked up by predators.

DIVING SITES
The best diving sites are off the Cayman Islands, particularly Little Cayman, with sheer drops to limit-less depths, and Bonaire, where the coral-clad slopes are gentler. Saba, a steep-sided volcanic cone, has an abundance of corals and the Grenadines' waters are not as crowded.

95

As well as the natural beauties of the sea, shipwrecks are a source of endless fascination and near some islands ships have been sunk deliberately in order to provide artificial reefs for underwater explorers. Off the shores of Anguilla, divers can swim over a 60m hulk sitting upright on the seabed.

Scuba-diving was invented in the early 1940s and developed rapidly as a sport, popularised by divers such as Jacques Cousteau, one of its inventors. There are several suppliers in the Caribbean and diving can be easily arranged on most islands. Many hotels offer qualifying courses with the affiliated dive organisations (PADI and NAUI); there are also non-qualifying resort courses that enable novices to dive almost immediately. (Remember to arrange personal insurance before leaving home if you intend to go diving.)

MARINE PARKS
Several islands, including the US and British Virgin Islands, Saba and Bonaire, have created marine parks around their shores in order to protect their corals and fish. Divers are forbidden from picking coral or hunting fish with spear-guns within these areas. Never buy coral jewellery on the islands – it is made from live coral that is culled from the reef.

BVI FERRIES

Regular ferries criss-cross the waters of the Virgin Islands. There are frequent services between Road Town on Tortola and The Valley in Virgin Gorda. The sleek North Sound Express runs between Beef Island (the airport at the eastern end of Tortola) and the expensive hotels of the North Sound (the east end of Virgin Gorda), while a daily service links The Valley and Beef Island. Several daily sailings carry passengers to Jost van Dyke from West End on Tortola. Some offshore islands have their own water ferries: Peter Island's ferry, for example, leaves from the CSY Marina just out of Road Town and Marina Cay (from Beef Island).

Smaller British Virgin Islands

Anegada▶ is not a typical Virgin Island. It stands alone, 30km out in the ocean and whereas the other Virgins are tall and volcanic islands, Anegada is an 11km curve of coral. The island is scrubby and flat (only 9m at its highest point) and culminates in a submerged tail called Horseshoe Reef, a magnificent living coral expanse, which has claimed more than 300 unwary ships over the centuries. The name Anegada means "inundated" – which it occasionally is, by passing waves. Only 200 people live here, sharing the island with goats and iguanas; their sole collection of houses is called The Settlement. The island is not much visited by tourists, but there are a couple of places to eat and stay, and Loblolly Bay on the north coast is the best of many beaches.

Jost van Dyke▶▶▶ is almost devoid of tourism, other than visiting yachts. It lies north of Tortola and takes its name from a Dutch pirate. Just a few hilly square kilometres in area, the island is reached by ferry from West End on Tortola. Great Harbour, the main port, is a port of entry to the Virgin Islands and has a church, a police

Perfect peace in an ideal anchorage: Jost van Dyke

station and a few beach bars (one of whose owners, Foxy, welcomes visitors with a personalised calypso). There is an excellent beach at White Bay and yachts put in at Sandy Cay, one of a couple of sheltered cays off the island. The best time to visit Jost van Dyke is on New Year's Eve, when 2,000 or so revellers sail in for a night's drinking and dancing on the sand.

Necker Island▶▶▶ is an idyllic green speck rimmed with blinding white sand and translucent blue water. Set off the northeastern tip of Virgin Gorda, it is owned by the founder of Virgin Airlines, Richard Branson, who has built a Balinese house and rents the island to groups, families or companies – at a high cost.

Sir Francis Drake Channel

Sir Francis Drake Channel is the sailing heartland of the Virgin Islands – a magnificent stretch of water off Tortola, where the white triangles of yacht sails beat back and forth over an unbelievably blue sea. On its southern side the channel is bounded by a necklace of small, irregularly shaped islands, which run southeast in a graceful curve from Virgin Gorda to St John in the USVI. In their isolated coves are some superb, secluded stretches of sand.

Starting in the northeast (most sailing trips sail out of Road Town south towards Peter Island, then northeast towards Gorda and Anegada), **Fallen Jerusalem** and **Round Rock** lie off Virgin Gorda. Designated a National Park, Fallen Jerusalem has rocky terrain that gives it the appearance of an ancient city in decay. **Ginger Island** is uninhabited, but the next in line, **Cooper Island▶ ▶ ▶**, has about 10 inhabitants – the staff of the Cooper Island Beach Club on Manchioneel Bay, which often attracts a lively crowd of "yachties" at lunchtime and in the evenings. Scuba-diving facilities are available and there is a very beautiful beach.

Salt Island▶ ▶ takes its name from a salt pond that is still farmed. Rent, payable to the Queen of England, is set at a sack of salt a year, but apparently it has not been collected recently. This is one of the Virgin Island's most popular dive sites, with the wreck of the RMS *Rhone*, which sank in the 19th century, lying offshore. Part of the wreck is shallow enough to snorkel in and you will find yourself bathing in the exhaled bubbles of divers below you. Next in line is **Peter Island▶ ▶**, where there is just one chic island resort with rooms scattered along Deadman's Bay (a charming place, despite its name; tel: 495 2000). Offshore is a small outcrop called Dead Chest, where Bluebeard, a.k.a. Long John Silver, put his mutinous crew ashore with one bottle of rum. **Norman Island▶**, the last island in the chain before St John, is also uninhabited, but is worth visiting for the eerie, waterbound caves at Treasure Point, which have snorkelling and the floating bar, the *Willie T.*

BVI DIVING
The Virgin Islands have some excellent diving sites. In Sir Francis Drake Channel there are caves, pinnacles and submerged rocks. These are smothered in corals and teeming with fish, some of which have become tame enough to feed. Blonde Rock, off Dead Chest and the Dogs, off Virgin Gorda, are good examples. Anegada has many wrecks, some of them still poking above the waves where they foundered, but the most famous is that of the *Rhone*, which sank off Salt Island in 1867. This wreck was used in the filming of *The Deep* and it is possible to dive inside its bow section, which lies in 24m of water. The broken pieces of its stern, including the propeller gear, are at about half this depth.

97

Sailing – the only way to travel between the many beautiful Virgin Islands

St Croix

St Croix (pronounced "St Croy") is the largest of the Virgin Islands and lies alone, 50km to the south of the main USVI group. This was the senior island in Danish colonial days because of its successful plantation economy, but whereas St Thomas has been overtaken by the hustle of modern America, St Croix has retained a quieter, historic feel, with two attractive harbour towns, one at either end of the island. Roughly twice the size of St Thomas, it is a sparsely populated island, with varied scenery: mountains, rain forest, beaches, and dairy and cattle-breeding farmlands.

St Croix's main town is **Christiansted▶▶**, on the waterfront in the east. The Danish influence can still be seen in the town's architecture, with its terraces, patios and arched yellow colonnades. Fort Christiansvaern was the town's old defence. The commercial centre is around the Old Customs House and the Scale House near the wharf, where merchants once weighed their goods. The Steeple Building is a museum of Native American artefacts and on King Street Government House still houses government offices. The **St Croix Aquarium▶▶▶** (tel: 773 8995. *Open* Tue–Sat 11–4. *Admission: inexpensive*) in the Cavarelle Arcade is worth a visit. The dry east has most of the island's hotels and there are golf courses at Buccaneer and Teague Bay. One of the best beaches is on Buck Island, a national park known for its snorkelling.

Centerline Road heads west towards Frederiksted through agricultural land that made St Croix wealthy during the 19th century. The **St George Village Botanical Garden▶** (tel: 773 5575. *Open* Mon–Fri 9–2. *Admission: donation*) is a peaceful retreat on an old plantation estate, growing Amerindian and other Cruzian plants. Also off the main road is the **Cruzan Rum Factory▶** (tel: 692 2280. *Open* Mon–Fri 9–11:30, 1–4:15. *Admission: inexpensive*) offering guided tours, tastings and sales . Further on is the moated **Whim Great House▶▶** (tel: 772 0598. *Open* Mon–Sat 10–3. *Admission: moderate*), an unusual rounded estate building restored with colonial-style antiques; in the kitchen, old utensils and sugar machinery are displayed. There are more colonnaded trading buildings in **Frederiksted▶▶**, including restored Fort Frederik and its museum. Mahogany Road leads northwards through rain forest.

FACT OR FICTION?
Herman Wouk's *Don't Stop the Carnival*, one of the finest books to have come out of the West Indies, was inspired by life on the Virgin Islands. His Gull Reef Club is supposed to have been modelled on a hotel on Hassel Island, in Charlotte Amalie harbour and on the hotel on the Cay off Christiansted in St Croix. The book tells of the succession of disasters that befall a hotelier and rumour has it that Wouk didn't dare return to the island because the story was so painfully accurate and because so many of the hoteliers thought they recognised themselves in the main character, Norman Paperman.

For the finest sunset, a Frederiksted beach bar on the west coast is what is required

St John

One of the most beautiful islands in the Caribbean, St John is the smallest and least developed of the USVI. It lies just a few kilometres east of St Thomas, which is a short ferry ride across the Pillsbury Sound, but is so tranquil that it seems a world away. Approximately two-thirds of the island are given over to the Virgin Islands National Park, so most of its steep, volcanic hills are left to grow as natural jungle.

There are numerous trails through the Park (on foot, on horseback and even underwater through the corals of Trunk Bay) with hikes and activites led by well-informed rangers. Schedules are available from the National Park Visitor Center in Cruz Bay (tel: 776 6201). On the north coast you can see the ruins of the **Annaberg Plantation▶▶**, a relic of Danish days, when the island was covered with sugar cane. Camping facilities can accommodate travellers with or without tents.

Around the fringes of the National Park St John's coastline has been developed. **Cruz Bay▶▶**, at the western tip of the island, is the main town and here you will find many good bars and restaurants, as well as the Elaine Ione Sprauve Library and Museum, with marine life displays and artefacts dating from a slave revolt against Danish planters in 1733; after nearly a year, the rebels were defeated by imported French troops and many committed suicide rather than return to slavery.

The sand is crystalline and the surf gentle at Trunk Bay, on St John's north shore

TRAVEL BETWEEN THE ISLANDS
Most of the Virgin Islands are linked by ferry: regular links connect St Thomas (Charlotte Amalie and Red Hook), St John (Cruz Bay) and Tortola (West End and then Road Town). Sometimes the link continues to Virgin Gorda (The Valley). A hydrofoil service now connects Charlotte Amalie and Christiansted on St Croix. The oft-choppy trip takes about an hour and a half each way. St Croix is best reached by air – a novel way to make the link is by sea-plane.

Three centuries ago the Caribbean waters were infested with pirates. Bands of seaborne outlaws would lie in wait in hidden coves before taking to the high seas in their fast ships and attacking passing trade. Piracy was a dangerous lifestyle – capture usually meant death – but the rewards were great; a good haul could provide life on Easy Street for months on end.

The infamous Blackbeard

100

WOMEN AT SEA
Two women joined the macho world of piracy in the 18th century. Anne Bonney was the fiery daughter of an Irish lawyer and Mary Read was brought up as a boy and served as a soldier and sailor before setting off to the Caribbean. Both women fell in with Jack Rackham and joined his pirate crew. They were all caught off the shores of Jamaica and sentenced to death; both women "pleaded their bellies" (pregnancy) and Bonney escaped execution, but Read died in prison.

Piracy started in the Caribbean soon after the word spread that the Spaniards were taking gold from the Aztecs. The stakes were high from the start – intrusion into Spanish waters was punishable by death – but adventurous interlopers like François le Clerc and Pie de Palo ("Pegleg") were willing to take the risks. British adventurers arrived in the late 16th century, including Sir John Hawkins and Francis Drake, who made their fortunes on slave-trading expeditions and later by ransacking cities on the Spanish Main. Known variously as freebooters, buccaneers and sea rovers, pirates often started out as privateers, permitted by local governors to attack enemy shipping in times of war – but the rewards were so good that the practice was extended to include any ships that might bring in a prize and was continued in peacetime. A single capture could bring vast riches (usually a cargo of goods – silks, arms, animals and grog). Once these had been sold the pirates would spend their loot on alcohol and women until the money eventually ran out and they had to go in search of more.

On board ship, however, there was a strict regime. Generally pirates were accomplished sailors who operated small, fast ships. The crew would sign "articles" stipulating their obedience to the captain and their duties: keeping their weapons clean, dispatching themselves bravely in battle and refraining from playing cards and bringing women aboard (which carried a death penalty). Punishments included lashes of the whip and "marooning" (being left ashore on an island with water, a pistol, gunpowder and shot). Each man had a share in any prizes captured on the venture and injured men were compensated from the loot. There was usually a musician on board, who was expected to play six nights a week but rested on Sundays.

When faced with a pirate attack, a captain knew that he would be killed if he put up a fight. There are some particularly gruesome stories of pirates' cruelty: the Frenchman Montbars was said to cut out men's guts and make the victims dance till they died; and his compatriot l'Ollonios removed the heart of one man and fed it to another.

Gallery of rogues For a century until 1700, no ship was safe in the Caribbean and pirates were feared and reviled. They operated from hideaways on Tortuga and, after 1691, the Bahamas. However, there is no disputing

that there were colourful characters among their ranks. Perhaps the best-known Caribbean pirate was Blackbeard (Edward Teach). This huge man cultivated a diabolic image, tying ribbons in his long pigtails and beard and putting slow-burning fuses under his hat so that he appeared to be on fire. A reward of £100 was offered for his capture and he was eventually caught after a chase at sea. Blackbeard died fighting rather than suffer the ignominies of surrendering and his head was hung from the bowsprit of his ship.

Bartholomew Roberts is thought to have captured 400 ships in two years. He drank only tea (even when his crew was getting drunk on rum) and he always kept the Sabbath. Roberts was a dandy, going to battle in fine dress; he was killed in a skirmish with a British ship.

Stede Bonnet was a Justice of the Peace and a landowner from Barbados, who decided to buy a ship and become a pirate. Known as the "gentleman pirate", Bonnet was eventually captured. Their stories are told by Exquemeling in his *History of the Pirates*.

HENRY MORGAN
Henry Morgan was an indentured labourer who became the leader of the Port Royal buccaneers in the 1660s, directing expeditions against Spanish cities and netting 750,000 pieces of eight in an attack on Panama City, which he destroyed in the process. Having made his fortune, Morgan switched sides, becoming the Lieutenant Governor of Jamaica, a position that entailed stamping out piracy.

101

Treasure from the New World is loaded onto a 16th-century ship

PUTTING ON THE STYLE
As dandies and natty dressers, some pirates wore tricorn hats, coats and cordoba boots – but looting was hot work in the Caribbean and most wore baggy shirts and trousers with no shoes. Hats included Jacobin caps and turbans, and hair was often braided and then stiffened with water and flour. Earrings were believed to improve the eyesight – and the pirate who sighted a prize gained an extra share.

St Thomas

Cruise ships and yachts anchor side by side in St Thomas's harbour

HURRICANES LUIS AND MARILYN
The last decade or so has been pretty cruel to the USVI. In 1989, Hurricane Hugo caused terrible destruction in St Croix. It was the turn of St John and particularly St Thomas, which was dealt a double blow in September 1995. First Hurricane Luis swept through, causing some destruction, and then a week later Hurricane Marilyn tore through the islands, causing maximum damage because it brought very heavy rains. The island was declared a disaster area. Many long-term residents left for good. It took over a year to rebuild because many people were uninsured (rates were so high that they could not afford insurance).

St Thomas is the USVI capital island and is the most developed of all the Virgins. It is a mountainous 19km by 5km and has a population of over 50,000, so this is hardly a secluded tropical retreat; it does, however, have excellent bars, restaurants and clubs, many of which are concentrated around **Charlotte Amalie**▶▶▶.

Charlotte Amalie owes its birth and its still-thriving life to a fine harbour, sheltered by hills and protected by islands. Pirate ships and ocean traders once brought business here; now it arrives on cruise ships and yachts. A major trading centre for centuries, the waterfront is still a magnet for shoppers looking for gold, French perfume, Colombian emeralds and fashions. The town has another side, however: the arched façades of its stone trading buildings downtown and the elegant hillside mansions retain an atmosphere of centuries past.

The cooler slopes above Charlotte Amalie are dotted with grand mansions, linked by stepped alleyways and sinuous roads. **Government House**▶ (1867), once the seat of the Danish council and now the Governor's official residence, stands above the town centre. Just above it is Blackbeard's Tower (where the pirate was supposed to have lived), reached by the 99 Steps (there are actually 102 of them). Even beyond Charlotte Amalie, the hillsides are covered with houses. On the spine of the hills above the town is Drake's Seat, where the mariner supposedly watched for Spanish ships. It is worth the climb as the view is magnificent. There are botanical gardens at **Estate St Peter Greathouse**▶▶ (tel: 774 4999. *Open* daily 9–5. *Admission: moderate*) high above the north coast. In the east of the island beyond Red Hook, the ferry point for St John, you will find **Coral World**▶▶ (tel: 775 1555. *Open* daily. *Admission: expensive*) with an underwater observation tower, 50,000-gallon Predator Tank and living coral reef display, plus all sorts of aquariums, touch tanks and a tropical nature trail.

Most of the beaches on St Thomas are heavily developed (except Magens Bay, on the National Geographic's Top 10 Beaches list), so it is easy to find watersports.

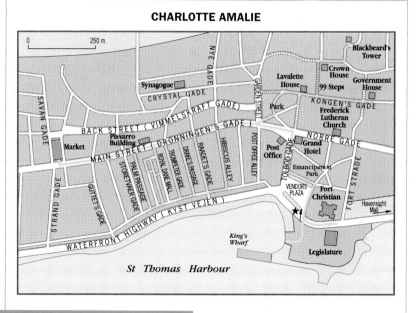

CHARLOTTE AMALIE

St Thomas Harbour

Charlotte Amalie

Ferries arrive at this downtown waterfront, but many disembark at the cruise-ship dock across the harbour and head straight for Havensight Mall, the first of the island's shopping centres, which has been converted from a series of warehouses. Safari buses and taxis provide transport for passengers from here into town. Opposite the entrance to Havensight, the **Paradise Point Tram**▶▶ (tel: 774 9809. *Open daily 9–5. Admission: expensive*) provides visitors with a 7-minute, 215m lift to a spectacular viewpoint overlooking the town and bay. On a clear day St Croix may be visible.

Charlotte Amalie's old trading streets are laid out in a gridiron pattern with a series of narrow alleys with stores and restaurants running down to the waterfront. As you arrive, you will pass the light green **Virgin Islands Legislature Building**▶, which was built by the Danes as a police barracks in 1874 and now houses the

USVI Senate. Across the road is the dark red and gold **Fort Christian**▶▶, which dates from the Danes' arrival in the 1660s. It now contains the Virgin Islands Museum, tracing early and colonial life on St Thomas.

Beyond the old Grand Hotel and the neoclassical Post Office, at the head of Main Street, is the main shopping area. Here, the old brick and stone warehouse buildings bear well-known names alongside local shops such as A H Riise (selling perfumes, jewellery, crystal and watches).

Wander through the passages and alleys between Main Street and the waterfront, where there are yet more shops and pleasant cafés. A plaque on Main Street, between A H Riise and the town's market, marks the birthplace of the Impressionist painter Camille Pissarro.

The 19th-century Virgin Islands Legislature Building, on the waterfront, has become the headquarters of the USVI Senate

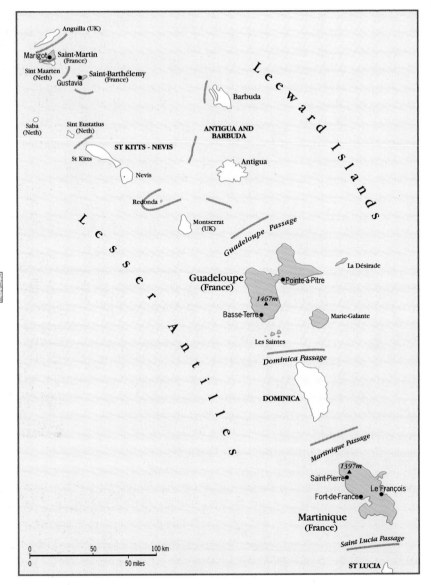

Anguilla (UK)

Marigot • Saint-Martin
(France)

Sint Maarten
(Neth)
Gustavia • Saint-Barthélemy
(France)

Barbuda

Saba
(Neth)

Sint Eustatius
(Neth)

**ANTIGUA AND
BARBUDA**

ST KITTS - NEVIS

St Kitts

Antigua

Nevis

Redonda

Montserrat
(UK)

Guadeloupe Passage

La Désirade

Guadeloupe
(France)

• Pointe-à-Pitre

1467m ▲

Basse-Terre •

Marie-Galante

Les Saintes

Dominica Passage

DOMINICA

Martinique Passage

1397m ▲

Saint-Pierre •

Le François

Fort-de-France •

Martinique
(France)

Saint Lucia Passage

| 0 | 50 | 100 km |
| 0 | 50 miles | |

ST LUCIA

L e e w a r d   I s l a n d s

L e s s e r   A n t i l l e s

FÊTES PATRONALES

Fêtes patronales take place on the French- and Spanish-speaking islands to celebrate the saint's day of each town's patron saint. Check for dates with each island's tourist board.

Above right: Chutes du Carbet, Guadaloupe

THE FRENCH ANTILLES Unmistakably French in their food, culture and general outlook, the "overseas depart-ments" of Martinique and Guadeloupe combine tropical scenery with a noticeably European-influenced lifestyle. Visitors can explore Guadeloupe's bustling capital Pointe-à-Pitre, its sandy beaches and rain forests, Martinique's historic towns and villages, the restaurants of Saint Martin, and the chic beach resorts of Saint-Barthélemy; while the tiny isles of Les Saintes, La Désirade and Marie-Galante offer white sand beaches and quiet island life. Variety and beauty are the hallmarks of the French West Indies, made up of the single island of Martinique and the six islands which comprise the *Région* of Guadeloupe.

The main island, Guadeloupe, is actually two islets of contrasting landscapes, linked by a small land bridge. The administrative *Région* of Guadeloupe is an archipelago, consisting of the islands of Les Saintes, La Désirade, Marie-Galante, and Saint-Barthélemy, as well as the half-French, half-Dutch island of Saint-Martin/Sint Maarten. As the French islands are in the northern and centre sector of the Antilles, they enjoy similar climates and vegetation. Only one of the islands (Martinique) is in the region that is defined by the Windward group.

Lying between the Caribbean Sea and the Atlantic Ocean, the French Antilles, spread across 560km of sea, include two of the region's three volcanically active

French shops under the tropical sun in Guadeloupe

▶▶▶ **REGION HIGHLIGHTS**

Anse de Grande Saline
page 121

Aquarium page 110

Baie de l'Orient
page 123

Cascade aux Ecrivisses
page 112

Grande Anse des Salines
page 118

Grande-Case
page 123

Gustavia Harbor
page 121

Jardin de Balata
page 119

Maison de la Canne
page 118

Terre-de-Haut page 113

islands. Apart from the inner, Caribbean side of Guadeloupe and central/northern Martinique (which are covered in tropical mountain forest), the islands are green and humid, with excellent beaches and deep coves and bays. The eastern section of Guadeloupe remains part of an arc of limestone isles, and the western parts are a continuation of the volcanic link. Also in this chain, Martinique, the largest volcanic connection of the Windward islands, has three major peaks. At 1,467m Guadeloupe's volcano, Soufrière, is the highest peak to be found in the Eastern Caribbean.

The names given to the main islands in the Carib language – *Karukera* ("Island of Beautiful Waters") for Guadeloupe and *Madinia* or *Madinina* ("Island of Flowers") for Martinique – illustrate the mystical appeal of these islands. Even the French half of Saint-Martin has relatively fertile, scrub-clad, hilly terrain. The smaller islands off Guadeloupe and the most northerly island of the French Antilles, Saint-Barthélemy, are arid and rocky, with sparse, drought-loving vegetation; Guadeloupe's limestone islands and the volcanic Les Saintes feature coral reefs and beautiful, sandy beaches. The karst landscapes on Marie-Galante and Saint-Barthélemy (and on parts of Guadeloupe), together with poor soil, generally restrict arable cultivation, unlike the rich, watered lands of most of Guadeloupe, Martinique and Saint-Martin.

Although situated in and among staunchly British or Dutch islands, the French Antilles have maintained their unmistakable French air. Rather than negotiating a political break with her colonies, France has taken the view that they should be a full part of the republic, and since 1974 Guadeloupe and Martinique have had the right to elect their own representatives to the National Assembly. A small independence movement has emerged in Guadeloupe, and there are still occasional protests. In Martinique, the statue of Josephine Bonaparte, who was born on the island, was beheaded as a protest against French colonial dominance (her head was never found).

HISTORY French settlers first colonised Guadeloupe and Martinique in 1635, and African slaves were shipped in to work the new sugar plantations. By 1669, Martinique was such a successful colony that the French moved their administrative base there from St Kitts. In the wake of the French Revolution, Guadeloupe's slaves were freed, their colonial masters were killed and their plantations wiped out. Martinique reacted differently, calling on the British to maintain the status quo. Slavery was re-introduced in

1802 and the British occupied Guadeloupe, but France confirmed her hold on the island in 1815 – which was unfortunate for the slaves, for although slavery was abolished in the British colonies in the 1830s, emancipation did not come to the French territories until 1848. To fill the labour gap, the French Antilles encouraged the immigration of thousands of East Indians, who moved in as indentured labourers.

In the 1930s, Martinique became a centre for the black consciousness movement known as *Négritude,* led by Aimé Césaire and Etienne Lero. Guadeloupe and Martinique were granted departmental status in 1946, giving them equal rights with every other *département* in mainland France.

ISLAND LIFE The French Antilles have capitalised on their greatest assets: the vivacious mingling of races from many lands, and the enchanting surroundings. Tourism has brought an unprecedented influx of revenue and has transformed the lot of the islands without undermining their natural beauty or affecting the local way of life. The people of Martinique and Guadeloupe are known for their physical beauty and Gallic style. Although French is the official language and French influence permeates island life, from the food and buildings to the designer shops and the *boules* games, there is also a distinctively Caribbean side to the culture. The air pulses to zouk, a classic Caribbean beat; the countryside is laden with rain forests, sugar cane, and tropical fruit; and the people speak a form of Créole, heard everywhere – although its exclusion from official life has made it something of a poor relation.

With the mingled attributes of a robust culture, fertile soil and abundant seas, a climate combining aridity with high rainfall and all the requisites of the voracious tourist trade, the French Antilles seem to have arrived at a fairly happy balance of nature and development. Certainly they are among the most attractive and peaceful islands to be found in the entire Caribbean region.

CRÉOLE CUISINE
The French Caribbean has a strong tradition of Créole cooking, turning the techniques of French cuisine to Caribbean ingredients, including seafood and tropical fruits. Many restaurants serve classic and *nouvelle* French cuisine and some also offer the Caribbean equivalent, *nouvelle cuisine créole. Blaff* is a traditional manner of frying fish in spices; for *court bouillon*, fish is poached in a special mixture of lime, wine, onion and tomatoes. *Touffé is* a casserole and *colombo* is a sort of Caribbean curry. You may come across *z'habitants*, a local dish of crayfish. *Accras* are batter balls, usually made with fish and *souskaï* is a savoury way of marinating fruit.

Hobie cats on a Saint-Martin beach

Hobie Cat

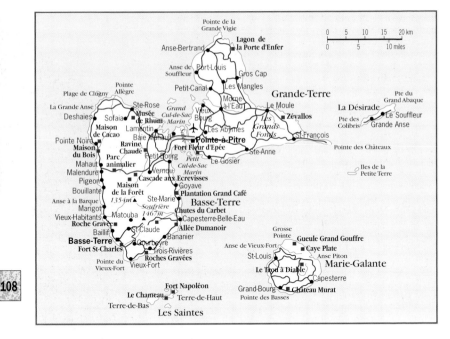

Pointe de la
Grande Vigie

Lagon de
Anse-Bertrand ■ la Porte d'Enfer

0 5 10 15 20 km
0   5   10 miles

Anse de Port-Louis
Souffleur Gros Cap

Plage de Clugny Pointe Allègre Petit-Canal Les Mangles **Grande-Terre** Pte du
Grand Abaque

La Grande Anse Ste-Rose *Grand* Vieux Le Moule **La Désirade**
Deshaies Sofaia *Musée Cul-de-Sac* Bourg ■ **Zévallos** Pte des Le Souffleur
de Rhum Marin Les Colibris Grande Anse

Pointe Noire Maison de Cacao Baie Mahault ■ **Pointe-à-Pitre** St-François
du Bois Parc Chaude Petit-Bourg **Fort Fleur d'Epée** Pointe des Châteaux
Mahaut animalier *Cul-de-Sac* Ste-Anne
Malendure Verneuil *Marin* Iles de la
Pigeon **Cascade aux Ecrevisses** Le Gosier Petite Terre
Bouillante Maison Goyave
Anse à la Barque de la Forêt Ste-Marie ■ **Plantation Grand Café**
Marigot *1354 m* ▲ Soufrière
Vieux-Habitants Matouba *1467 m* ▲ **Chutes du Carbet** **Basse-Terre** Grosse
Roche Gravée Capesterre-Belle-Eau Pointe **Gueule Grand Gouffre**
Baillif St-Claude **Allée Dumanoir** Anse de Vieux-Fort ■ **Caye Plate**
Basse-Terre Courbeyre Bananier St-Louis Anse Piton
Fort St-Charles Trois-Rivières **Le Trou à Diable** **Marie-Galante**
Pointe du **Roches Gravées** Capesterre
Vieux-Fort Vieux-Fort **Fort Napoléon** Grand-Bourg ■ **Château Murat**
Le Chameau Terre-de-Haut Pointe des Basses
Terre-de-Bas **Les Saintes**

Guadeloupe

Guadeloupe has two distinct halves, like the wings of a butterfly. In the west is Basse-Terre, a rain-forested volcanic monster which is similar in appearance to Dominica, further south. The eastern wing, across the narrow Rivière-Salée (Salt River), is Grande-Terre, a relatively flat, coral-based outcrop from a much older range of volcanoes.

Many of Guadeloupe's hotels are located along the southern shore of Grande-Terre, which offers watersports and good waterfront restaurants and bistros. This "wing" of Guadeloupe is composed of a shattered limestone outcrop with karst hills, known as *montagnes russes*. Low plains (*fonds*) reach out to the white, sandy beaches and spectacular rocky cliffs along its coastline. The terrain on Basse-Terre is for the most part mountainous, rain

FRENCH FESTIVALS
In keeping with their love of food, the French Antilleans stage a Chefs' Festival each year (in April on Martinique, May on Saint-Martin and in August on Guadeloupe). Each island's leading cooks are invited to bring along their finest creations for judging, and there follows a general feast. Carnival in the French Caribbean features the main processions on Mardi Gras (Shrove Tuesday) and Mercredi des Cendres (Ash Wednesday). On the Wednesday the colour scheme is black and white, and the day culminates in the burning of the carnival figure, Momo.

A cocoa tree growing on Guadeloupe

forested and nourished by cascading waterfalls and mountain streams such as the Grande Rivière Goyaves, the island's longest river at nearly 32km. Inlets of black, volcanic-sanded beaches lie on the south and southeast coast of the island, but there are excellent golden sand beaches in the northwest.

Guadeloupe's climate is tempered by the cooling north-east Trade Winds, generally no more than breezes – Les Alizes. Hurricanes occurred in 1979 and 1989, but the islands generally enjoy idyllic weather.

ISLAND LIFE About 420,000 people live in the archipelago of Guadeloupe, almost 50 per cent of whom are under 20 years of age. Most are of African descent; some are descendants of early settlers – *Békés* – or of East Indian

indentured workers. Tourism and administration provide work for nearly half the population; agriculture and industry are the other economic mainstays.

Officially, the language in Guadeloupe is French. Créole, however, is the language of the people – although once banned from educational establishments, it is now a proud demonstration of individualism.

Waterfront market and ferry departure point, Place de la Victoire

POINTE-À-PITRE This large city, sprawling along the coastline in the crook of Guadeloupe's two large islands, has a population of about 100,000. Its heart is the **Place de la Victoire►►**, a large square set with royal palms, mango trees, statues of famous Guadeloupeans and lined with cafés, overlooking the busy harbour, La Darse, where ferries depart for the offshore islands. The tourist information office can be found near La Darse and the cathedral, built mainly of metal in order to withstand the occasional fierce Caribbean hurricanes.

From here the crowded streets stretch in all directions, overlooked by tall houses with intricate balconies and shutters. On the rue Frébault, in the

Boats on Ste-Anne

GETTING AROUND GUADELOUPE

110

As one half of the island is flat, with plantations and beaches and the other is mountainous (with a 30,350-ha national park), Guadeloupe is no easy place to view on one excursion. Grande-Terre is criss-crossed with roads that do not give straightforward access to all its attractions, and should be divided into at least two journeys. Basse-Terre has few roads crossing its peaks and gorges; one circumnavigates the area, running around the coastline, but sightseeing needs at least three full excursions. The island's "neck", between Grande-Terre and Basse-Terre, takes yet another trip.

Chengy Hindu temple

main shopping district, a **covered market**►► provides Caribbean mayhem and every imaginable kind of produce. The **Musée Schoelcher**►► (tel: 82 08 04; call for hours. *Admission: inexpensive*), set in a stone and stucco house at 24 rue Peynier, displays memorabilia associated with Victor Schoelcher, the 19th-century anti-slavery campaigner; and the **Musée St-John Perse**► (tel: 90 01 92. *Open* Thu–Tue 8:30–11:30, 2:30–5:30. *Admission: inexpensive*), on rue Nozière, traces the life of Alexis Saint-Léger, the Nobel Prize-winning Guadeloupean poet. East of the town, the **Aquarium de la Guadeloupe**►►► (tel: 90 92 38. *Open* daily 9–7. *Admission: expensive*) in Bas du Fort displays tropical fish and the **Fort Fleur d'Epée**►, an 18th-century defensive bastion built of coral rock, has been partly restored.

OUTSIDE POINTE-À-PITRE Tourism centres around the towns along Grande-Terre's south coast – Le Gosier, Ste-Anne and St-François – where beaches and waterfront restaurants are packed. Further east, the beaches are emptier and at the Pointe des Châteaux there are superb strips of sand where nudism is permitted.

North of this coastal strip the country opens out and cane fields rustle in the breeze; here, the towns are quieter and isolated from the tourist clamour. In Morne-à-l'Eau, the cemetery is full of the distinctive local checked gravestones, covered with black and white tiles. Some *Blancs Matignons* live in this area, the descendants of impoverished white settlers who have stayed here for centuries, choosing not to mix with black Guadeloupeans.

To the west of Pointe-à-Pitre, across the Rivière-Salée, the scenery suddenly changes and Basse-Terre's mountains tower ahead. The quickest road to the capital town, also called Basse-Terre, runs south along the island's eastern shore. At the **Plantation Grand Café**► (tel: 86 33 06. *Open* May–Oct, Mon–Fri and Sat. *Admission: expensive*), you can see a working banana plantation. Past Ste-Marie, where Columbus is thought to have landed on his second voyage, the route runs through the **Allée du Manoir**►►, an avenue of 30m high royal palm trees. Inland, the Etang Zombi and the Grand Etang lakes and three waterfalls known as the **Chutes du Carbet**►►, grace the slopes of the Soufrière. The coast road continues to the charming town of Trois-Rivières, scattered down the steep hillside; near the coast, where ferries depart for the nearby Iles des Saintes, there are Arawak carvings on the rocks at the **Parc Archéologique des Roches Gravées**►► (tel: 92 91 88. *Open* daily 9–5. *Admission: inexpensive*), dating from around AD 1000.

One of Guadeloupes's historic trails is the "Trace des Contrabandiers" (The Smugglers' Trail). It follows the spine of Basse-Terre's mountain range and carves its way through the magnificent rain forest. Two centuries ago, this was a long and possibly dangerous hike, but if no ship was available travellers simply had to walk. Such routes are now opening again as beautiful walking trails.

Waterfalls and luxuriant ferns in Guadeloupe's rain forest

PERPETUAL RAIN
Rain forests create their own rain. Atlantic winds are laden with water and when they hit the island slopes they are forced upwards, condensing into huge white clouds above the mountain peaks. These clouds drop their loads onto the forest and when the sun comes out it causes evaporation, putting water from the forest back into the sky, where it joins a never-ending cycle.

The Caribbean's mountainous islands are criss-crossed with paths. Most were cut by armies, but used by rebel maroons who hid out in the hills and by runaway slaves. In the 19th century, walking traders would carry up to 50kg of goods for sale on trays placed on their heads. These *porteuses* were immensely fit, capable of walking up to 40km a day across the mountains.

Tropical rain forests grow on all the tall, well-watered islands of the Eastern Caribbean and in the Greater Antilles. At lower elevations, gommiers and other hardwood trees such as mahogany tower over fern-covered floors, with canopies at about 24m, their trunks grappled by creeping vines. Above 975m are the montane or cloud forests, where ferns and orchids form curves from the upper branches of the trees. Higher still, above 1,500m, are the elfin forests of stunted trees covered with mosses and lichens.

Most of the Eastern Caribbean islands have designated national parks to protect their precious rain forest areas and the flora and fauna they support. Forest trails have been created in Dominica, St Lucia, Martinique and Guadeloupe amongst others. In the Greater Antilles, Jamaica has excellent walking in the Blue Mountains and Puerto Rico has a number of national parks. Virgin Islands National Park on St John (USVI) also has many hiking trails.

Guided tours are the safest; even on small islands it is easy to get lost. Guides also usually know local flora and the uses of plants in traditional medicine. Trainers or light ankle-height boots are normally adequate; a sweater is needed for higher climbs and a waterproof jacket is useful for protection against downpours.

Maison de la Forêt, Guadeloupe

Morne-à-l'Eau cemetery

INTRODUCING THE PINEAPPLE

Columbus was "astonished and delighted" with the pineapple when he was presented with it on his arrival in Guadeloupe, during his second voyage to the Caribbean. After its introduction to Europe, it was regarded as a luxury and became a symbol of hospitality; pineapples can still be seen crafted in stone on the entrance gates to many country houses in Europe.

Spread over the hillside, the namesake capital of Basse-Terre has a number of attractive stone and wooden town buildings. The former **Fort St-Charles**▶▶ (1650), overlooking the harbour, is a huge defensive bulwark with a small museum. It was renamed Fort Delgrés in 1990 after a noted abolitionist, Louis Delgrés. Inland from Basse-Terre, on the slopes of the Soufrière volcano, is the town of Matouba, where a 200-year-old trail, Trace Victor Hugues, leads to hot baths fed by volcanic springs (a 28km haul, not to be undertaken lightly). Near the Bains Jaunes hot springs, the narrow road strikes on up to Savane à Mulets and stops 305m short of the crater itself, which still occasionally spews out dust and even lava.

The north of Basse-Terre makes a day trip tour in itself. Heading north up the east coast, through traditional cane-growing flats, a working sugar factory complete with steam-driven crusher operates at the **Domaine de Séverin**▶▶, at Ste-Rose and the story of sugar production is told at the **Musée de Rhum**▶▶ (tel: 28 70 04. *Open* Mon–Sat 9–5. *Admission: inexpensive*). On the northwestern corner of the island are some of Guadeloupe's best beaches, particularly the Plage de Cluny and la Grande Anse, a 4km sweep of golden sand and palms. Near the 17th-century town of Pointe-Noire is the **Maison du Bois**▶ (reopening 2002), which shows local building techniques. Also look for the **Maison du Cacao**▶▶ (tel: 98 21 23. *Open* daily 9–5. *Admission: inexpensive*), to view a pictorial illustration of the history of cocoa and chocolate.

La Traversée crosses through the middle of Basse-Terre, passing the **Cascade aux Ecrivisses**▶▶ and the **Maison de la Forêt**▶▶ (tel: 80 86 00. *Open* daily 9–5. *Admission free*), which traces the development of the island's natural life. Past a small zoo, where forest animals are kept, the road descends to the sea and rejoins the coast road, turning south towards Basse-Terre. The Jacques Cousteau Marine Reserve is located off the popular black sand beach at Malendure.

Malendure has a string of beach bars; the Ile de Pigeon is an excellent site for scuba-diving

LA DÉSIRADE Virtually unspoilt by tourism, La Désirade offers a quiet getaway and white beaches. The "Desired One" was often the first island spotted by 16th-century sailors longing for land after a tedious Atlantic crossing. Their desire was frustrated, however, as ships would sail past this barren, windy island.

Only 11km by about 2km, La Désirade is a table mountain lying 8km east of Grande-Terre in the Atlantic. Its population of under 2,000 is spread along the southern shore between the town of Grande Anse and the village of Le Souffleur.

La Darse, Pointe-à-Pitre

113

MARIE-GALANTE The beach at Petit Anse is the draw of Marie-Galante, the largest of Guadeloupe's offshore islands. Almost circular in shape, it measures nearly 155sq km and has a population of 12,400, about half of whom live in the main town of Grand-Bourg. Named by Columbus in 1493 after his flagship, *Santa Maria de Galante*, it was a long-time Carib stronghold but was eventually captured by Europeans and turned into a sugar island (Marie-Galante rum is still renowned). Beyond Grand-Bourg, ruined windmills are reminders of the sugar trade's peak. The **Château Murat►** (tel: 97 94 41. *Open* Mon–Fri 9–12, 2:30–5:30, Sat–Sun 9–2:30. *Admission free*), a restored 18th-century plantation house east of Grand-Bourg, contains a museum, and further inland Le Trou à Diable cavern can be explored (but sturdy footwear, a torch and caution are needed). There are also excellent walking paths around the island.

LES SAINTES The lures of Les Saintes include a nudist beach, scuba-diving and a beautiful bay that's been called a mini Rio. These volcanic peaks lie to the south of Basse-Terre. Only two are inhabited: Terre-de-Bas and Terre-de-Haut. The population of the former is descended from plantation slaves. **Terre-de-Haut►►**, which was never planted, centres around tourism, with hotels on the waterfront of Bourg, its only town. White fishermen – descended from French colonials – wear *salako* hats, similar to Chinese "coolie" hats, which are made in Terre-de-Bas. There are good beaches on Terre-de-Haut and sights include Fort Napoléon, with a museum and exotic garden (tel: 61 01 51. *Open* daily 9–12. *Admission: inexpensive*), on the island's highest point.

THE BATTLE OF THE SAINTS
The Battle of the Saints, so-called because it took place just off Les Saintes in 1782, was a turning point in the fight for European imperial supremacy over the Caribbean islands. It was also a first in naval terms; the British Admiral Rodney saw a gap between the French ships and managed to "break the line", splitting the French fleet into two parts so that the flagship could not communicate with most of its fleet. The battle ended in victory for the British, who held sway over Caribbean waters for the next two decades.

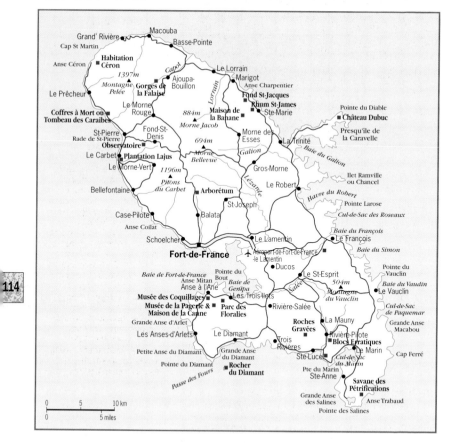

Grand' Rivière
Cap St Martin
Macouba
Basse-Pointe
Anse Céron
Habitation
Céron
1397m
Montagne
Pelée
Gorges de
la Falaise
Cabet
Le Prêcheur
Le Morne
Rouge
Ajoupa-
Bouillon
Le Lorrain
Marigot
Anse Charpentier
Fond St-Jacques
Rhum St-James
Ste-Marie
Pointe du Diable
Château Dubuc
Coffres à Mort ou
Tombeau des Caraïbes
St-Pierre
Rade de St-Pierre
Observatoire
Fond-St-
Denis
884m
Morne Jacob
Maison de
la Banane
Morne de
Esses
694m
La Trinité
Presqu'île de
la Caravelle
Le Carbet
Plantation Lajus
Le Morne-Vert
1196m
Morne
Bellevue
Galion
Baie du Galion
Bellefontaine
Pitons
du Carbet
Arborétum
Gros-Morne
Le Robert
Ilet Ramville
ou Chancel
Pointe Larose
Case-Pilote
Anse Coilat
Balata
St-Joseph
Havre du Robert
Cul-de-Sac des Roseaux
Schoelcher
Le Lamentin
Baie du François
Le François
Baie du Simon
Fort-de-France
Aéroport-de-Fort-de-France
-le Lamentin
Ducos
Le St-Esprit
Pointe du
Vauclin
Baie de Fort-de-France
Pointe du
Bout
Anse Mitan
Anse à l'Âne
Baie de
Genipa
Les Trois-Ilets
504m
Montagne
du Vauclin
Baie du Vaudin
Le Vauclin
Musée des Coquillages
Musée de la Pagerie &
Maison de la Canne
Parc des
Floralies
Rivière-Salée
Salée
Cul-de-Sac
de Paquemar
Grande Anse d'Arlet
Les Anses-d'Arlets
Le Diamant
Roches
Gravées
La Mauny
Rivière-Pilote
Grande Anse
Macabou
Petite Anse du Diamant
Grande Anse
du Diamant
Trois
Rivières
Ste-Luce
Blocs Erratiques
Le Marin
Cap Ferré
Pointe du Diamant
Rocher
du Diamant
Passe des Fours
Pte du Marin
Ste-Anne
Cul-de-Sac
du Marin
Savane des
Pétrifications
Grande Anse
des Salines
Pointe des Salines
Anse Trabaud

0   5   10 km
0   5 miles

114

PETIT PUNCH
This popular French
Caribbean drink is taken
before lunch. A heap of
brown sugar crystals is
dashed with local white
rum and stirred. A quarter
of lime is squeezed in and
the mix is downed in one
gulp. Ice water is then
swilled around to collect
the last of the sugar and
downed as a chaser.

Martinique pâtisserie

Martinique

Martinique – which is far more tourist-orientated than
Guadeloupe – has always been the heart of the French
Caribbean. St-Pierre, once its most important town, was
known as the Paris of the Lesser Antilles and its booming
sugar trade was vitally important to the French, who were
even prepared to give up their claims to territories in
India and Canada in return for keeping the island in the
18th century. As its Amerindian name, *Madinina* ("Land
of Flowers") implies, this is a fertile island and since the
French arrived in 1635 (they have owned it almost contin-
uously ever since) it has been successfully farmed.
Agriculture and fishing are still important and there are
vast hectares of bananas, pineapples
and sugar cane. Martinique lies mid-
way down the chain of the Lesser
Antilles, between the independent
islands of Dominica and St Lucia.
Shaped something like a boxing
glove, it measures 80km by 32km at
its widest point. In the mountainous
north, the highest peak, the active
volcano Montagne Pelée, stands

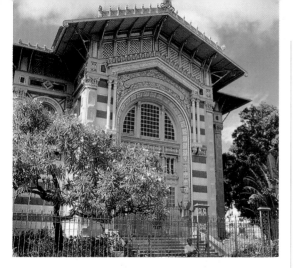

*The flamboyant
Schoelcher Library on La
Savanne, Fort-de-France*

THE HEAD CODE
There is a certain
elegance and coquettish
air about some French
Antilleans that mirrors
their metropolitan counter-
parts. A century ago there
was even a flirtatious
message in the way island
women wore their madras
headdresses. Tied with
chequered silk material,
the headdress indicated a
code in the number of
points protruding. One
corner meant that the
woman had no lover; two
points meant that her
heart was taken. Three
points meant that officially
her heart was taken, but
that a man might try
his luck.

1,396m high; rain forests cover the Pitons du Carbet and to the south, the land descends to fertile plains and *mornes* (or foothills).

The island's relatively large tourist industry is not immediately visible, as there is a strong local community. The population is made up of a diverse mix of French, African, East Indian, Chinese and Arab races; French is the official language and the French influence can be seen in everyday life, from the croissants to the Peugeot cars. But there is also a lively Créole culture and good Caribbean restaurants, shops and bars.

FORT-DE-FRANCE Martinique's capital is a modern town set in a bay on the calm Caribbean shore. It has grown enormously since the eruption of Montagne Pelée devastated St-Pierre in 1902, and over 100,000 inhabitants now live in the centre and in the suburbs that have clambered all over the surrounding hills. Overlooking the waterfront on the Baie des Flammands, the centre of the town is **La Savanne**▶ ▶, an open park studded with 30m-tall royal palm trees, where the Martiniquans take their evening walks. There is a headless statue of Josephine Bonaparte, the French empress, who was born across the bay at Trois-Ilets. You can visit **Fort St Louis**▶ (tel: 60 54 59. *Open* Mon–Fri 9–3:30, Sat 10–3. *Admission: inexpensive*), the huge fortress that protected the town from invasion in the days of the empire. The **Musée Départemental d'archéologie précolombienne**▶ (tel: 71 57 05. *Open* Mon–Fri 8–5, Sat 9–12. *Admission: inexpensive*) has a well-presented display of Amerindian pottery. Nearby, the striking **Bibliothèque Schoelcher**▶ ▶, a domed structure of brightly coloured metal and glass, was built for the 1889 Paris Exhibition and transported here to house a library commemorating Victor Schoelcher's anti-slavery campaign.

Driving in Fort-de-France is not a good idea. The streets are crowded and several are given over to markets – such as the fish market on the Rivière Madame, near the geological displays of the Parc Floral. Beyond the suburbs, the scenery turns into mountainous rain forest to the north and sugar cane flats to the south and east. Here, life is simpler: Catholic churches overlook town squares and orange and green fishing boats are moored in the bays.

Jardin de Balata

Ian Fleming, the creator of James Bond, lived on the north coast of Jamaica and took the name for his famous spy from a real ornithologist, the author of The Birds of the West Indies. *The Caribbean is on migratory routes north and south and many birds from further north like to winter in the Caribbean. With so many habitats (shoreline, mangrove swamp, forests) within a relatively small area, human visitors can expect to see a striking variety of different species.*

116

Top: scarlet ibis
Right: Jamaican
mountain goats

ZOOS

The Caribbean islands have a small number of zoos. In Santo Domingo, the capital of the Dominican Republic, the Parque Zoologico Nacional keeps elephants as well as tropical animals, and in Port of Spain, Trinidad, the Emperor Valley Zoo has tropical animals seen in Trinidad, including the tree porcupine, the crab-eating racoon and monkeys such as the weeping capuchin and the red howler. Animals are free to roam in the Barbados Wildlife Reserve, in the north of the island and on Guadeloupe the Parc Zoologique et Botanique, on the Route de la Traversée (D23) in Basse-Terre, has walkways through the rain forest. There are also small zoos in Sint Maarten and in Mayaguez, Puerto Rico.

Mangrove swamps and coastal lagoons are good places to look out for herons, ducks and more exotic creatures such as gallinules and jacanas, whose long toes enable them to walk over lilies. Colonies of flamingoes nest on the island of Bonaire and kingfishers can often be spotted flitting along rivers.

Pelicans are a familiar sight on many islands, flying in formation around the shoreline or diving into the sea for food. Tropicbirds occasionally soar near the coast and the magnificent frigatebird cruises high in the air, waiting for passing meals. Gulls, terns, gannets and boobies skim along the surface of the sea before rising and plunging to catch fish, while small crowds of oystercatchers and sandpipers walk along the beaches as they feed, dodging the breaking waves.

On open ground, the white cattle egret can be seen wherever there are grazing cows, and thrushes, finches and larger birds, such as crows (called John Crows), are common. Slightly harder to spot are mocking birds and flycatchers, which snatch up insects on the wing, and tanagers, which feed on fruit.

In contrast, some of the most familiar birds are self-assured enough to try stealing the sugar from breakfast tables: the carib grackle, which is also called a blackbird in some areas, has a V-shaped tail and displays by puffing up its feathers. The cheeky bananaquit has distinctive yellow and black plumage.

It takes a lot of luck to see the Caribbean's more exotic birds. Shimmering hummingbirds flit around the flowers on a permanent search for nectar; the purple-throated and green-throated hummingbirds and the Antillean crested hummingbird live in most islands of the Eastern Caribbean. High in the forests there are still Caribbean parrots, though these are now an endangered species, particularly in the Eastern Caribbean, where there are parrots unique to St Vincent, St Lucia and Dominica (the imperial and red-necked parrots).

The island of Trinidad is an exception in the Caribbean, both in its animal and its bird life, because it has considerable spill-over from the South American continent. Over 400 bird species make this the best island for bird-watching, but the most spectacular sight is the scarlet ibis, with its vivid red plumage and downwards-curving bill. It might just be possible to see a bright blue motmot or maybe a mannikin; the male mannikin, with its white breast and black cap and wings, spends about 70 per cent of its time displaying, strutting with its competitors around the female, making noises like a little firecracker and even turning somersaults.

Caribbean animals Most animals on the Caribbean islands – goats, chickens, donkeys, cattle and even monkeys and mongeese – were imported by settlers. Indigenous survivors, most of which are endangered, include the coney, which is something like a guinea pig and lives in the Jamaican John Crow mountains and in Hispaniola; the agouti, a tail-less rodent the size of a rabbit, living in the Eastern Caribbean; the American racoon; and the tatou, an armadillo that survives in Grenada. Reptiles are more widespread. Tiny geckos and lizards crawl over walls and tree frogs peep noisily in gardens. Iguanas, which can grow to nearly 1.5m, are found on a number of islands and the few snakes include small constrictors and the notorious fer de lance, with eyes that glow orange at night.

Perhaps the most curious of a wide range of insects are Hercules beetles, which can measure 15cm long and have claws protruding from their heads and Cuban tarantulas, which can grow to the size of a man's hand.

ANIMAL SETTLERS
In the early days of European settlement, sailors would leave animals ashore and plant fruit-bearing trees on remote islands so that there would be a supply of food for anyone who might be shipwrecked. Père Labat, an early French traveller, recounts that a sailors' tale that a ship-wrecked crew with a pig on board should throw it into the sea and row after it, as it would know innately the direction of the nearest land.

SANDFLIES
Apart from mosquitoes, the most annoying insects that frequent beaches are sandflies. So small that they are virtually invisible, sandflies are known on some islands as "no-see-ums", and their bite causes an infuriating itch.

117

Iguanas live on many Caribbean islands

DIAMOND ROCK
The sheer-sided Diamond Rock stands just off the south coast of Martinique and is rarely visited, but for 18 months in 1805 it was occupied by 100 British sailors, who built a fort there in order to deny the channel to French ships. All the supplies, building materials and food had to be winched up from ships below. Eventually the French made a serious effort to take it back and bombarded the Rock for three days before the commander surrendered.

St-Pierre, once a bustling city

OUTSIDE FORT-DE-FRANCE Martinique is a large island and although the roads are good, a leisurely circuit can take a couple of days. Buses run from the waterfront at Fort-de-France and shared taxis follow regular routes. Car hire companies operate in Fort-de-France and the main tourist areas and at the airport.

The closest tourist resort to Fort-de-France is Pointe du Bout and its beach, Anse Mitan, south across the bay (take a ferry from the waterfront). This is a lively area with good restaurants and cafés, though the beaches are not the best. To the south, beyond Trois-Ilets, is the **Musée de la Pagerie**▶ ▶ (tel: 68 38 34. *Open* Tue–Fri 9–5:30, Sat–Sun 9–1, 2:30–5:30. *Admission: inexpensive*), dedicated to Josephine Bonaparte and set in the farm where she was born. There is a golf course and a museum of sugar, the **Maison de la Canne**▶ ▶ (tel: 68 32 04. *Open* Tue–Sun 9–5:30. *Admission: inexpensive*), nearby.

West along the coast, there are three attractive coves at **Les Anses-d'Arlets**▶ ▶, isolated on the southwestern shore, and worth a detour. As the coast road winds its way to Le Diamant, it passes the solitary Diamond Rock, a few kilometres offshore (see panel). For an excellent potted history of the island (in French) and Amerindian and colonial artefacts, visit the **Écomusée de la Martinique**▶, Anse Figuier (tel: 62 79 14. *Open* Mon, Wed–Sat 9–1:30, 2:30–5. *Admission: inexpensive*). Le Martin, which has a large marina, and Ste-Anne, further south, are the two main tourist towns in the southeast. The best beaches in Martinique are at the southern tip of the island: **Grande Anse des Salines**▶ ▶ ▶, a 4km sweep of palm-backed sand, and nearby Anse Trabaud.

The east coast of Martinique is mainly agricultural and the sea can be rough, though there are beaches tucked into the folds of the coastline. Near Le François, **Habitation Clément**▶ ▶ (tel: 54 62 07. *Open* daily 9–6. *Admission: expensive*) is one of the most attractive plantation houses in the Caribbean. The **Rhum St James rum distillery**▶ ▶ (tel: 69 30 02. *Open* daily 9–6. *Admission free*) at Ste-Marie and the **Maison de la Banane**▶ ▶ (tel: 69 45 52. *Open* daily 9–4:30. *Admission: inexpensive*), which is further inland, are open to visitors.

ST-PIERRE'S SURVIVOR
At one time, St-Pierre was the most chic and stylish town in the Eastern Caribbean. It boasted a theatre and a cathedral and "Pierrotins" followed Paris fashion to the letter. Although the town was almost totally destroyed by the volcanic eruption of 1902, one man was saved because he had been put in a police cell overnight after a drinking spree. The walls of the cell protected him from the heat and gases of the explosion. He later joined a circus, exhibiting himself in a reproduction of his cell.

Two spectacular roads lead north from Fort-de-France to the town of St-Pierre, one climbing into the rain-forested mountains and the other following the coast. The Route de la Trace, an old forest road cut by the Jesuits three centuries ago, climbs up through the suburb of Didier and passes through Balata, where a replica of the Sacré-Coeur in Paris was built in 1923 as a World War I memorial. The road continues to the **Jardin de Balata**▶▶ (tel: 64 48 73. *Open* daily 9–5. *Admission: inexpensive*), where walkways lead past hundreds of tropical plants. From here, La Trace forges into the peaks of the Pitons du Carbet.

The coast road passes through fishing villages such as Case-Pilote, named after a Carib chief and Le Carbet, where Paul Gauguin lived for two years in the 19th century; the **Musée Gauguin**▶ (tel: 78 22 66. *Open* daily 9–5:30. *Admission: inexpensive*) exhibits reproductions of his works.

Though it was never the official capital, St-Pierre was the business and social centre of Martinique – until 8 May, 1902, when the whole town was engulfed by a volcanic ash and nearly all the 26,000 residents were killed. The town is still inhabited and many of its old buildings, including the theatre and some waterfront warehouses, still exist, though as ruins. There are a couple of museums on the rue Victor Hugo – the **Musée Historique**▶ (tel: 78 15 16. *Open* Mon–Sat 9:30–5. *Admission: inexpensive*) with displays about town life before 1902 and the **Musée Volcanique**▶▶ (tel: 78 15 16. *Open* daily 9–5. *Admission: inexpensive*), which has grim exhibits from the day of its destruction. Montagne Pelée itself looms quietly over the remains of the town.

St-Pierre souvenir

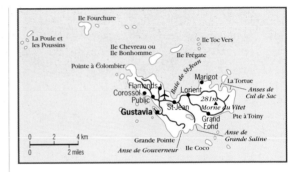

BRETON HERITAGE
St Barts was first colonised by Bretons and Normans and there is still a community of white Barthéleminois, whose language has retained some remnants of 17th-century Breton. Another curious hangover of their ancient heritage, still occasionally seen, is their *calèche* hats, cotton bonnets fitted with wooden slats that stick out above the face like a visor. Apart from shading the wearer from the sun, they keep away other intrusions, earning them the nickname *quichenotte* – supposedly a corruption of "kiss-me-not".

Saint-Barthélemy

Saint-Barthélemy, a tiny speck set in an aquamarine sea, has seen the full ebb and flow of Caribbean fortune. From a backwater visited occasionally by pirates it became a thriving trading post for 50 years before slipping back into obscurity. Today, the island is one of the Caribbean's most luxurious and desirable destinations.

St Barts (or Saint-Barth in French), as this most French of the French Caribbean islands is affectionately known, has a rarified and exclusive air. It is the favoured retreat of a chic clientele of stars and the seriously rich, who zip around the island's boutiques and beaches in Suzuki jeeps and on *mobylettes* (mopeds). Tropical sophistication is taken to perfection here – at a very high price.

Although St Barts is just under 21sq km in size, with no hill rising above 280m (Morne Vitet), the scrub-covered scenery is rough and dramatic and six large lagoons are scattered across the landscape. The island lies 24km to the southeast of Saint-Martin, on the same coral geological shelf, and this gives it magnificent white sand beaches. More than 20 tiny islets and islet groups lie in its waters, of which the largest is Ile Fourchue; others include the Ile Frégate twin islands, Les Balines and La Baline

Offshore islands near Saint-Barthélemy

("The Whales" and "The Whale") and La Poule et Les Poussins ("The Hen and Chickens").

Like Saint-Martin, St Barts is a *commune* of Guadeloupe, 250km to the south, administered by a *sous-préfet* from Paris, but it has not always been French. After 100 or so years of trading with smugglers and pirates, the 1,000 French settlers learned in 1785 that the island had been leased to the Swedes in return for trading rights in the Baltic. Sweden made St Barts a free port and for half a century the island prospered. When it was handed back to the French in 1878, its duty-free status was retained.

The capital of St Barts is **Gustavia►►►**, named after Gustav III, the Swedish King who made the 1785 exchange. It has just a few pretty streets, some with Swedish names, set on three sides of a natural harbour. In its heyday the town was defended by four fortresses, of which two, Fort Gustav and Fort Karl, can be visited. The **Museé de Saint-Barth►►** (tel: 29 71 55. *Open* Mon 2:30–6:30, Tue–Fri 8:30–12:30, 2:30–6:30, Sat 9–1. *Admission: inexpensive*) is set in the restored Wall House on the seaward arm of the bay. Unfortunately, much of the original town was destroyed by fire in the 1850s, but some of the old stone warehouses have been restored and now provide atmospheric settings for bars and restaurants.

St Barts can easily be explored in a day. A drive around the steep, switchback roads takes in the occasional old church or traditional country house with plastered walls and tin roofs dotted among the modern villas. You might even hear a bit of local dialect or see an islander dressed traditionally in a long white skirt and bonnet or *calèche*. Good beaches include Anse du Gouverneur and **Anse de Grande Saline►►►** on the south coast; also the Baie de St John and Anse de Grand Cul de Sac on the north.

North of Gustavia, the road runs through Public to Corossol, an old fishing village with a shell collection at the **Inter Oceans Museum►►** (tel: 27 62 97. *Open* Tue–Sun 9–12:30, 2–5. *Admission: inexpensive).* The village is also the best place to find St Barts weaving, made from the latanier palm, which grows all over the island.

To the northeast of the capital, the Plaine de la Tourmente is the site of the island's airstrip and of a graveyard. St Jean, to the east, is one of the centres of the tourist industry, with boutiques and restaurants. At Lorient, further east, local fishermen work as they have for centuries; beyond this point, the country opens out, though there are hotels tucked away in the bays. When the winds are up, the windsurfing is excellent in the east.

The hair-raising landing strip at St Barts only accommodates small planes

121

The Hôtel la Banane – a tourist's-eye view of St Barts

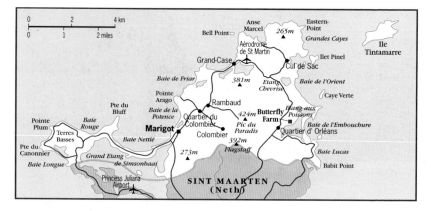

THE PARTITION
A fanciful story describes the partitioning of Saint-Martin/Sint Maarten between the French and the Dutch. Two men, one from each side, stood back to back and set off around the coastline until they met up again; the line between the departure and meeting points was to be the border. The French ended up with the larger share of the island – so the Frenchman presumably walked faster – but there are tales that the Dutchman was delayed by snoozing after too much French wine, or by a pretty French girl who happened to be passing.

Saint-Martin

The border that divides the island of Saint-Martin between France and Holland (see also pages 140–142) is barely noticeable. The countryside is much the same on both sides. Only an obelisk and a bilingual sign mark the fact that this is the smallest island in the world to be divided between two sovereign states. France, which owns the northern half of the island, looking towards Anguilla, marginally got the better of the division (see panel), with 54 of the total 95sq km.

This is a rugged island with tall, green and yellow concave slopes (the tallest is Pic du Paradis, at 424m) and a tortuous coastline indented with coves and superb white sand beaches. The main landmass is pierced with lagoons and salt ponds and one "wing" is almost entirely occupied by a vast lake – one of the largest natural lakes in the Antilles, divided between the Dutch and French territories; the French part is attended by two low islands, Ilet Pinel ("Penal Island") and Caye Verte, to which there are daily ferry trips.

Saint-Martin is a *commune* of Guadeloupe and has a distinctly French air – policemen wear *képis* and French restaurants, cafés, bistros and boutiques abound in the main resorts. But the atmosphere of the island is basically international and modern, having boomed, like the Dutch side, from a lazy backwater 20 years ago to a large tourist destination. The population has likewise exploded to cope with the influx of tourists; this is not the best Caribbean island for getting away from the crowds.

Marigot▶▶ is the capital on the French side, a small nexus of streets set between the Baie de Marigot and the Simpson Bay Lagoon. The few old townhouses with wrought-iron balconies and the waterfront warehouses have been restored and now buzz with shoppers and drinkers taking time out from the beach. On the Boulevard de France, overlooking the bay, is the **market square▶▶** and the tourist office. The ruined Fort St Louis, the town's defence in the days of imperial wars, still has a magnificent view over Anguilla and the town's approaches, as well as the lagoon, where the busy **Marina Port la Royale▶▶** yacht basin is packed with pleasure craft and lined with cafés and restaurants.

Heading west out of town you will come to the **Musée de Saint Martin▶▶** (tel: 29 22 84. *Open* Mon–Sat 9–1, 3–6. *Admission: inexpensive*), which traces the indigenous and colonial history of the island.

Beyond here, some of the island's best beaches can be found in Baie Rouge and Baie Longue at the western tip of the island. The road south out of Marigot leads past the obelisk, which marks the border, to the main airport.

North of Marigot is a more natural Saint-Martin, although the hills are dotted everywhere with modern villas. There is a lookout near the summit of the Pic du Paradis that gives marvellous views of the nearby islands.

Beyond the local settlement of Colombier and an excellent, often uncrowded beach at Friar's Bay, is the appealing town of **Grand-Case**, set along the sandy waterfront. Known as the gastronomic capital of the island, it has a row of excellent restaurants and bars set above the sea.

Past the airstrip to the east the countryside does become surprisingly sparse, although most bays are now developed with hotels. Of the east coast beaches, the best for windsurfing are Baie de l'Embouchure and **Baie de l'Orient**, partly a nudist beach.

Marigot harbour…

…and café society

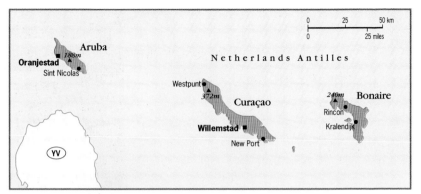

Aruba's white-sand beaches

Boca Tabla, on Curaçao's northern shore

THE NETHERLANDS ANTILLES The six Dutch islands of the Caribbean carry the imprint of their colonial history; on Curaçao, even canals and gabled warehouses can be seen. The dry island of Aruba has superb beaches and Bonaire has some of the region's best preserved reefs. Aruba, Bonaire, Curaçao and especially Sint Maarten all have developed tourist infrastructures, while the tiny outcrops of Saba and Sint Eustatius see far fewer visitors. The islands lie in two groups, separated by 800km of sea: the volcanic Dutch Windwards, Sint Maarten, Saba and Sint Eustatius, nicknamed Statia (the SSS islands), near the northern end of the Lesser Antilles; and the Dutch Leewards, Bonaire and Curaçao, off the coast of Venezuela. Aruba was politically part of this group until it separated from the Netherlands Antilles in 1986, but many still refer to these as the ABC islands. The two groups contain some of the more beautiful – as well as the most inhospitable – landscapes found in the West Indies islands.

A Dutch heritage spanning 350 years has formed much of the character of each island. The official currency is the Netherlands Antilles florin or guilder (Aruba has its own Aruban florin), island cuisine includes dishes such as *keshi yena* made with melted Gouda cheese, and souvenir shops are as likely to stock Delft blue chinaware as they are more

traditional Caribbean crafts. Red-bricked, pastel-painted and gabled houses recall the heyday of the Dutch Empire, contrasting with the modern buildings erected since the oil boom of the 20th century, all set incongruously among golden beaches and coconut palms. The ABC islands have their own language, Papiamento, a curious-sounding mix of Spanish and Dutch, seeded with Portuguese, English and African.

HISTORY The Dutch West India Company first spotted the strategic and economic significance of the Lesser Antilles in the 1620s; Sint Maarten was a neat stepping stone to Dutch colonies in Brazil; and Aruba, Bonaire and Curaçao (colonised on a small scale by the Spanish in 1511) provided salt for the profitable herring industry at home. As trade increased, Curaçao became a centre for the slave trade attracting the interest of rivals and during the 18th century the islands were seized by one European power after another. The other great Dutch success story was tiny Sint Eustatius, nicknamed the Golden Rock after the riches its traders piled high in their waterfront warehouses. Its rather bizarre downfall occurred when the island's governer saluted an American brig flying the Stars and Stripes as it sailed into the harbour on 16 November, 1776. This innocent gesture made Holland the first nation to recognise the newly constitued United States, provoking an outraged Britain to send a naval expedition to sack the island in 1781, a blow from which it never recovered.

In 1816 the Dutch regained their hold, but the era of booming trade was over and the islands fell into decline until the arrival of the oil companies in the early 20th century. Refineries were set up on Aruba and Curaçao, bringing in workers from neighbouring islands and new prosperity. In the 1980s the oil industry, faced with falling profits, reduced its Antilles operations and islanders have become increasingly reliant on the tourist trade.

The Netherlands Antilles

A yacht-borne picnic excursion passes Saba at sunset

▶▶▶ REGION HIGHLIGHTS

Bonaire Marine Park (scuba-diving)
page 130

Curaçao's Floating Market *page 133*

Curaçao Liqueur Distillery *page 135*

Eagle Beach and Palm Beach *page 129*

Koningin Emmabrug *page 134*

Sint Eustatius Historical Museum *page 139*

Windwardside *page 137*

126

PATH TO INDEPENDENCE?

The Dutch islands were in step with the rest of the Caribbean in their growing desire for political self-government in the early part of the 20th century. Labour union movements in the oilfields increased the political awareness of the islands and, in 1936, a *Staten*, or parliament, was formed. During World War II, while Holland was occupied by the Germans, the Dutch islands were left to fend for themselves and gained experience of self-government. There was not the headlong rush for independence after the war that was seen among the British islands, but autonomy was granted in 1954. Holland has stated that it will allow the islands to become fully independent when their economies are reliably stable, but many islanders prefer to remain within the Kingdom of the Netherlands for the foreseeable future.

Red roofs in The Bottom, the capital of Saba

Today the Netherlands Antilles are divided into three territories: Curaçao (the administrative capital), Bonaire and the three Windward islands, Sint Maarten, Sint Eustatius and Saba. Each has its own representative body (the Island Council), elected every four years, which chooses commissioners. Together they form the Executive Council for each island or island group. The Queen of the Netherlands appoints the Lieutenant-General and the island Governor, who serves a term of six years and appoints Antillian ministers. Aruba was deemed a state apart (*Status Aparte*) from the other administrations in 1986 and is now an autonomous part of the Netherlands, preparing for full independence in the near future.

"African" carvings at a craft stall in Aruba

The Netherlands Antilles

PAPIAMENTO

Some expressions in Papiamento (spoken in Aruba, Bonaire and Curaçao):

Welcome	Bon bini
Good morning	Bon dia
Good afternoon	Bon tardi
Good evening	Bon nochi
How are you?	Con ta bai?
Thank you	Masha danki
Goodbye	Ayo

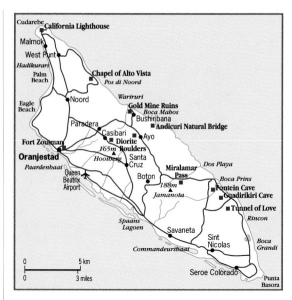

STATUS APARTE

Status Aparte was the eventual solution reached by the Arubians to give them autonomy from Curaçao, the capital island, and traditionally the centre of the Netherlands Antilles. Arubians felt it unjust that wealth generated by their own oil business should have to be channelled via Curaçao before being returned to them. It took over 50 years to change the island's status; the act had to be passed on Curaçao, where the Curaçaoans themselves had a majority of the seats, but Aruba eventually severed the link in 1986 and the island now has its own parliament, as well as its own currency and flag.

Oranjestad: a modern interpretation of traditional Dutch-Caribbean style and colours

Aruba

From the air, Aruba seems small and flat, with a ribbon of blinding white sand running down its western side. In fact, although the island is only 31km by 9km, its hills rise to over 150m and the combined stretch of Palm Beach and Eagle Beach is one of the Caribbean's finest strips of sand. The island's distinctive beauty lies in its countryside – an almost extraterrestrial landscape of arid rocky deserts, cactus jungles and secluded coves. With its low humidity and average temperature of 28°C, Aruba has the climate of paradise; any rain falls mostly during November.

The 78,000 Arubians have a wide range of origins, including Spanish, Portuguese, East Indian and the Caribbean, as well as Dutch.

The official language is Dutch, and English is widely spoken, but most Arubians speak Papiamento, a dialect drawing from Spanish, French, Portuguese, Dutch, African and English (see panel). Colonisation came relatively late to Aruba, which was virtually ignored by European powers until the

20th century and this has resulted in its people retaining a strong sense of independence.

The capital, **Oranjestad▶▶**, lies on the protected south-western shore of the island; the town and its outlying suburbs are the centre of Aruban life. Named after the Dutch royal house of Orange, this is Aruba's main port. Some of the older buildings around the main street, Nassaustraat, date from the oil boom early in the 20th century, but most are modern imitations with traditional flourishes, containing the banks and shopping complexes of the modern town. A line of fishing boats forms the quay-side Schooner Market, selling produce from Venezuela.

Fort Zoutman (1796) is the island's oldest building and contains the **Historical Museum▶** (tel: 826099. *Open* Mon–Fri 9–12, 1:30–4:30. *Admission: inexpensive*), tracing Aruba's history and the **Archeological Museum▶** (tel: 828979. *Open* Mon–Fri 8–12, 1–4:30. *Admission free*), depicting indigenous life. The **Numismatic Museum▶▶** (tel: 828813. *Open* Mon–Fri 7:30–noon, 1–4. *Admission free*), on Irausquin Plein, has a collection of 30,000 bills and coins.

To the west of Oranjestad, the coastal road runs past the cruise ship dock to Aruba's magnificent beaches: **Eagle Beach▶▶▶** ("low rise strip") and **Palm Beach▶▶▶** ("high rise strip"). There is no shortage of watersports or bars here – nor is there any lack of crowds, especially in June, when Aruba hosts a windsurfing festival.

East of the town, the road passes through suburbs into the scrub. Sprinkled among the new houses are traditional buildings, with talismanic symbols painted on the clay walls and roofs made of cactus wood and grass.

Aruba's highest hill is Jamanota (188m), but its most distinctive is the **Hooiberg▶**, standing over 165m high, with a stairway that will help to ease the climb. To its north are the huge, grey and rounded **diorite boulders▶▶** at Casibari and Ayo and on the north coast, east of Oranjestad, are the ruins of the Bushiribana gold mines, whose discovery in 1825 led to a brief gold rush. One particular smelting site at Balashi produced over a million kilogrammes of gold.

Also in this area are the ruins of a 16th-century fortress and at **Andicouri▶▶**, the sea has carved the spectacular Natural Bridge from the coral rock. San Nicolas is the island's second town and the site of the former oil refinery.

129

Aruba's Dutch legacy is still apparent…

…while tourism is taking over on its inviting beaches

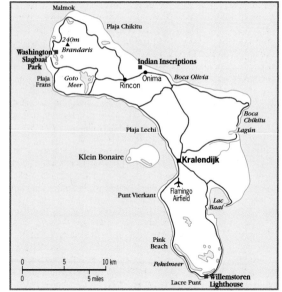

Above and far right: salt stacks awaiting shipping glare in the tropical sun of Bonaire

Bonaire

Bonaire is a stark desert island, perfect for the rugged individualist who is turned off by the commercialised high life of the other Antillean islands. A magnet for divers, the island has one of the most unspoiled reef systems in the world. The water is so clear that you can lean over the dock and look the fish straight in the eye. This is not the island for connoisseurs of fine cuisine, nor for shopping addicts, but what lies off its shores is guaranteed to keep divers enthralled. Most visitors to the island come for the amazing scuba-diving. The **Bonaire Marine Park▶ ▶ ▶** – a model of ecological conservation – almost surrounds Bonaire itself as well as Klein Bonaire from the high-water tidemark to a depth of nearly 60m. The corals and fish are some of the finest and least disturbed in the Caribbean and they make Bonaire well worth visiting for a relaxing holiday with a sporting focus.

Shaped somewhat like a foot, Bonaire is a crooked 38km long. In the bight of the protected coast is the football-shaped Klein Bonaire, about to be kicked towards Curaçao. Like its neighbours, Bonaire is dry and windswept, covered in scrubby vegetation and dotted with tall cacti. From the salt flats in the south, the land rises to the 240m Mount Brandaris in the northwest. Much of the coastline is limestone coral shelf, but there are breaks in the wall where the sand collects to form decent beaches. Two colonies of flamingos nest on the island and can be seen feeding in the lagoons during the day. A circuit of the island can be completed in a day; cars can be hired from hotels or car hire companies.

Industries on Bonaire include oil bunkering (storing oil fuel for ships), salt harvesting and radio transmitting stations, but tourism (mainly diving) is the most important economic sector and it has changed the island

THE SALT INDUSTRY
As you drive south on Bonaire you will come to the vast white stacks of Bonaire's salt, beneath which several cranes bustle about. Salt production has recently been revived for industrial purposes; sea water is let into shallow "pans" and the sun and the wind then do their work, evaporating the water. The resulting brine is channelled into other pans to increase the evaporation effect and eventually a bed of white crystals appears. These are harvested and cleaned before being stacked by a crane on rails in mounds ready for shipping.

radically in the last 15 years. From a lazy backwater (which the island had remained from the moment the Dutch arrived in 1636) it has suddenly geared up for large numbers of visitors, but a certain funky sleepiness has survived. Bonaireans speak Papiamento, although Dutch is the official language and English is widely understood.

The capital, **Kralendijk**►►, lies in the protected bight of the western shore, on the coral (*kralen*) wall (*dijk*). A few traditional Bonaire houses, painted gold with white stucco, stand among the mostly modern buildings; bars and restaurants line the waterfront and hotels are spread along the shores on either side of the town.

Fort Oranje, the town's old defence, now contains the island museum, displaying indigenous native American and colonial Bonairean artefacts. The whole town comes to life for the Lentern Carnival and for parades and festivals during late June.

Beyond the hotel strip, going north, the road passes the oil storage depot and continues to **Goto Meer**►, one of the flamingos' favoured nesting spots. The island's north-western tip is made up of the 5,458-ha **Washington Slagbaai Park**►►, where marked roads give views of Bonaire's semi-arid flora, as well as possible glimpses of iguanas and some of the estimated 130 species of birdlife (including pelicans, bananaquits and sandpipers). Visits can be made by car and by bicycle. Another road heads back to Kralendijk via Rincon, the island's second town and Indian inscriptions at **Onima**►.

A circular road runs around the southern toe of the island beyond the airport to **Pink Beach**►►, named for the striking colour of its sand and then to the vast white stacks of harvested salt at the **salt works**►► (see panel opposite). Another flamingo colony nests here. Coloured obelisks stand on the coast, built as shipping guides on an otherwise indistinguishable coastline. Two groups of small huts huddled on the shore were once two-man dormitories for slaves who worked the salt pans in 1850. Lac Baai has two good beaches; nudism is permitted on one.

NATURE AND WILDLIFE
The divi-divi tree, which grows in the Dutch Leewards, has a gnarled but vertical trunk about 50cm high, but the strong Caribbean wind forces its branches to grow at 90 degrees to the trunk. The ABC islands are mainly dry and covered with cactus and scrub. Birds include the orange and black troupial, Curaçao's national bird, and the oriole, which lays its eggs in a nest 1m high.

131

Kralendijk waterfront at dusk

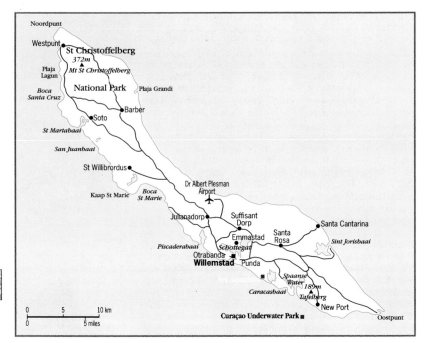

Curaçao

In Willemstad, Curaçao's capital, handsome rows of pastel-coloured townhouses look as though they were transplanted from Holland. The island's Dutch architecture makes a cheerful contrast to the cactus-dotted back country scrub known as the *Kunuku*. Curaçao's soft white sandy beaches are small, but watersports attract enthusiasts from all over the world and some of the best reef diving is here. The shopping is first-rate too, and the sun smiles down, but thanks to the gentle trade winds it never gets too hot. The largest of the Netherlands Antilles, the island lies between Aruba and Bonaire, 55km from the coast of Venezuela. Curaçao is a long and thin island, measuring 60km by 15km, created from lava emissions encrusted with coral limestone.

HISTORY Curaçao is the traditional heart of the Dutch Caribbean and has been the administrative capital since the Dutch arrived in 1634. Dubbed the "Land of Giants" by explorer Amerigo Vespucci, who felt dwarfed by the indigenous Caiquetios tribe, Curaçao was left alone by early colonisers, though many of its inhabitants were taken as slaves to the Hispaniola gold mines. By the early 17th century, there was a handful of Spanish settlers, but these were chased out by Dutch merchants. Slave-trading was the island's prime source of wealth and emancipation signalled its decline. In 1915 a new source of prosperity was introduced with the building of an oil refinery and the population soared as workers moved in. During the 1960s and 1980s the oil industry was dealt two blows: "automation", which reduced the number of employees,

DUTCH CUISINE

Food in the Dutch Leewards is very different from dishes elsewhere in the Caribbean. A number of restaurants specialise in local cuisine, made even more exotic by its Papiamento names. Dishes include *sopi* (soup) and *stoba* (stews), made with *galina* (chicken), *bestia* (lamb), *carco* (conch) and *kreeft* (lobster) or even *juwana* (iguana). Side dishes include *snijboonchi* (string-beans), *giambo* (cactus fruit), *funchi* (maize meal) or *toetoe* (cornmeal mixed with beans and bacon, topped with Edam cheese). *Keshi yena* is spicy chicken, covered with Dutch cheese.

and the effects of rising prices. Eventually the business was wound down and there are now plans to expand the tourist industry. Curaçao's hotels are concentrated on the larger beaches to either side of Willemstad, but within easy reach of the capital's shops and restaurants. The island has some excellent restaurants and it is well worth experimenting with local cuisine. Venture off the beaten track and seek out some of the picturesque and secluded craggy coves carved into the rugged north coast.

ISLAND LIFE Curaçao is the most populous of the Netherlands Antilles and its life as a trading port has given it an extremely varied mix of people. Though Dutch is the official language, Curaçaoans generally speak Papiamento as a first tongue; most also speak English and Spanish. Of all the Dutch Caribbean islands, Curaçao shows the strongest Dutch influence, in its buildings, its food and its faces.

The Penha building: Dutch-influenced architecture on the Handelskade waterfront

WILLEMSTAD Lying on the protected southern shore, Willemstad has developed around the Schottegat, a huge natural harbour, which attracted the first Dutch colonisers. The oldest part of the town is **Punda▶** ("the Point"), of which the main quay, the **Handelskade▶▶**, is one of the most striking sights in the Caribbean; its buildings (such as the 1708 Penha House) combine the curly gables of Amsterdam with the bright colours of the West Indies. Like the streets behind it, the Handelskade still works as a trading area, now serving cruise-ship passengers attracted by duty-free shopping. At right angles to it is the **Floating Market▶▶▶**, a line of wooden boats docked at the quayside, where you can buy fresh fruit and vegetables shipped in from Venezuela and displayed on slab tables shaded by awnings attached to the masts.

133

The **Mikve Israel Synagogue▶▶** (tel: 461 1633), which is situated on Columbusstraat, dates from 1732; the Jewish Historical Museum, in its courtyard, displays among other artefacts a 250-year-old ceremonial bath and other ritual and Torah objects are still in use today. **Fort Amsterdam▶**, the town's original defence, was built in 1634. It is now the residence of the Governor of the Netherlands Antilles and the seat of their Parliament.

Willemstad's main quay, Handelskade

134

A museum in the **Fort Church▶** (tel: 461 1139. *Open Mon–Fri 9–12, 2–5. Admission: inexpensive*) displays maps and religious artefacts dating back to 1635. Four other 17th-century forts surround the port, two of which are now restaurants. There is a good "Restaurant Row" under the arches of the Waterfort, and the Old Mamet, near Koningin Wilhelminabrug, is an excellent stop for lunch; customers sit at long tables, watching the cooks serve up such popular Curaçao dishes as *stoba* (stew) and *toetoe* (see

Above and above right: shading under the sails at the floating market at Willemstad

panel on page 132). The **Numismatic Museum▶▶**, Breedestraat 1 (tel: 461 3600. *Open Mon–Fri 8:30–11:30, 1:30–4:30. Admission free*) displays early banknotes and coins from Dutch Antillean history and precious stones.

Otrabanda, on the other side of the main harbour channel, is reached by the **Koningin Emmabrug▶▶▶**, a pedestrian pontoon bridge formed by about 15 barges that move constantly on the waves. Occasionally the bridge opens to let ocean-going vessels through; small passenger ferries operate at these times. In Otrabanda there are more excellent examples of the distinctive Dutch Créole architecture: colonial houses, with their orange tiles and curly gables, many painted with Curaçao gold. **The Curaçao Museum▶▶** (tel: 462 3873. *Open Mon–Fri 9–12, 2–5, Sun 10–4. Admission: inexpensive*), in an old townhouse once used as the naval hospital, exhibits among other interesting items part of the first airplane to fly here from the Netherlands. The Beth Haim Cemetery has some of the oldest European tombs in the Americas.

OUTSIDE WILLEMSTAD The suburbs of Willemstad creep around the Schottegat harbour. The autonomy monument, on the eastern side, is a 1954 sculpture of six birds, commemorating the year when the six Netherlands Antilles were granted self-rule. Further along is the **Curaçao Liqueur Distillery►►** (tel: 461 3526. *Open* Mon–Fri 8–12, 1–5. *Admission free*), in the Landhuis Chobolobo, where Curaçao liqueur is produced from the peel of small, green oranges. Nearby, the Amstel Brewery can be visited on Tuesdays and Thursdays. The oil refinery on the northwest shore was once the largest in the world, best viewed from the hills around Fort Nassau, behind Punda. Near the sports stadium is the restored 18th-century **Landhuis Brievengat►►** (tel: 737 8344. *Open* Mon–Fri 9:15–12:15, 3–6. *Admission: inexpensive*), a cochineal plantation house. Close to the airport are the **Hato Caves►**, with Indian petroglyph drawings, as well as stalactites and stalagmites.

East of Willemstad is the **Curaçao Sea Aquarium►►** (tel: 461 6666. *Open* daily 8:30–6. *Admission: expensive*), with re-created reefs and tropical fish. Glass-bottom boat trips and scuba-diving are available in the nearby Curaçao Underwater Park, a restricted marine area, where divers can swim with rays and feed sharks through a mesh.

Westward is the bush countryside, where isolated plantation houses (*landhuisen*) stand among scrub and cacti. Near the island's western tip is **Christoffel National Park►►** (tel: 864 0363. *Open* Mon–Sat 8–5, Sun 6–3. *Admission: expensive*), on the slopes of the Christoffelberg (372m), with marked driving and walking trails and a natural history museum. Curaçao's best beaches are towards the western end, on the south shore.

135

SIMON BOLIVAR
Simon Bolivar (El Libertador) was forced to spend a period of exile on Curaçao after a failed South American uprising in 1811. His revolutionary campaigns in the northern part of South America eventually helped liberate the countries that became Venezuela, Bolivia, Peru, Ecuador and Panama from Spanish rule during the early 19th century.

Fishing in Spaanse Water, eastern Curaçao

FLAT POINT AND THE ROAD

Flat Point is, in fact, on a gentle slope, but it is the only area of Saba large enough to have an airstrip (396m long). The Road is a feat of engineering that it was said would be impossible to build. Between Windwardside and The Bottom there is a plaque to Joseph Lambertus Hassell, who followed a correspondence course in engineering and then designed and built The Road, starting at Fort Bay and heading up to The Bottom, on to Windwardside and eventually via 19 hairpin bends down to Flat Point. The Road is still in good condition, after nearly 50 years.

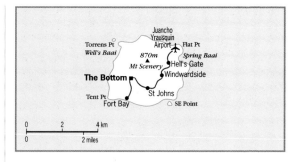

Saba

Not long ago, Saba almost passed a law decreeing that all the roofs on the island be painted red. Draconian, perhaps – but red roofs have long been a tradition on Saba. They go well with the white cottage walls, the picket fences and the striking greens of this fertile island.

Another draconian aspect of Saba is its geography. It is small, extremely rugged and difficult to reach. Mount Scenery, the waterborne peak of an extinct volcano, soars to 870m, on an island only 5km by 4km. The 1,500 hardy Sabians have their island neatly tamed; they must, in order to survive here.

Dutch colonists from Sint Eustatius were the first Europeans to settle on the island, in 1640. Twenty-five years later, Saba was taken by a British privateer and all non-English speakers were shipped away. In the 19th century the island was returned to Dutch possession and Saba survived on the money sent home by its menfolk, who earned a reputation as skilled sailors, and on the lace-making and threadwork of the women. The oil boom on Aruba and Curaçao provided work for islanders in the 20th century, but after its collapse the island turned to its small tourist industry. There are a few places to stay, which are more like friendly mountain guesthouses than Caribbean beach hotels. Saba has no natural beaches, but then visitors to the island mainly come for the excellent scuba-diving.

The island's four settlements are all linked by a sinuous artery, respectfully known as The Road (see panel). Its capital is a village by the name of **The Bottom▶ ▶**, thought to derive from the Dutch *Botte* (bowl), though ironically it's situated 250m above sea level. Most of the houses do, indeed, lie at the bottom of a bowl, but new buildings are steadily creeping up the towering, forested peaks that surround it. The Governor's Residence, in the village, is an attractive balconied Caribbean house. A number of bars are run from timber-frame houses, such as Cranston's Antique Inn, where you can join the Sabans for an afternoon drink.

One of Saba's pretty white cottages

On the sheltered coast beneath The Bottom are Saba's two harbours: Ladder Bay and Fort Bay. The first is reached by steps; in the days before The Road, Sabans had to carry all their supplies up here on their shoulders. Fort Bay has been the principal port here since 1972, when the jetties were built. It is also the departure point for scuba-diving operations. From here there is nowhere to go but back up to the village, from which The Road leads to St John's, a small collection of houses built on an expanse of relatively flat ground.

Magnificent views of the coast open out 365m below as The Road reaches **Windwardside▶▶**, Saba's other principal village. The tourist office can be found here, as well as banks and hotels. Windwardside is even neater and prettier than The Bottom, its white houses set behind stone walls, with gardens of bougainvillea and hibiscus. The **Saba Museum▶** (*Open* Mon–Fri 10–12, 1–4. *Admission: inexpensive*), set in a private home, shows Amerindian artefacts and 19th-century exhibits. Older village women still knit the renowned Saba lace, which can be bought at the Island Craft Shop, and brew "Saba Spice", a potent concoction of rum and various herbs and spices.

Beyond Windwardside is the village of Hell's Gate, and from here The Road descends tortuously to the optimistically named Flat Point, site of the island's airstrip (see panel opposite).

Like many of the old trails used by the islanders before The Road was constructed, the steep path to the top of Mount Scenery has carefully laid steps (they start just outside Windwardside) leading through the rain forest and elfin forest; on a clear day the views from this laborious climb are superb.

Houses stacked top-to-toe in Windwardside village

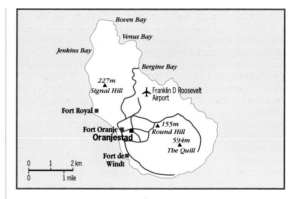

**SINT EUSTATIUS
MUSEUM**
For further details on the
the Sint Eustatius
Historical Foundation
Museum, tel: 318 2288.
Open Mon–Fri 9–5,
Sat–Sun 9–noon.
Admission: inexpensive.

Sint Eustatius

Two hundred years ago, Sint Eustatius was one of the richest and most important islands in the West Indies. As many as a hundred ships would put in to this busy trading port at a time. But the stretch of warehouses that once ran along the Lower Town's shore has gone and only a few walls remain from the island's era as the "Golden Rock".

Almost all of the 18th-century's booming business was breaking the trade laws, as goods which should have been sold to the colonies' governing countries were smuggled to Statia (as the island is usually known) for quick and direct payment. A brisk arms trade developed during the Revolutionary War and as colonial powers battled over their possessions, the island changed hands over 20 times.

*A Statian resident
contemplates island
philosophy*

Statia's golden age came to an end after the British, led by Admiral Rodney, captured the island and sold off all its goods (see panel opposite).

Today Statia is a quiet backwater with only 2,800 inhabitants, mainly of African descent and English-speaking, although the official language is Dutch. The island is undeveloped – there are only a few hotel rooms and no white sand Caribbean strands – though with the help of the EC, Statia has renovated its historical buildings. Lying 48km south of Sint Maarten (the main access to Statia), between the volcanic peaks of Saba and St Kitts, the island is just 31sq km in size. In the south rises a perfectly formed extinct volcanic cone called the Quill; the volcanic sand makes all Statia's beaches dark.

The capital and only town, Oranjestad, sits on a cliff 160m above the island's sheltered Caribbean coast. Its **Upper Town▶ ▶** has cobbled streets and a few old stone houses with wooden wraparound balconies among the newer buildings and from its clifftop courtyard of cobbles, date palms and cannon, **Fort Oranje▶** enjoys a superb view of the bay. The **Sint Eustatius Historical Foundation Museum▶ ▶** is set in de Graaff House, named after the Governor who was responsible for the First Salute (see page 125). There are rooms devoted to Arawak and Carib culture, the colonial years and more recent island history. Some of the Upper Town's historical buildings are no more than shells, but it is worth climbing the tower of the Dutch Reform Church for its fine view. The ruined Honen Dalim synagogue, on Synagoogpad, is one of the oldest in the western hemisphere.

Lower Town▶ ▶ is where the trading warehouses once stood; as trade expanded, a dyke was built to reclaim more land from the sea. An ancient stone walkway descends from Fort Oranje to the small line of restored buildings recreated with the original bricks. Statia has a growing reputation for scuba-diving and boats depart from here, heading out to the reefs offshore. Occasionally divers find blue beads, which were used as a currency on the island two centuries ago.

Beyond the town, Statia's countryside is relatively open, although modern homes are steadily filling the available space. An older Statia is still just visible in the fences of spiky agave and cactus plants and the inevitable goats. It is an easy walk to the lip of **the Quill's crater▶ ▶**, where lush rain forest grows down in the bowl (it can be a very slippery climb). In the south of the island there is a good view of St Kitts from the tiny Fort de Windt; in the north, an area of uninhabited hills is the site of Statia's only major industry, an oil bunkerage and a refinery that produces 250 barrels a day.

139

ADMIRAL RODNEY'S REVENGE
A few years after the First Salute the British had their revenge when Admiral Rodney captured the harbour and kept the flags flying as though the island were open for trade, impounding 150 ships that unwittingly came into harbour. Rodney carried off the merchandise and destroyed the retaining walls. His suspicions were aroused by a sudden rise in the number of deaths on the island: Rodney had several coffins dug up, to find that merchants were hiding their gold in them.

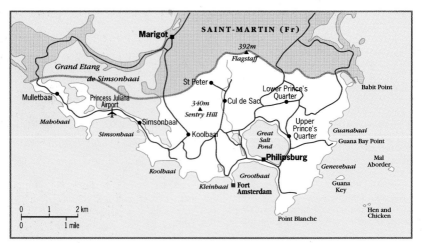

SHOPPING SPREES
Amid the vast cruise
ships that dock at Sint
Maarten's capital are
smaller, wooden craft,
whose captains also
come to enjoy some of
the Caribbean's best
shopping. Sint Maarten is
where many West Indians
go at Christmas, for wine,
electrical goods, tobacco
and alcohol. Local yachts
make the run from as far
down as the Grenadines,
where many were built.

Philipsburg's beach

Sint Maarten

Seen from a distance, Sint Maarten (or Saint-Martin)
appears serene, rising from the sea in graceful curves to
form steep mountain peaks. But this peaceful air belies
the hectic activity of Sint Maarten, one of the busiest and
most developed territories in the Caribbean.

Despite being just 96sq km in area, the island is divided
between two countries (the smallest island in the world to
fly two flags). Since it was first settled in 1648, it has been
shared between the Dutch and the French (see pages
122–123 for the French territory, Saint-Martin) and give or
take the odd invasion, relations have been pretty amica-
ble. There is even a peak called Mount Concordia as a
tribute to their goodwill. The island stands on the same
landmass as Anguilla and St Barts, an ancient volcanic
bank, inactive and coral-encrusted and has superb white
sand beaches. Dutch Sint Maarten occupies 41sq km in the
southern part of the island.

Given its size, Sint Maarten's tourist industry is huge
and this has changed the island dramatically over the last
20 years. There has been extensive building and rebuild-
ing after Hurricane Luis in 1995 and the population has
boomed. Though Dutch is the official language, a whole
range of spoken languages can be heard here, from
Haitian Kreyol and Papiamento to English.

The island is crammed to the hilt
with hotels, restaurants, bars, clubs,
casinos and heavy traffic, fre-
quently jammed up. The airport at
Juliana is a hive of activity, with
flights arriving from the main
Caribbean islands as well as from
European and US cities. Sint
Maarten is also popular as a cruise
ship stopover and its status as a
duty-free port brings in streams of
high-spending tourists, as well as
neighbouring islanders keen to take
advantage of the bargain prices.

One of the most attractive features of Caribbean architecture is "gingerbread" design, which embellishes houses with an elaborate latticework of wood carved into squiggles, sweeps and twirls. The term is supposedly derived from 16th-century German pastry-makers, who were known for their ornately decorated gingerbread creations.

The flamboyance of gingerbread appealed to plantation owners and estate managers, who had grand houses built to show off their wealth, with elaborate verandas overlooking their estates. Public buildings were also given the gingerbread treatment, the most fanciful of which are in Haiti. Saba, one of the Dutch Windward Islands, has several well-maintained gingerbread houses with green or red window frames, surrounded by pretty tropical blooms, concentrated in a small area (Windwardside and The Bottom). Gingerbread's popularity spread and the style was taken up in the USA during the prosperous 1860s and 1870s, after the Civil War. Good examples can be seen in the beach resort of Cape May, New Jersey.

Traditionally, Caribbean houses were constructed in wood, as there was no need for the warmth provided by stone and brick. Wood was cheaper and buildings could even be dismantled and taken away (in Barbados, farmers' homes were known as "chattel" houses because they could be moved with other goods and chattels). These houses, their walls made from strips of clapboard and their roofs tiled with wooden shingles, are steadily disappearing as the islands develop, but you will see examples of them if you drive through the countryside.

Curaçao, Bonaire and Aruba's houses are made with brick and plaster – wood was scarce and at risk from fire, so its use in building was banned. The walls are painted in gold, light brown, purple and deep green and the effect is completed with orange "dakpannen", clay roof tiles and white borders. The story goes that Admiral Kikkert, a Governor of Curaçao, suffered from headaches brought on by the reflection of the sun bouncing off Willemstad's whitewashed buildings, so he ordered that they be painted any colour other than white.

Old San Juan's city hall, Puerto Rico

COUNTRY SHACKS
Traditional Caribbean country shacks were made with "wattle and daub", a latticework of springy twigs covered in mud and dried in the sun. The roof was topped with thatch, providing a cool indoor environment. More recently, concrete has become popular as a hurricane-resistant building material.

A restored colonial house in French Saint-Martin

A West Indian market in the mural – tourists shopping in real life at Philipsburg

PETER STUYVESANT
Peter Stuyvesant was an early Governor of Curaçao (in 1638) and later of all the Dutch possessions in the Americas, which he governed from Nieuw Amsterdam (New York). An autocratic leader, he lost his right leg in a fight for Sint Maarten in 1644 and wore a silver ornamented false leg as a replacement. Stuyvesant was forced to surrender the North American possessions to the British in 1664, but later returned to live in the Great Bouwery in Manhattan until his death in 1672.

The capital and main town on the Dutch side of Sint Maarten is **Philipsburg▶**, set on a narrow spit of land between Great Bay and the Great Salt Pond (the source of the salt which originally attracted the Dutch West India Company to the island). It has just four streets and a sprinkling of traditional houses among an otherwise modern town that has sprouted since the tourist boom. The town faces south, towards Saba and Sint Eustatius, the other two Dutch Windward Islands.

Visitors who stream off the cruise ships arrive at de Ruyterplein, a small square which is the setting for the pretty Old Courthouse Building and a tourist information office. Leading through it is Front Street, Philipsburg's mile-long shopping arcade, where the best of the duty-free bargains can be found – cameras and electronic goods, jewellery, crystal and porcelain – as well as plenty of cafés and bars. In an arcade at the head of Front Street, the **Sint Maarten Museum▶** (tel: 542 4917. *Open* Mon–Fri 10–4, Sat 10–2. *Admission: inexpensive*) has exhibits of pre-Columbian and colonial island life. Its displays highlight the contrasting lifestyles with items such as Native American pottery and Delft dinner services.

Philipsburg's outlying areas completely encircle the lagoon and determined shoppers will find yet more arcades around its shores, but generally this is where the islanders themselves live. The **Sint Maarten Zoo▶** (tel: 543 2020. *Open* Mon–Fri 9–5, Sat–Sun 10–6. *Admission: inexpensive*) on the Madame Estate keeps animals from both South America and the Caribbean area. Further afield, Sint Maarten's eastern side is relatively untouched and secluded.

The main route out of Philipsburg is often clogged with traffic; in Koolbaai (Cole Bay), a left turn leads alongside the Simpson Bay Lagoon to the busiest tourist area. Simsonbaai (Simpson Bay) itself has a good beach and beyond the airport are Mandsaoi (Mano Bay) and Mulletbaai (Mullet Bay), with watersports, shops and a golf course. The road to Marigot crosses the border, which is marked only with an obelisk and a sign saying *Bienvenue à la Partie Française*.

Almost every brochure for a Caribbean holiday includes a picture of a waiter with a tray of sweet and exotic tropical fruit. Not all will be in season at any one time, but a visit to the market is always worthwhile for the displays of this fertile region's appetising produce.

The pineapple, used by Native Americans for food and wine-making, grows on a stem in the centre of a low bush of about 30 stiff, spiky, cactus-like leaves and takes about 15 months to mature. Black pineapples are slightly smaller and sweeter.

Pawpaw, or papaya, grows on a tall and slender tree of very light wood. The fruit, which matures to yellow and orange, can grow to 0.5m in length. Papaya is said to be good for high blood pressure and the seeds are used as a remedy for constipation.

The fruit of the soursop, which is not sour at all, is irregularly shaped, sometimes oval, with small, black hooks protruding from its aromatic, light green skin. Inside, black seeds sit in a white, pulpy flesh that tastes like a combination of mango and pineapple. Its seeds make it difficult to eat fresh – so it is probably best tasted in ice-cream.

Related to the soursop, the sweetsop looks like a fleshy green pine cone. It is known locally as the sugar apple or custard apple; its seeds are contained in a sweet, creamy pulp, rather like custard.

Guava fruit is really an outsize berry, which turns from green to yellow when ripening. Inside, its seeds sit in a

white or pink pulp. Guava has a bittersweet taste and provides five times as much Vitamin C as orange juice.

Mango trees, although not native to the Caribbean, grow throughout the region; their yellow and red fruits have some of the sweetest-tasting flesh of all. Other exotic fruits include the Otaheite apple, shaped like a pear with a red skin and a crisp white pulp, or the carambola, yellow-skinned with crunchy white flesh, which is shaped like a five-pointed star when cut cross-section.

TENDER FRUIT
Papain, from the papaya, is used as a meat tenderiser; West Indians simply wrap their meat in pawpaw leaf and leave it to stand. Pineapple is also a meat tenderiser, with pretty powerful effects: stranded soldiers on a South Sea island during World War II found that their teeth fell out if they ate too much of the fruit.

Young breadfruit, usually eaten baked or roasted

HYBRID FRUIT
Jamaica has created two hybrids of other citruses. The ortanique is part orange, part tangerine; the size of the former but with a skin that peels like the latter. The lumpy ugli fruit is a cross between a grapefruit, an orange and a tangerine.

Great Courland Bay, one of a number of deep, palm-fringed coves cut into Tobago's northern shore

OTHER CARIBBEAN STATES The larger, independent nation states of the Caribbean, separated by physical and cultural obstacles (and often suspicious of each other, if not openly hostile), are marked by their diversity. Jamaica's lushness and extensive rain forests are a reminder of what Haiti, 160km east, must have been before generations of impoverished peasants cleared the hillsides in search of charcoal. Jamaica has all the attributes of the travel agency clichés – beaches, rivers, mountains – but it also has social and economic problems, as any visitor to downtown Kingston will see. Cuba is cracking and crumbling behind its wall of isolation. The colonial splendour of old Havana is gradually collapsing

from neglect; yet this was once the most inviting tropical resort in the world. Haiti and the Dominican Republic share an island, but their border is more often closed than open. For all the Dominican Republic's colonial treasures and natural beauty, thousands of poor islanders risk their lives each year to cross the Mona Passage to Puerto Rico, where rural and US-influenced lifestyles exist side by side. The oil-producing nation of Trinidad and Tobago, famous for its Carnival and calypso, faces an uncertain future after years of wealth; while Barbados is perhaps the most developed of all the islands. No two islands are similar. If you want to know more than a little piece of the Caribbean, explore some of these fascinating states.

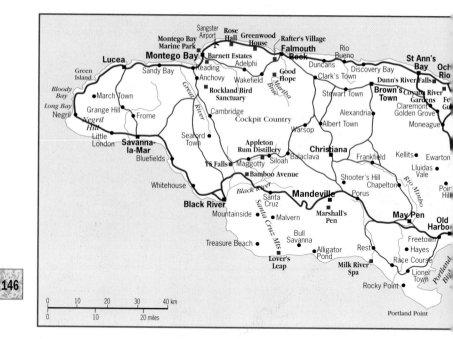

▶▶▶ REGION HIGHLIGHTS

The Blue Mountains
pages 148–149

Caribbean West Coast, Barbados *page 218*

Colonial Santo Domingo *page 192*

El Yunque Rain Forest *page 211*

Negril *page 157*

Old Havana, Cuba *page 170*

Old San Juan *pages 204–205*

Samaná peninsula *page 190*

Trinidad Carnival *page 227*

Trinidad, Cuba *pages 174–175*

Jamaica

The third-largest island in the Caribbean (after Cuba and Hispaniola), the English-speaking nation of Jamaica enjoys a self-sufficiency based on tourism, agriculture and mining. Its attractions include jungle mountaintops, clear waterfalls and unforgettable beaches, yet the country's greatest resource may very well be the Jamaicans themselves. Although 95 per cent of the population trace their bloodlines to Africa, their national origins lie elsewhere: in Europe, the Middle East, India, China, South America and many of the other islands in the Caribbean. The music, art and cuisine of Jamaica are vibrant, with a spirit easy to sense but as hard to describe as the rhythms of reggae or a flourish of streetwise patois.

HISTORY Jamaica was born of strife, as a colonial outpost, first of 16th-century Spanish settlers (who destroyed the Arawak inhabitants) and then of the British, who cut their plantations in the hills. Pirates brawled on the coastline, and the flourishing plantations, worked by slaves, were attacked by runaway maroons (see panel). Uprisings

Jahbah's health food centre in Negril

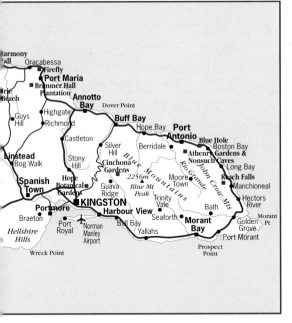

MAROONS

The maroons were a community of runaways who lived high in the inaccessible Jamaican interior, in the John Crow Mountains in the northeast and the Cockpit Country in the northwest. Their name comes from the Spanish word *cimarrón* ("wild"); the earliest maroons were slaves left behind by the Spaniards when they fled from the British in 1655. Maroons were highly successful guerillas and were never conquered; eventually the colonial authorities were reduced to negotiating with them, agreeing to guarantee their freedom and a considerable measure of self-government (which they still have today), in return for certain conditions, which included returning runaway slaves.

among the slaves led to several serious rebellions and terrible bloodshed, and even after emancipation in the 19th century the cycle of hardship and violence continued. A number of demonstrations marked the run-up to full enfranchisement in 1944, and preceded complete independence from the UK in 1962.

Over the past 40 years the island has built one of the biggest tourist industries in the Caribbean, providing easy access from Europe and the US and a full range of accommodation: beachfront luxury, all-inclusives (offering entertainment and accommodation), guesthouses on the cliffs in Negril, villas and mountain retreats. The resort towns of Montego Bay, Ocho Rios and Negril have good restaurants and lively bars and nightclubs.

ISLAND LIFE Jamaica is a cultural leader in the Caribbean; its boisterous culture of reggae and rastafari is known throughout the world and attracts visitors who are looking for a little more than the traditional Caribbean image of sun, sea and sand. Economically, though, the 2.6 million islanders have not had an easy ride recently; rising prices for imports and a fall in earnings from the main export, bauxite, led to austerity measures in the 1980s and there is still considerable unemployment and inflation. From time to time there are outbursts – troubles tend to come to a head, particularly in Kingston, during the fiercely contested elections, when traditional political rivalries are at their height.

There is no reason why this should affect visitors to the island, most of whom will be on the north coast anyway. Besides, the majority of Jamaicans are welcoming and friendly. Jamaica remains primarily a place of peace and beauty, with all the character and vibrancy that has come to characterise the Caribbean.

JAMAICAN JERK

Jerking is a special way of cooking meat that was started by the maroons in their hideaways. Originally it was wild hog, shot in the hills, that was cooked slowly in a barbecue sunk into the ground, but now you can buy jerked chicken, sausages and fish. These days there are "Jerk Centres" all over the island, but the traditional home of jerk pork, a very hot and spicy dish, is Boston Bay, near Port Antonio, where you can choose your meal, as it is cooked at a number of roadside shacks.

A safari cruise on the Black River into the mangroves of the Great Morass

SWIMS
On the road between Black River and Bamboo Avenue you will see vendors holding plastic bags of pink "swims" – local shrimps cooked in pepper sauce. Swims are tasty, but the pepper sauce, made from Scotch bonnet peppers, is very hot. The peppers get their name from their shape, said to look like a Scottish high-lander's headdress.

COFFEE FACTORIES
Blue Mountain coffee is renowned as some of the best in the world. At the Mavis Bank and Silver Hill coffee factories, berries are pulped and fermented to reveal the beans, which are then dried and husked before being bagged for export (much of the crop goes to Japan). Take a formal tour at Mavis Bank, or an informal one elsewhere.

▶▶ Black River

Southwest Jamaica, around Black River, is a little-known corner of the island, where a quiet, rural lifestyle still exists, relatively untouched by the development and tourism of the north coast. The fishing town of **Black River**▶ is somewhat run down, although there is still some charm in its old wooden buildings, set up when log-wood exports (the source of indigo before synthetic dyes were developed) brought prosperity a century ago. On the **Black River Safari**▶▶ (tel: 965 2513), you can cruise along the river itself into Jamaica's largest swamp, where mangroves form a tunnel around you and you may glimpse herons, egrets and even crocodiles.

There are a few isolated, usually deserted bays scattered along this coastline. From Crane Beach, just outside the town, the scrubby savannah land extends to the south-east, where lone cows graze attended by white cattle egrets. It eventually reaches **Treasure Beach**▶▶, a lost and lazy settlement set on a superb strip of sand. There is a wonderfully relaxed atmosphere, providing a perfect antidote to the more commercial resorts in the north. Another good beach can be found at Bluefields, to the northwest of Black River.

Inland, north of Black River, the main road skirts the swamp and then leads to **Bamboo Avenue**▶▶, a fine sight that is worth a quick detour. For just over 5km the huge bamboo plants form an arch over the road, hanging in graceful bushy curves. Just north of here are the **YS Falls**▶▶, a series of waterfalls and ponds where you can swim. These can sometimes be crowded with tourists, but the falls themselves are stunning.

▶▶▶ Blue Mountains

The heavily forested **Blue Mountains** tower above Kingston, but the pace of life in the small mountain communities there is much slower than the capital. Granted the status of a National Park, these mountains are the second tallest in the Caribbean after the Dominican Republic's Cordillera Central and, in the distance, they do appear a hazy shade of blue. You can walk the Blue Mountains, including the 2,255m Blue Mountain peak, with guides arranged at the less formal **Maya Lodge**▶▶, close by (tel: 927 2097). Another great place to head for is higher up: Strawberry Hill, in Irish Town, is an elegant hotel with traditional architecture (tel: 944 8400). You reach it from Papine; at this point the road passes into gorges and steep-sided valleys where fruit and vegetables are grown.

At Castleton, on the road to Annotto Bay on the north coast, botanical gardens dating from 1862 are laid out beside a river; here, guides will show you exotic flora, birds, butterflies and the ingenious trapdoor spider. There are gardens at Cinchona (reached from Clydesdale), where quinine was once extracted from cinchona trees; other places worth visiting include the World's End Rum Distillery at Guava Ridge and the coffee factories at Mavis Bank, nearby and at Silver Hill (see panel opposite). The Pine Grove Hotel is a good stop for refreshment.

▶ Cockpit Country

Cockpit Country lies in the northwest of Jamaica, to the south of Falmouth. This has always been one of the most inaccessible and remote areas of the island and for years it provided a hideout for the guerilla-style runaway maroons. Its romance lies in its appearance – shaggy, pointed mountains of karst limestone – and in its names. During the maroons era, it was known as the Land of Look Behind and had districts such as "Quick Step" and "Me No Sen, You No Come", which were so dangerous that British soldiers would ride back to back on their horses until a peace treaty was signed in 1739. Even today Cockpit Country is rarely visited and the few roads are rough and little used.

In the cane fields among Maggotty, the **Appleton Rum Estate**▶▶ (tel: 963 9215. *Open* for tours Tue, Thu–Sat 9–3:30. *Admission: expensive*) is a working sugar cane factory and rum distillery that is well worth a visit during the cane-cutting season from January to July. Tours show the newly cut cane being rolled through crushers to release the juice, which is boiled at high temperatures before being crystallised into sugar using massive centrifuges. There is a restaurant and bar at the distillery.

MANATEES
The endangered manatee is a large marine mammal that occasionally appears on the shores around Milk River and in the river estuary. Also known as the sea cow, it can grow to 4m in length and can weigh up to 140kg. With its small, rounded tail, front flippers and tiny, underdeveloped eyes, the manatee is believed to have been the source of many sailors' tales of mermaids on distant rocks.

149

TREE OF LIFE
The national flower of Jamaica is the delicate, light blue bloom of the *Lignum vitae* tree. Its name means "wood of life", and it is valued for many things. The wood, which is extremely hard, can be used to make axle shafts, bowling balls and even to replace metal ball-bearings and the resin is used in the treatment of breathing disorders.

A dance troupe in traditional costume in Kingston

►► Kingston

Kingston, the capital of Jamaica, sits on the southern shore of the island, between a huge natural harbour and the Blue Mountains. It is a far cry from the north coast resort towns; Kingston is very much a Jamaican city, whose character is unaffected, in the main, by tourism. Downtown it is a mêlée of traffic, people and streetside trade: noisy buses, neatly dressed schoolchildren, stray goats and vendors touting their wares. There are not many formal "sights" here, nor much left of architectural interest, but with a population of well over half a million, Kingston is a good place to catch some genuine Jamaican life. Unfortunately, this includes a criminal element, as in most busy cities, so be careful when walking around. Avoid garrison towns and ghetto areas like Trenchtown.

The heart of downtown Kingston pulses around the **Parade►►**, a bus terminal and market area, where vendors sell every conceivable consumer item from the sidewalks and "busmen" – the good-humoured bus ticket collectors – do their utmost to persuade passengers onto their buses, watched over by the stately Ward Theatre and Kingston Parish Church. The **National Gallery of Art►►** (tel: 922 1561. *Open* Mon–Thu 11–4:30, Fri 11–4. *Admission: inexpensive*) offers a formal view of the island's art and then you might visit the Statuary in **National Heroes Park►►** (see panel).

Most visitors to the capital stay uptown in New Kingston, a business and residential area with a more relaxed tempo and good restaurants and bars. **Devon House►►►** (tel: 929 7029. *Open* Tue–Sat 9–5. *Admission: inexpensive*) is a historic oasis in the modern town and it is worth spending time in its atmospheric grounds. The main house was constructed in 1881 in neoclassical style adapted to the tropics and is open to visitors. Its courtyards contain shops and restaurants . Further along Hope Road, you pass Kings House, the Governor General's residence and the **Bob Marley Museum►►** (tel: 927 9152. *Open* Mon–Sat. *Admission: moderate)* in the Tuff Gong Studio that was also the reggae legend's home from 1975 until his death in 1981. The **Hope Botanical Gardens►►** (tel: 927 1257. *Open* daily 8:30–6:30. *Admission free*) has an orchid house and a small zoo (*Admission: inexpensive*).

THE NATIONAL HEROES
The Jamaican national heroes, whose statues stand in Heroes Park, are Paul Bogle, a preacher, and George William Gordon, who were both blamed and executed for a rebellion in Morant Bay in 1865; Marcus Garvey, the activist and founder of the Universal Negro Improvement Association, which was so influential among black people in the early part of this century; and Independence leaders Alexander Bustamante and Norman Manley. Nanny, a female maroon leader, has also joined the ranks of the national heroes.

SPANISH TOWN
Kingston did not become Jamaica's capital until 1872. Before that the capital was Spanish Town, where you can still see the grand old Georgian colonial administrative buildings and courthouse in the main square. In the cathedral there are tablets in the floors and walls dating back to the late 17th century. It is worth the half-day's trip from Kingston by bus or taxi to see these reminders of the past.

Devon House, New Kingston, built by George Stiebel, Jamaica's first black millionaire

Rich and debauched Port Royal earned the names "Gilded Hades" and "the wickedest city in Christendom" in the 17th century, when pirates would sail into town laden with loot and binge until their next escapade. In 1692 the revelry came to an abrupt halt. At about noon on 7 June a massive earthquake struck and the city disappeared under the waves, killing 2,000 people.

Port Royal lies on the tip of the Palisadoes Peninsula, at the mouth of Kingston Harbour. It was fortified by the British in 1655 and became a gathering place for English buccaneers. Soon, this was the Caribbean's richest town; merchants shipped their wares here for onward sale and buccaneers, hounded from their base on Tortuga, off Haiti, brought their own loot. Taverns (one for every 10 inhabitants) were crowded with prostitutes and men were killed at the drop of a hat. When the earthquake struck, the townspeople thought it was Judgement Day. Whole streets slipped into the bay and ships were flung into the town's remains on a tidal wave. Of 3,000 houses, only 200 were left standing – but the spirit of Port Royal wasn't immediately extinguished; as the dust settled, some of the survivors simply carried on drinking.

After the earthquake, Port Royal was rebuilt, only to be devastated by a fire in 1703. Its remaining residents then moved to Kingston, leaving their town to the navy.

Port Royal today Nowadays Port Royal is a quiet village, reached by ferry from the Kingston waterfront and known for its fried fish and bammy (a flat Jamaican cake made with cassava). Fort Charles, a lumbering stone fortress whose embrasures are still lined with cannons, survived the earthquake, although it sank a few metres. Inside, in quarters where Nelson stayed in 1779, the **Maritime Museum** (tel: 967 8438. *Open* daily 9:30–4:30. *Admission for tours: inexpensive*), has models of ships and maritime memorabilia. The nearby Giddy House is a Victorian armoury that ended up at its weird angle and received its name in 1907, after another earthquake.

LUCKY BREAK
In the graveyard of St Peter's Church (1725), the story of Lewis Galdy is written on his tombstone: he was "swallowed up in the Great Earthquake", but was disgorged into the sea a few minutes later as another shockwave passed and kept swimming until he was eventually rescued by a boat. Next to him are buried the remains of three children found underneath a collapsed wall by marine archaeologists and who were reburied in 1992.

151

Cannons at the ready at Fort Charles

Jamaica is musically the loudest and the most productive of all Caribbean islands. Folk culture and religious traditions have given birth to a wealth of dance rhythms and music has a strong element of protest, developed by singers ranging from the "rude boys" of the 1960s to the dancehall singers of today. But this does not restrict the scope of musical life; tune the radio to Irie FM for certain proof that Jamaicans can put just about any song to reggae and make it sound good.

MARCHING BANDS
In the British Caribbean there is still a tradition of marching bands, very much in the British military fashion. Musicians dress in suitably formal and colourful tunics, but when marching, rather than keeping to a formal, disciplined style, they swagger and swing their instruments around.

Until 50 years ago, the popular dance rhythm in Jamaica was mento. With its slow, melodic sound and strong lyrics, this was similar to the old calypsos of Trinidad – and, like them, mento had a satirical edge. Ska dance music emerged in the late 1950s, at a time of political upheaval, as Jamaica moved towards independence, and was initially frowned on by the establishment; it introduced "rude boys" and usually delivered a socially conscious message.

Rocksteady, a slower version of the ska rhythm, incorporating a heavier bass riff and stronger vocals, put in a brief appearance in the mid-1960s, but it was soon

Maxi Priest and Shabba Ranks; Shaggy, top

TOASTING
Toasting developed in clubs, as DJs sang their quickfire lyrics over popular tunes when introducing records. This rapid, off-the-cuff patter is difficult for the uninitiated to understand, requiring a lightning mind and a good deal of skill.

superseded by reggae. This immensely popular music combined elements of ska and rocksteady and its "chaka-chaka" rhythm was given international appeal by bands such as Bob Marley and the Wailers, and Third World.

Reggae has had lasting success, spawning new bands in many other countries, but in Jamaica the music scene has moved on. In the 1980s it adapted rap music to produce "dancehall", a hard and repetitive rhythm overlaid with a heavy rapping voice. The strutting rude boys came to the fore again, headed by DJs such as Shaggy and Yellowman, the king of "slack" (vulgar songs). Other singers have begun to sing softer, more melodic songs and culture reggae.

▶▶ Mandeville

The central town of Mandeville is 610m above sea level and enjoys a cooler climate than the coast. In imperial days beaches were considered unhealthy and the British colonials would come here for their summer retreat from Kingston. Nowadays the town is the centre of a rural (and recently industrialised) area – a far cry from the beach-hustling and resorts of the north coast. There are just a few places to stay and they have a relaxed and stately (if faded) air.

Mandeville itself was built along the lines of an English country town, with a parish church and a Georgian court-house facing each other across the grassy common, or green. The colonials would have taken their constitutional walks here, but the green now serves as the bus terminal and is a focus of chaotic Jamaican life.

On the hills around Mandeville is some of Jamaica's most fertile land; the roadsides are lined with stalls selling all the fruits and vegetables in season: mangoes, oranges, bananas, peanuts and cashews. Just south of town is **Marshall's Pen▶▶** (by appointment, tel: 963 8569. *Admission: moderate*), a classic Jamaican mansion surrounded by gardens on what was once a coffee plantation. Built in the late 18th century, the wooden house is furnished in period style. It is possible to arrange bird-watching trips on the estate. On the coast to the south of Marshall's Pen is Lover's Leap, where there is a spectacular lookout. There are also superb views from Spur Tree Hill, southwest of Mandeville.

The region around Mandeville is Jamaica's bauxite mining country. Used to make aluminum, bauxite is a major export and open cast mines form orange scars across the landscape before being returfed and returned to grazing land. At Shooter's Hill, to the northeast, you can arrange a tour of the **Pickapeppa Factory** (manufacturing a popular spicy sauce); ask when they are likely to be boiling up – this is the best time to visit (by appointment, tel: 962 2928. *Admission free*). Milk River, on the south coast, is an old spa town, popular before beach holidays.

Stately Mandeville, once a colonial retreat

JAMAICAN BIRDS
Of the 250 or so birds that spend time in Jamaica (the island is on a migratory route), there are 25 native species. These include the Jamaican owl, with its eartufts and guttural whirring call; the Jamaican woodpecker, black and white except for its red head; the yellow-bellied cuckoo, which can be seen in the Mandeville area; and the Jamaican becard, which suspends its nest from a tree, entering through a hole in the bottom.

CASHEWS
The cashew nut, cultivated in the Mandeville area, grows in a shell at the end of the cashew apple on an ever-green tree. Inside the shell is an oil that can blister human skin and is poisonous if burnt; it must be dried in the sun and roasted to remove the oil before an inner shell can be broken off to reveal the nut. This laborious process is the reason why cashews are so expensive.

BEACHES

Many hotels are set on beaches and most of these have watersports facilities. In Montego Bay itself Doctor's Cave Beach is the most popular choice and tends to get very busy. There is an entry fee, but facilities include changing rooms and bars. Other strips of sand are accessible at Walter Fletcher Beach and Cornwall Beach.

154

THE WHITE WITCH OF ROSE HALL

The most famous mistress of Rose Hall was Annie Palmer, who lived there around 1820. Her story has no doubt been embellished over the years, but she is said to have murdered three husbands and had many lovers, including some of her terrified slaves, maintaining her power over them through witchcraft and sometimes killing them when she lost interest. Finally she herself was murdered by one of her lovers who realised he was losing favour with her.

►► Montego Bay

Montego Bay, in the northwest, is the most famous of Jamaica's resorts. Mo Bay, as it is known, is a lively town; there are plenty of bars along Gloucester Avenue and some good restaurants, both international and local, set in the old stone buildings and down on the waterfront. The hotels include some of the Caribbean's snazziest, such as the Tryall Club and Round Hill: these are not in the town itself, but scattered in coves along the coast to the east and west. There are many package hotels around Montego Bay, but independent travellers will also be able to find cheaper accommodation, particularly on Queen's Drive and Sunset Boulevard, and in the suburbs. Activities in the area include river rafting trips and visits to a number of great houses, which can be arranged by tour operators (see **Travel Facts**).

The heart of Montego Bay itself is **Sam Sharpe Square►►**, where vendors hawk their coloured T-shirts, peanuts and sky-juice (plastic bags of ice crystals with a dash of fruit concentrate) to passers-by. In the corner of the square is the Cage, a jail for errant slaves from the days before emancipation, and a statue of Sharpe himself, a slave leader who was executed after an uprising in 1831. Towards the sea from here you will find the **Craft Market►**, with souvenirs, wooden carvings and straw hats on sale for tourists. North along Gloucester Avenue is **Doctor's Cave Beach►►**, the most popular beach in the town and another fine Jamaican institution: the **Pork Pit►►**, where you can buy jerked chicken and pork. Tours can be made of the **Montego Bay Marine Park►** (tel: 979 2281) in glass-bottomed boats, arranged on the main beaches, or by mini-sub with Mobay Undersea Tours (tel: 952 5619. Daily. *Tours expensive*).

As you leave town heading east along the north coast you pass the Half Moon Club hotel and its golf course and come eventually to **Rose Hall►►►** (tel: 953 2341. *Open daily 9–6. Admission: expensive*), Jamaica's best-known great house. Set in stately gardens overlooking the coast, Rose Hall was built in the 1770s in imitation of British mansions of the period. The grand interior is furnished with antiques, but the guides concentrate on telling you about the house's former mistress, Annie Palmer (see panel). The less pretentious **Greenwood Great House►►**

Doctor's Cave Beach, Montego Bay; Jamaica's first and best-known public beach

Bargaining at the craft market, downtown Mo Bay

JAMAICAN DOCTOR BIRD
The doctor bird, or the red-billed streamertail, is the Jamaican national bird and one of the prettiest hummingbirds. As its name suggests, it has a red bill; the male's chest is a shimmering fluorescent shade of green. In flight it displays a pair of back tail feathers about three times as long as its body.

SEAFORD TOWN
Seaford Town, south of Montego Bay, looks like a normal Jamaican town but has an unusual history. Lord Seaford granted the land to German settlers who came here to farm it in 1835 and their blond descendants can still be seen. A similar experiment involved importing Indian labourers to Little London on the south coast, near Savanna-la-Mar; they, too, were absorbed into the local community and culture.

(tel: 953 1077. *Open* daily 9–6. *Admission: expensive*) stands on a hill about 8km beyond Rose Hall. Built during the same period, it was owned by the family of the poet Elizabeth Barrett Browning. But perhaps the most attractive plantation house is **Good Hope**▶▶▶ (tel: 954 3289), which has a wonderful view over the fertile Jamaican lands. It is a hotel, but also offers horse-riding (*Open* Thu–Tue 7:30–4:30. *Admission: expensive*).

Beyond the town of Falmouth is the Martha Brae river. Hour-long rafting trips with **Martha Brae Rafting**▶▶ (tel: 954 5168. *Open* daily 8:30–4:30. *Admission: expensive*) start upstream at Rafter's Village. At Rock, a phosphorescent lagoon glitters at night when disturbed.

Heading west from Montego Bay, the road skirts the bay itself and heads for the area of Reading, passing hillsides dotted with expensive villas. Beneath them is Catherine Hall, where the Bob Marley Performing Centre hosts the annual reggae gathering, Reggae Sunfest. From here the coast road leads to Negril, passing on its way the mouth of the Great River and the hotels at Round Hill and Tryall, with its golf course.

Turn south at Reading and climb into the hills. Near Anchovy is the delightful **Rockland Feeding Station**▶ (tel: 952 2009. *Open* daily 2–5. *Admission: moderate*), a bird sanctuary best visited after 3:30 PM. Set among fields of banana and citrus, the **Belvedere Plantation**▶▶ (tel: 956 7310. *Open* Mon–Sat 10–4. *Admission: moderate*) gives tours of a re-created village from the last century, displaying various trades and a fascinating herb garden. There is also a garden walkway along the river with labelled plants. At Catadupa, **Croydon in the Mountains**▶▶ (tel: 979 8267. *Open* Tue–Wed, Fri 10:30–3 for half-day tours. *Admission: expensive*) is worth visiting for a view of a working plantation where they grow coffee, pineapple, cocoa and bananas.

Bob Marley shot to international fame in the 1970s, popularising reggae and rastafari across the world. Although he had the toughest Jamaican roots, Marley was awarded Jamaica's highest public honour, the Order of Merit, and his legacy remains in the hundreds of songs that are still played all over Jamaica.

TUFF GONG

The Tuff Gong Studio was bought by Marley as his home and recording studio in 1975. Set on Hope Road in New Kingston, an uptown area of Kingston, it is a far cry from the shanties of Trenchtown. Tours of the studio show the gold records awarded for Marley's top-selling discs and video recordings of Marley performing his songs.

Robert Nesta Marley was born on 6 February 1945. Deserted by Norval Marley, her white Jamaican husband, Marley's mother, Cedella, raised Nesta in Nine Miles village, in the parish of St Ann's, on Jamaica's north coast. When he was a youth they moved to the poorest shanty area of Kingston and he worked as a welder.

Determined to succeed as a musician, Marley formed "The Wailing Wailers" in the early 1960s with Bunny Wailer and Peter Tosh. Together, they typified the "rude boy" image and found popular success with over 30 ska songs; but, having made little money, the band split up and Marley had to turn to welding again to make a living.

The 1970s finally brought financial success and the new Wailers were signed by Island Records. By this time Marley had become a rastafarian and the band began

MARLEY MAUSOLEUM

Bob Marley's mausoleum, in his home village of Nine Miles, is a site of pilgrimage to many fans and can be toured. Prepare for a mild onslaught of high-pressure selling, but it is interesting to see the small house and the tomb itself, which is decorated with memorabilia important to the great singer.

playing reggae. The album *Catch a Fire* hit the international charts and was followed by *Natty Dread*, *Exodus* (the best-selling album of all), *Kaya* and *Uprising*.

By now a world-famous celebrity, Marley emigrated from Jamaica after an attempt on his life, but returned in 1978 to stage the One Love Peace Concert, in which he persuaded Prime Minister Edward Seaga and opposition leader Michael Manley to make a gesture of unity against the gangland wars that were then plaguing the island.

Bob Marley died of cancer at the early age of 36 on 11 May, 1981. His body was laid to rest in a mausoleum at Nine Miles in St Ann's (see panel).

▶ ▶ ▶ Negril

The town of Negril lies at the far western tip of Jamaica and, more than any other place on the island, typifies the Jamaican image of a hedonist's hideaway on an idyllic beach. Sunset-watching has been a hallowed pastime here since the 1960s, when the village was adopted as a home by hippies. Since then Negril has been discovered by tourists; there are large hotels on the beach and people are bussed in daily to watch the sunset from Rick's Café. But the old laid-back life still exists and it is just possible to escape the crowds. There is not much to see in Negril – but then that is hardly the point of the town. You can expect to be hustled there – but then who could resent a vendor who arrives by canoe bearing a briefcase, or who greets you by massaging your leg with aloe?

Negril divides neatly into two halves: the beach and the cliffs. If there is a town centre it is at the rotary, from where the road runs inland towards Savanna-la-Mar. To the north, the road reaches Montego Bay, alongside **Long Bay▶ ▶ ▶**, one of Jamaica's best beaches – 8km of superb sand with hotels and beach bars (try Cosmo's at the top end) scattered along it. Beyond Hedonism II, on the point, is **Bloody Bay▶ ▶**, which takes its name from the days when whalers used to clean their catch here. Behind the beach is the Great Morass, a mangrove swamp that can be visited by boat to see wading birds.

South of the rotary, the coastal road of Negril's West End winds its way along the clifftops, where there are small hideaway hotels, guesthouses and plenty of bars or try the more "jet-setty" Xtabi and Rock House. The cliffs are not very high – although they might seem so to people about to jump off into the sea, a tradition in some bars. Negril has a number of outdoor music parks where you can sometimes hear big Jamaican bands. At the southern end of Negril is the 30m **lighthouse▶** (tel: 957 4875. *Open* daily 10–6. *Admission free*), which has good views of the surrounding area.

HEDONISM II

Hedonism II (there was no Hedonism I) was one of the first of Jamaica's all-inclusive hotels. Once inside the gates there is no charge for the facilities, which include scuba-diving, sailing, trapeze instruction, toga-tying, finger-painting for adults and even "nudes versus prudes" volleyball.

CALICO JACK

The infamous pirate Jack "Calico" Rackham (named for his penchant for calico underwear) was captured in Negril in 1720 and executed. With him were two women pirates, Mary Read and Anne Bonney, who was pregnant and escaped execution and said of him: "If he had fought like a man he would not be dying like a dog".

157

A sunset cruise off Rick's Café on the cliffs of Negril

Other Caribbean states

►► Ocho Rios

Halfway along the north coast, Ocho Rios is Jamaica's second biggest resort town. As in Montego Bay, the resorts are scattered for several kilometres on either side of the town, which itself stretches along the seafront and has become a much-frequented holiday spot for Kingstonians. Ochie, as it is affectionately known, is well provided with beaches, watersports and entertainment; there are expensive resorts and some cheaper hotels and a clutch of lively bars can be found on James Avenue, near the centre of town. The main beach is the Ocho Rios bay public beach directly beneath the twin skyscrapers on the seafront; to the west of Ocho Rios there is a good strip of sand at Mammee Bay. Many excursions can be made into the surrounding countryside, making this a popular cruise ship destination.

The town centres around the clock tower, where cars and buses, market vendors and the occasional goat vie for supremacy. There is nothing much to see in Ocho Rios itself, but Jamaica's best-known tourist attraction, **Dunn's River Falls►►** (tel: 974 2857. *Open* daily 9–5. *Admission: moderate*), lies to the west of town. The falls are a remarkable sight, as the river cascades over limestone outcrops, dropping steadily nearly 200m. Most people start at the bottom and climb through the lips and falls, pausing occasionally to swim in the pools (bathing suits are essential and trainers are recommended). The falls are popular with tour buses and tend to be crowded.

Further along the coast road to the west of Dunn's River Falls are a number of small towns and occasional hotels in an isolated bay. **St Ann's Bay►** is the birthplace of black activist Marcus Garvey. There is not much to detain you here, but spare a moment to think of Christopher Columbus, who was forced to spend over a year here

Tourists climb up Dunn's River Falls, Ocho Rios

waiting for rescue when his ships sank (see panel). Close by is the site of Jamaica's first Spanish settlement, Seville Nueva, restored as an archeological park.

The road south from Ocho Rios climbs immediately into the hills. **Coyaba River Gardens**▶▶ (tel: 974 6235. *Open* daily 8–5. *Admission: inexpensive*) makes a pleasant stop, as the Gardens are festooned with flowering bushes and trees set among streams and ponds. The **Shaw Park Botanical Gardens**▶▶ (tel: 974 2723. *Open* daily 8–5. *Admission: inexpensive*) also make an interesting tour of tropical plants and lily ponds. The main road to Kingston then passes into **Fern Gully**▶▶, a deep, cool cleft in the hills. Huge ferns flourish on the banks and trees hang over the road, blocking out the light.

Heading east from Ocho Rios, you cross the White River, hosting daytime rafting trips and torchlit night excursions with dinner; these can be arranged at hotels. **Prospect Plantation**▶ (tel: 974 2058. *Open* daily for tours. *Admission: expensive)* is a working plantation where native fruit and vegetables, including soursop, cocoa, tamarind and ackee, are grown and trees (bearing plaques) were planted by celebrated visitors including Winston Churchill and Charlie Chaplin. It can be toured by tractor-drawn carriage or on horseback. **Harmony Hall**▶▶ (tel: 975 4222. *Open* daily 10–6. *Admission free*) is an art gallery set in a restored house, exhibiting works by Caribbean artists. At **Irie Beach**▶▶ – not actually a beach, but a gulley inland where a river cascades over small falls into rockpools – you can swim and sit in the sun.

About 24km further on is **Firefly**▶▶▶ (tel: 997 7201. *Open* Mon–Sat 8:30–5. *Admission: expensive*), where Noel Coward lived until his death in 1973. The house itself is simple and has a few furnishings and musical scores still as Coward left them. However, the most spectacular feature of the house is its view, extending along the north coast as far as the Blue Mountains. As you travel to Firefly, you will pass another literary-connected establishment: Goldeneye, the house of James Bond's creator, Ian Fleming. This can be rented as a villa.

Relaxation at the north-east resort of Ocho Rios

MARCUS GARVEY
Marcus Mosiah Garvey was a black activist during the early 20th century. His aim was to help Africans and their descendants improve their situation in a white-dominated, colonial world. Through his Universal Negro Improvement Association he built up a massive following in the Caribbean and the US, keeping in touch with the organisation's branches throughout the world by means of its newspaper, *Negro World*. Garvey died in relative obscurity in Britain, but in 1964 his bones were brought back to Jamaica, where he was proclaimed the first Jamaican national hero.

Other Caribbean states

BEACHES
Set against the backdrop of the John Crow Mountains, the beaches around Port Antonio tend to be steep-sided coves, but there are pleasant strips of golden sand in the area. Be careful of currents – the sea can become rough when onshore winds are blowing. There are good beaches at Winifred and at Boston Bay and Frenchman's Cove is often deserted. Although not a beach, the Blue Lagoon is a favourite spot: a stunningly blue sea pool with edges fringed by palm trees and a waterfall restaurant.

Street scene, Port Antonio: red roofs and telegraph poles

BANANAS GALORE
The banana trade made Port Antonio rich at the turn of the century, reaching its heyday in the 1920s. The fruit was brought down the Rio Grande on bamboo rafts, to be shipped out to the US. When Errol Flynn bought Navy Island in Port Antonio harbour in the late 1940s he popularised the use of these rafts for pleasure; it has since become a staple of a Jamaican holiday.

▶▶▶ Port Antonio

The northeast is a lesser-known corner of Jamaica, but one of the most rewarding. Although there are hotels here, the area is distinctly less commercial than the big resort towns on the north coast. Small rural communities are dotted along the steep slopes of the John Crow Mountains, which tumble down to the coast. The scenery is fertile and unspoilt; nature quickly reclaims any human invasion, with fences becoming hedges and telephone wires covered with vegetation in no time.

Port Antonio itself is a charming town with an easy, relaxed pace, set between mountains and a magnificent double harbour. The few streets of clapboard houses have become a bit run down since the decline of the town's prosperity, which flowed from the banana industry early this century and then from its brief reign as Jamaica's most exclusive resort in the 1950s, when the likes of Errol Flynn and Bette Davis were frequent visitors.

There is a fine panorama of the town from the Bonnie View Hotel. Beneath it, behind the harbour, is the oldest part of town, with stone buildings such as the courthouse and parish church; beyond is the Point, with beautiful old wooden town houses. Just off the Point is Navy Island (guided tours by reservation; tel: 993 2667), once owned by Errol Flynn; his former residence is now a hotel. Not far southeast of town are Athenry Gardens and the Nonsuch Caves, illuminated caverns festooned with stalactites.

East of the town, beyond the Blue Hole (see panel), is **Boston Bay**▶▶▶, the home of jerk, which is freshly cooked at roadside stalls. Also worth a visit are the **Reach Falls**▶▶▶, some of the island's prettiest and normally free of tourist buses.

Inland from Port Antonio, Berridale marks the start of two-hour river-rafting trips on the **Rio Grande** (tel: 993 5778. *Open* daily 8:30–4:30. *Admission: expensive*; transport is provided from the Rafter's Rest, on the river mouth). You descend gradually through magnificent, fertile scenery punted by a raftsman with a bamboo pole. The road then climbs further into the John Crow Mountains and leads to **Moore Town**▶, an old maroon settlement; visits can be arranged by the Port Antonio tourist office. Walking tours in the hills above Port Antonio are offered by Valley Hikes (tel: 993 3881. *Open* Mon–Fri 9–4:30, Sat–Sun 9–12. *Admission: expensive*).

The word "rasta" tends to conjure up a picture of musicians dressed in red, gold and green and sporting hydra-heads of dense dreadlocks. But the picture is a misleading one. In Jamaica, most of the rastafarians live quiet, religious, often reclusive lives and rarely set foot in tourist-dominated towns.

Rasta beliefs first emerged during the 1930s in the poor ghettos of west Kingston as the religious crystallisation of anti-colonial black consciousness movements. Although it has often been sensationalised and misunderstood, rastafari is still a Judeo-Christian-inspired faith and many believers carry bibles and go to services.

Rastas have no central church, but there is a system of recognised beliefs common to all followers. According to the rastafarian interpretation of the Bible, Ras (prince) Tafari is a divine incarnation, believed to have taken earthly form as the Emperor Haile Selassie of Ethiopia. To rastas, Africans are God's chosen people and some look ahead to eventual black supremacy. Ethiopia is believed to be Zion, or heaven on earth – a belief linked with the "back to Africa" movement. Other countries, particularly Jamaica (to which blacks were forcibly brought to atone for their ancestors' sins) and white nations, are regarded as Babylon, or hell on earth.

True believers lead simple, austere lives, rejecting the trappings of modern Western life. They eat "ital" (from "vital" or natural), mostly vegetarian foods and usually prefer herbal remedies to Western medical treatment. Most rastas wear their hair uncut and uncombed, in long, thick "dreadlocks", and most regard smoking marijuana, or "ganja", (illegal in Jamaica) as a sacred activity.

Rasta beliefs have been obscured as the following has become internationally known; many of the famous Jamaican reggae stars adopted the faith and to the west it became associated with messages of militancy and ganja-smoking.

Unfortunately, the trappings of the movement have been hijacked in the Caribbean by small-time opportunists and hustlers, who don rastas' clothing and are known as "wolves" or "dreads".

LION OF ZION
Haile Selassie was known as the "Lion of Judah"; as a proud, African animal, the lion is often used in rasta art. A full head of dreadlocks is taken to symbolise the lion's mane and followers will consciously emulate the lion's slow, proud bearing.

Rasta craft market in Montego Bay

GANJA
Marijuana was introduced into the Caribbean by agricultural workers from India, who arrived as indentured labourers on contracts to work the canefields after the abolition of slavery in the 19th century. Smoked in a "chalice", and believed by rastas to bring wisdom, the leaf has several names in Jamaica, including ganja, cully weed, holy herb and wisdom weed.

Sunrise at Cayman Brac

The Cayman Islands

Thousands of visitors fly down to the Cayman Islands for reliable sun and sand and the finest diving seas close to the mainland US, and the islands are well geared up to receive them. The Caymans' successful tourist industry is supplemented by the offshore finance sector; the islands' status as a tax haven and the presence of numerous millionaires has given the 36,000 Caymanians the highest average per capita income in the Caribbean – although many islanders have menial, low-income jobs.

The Cayman Islands are formed by limestone caps of submerged mountain peaks, rising 7,680m from the valley floor. These three British-dependent islands have distinctly different atmospheres. They lie to the northwest of Jamaica, separated into two groups. Grand Cayman, the senior island and site of the capital, George Town, is 32km by 12km and is busy, commercial and flat. It is also by far the most developed island of the three. About 137km to its northeast are the twin cays of Cayman Brac (with a population of about 1,200) and Little Cayman (which has only about 70 people), offering some of the region's best fishing. The gradual development of a tourist industry is distinctly low-key here.

All three islands are generally dry and scrubby, with areas of swamp, and lie very low in the water. But for all their featureless appearance above the waterline, they boast some of the most impressive underwater scenery and marine life in the Caribbean.

There are a number of scuba operations on the islands, diving mainly off the walls – vertical underwater drops clustered with coral – in the north and west of Grand Cayman. If you are not a diver, you can see the corals from the Atlantis Submarine (tel: 949 7700), which offers reef trips some 36m down near George Town.

Tourism on Grand Cayman has mainly taken hold along Seven Mile Beach, where bars and restaurants stand shoulder to shoulder among the many hotels and from where there is an excellent view of the sunset most days. You can dine extremely well here, in chic restaurants, but there are also a number of fast food chains and rib joints.

From Mondays to Saturdays, bars and clubs provide plenty of nightlife and there are shows in the hotels and a couple of places to dance. Cayman Brac and Little Cayman are, on the other hand, very peaceful and quiet and their inhabitants, like those of Grand Cayman, are generally known as some of the most easy-going people in the Caribbean.

A Cayman Islands totem pole

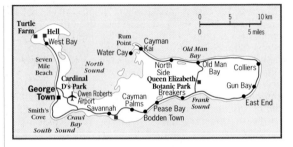

BEACHES

Seven Mile Beach is an archetypal Caribbean beach with perfect golden sand that shelves gently away to the west. The water is calm on this protected side of the island and there are magnificent sunsets. All kinds of watersports are available here, from waterskiing to parasailing; the only problem is that it is sometimes pretty crowded. Caymanians tend to go to Smith's Cove, an inlet between the coral rocks to the south of George Town. Other beaches that are worth exploring include Cayman Kai and Water Cay, on the north coast.

Swimming with stingrays off the Cayman Islands

GRAND CAYMAN This is the largest and most developed of the Caymans and it is here that you will find the capital and the only real town, George Town, a small collection of wooden and concrete buildings on the waterfront in the protected southwest of the island. Its quiet streets come alive with the arrival of cruise ships and during the annual festivities, the Batabano Carnival (April) and Pirates' Week (late October), when choreographed hordes of swash-bucklers carouse there. The **Cayman Islands National Museum►►** (tel: 949 8368. *Open Mon–Fri 9–5, Sat 10–4. Admission: inexpensive*) set in a traditional Caymanian building, is run by the National Trust and has excellent displays illustrating the islands' history and natural life. It includes an interesting section on the old seafaring traditions with artefacts found both on land and in the sea.

Life for most visitors to Grand Cayman is centred on Seven Mile Beach, which is heavily built up with hotels and condominiums along its 9km length. Here you will find the liveliest bars and restaurants. In their prosperity, the Cayman Islands have been swamped with satellite dishes, big cars and other trappings of North American culture, but as the tourist development thins out to the north and further afield in the east, you will occasionally see the neat, wooden buildings of the old-time Caribbean; the white clapboard houses, with their pink or blue shutters and shingle tiled roofs, are often set in carefully tended gardens blooming with hibiscus and bougainvillea.

In West Bay, north of Seven Mile Beach, **Hell▶** is a pitted and scorched terrain of worn coral limestone. At the **Cayman Turtle Farm▶** (tel: 949 3894. *Open* daily 8:30–5. *Admission: moderate*) you can learn about the life cycle of the turtle. There is a turtle release programme, but this is a sad place, as the animals are cooped up quite severely. Off the east coast, **Stingray City▶ ▶** is the island's most famous (and touristy) dive and snorkel site, which is visited by friendly stingrays.

East of George Town, on the coast, seek out **Pedro St James Historic Site▶ ▶** (tel: 947 3329. *Open* daily 9-5. *Admission: moderate*), which is a heritage park arranged around a restored 1780s great house. Built with slave labour, it was a fitting backdrop for the announcement of the abolition of slavery in 1835. Further east and inland, the award-winning **Queen Elizabeth Botanic Park ▶ ▶** (tel: 947 9462. *Open* daylight hours. *Admission: moderate*) showcases exotic local flora and fauna.

Local straw craft in the making, Cayman Brac

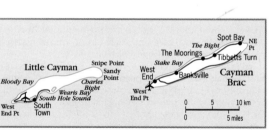

LITTLE CAYMAN AND CAYMAN BRAC The other two Cayman Islands, both thin and each about 20km long, lie tip to tail some 136km to the northeast of Grand Cayman. The channel in between them may not look dangerous but it is, in fact, a treacherously deep stretch of water. It is possible to arrange day trips by airplane to both Cayman Brac and Little Cayman.

Cayman Brac takes its name from the "brac" or cliff at its eastern end, the highest point in the Caymans (a princely 45m). There are just 1,200 Brackers and they have a reputation for their friendly hospitality. Cayman Brac has a museum in Stake Bay and a few shops, but generally it is as sleepy today as it has been for the last 100 years. Apart from the people and the opportunity to do nothing in warm surroundings, the best reason to visit is the coral. Superb dive sites and snorkelling grounds can be explored around the western tip of the island.

There are a handful of hotels on Little Cayman; these offer diving in the stunning Bloody Bay Wall Marine Park and fishing facilities. The island is also home to hundreds of birds, including the Caribbean's largest population of red-footed boobies, and a rare frigate bird breeding site.

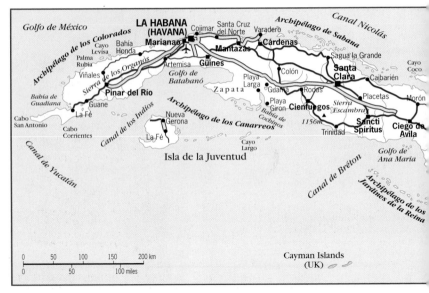

Other Caribbean states

166

CUBAN RHYTHMS
Music is essential to Cuban life, and you will hear it everywhere – at Sunday afternoon concerts in town bandstands, at night-time cabaret and, of course, during Carnival in July. Many of the rhythms that originated in Cuba are closely associated with dancing: the rumba, the cha cha, danzon and son. The most popular modern rhythm nowadays is salsa, but the best known of all the Cuban songs, *Guantanamera*, is in the guajira rhythm.

A Cuban passion: 1950s cars

Cuba

An extraordinary, enigmatic country, Cuba is strikingly different from other Caribbean islands – a place of revolution, violence and hardship; but also a beautiful land where ancient and modern exist side by side.

Havana (La Habana), Cuba's capital, is less than 160km from Florida's Key West, but its proximity belies the political gulf between the two countries. Before the 1959 Revolution, 90 per cent of visitors to Cuba were from the US. Today, US citizens are forbidden to spend their dollars in Cuba; only excursions for scientific or research purposes are permitted, although many US tourists now travel there from countries such as Canada, Jamaica, and Mexico. US citizens wishing to travel in Cuba should contact the Department of Treasury, Washington, DC 20220 (tel: 202/622-2111).

Cuba lies at the gaping mouth of the Gulf of Mexico and is the largest of the Caribbean islands, a snake-like 1,250km long, though never much more than 121km wide. Much of the fertile, agricultural land is covered in sugar cane. There are three mountain ranges: in the west, the karst formations of the Sierra de los Organos, whose red earth is covered with tobacco plants; the Sierra Escambray, halfway along the island; and the Sierra Maestra, in the island's eastern province, and includes the highest peak of Pico

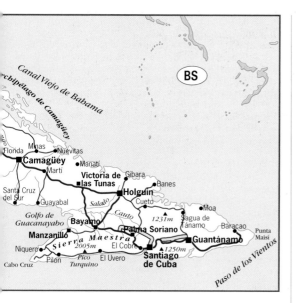

CUBAN COCKTAILS
Two of Cuba's best-known cocktails were favourites of Ernest Hemingway and he was supposed to have had a saying: "My mojito in the Bodeguita, my daiquiri in the Floridita" (the Bodeguita del Medio and El Floridita are long-established Havana restaurants). A mojito is made with rum, sugar, fresh mint leaves and Angostura Bitters (from Trinidad). It is then shaken with ice and strained into a glass. A daiquiri is also based on rum, which is blended with cane sugar and fresh fruit, so that it comes out as an ice-cold, crystalline sludge. A Cuba Libre, named soon after the Revolution, consists of rum on ice with the juice of a lime, topped with cola (a version of which the Cubans still produce).

Turquino at 1,980m, where revolutionaries hid in the 1950s. The entire island is ringed with around 6,500km of sandy beaches, coral cays, and large, secluded bays.

Even without official American visitors, Cuba lays great emphasis on tourism. It has to, in order to bring in much-needed hard currency – especially now that financial support from the former USSR has dried up. Europeans and Canadians flock here for inexpensive holidays; Havana and Santiago de Cuba, the second city, are now linked by air to many European capitals, including, of course, London.

HISTORY Cuba was Columbus's second landfall in 1492, and for the next four centuries Spanish adventurers arrived here expecting to make their fortunes. They decimated the indigenous population, replacing them with African slaves, who worked the prosperous sugar plantations. Over the years the slaves mingled with Spanish colonists to form today's mixed Cuban race. During the 16th and 17th centuries, "New World" treasure flooded into Spain via Havana, which quickly became the richest city in the Caribbean.

Spanish colonisation gave way briefly to British rule; then the US took control of the island until, in 1902, Independence was declared. During the early 1940s, Americans began to exploit Cuba and its cheap labour. The island played host to thousands of visitors from the US, and a wide variety of entertainments and diversions became available, ranging from privately organised gaming casinos to explicit shows. Havana's streets were the setting for extortion, illicit alcohol distribution, trade in narcotics and prostitution. The state, under the dictatorship of Fulgencio Batista, exploited tourism at the expense of the Cuban population and the country.

Embittered Cubans, led by Dr Fidel Castro, rose up against the Batista regime but were incarcerated on the Isla de Pinos (renamed the Isla de la Juventud after

Main square, Trinidad, Cuba

REVOLUTIONARY ART

There are no billboard advertisements in Cuba, but revolutionary posters are an art in themselves – brightly coloured and featuring famous Cuban faces or working scenes. Some rail against the "Yankee Imperialists" of the United States; others show Fidel and other state heroes (such as José Martí, the poet and journalist who was killed soon after taking up arms against the Spanish in 1895) and the Argentinian Che Guevara, encouraging the Cubans to fulfil their social duties.

the Revolution) in 1953. On their release, Castro and the revolutionaries undertook military training in Mexico, joined by the Argentinian doctor, Che Guevara. In 1956 they sailed to Cuba on the *Granma* and hid in the Sierra Maestra, with a band of guerillas that at one stage numbered only 12. Their following grew as soldiers deserted Batista to join the rebels. Batista fled Cuba on 1 January, 1959, and the revolutionaries took control. Castro defeated a US-sponsored invasion at the Bay of Pigs in 1961, and in 1965 he made the Communist Party of Cuba the island's sole legal political party.

STAYING IN CUBA The number of hotel rooms in Cuba has almost quadrupled in the last decade. However, facilities can vary dramatically. The most popular and largest of Cuba's beach resorts is Varadero beach, in Matanzas Province, east of Havana, but there are quieter resorts around the coast, such as the Isla de la Juventud, an offshore island in the southwest. Most hotels are mid-range resorts, but luxury resorts have risen on many beaches. Several are joint investment ventures between Cuba and Argentina, Canada, Spain or France, and meet high standards. Cuba's own hotels and casual accommodation can leave a lot to be desired, as Cubans are restricted by a lack of facilities and supplies.

ISLAND SIGHTS AND ENTERTAINMENT The world-famous Varadero beach, Havana's East Beaches, Santa Lucia, Guardalavaca and Daiquiri are just some of Cuba's better known seaside resorts. On the offshore cays, such as Cayo Sabinal and Cayo Coco, facilities are provided for

reef snorkelling and diving trips. The most popular cay is Cayo Largo, off Cuba's southern shores, a coral island resort with air links from Varadero making it an easy day's excursion. Beyond the beaches, Cuba has some of the Caribbean's most historic sites. The Old Town of Havana is 5sq km of cobbles, colonnades and Spanish colonial palaces. In the south is the "living museum" of 16th-century Trinidad, which has joined Old Havana as a UNESCO World Heritage site.

Although gambling is now forbidden in Cuba, there is still a lively entertainment scene, including renowned shows such as Havana's 50-year-old Tropicana.

Getting around is relatively easy these days with a good central highway and a 150-year-old railway running down the spine of the country, plus there are over 29,000km of roads. Car hire and chauffeur facilities are good, but expensive; cars available include VWs, Nissans and Mercedes. Cubans still drive 1950s American cars – when petrol is available – but ox-carts, horses and bicycles are common alternatives.

AFTER THE REVOLUTION

For the average Cuban, life improved after the Revolution, for instance, medical care and education became available to all. At the same time, Castro established a one-party constitution and political dissenters were simply locked up. Castro, usually known as Fidel, was a popular figurehead and to some extent he still is, though most of his population cannot now remember what life was like before the Revolution.

Domestic flights link most large towns and the Varadero beach resort, which is also joined by a highway to Matanzas in the south. Flights within Cuba are not expensive and are generally easily booked. Independent travel is possible except in restricted areas, though it can be difficult to find meals outside resorts and hotels can be basic. However, new lodges and camp sites, Cubatur's helpful guides and use of tourist buses and trains have made independent touring a realistic option.

ISLAND LIFE The Cuban currency, the peso, is rarely seen by tourists, as the US dollar is most readily accepted. The recently introduced Peso Convertible has parity with the US dollar and is widely accepted in resort areas. Dollar-only shops stock everything from bikinis to toothpaste. Seeing the best of the scarce resources being reserved for tourists has understandably caused resentment among Cubans, for whom life is very hard, although Cubans with dollars are now permitted to shop with them, too. Hustlers are appearing in larger numbers, and visitors should be particularly careful with their belongings in Havana and Varadero. Rationing has now reached a point where many people simply do not get enough food. Electricity is restricted and fuel for private vehicles is hard to find. Even the much-vaunted services of health care and education are under threat through lack of resources. Real progress is unlikely while the US embargo continues, and, for its part, the Cuban Communist Party has shown little inclination to change. However, since the embargo has loosened a little, things have improved slightly.

For all their difficulties, the 11 million Cubans are a lively nation, whose Latin Caribbean character shines through in their rhythmic music. It is well worth attending an evening at a *casa de la trova*, where professional musicians play in competition with one another; and in July each year the Cubans drop everything for *Carnaval*, a weekend of dancing through the streets.

MOTORISED ART
The cars driven by Cubans are a curious leftover from pre-Revolution days, when the island was almost an offshore state of the US. Dating from the 1950s – the last time Cubans were allowed to buy, or could afford, privately owned cars – these magnificent, fin-tailed beasts are adorned with a great expanse of chrome on their bumpers and fittings and are cared for lovingly.

169

TROVA
The trova is a special Cuban ballad which, like many Caribbean songs, has an element of social comment. Trovas are as likely to celebrate a national hero or take a swing at corruption in the Communist Party as they are to sing of love. The name "trova" is derived from the Provençal *trobar* (to compose) – as is the word troubadour, used to describe the medieval romantic poets of Languedoc.

A Cuban country house

Above: Wrought-iron balconies, vantage points for viewing the streets in Old Havana. Right: equally impressive are the views of Havana from across the water.

THROUGH THE KEYHOLE
It is always worth taking a look inside the buildings, both public and private, in Havana, if you can see or find your way through the front door. There may be glimpses of superb inner courtyards, with arched colonnades on each storey, constructed so that the sunlight and heat did not penetrate into the rooms. Others have elaborately decorated stairways or beautiful fan-shaped stained-glass windows.

▶▶ Havana (La Habana)

The modern city of Havana, on the north coast of Cuba near the western end of the island, has radiated outwards from the earliest colony, which was settled on the western shore of Havana harbour in 1514 and is now made up of four distinct districts: Old Havana, Central Havana, Vedado and Miramar.

Even in its dilapidated state, there is a charmed feel about **Old Havana**▶▶▶. Its tight alleys and cobbled squares, colonnades and colonial palaces built in coral rock are strikingly beautiful compared to the present-day city's high-rise hotels. Old Havana's finest square is the Plaza de la Catedral; the 18th-century baroque cathedral sits on its northern side, flanked by the Museum of Colonial Art and the renowned El Patio restaurant. Grassroots capitalism has emerged in various guises in Havana, including the appearance of a colourful arts and crafts market just off the Plaza de la Catedral.

Hemingway's favourite Bodeguita del Medio restaurant is nearby, as is the grand Plaza des Armas, which was originally the parade ground, with its imposing Palace of the Captain Generals. Also on the Plaza are the City Museum, and the classical-style El Templete portico, built to celebrate the first mass on Cuban soil. Just off the square, the Castillo de la Fuerza is Cuba's oldest fortress (1544), whose roof is topped by the city's symbol, the tiny golden statue of La Giraldilla. Numerous cannons, which were recently excavated near the ancient city walls, now surround the fortress.

To the west, Old Havana is bounded by the Paseo de Martí, an avenue giving easy access to the Memorial Museum, the National Museum (containing many old

masterpieces), the ornate Garcia Lorca Theatre and the Capitol (a copy of the one in Washington, DC's). Overlooking Old Havana is the 17th-century El Morro fortress, part of the Morro-Cabaña Historical and Military Park with the fortress of San Carlos de la Cabaña. It houses an extensive collection of antique weapons and a traditional cannon shot is fired from La Cabaña at 9 PM every evening.

Heading north through the open Parque Central, you emerge into the 19th-century Prado, a broad boulevard with a raised promenade where Habaneros sit and pass the time of day. Close by is the old Presidential Palace, an eclectic building of columns and balustrades, which now houses the Revolutionary Museum. This displays photographs, guerilla maps and stirring revolutionary memorabilia. Outside, military hardware on show includes tanks, planes and Castro's invasion boat.

Along the seafront, the 3km Malecon, a promenade where young Habaneros gather on summer evenings (and where *Carnaval* is staged), leads west to the modern districts of Havana, including Vedado. At the head of La Rampa, a bustling business street, stands the Habana Libre Hotel, built in the 1950s as the Hilton. The Bar Turquino, on the top floor, has a magnificent view of the city. South of here are the stately buildings of the City University and finally the open Plaza de la Revolución, where a statue of national hero José Martí stands beside a huge concrete column constructed in the shape of a communist star. Political rallies are held here and often draw up to as many as 500,000 people.

To the west of the square is the Cementerio Cristobal Colón (the Columbus Cemetery), with an impressive collection of magnificent mausoleums with exquisite stone carving – definitely not to be missed!

Elsewhere, there is a wealth of galleries, museums and palaces. A visit to the Casa de las Americas, which exhibits contemporary Latin American art and craft and has regular recitals and theatrical events, is particularly worthwhile – and Havana's excellent ice cream should be tasted at La Coppelita park on La Rampa.

THE BAY OF PIGS

The Bay of Pigs was catapulted into the headlines in April 1961 when 1,400 Cuban exiles staged an invasion of the island, partially backed by the US, in order to oust Castro and his revolutionaries. It was a military fiasco and most of the exiles were rounded up within a couple of days. In Cuban revolutionary lore it was written up as the first great defeat of imperialism on Latin American soil. Castro declared Cuba Communist a couple of days later.

HEMINGWAY'S ISLAND

Ernest Hemingway lived in Cuba during the 1940s and 1950s and he set two of his novels there: *Islands in the Stream* and *The Old Man and the Sea*, whose story supposedly takes place in the village of Cojímar. Two restaurants in Old Havana were particular favourites of his: the riotous Bodeguita del Medio on Calle Empredado and the more formal and stately El Floridita on Calle Obispo, where you can try some of the best lobster in the Caribbean. Hemingway lived in the suburb of San Francisco, in a hillside house called La Vigia, now open to the public. He was a keen deep-sea fisherman – a marina west of Havana bears his name.

The epic struggle in Hemingway's The Old Man and the Sea *is recalled in a statue*

An old West Indian legend tells of large Cuban women rolling the world's finest cigars on their thighs. Whether or not this was true, the reality nowadays is rather less picturesque, although it is still intriguing to watch Cuban cigars being rolled by hand, cut with large metal blades and pressed in antique wooden vices.

EARLY SMOKERS

Columbus was the first European to see Indians smoking tobacco, which is indigenous to the Americas. Twisted leaves would be wrapped in dried palm leaves or maize husk and smoked by Mayan Indians during religious ceremonies. The Mayans believed tobacco to be medicinal and the word "cigar" is derived from their own term for smoking, *sik'ar*. Tobacco quickly gained popularity in Europe, where, in the 17th century, smoking was a sign of great wealth.

172

CIGAR TYPES

The traditional Cuban cigar is a corona, which measures about 15cm and has straight sides, with one rounded and one cut end. The corona chica has the same shape, but is about 10cm in length. Ideales are slender and torpedo-shaped, tapered at the lighting end, as are the smaller bouquets. Panatellas are thin and cut open at both ends; a cheroot is even thinner.

Tobacco, a bright green plant with long, oval leaves, grows on many Caribbean islands for use in cigarettes – but only Cuba and the Dominican Republic have cigar industries. The finest Cuban tobacco, reserved for its cigars, grows in the northwestern province of Pinar del Río, where the earth is thick and deep red and the leaves grow with a minimum of starches and sugars. Dotted around the neat tobacco fields are drying houses, with wooden walls and palm-thatch or aluminium roofs, where the leaves are cured for up to three months after picking.

Once dried, the leaves are sorted according to age – older leaves have a stronger flavour but younger leaves are more elastic and better for rolling – and are bundled off to the factories. While one factory worker sits at the head of the room, reading aloud from a newspaper, the others sit at long tables, placing "binder" leaves in their hands, laying tobacco filler (the offcuts of the last rolls) on top and then making the first, skillful roll. Each cigar is then pressed in a vice to give it the correct shape. One half of the strong, evenly coloured "wrapper" leaf is then rolled around it, and finally the cigar is trimmed. After the manufacturer's bands have been slipped on, the cigars are packed in boxes, between leaves of aromatic cedar wood, for export.

Some of the most famous cigar manufacturers are based in Cuba, including Monte Cristo, Partagas, Romeo y Julietta, H Upmann and Davidoff. Within Cuba, cigars are remarkably cheap and factory tours can be arranged through Intur or Cubatur. Due to sanctions against the Communist regime, Cuban cigars are illegal in the US.

OUTSIDE HAVANA West of Havana is Pinar del Río Province, the home of the finest Cuban tobacco. It takes a good day's drive to see the neatly ranged fields of bright green tobacco plants and thatched drying houses. A worthwhile stop on the way is the lovely **Soroa Orchid Garden▶** where over 750 species of orchid flourish on a hillside site near the Manantiales waterfall. Around Viñales the landscape is punctuated with strange karst "haystack" hills, known in Cuba as *mogotes*. The town of **Pinar del Río▶** contains an attractive selection of neoclassical houses and a rum factory renowned for its wild guava-flavoured rum, Guayabita de Pinar. Also worth seeing is the cathedral of San Rosendo; the tobacco museum west of town; and one of the local cigar factories that are said to sell the best in Cuba.

UNEASY LEASE
Guantanamo, a remote, easterly province, is a curious anomaly, in that there is a US naval base there, on Cuban sovereign land. It was arranged on a lease in 1902, but since the Revolution the Cubans have refused to accept the nominal annual payment of $5,000.

Cienfuegos traffic

North of Pinar, the charming small town of **Viñales▶** is situated amid the *mogotes* of the Sierra de los Organos, in an area that has been declared a national monument. Just over a kilometre west of town, the **Prehistory Wall**, a mural painted by Leovigildo Gonzalez, a disciple of the great Diego Rivera, can be seen; 5–6km north, look for the Cueva del Indio, a lovely Indian cave that can be toured by foot and by boat. Catch a boat at Palma Rubia to get to Cayo Levisa, part of the Archipelago de los Colorados, with a long, sandy beach with good snorkelling and scuba-diving around a reef that parallels the beach.

Hemingway aficionados might want to visit **Cojímar▶**, the village where he set his tale *The Old Man and the Sea*. Hemingway himself fished from Cojímar and his International Fishing Tourney originated there, although it now takes place at the Hemingway Marina near Havana.

To the east of Havana is Cuba's best resort town, **Varadero▶**, where hotels and restaurants stand on the Peninsula de Hicacos' 19km of powder-like sand. Windsurfing and parasailing can be arranged here and there are lively evening bars, including the Cueva del Pirata, a discotheque set in a cave. There is also an art gallery and municipal museum devoted to local history.

A short drive away at Punta Hicacos, the **Cueva de Ambrosio▶▶** was a ceremonial cave site decorated with dozens of Indian drawings an re-discovered in 1961. Look for the cave between the Marina Chapelin and the Marina Gaviota towards the north end of the peninsula. Varadero has its share of hustlers and prostitutes, who tend to congregate towards the south end of the resort area. The

173

MONCADA GARRISON
The Moncada Garrison in Santiago is honoured in revolutionary lore as the place where Castro made his first strike against the Batista regime. On 26 July, 1953, 130 young rebels assembled to the east of the city and although some were unarmed, launched an attack. Militarily, it was a dismal failure; most were rounded up as they tried to escape and many were killed. The survivors received long prison sentences. Moncada is recalled on the black and red party flag in the insignia "M-26-7", and 26 July has been made a national holiday.

BOTANIC GARDENS
About 16km east of Cienfuegos is the Jardin Botanico de Cienfuegos, set in part of an old sugar plantation. The gardens are devoted to medicinal plants, fruit trees, orchids, bamboos and a great collection of palm trees. It was founded by plantation owner Edwin F Atkins in 1901.

international hotels can be found further north and the very north end of the peninsula has been designated park area and is to be left undeveloped. In general, Varadero offers a fine beach holiday, but it is totally isolated and has more in common with a typical Caribbean beach resort of other islands than with the rest of Cuba.

On the south coast beneath Varadero is the swampy Zapata Peninsula, site of the infamous Bay of Pigs invasion in 1961 and now of the Bay of Pigs Museum and a number of tourist resorts. Further east, through the sugar flats, is the pretty town of **Cienfuegos▶**, also known as the Pearl of the South. It is one of Cuba's major ports, where interesting buildings include the 1870 neo-Gothic Catedral Purisima Concepción, the **Tomás Terry Theater▶** on the Parque Martí, decorated with an exquisite painted ceiling of muses and Cuban writers and the Moorish-influenced Valle Palace, an elaborate architectural folly on Punta Gorda. On the west side of Parque Martí, visit the Palacio de Ferrer, a 1894 building and climb the tower for wonderful views.

The southern slopes of the Sierra Escambray tumble into the sea around the town of **Trinidad▶▶▶**. Founded in 1514 by Diego Velázquez, Trinidad was a successful shipping town in the early 19th century and has been restored to its former grandeur. The cobbled central square, Plaza Martí, one of five main squares, has beautiful colonial Spanish buildings, complemented with bougainvillea blooms, as well as two museums: the **Museo de Arquitectura de Trinidad**, which traces the city's development during the 18th and 19th centuries; and the **Museo Romantico**, displaying furniture and decorative arts. Next door to the Museo Romantico is Trinidad's premier cathedral, the **Iglesia Parroquial de la Santisima Trinidad▶▶▶**

An interior in Trinidad's Museo Romantico

built between 1817 and 1892. The largest church in Cuba, it is famed for its acoustics. Other city museums include the **Museo de Archeológica Arqueologica Guamuhaya▶**, overviewing pre-Columbian to post-conquest times; and the **Museo de Lucha Contra Bandidos▶**, which focuses on the military campaigns waged against counter-revolutionaries in the Escambray Mountains in the 1960s. The Casa de la Cultura on Calle Zerquera showcases cultural events and has a gallery and shop; the Casa de la Trova has late night live music and open-air concerts on Calle Marquez, with singing on Sunday afternoons.

The fishing village of La Boca lies just 8km from Trinidad; you'll pass through *en route* to the beach at Playa Ancon, which has lovely turquoise water, good diving 275m offshore and a couple of resort hotels. To the east, the ruined Torre de Iznaga is an old watch-tower built to oversee slaves in the sugar cane fields.

Cuba's second town, **Santiago de Cuba▶▶**, commands a stunning position on a vast south-coast harbour, near the east end of the island. In the shadow of the great Sierra Maestra mountains, this city's cathedral is the oldest on the island (1514). Conquistador Diego Velázquez lived in the 1520 mansion on Cespedes Park, in Santiago's centre which now houses the Cuban Life Museum and its fine furniture collection. In all, the city has 14 museums, of which there are two notable examples: the Bacardi Museum, serving as a reminder of the rum family's origins and displaying pre-Columbian artefacts, national art and history exhibits, and the 26 de Julio Museum in the Moncada Barracks, attacked by Castro's revolutionaries on July 26, 1953.

Santiago has a more ethnically mixed population, having been the first Cuban city to receive slaves; French colonists fleeing Haiti's insurrection in the 18th century also arrived at Santiago, as did many migrating Jamaicans. Much of the city is organised around Cespedes Park, most prominently the recently renovated Hotel Casa Granda on the east side and the cathedral **Santa Iglesia Basilica Metropolitana▶** on the south side. Northeast of the centre lies the Plaza de la Revolución, dedicated to the 19th-century Cuban revolutionary General Antonio Maceo. The park is dominated by a bronze statue of the general on horseback surrounded by iron machetes, as well as a galvanised steel monument to the revolution.

Santiago's architecture is eclectic, offering everything from neoclassical to art deco. The pastel-hued buildings are in better shape than those in most Cuban towns. The Cementerio Sant Ifigenia, northwest of town, contains José Martí's mausoleum; inside, a statue of Martí – surrounded by six statues of women meant to represent 19th-century Cuba's six provinces – has been positioned to receive a shaft of sun all morning.

If you have a car, take the coastal road along the Sierra Maestra, checking out the deserted, black sand beaches. High points include **El Uvero▶**, about 65km west of Santiago, with a museum commemorating an early battle in the revolution; and **Pico Turquino▶** (reached via a turn-off 20km west of El Uvero), the highest peak in the Sierra Maestra at almost 1,830m. The road continues to Pilon; in the 1950s, Castro's revolution began in this area and there are sites devoted to those days.

Casa de Cultura in Cienfuegos

EL COBRE
About 9km west of Santiago lies El Sanctuario de Nuestra Senora de la Caridad del Cobre, or "El Cobre", the shrine to Cuba's patron saint, built above a copper mine. There's a legend attached, but more compelling is the idyllic setting in the Sierra Maestra. To get there hire a car from Santiago.

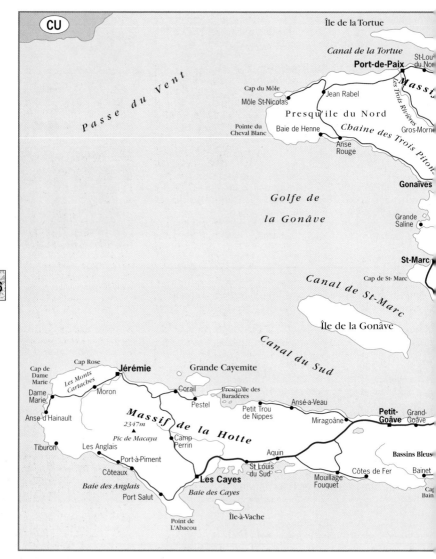

Haiti

Only 30 years ago, Haiti's excellent beaches, sophisticated hotels and proximity to the US made it one of the area's top holiday destinations. Since then, however, the political situation has become tense, with outbreaks of violence. Instability is the norm and Haiti cannot be recommended as a tourist destination at present. When things calm down again, by all means go. Few countries contain such striking contrasts of devastating poverty and luxurious lifestyles, hardship and hope. Travel there is a bombardment of the senses: the primitivist art, adorning buildings, walls and vehicles; the cramped, brightly painted buses and trucks, called *tap taps* (after the noise

BUCCANEERS
Buccaneers were
runaways from many
European nations who
crept into the remote west
of Hispaniola in the early
17th century. Renowned
as riflemen, they survived
by wandering the plains
killing wild cattle. The
meat was smoked over a
boucan, from which their
name derives. Later, working from a stronghold on
the Ile de la Tortue off the
north coast of Haiti, they
became pirates, known as
the Brethren of the Coast.

*Crowds in the streets of
Port-au-Prince*

made by the original trucks), with their carved wood and
religious maxims displayed along the sides and scenes
from the Bible on the hoods; the strange world of voodoo;
and the ceaseless hubbub of the markets. Love it or hate it,
there is nowhere in the world like Haiti.

This is not an easy island for travellers. White visitors
are particularly targetted with constant demands for
money, from people who are genuinely in dire need.
Haiti's currency is the gourde (five gourdes make a *dollar
haïtien*), named after the large, hard-shelled fruit of the
calabash tree and introduced by the country's despotic
leader, Henry Christophe, in the early 19th century.

Most flights from Europe and the US go to Miami for
connections to the main airport at the capital, Port-au-
Prince. Haiti's capital lies in the southwest, in the deep

A multicoloured tap tap

bight of the Golfe de la Gonâve. It is a buzzing city of over one million inhabitants, many of whom live in the shanty towns that cluster around the main town. There are good places to stay in Pétionville, the prosperous suburb above the capital, well priced now in their faded grandeur, not forgetting the beach hotels on the Côte des Arcadins about an hour north of Port-au-Prince. There is also a clutch of good restaurants.

Haiti occupies the western third (27,750sq km) of the island of Hispaniola, which it shares with the Dominican Republic. "Haiti", the original Amerindian name for the island, meaning "mountainous land", is an accurate description. Shaped like a crab's claw closing round the Golfe de la Gonâve, it is about 144km north to south and has two long mountainous ranges that stretch west like pincers towards Cuba and Jamaica. The highest peak is the Pic de la Selle (2,680m), in the southeast. The country is fertile and there is a variety of scenery: palm-backed beaches (the closest to Port-au-Prince are Ibo beach and Kyona; Cormier and Labadie are found outside Cap-Haïtien); cactus-covered plains and rain-forested mountains. However, in a country of around 6 million mainly rural inhabitants, deforestation and soil erosion have now become a serious problem.

Religious and nationalist graffiti, Port-au-Prince

HISTORY Haiti has a history of turmoil. The first 40 European settlers, left there in 1492 by Columbus, all died within a year. In 1697 the French were handed control of western Hispaniola (then called Saint Domingue) by the Spanish and made it an immensely wealthy colony, exporting sugar, coffee and indigo. At the end of the 18th century, after years of torture and starvation at the hands of their colonial masters, the African slaves finally rebelled, led by Toussaint l'Ouverture. In 1804 Haiti declared itself independent – the world's first black republic. Its political life since then has been troubled:

civil war between the north and the south was followed by a succession of tyrannical leaders and US invasion in 1915. The Americans left in 1934 and in 1957 François Duvalier, "Papa Doc", became the ruthless dictator, maintaining his grip on power through the notorious secret police, the *tontons macoute*. His son, Jean Claude ("Baby Doc") continued the reign of terror and corruption until, in the mid-1980s, a movement of revolt known as Operation Deschoukay drove him out of the country.

Haiti has continued to suffer political instability, which has been characterised by a series of coups d'états, failed elections and politicans who are unable to maintain a grip on this troubled nation despite American intervention, as in the case of Jean-Bartrand Aristide in the mid-1990s.

ISLAND LIFE Ordinary islanders, most of whom work on the land, have suffered the consequences of corrupt and repressive government and Haiti is now the poorest country in the western hemisphere. The majority of its population is descended from Africans; many of the small and powerful "mulatto élite" emigrated during recent troubles. French is the official language and its influence can be heard in the everyday spoken language, Kreyol.

Haiti has an amazingly vibrant artistic and religious life. Its primitive-style art, with primary colours and almost cartoon-like forms, has been copied all over the Caribbean. Many of the traditional themes of Haitian life are portrayed, including agricultural, biblical and voodoo scenes. Voodoo itself is a mix of Catholic and African beliefs, often sensationalised as "black magic", and running deep in the Haitian psyche. Haiti has its own dance rhythm – compas – which fills the streets during Carnival, from 6 January to Mardi Gras, before Lent. This is the best time to witness the extraordinary spirit of the Haitians, which survives despite years of insecurity and hardship. When stability returns to Haiti, it will hopefully resume its deserved place among the most interesting and popular Caribbean destinations.

THE BLACK JACOBINS
One of the far-reaching effects of the French Revolution was to bring to a head the tensions of Haitian society in the late 18th century. Political rights, granted in theory to the mixed race population by the French National Assembly, were denied within the colony and violence erupted. In 1791 the black population, who had suffered appallingly as slaves to the white colonists, themselves rebelled and the country was split between those of mixed race living in the south and the northern blacks (where Toussaint l'Ouverture rose to prominence). The story of Toussaint l'Ouverture and the Haitian revolution is told in CLR James's powerful book, *The Black Jacobins*. Published in 1938, this was an influential work at a time when British West Indians were re-assessing their history and turning their minds towards independence.

179

Fishing off the north coast town of Cap-Haïtien

Voodoo calls up sinister images: candle-lit ceremonies of dancing, chanting and mesmeric drum rhythms; initiates in trances flailing around, intoning predictions, eating hot coals, or making animal sacrifices. There is an element of truth in these images, but voodoo should not be written off as "black magic". Widely misunderstood outside Haiti, voodoo has a deeply rooted role in everyday island life.

DUPPIES

Duppies, also known as jumbies, are the wandering souls of the dead. People who die unhappy or without a proper wake are said to become restless spirits, returning to haunt those who knew them in life. Belief in duppies is widespread and even educated people who otherwise disregard obeah will acknowledge their existence.

Haiti is not the only island where voodoo is practised. Other forms of the religion exist elsewhere: santería, across the border in Santo Domingo and in Cuba; pocomania, in Jamaica; and shango, in Trinidad. In these parts of the Caribbean, however, the beliefs are gradually dying out, while in Haiti voodoo continues to touch everyone's life and was particularly prevalent in the days of Papa Doc, who made himself a high priest of voodoo.

Like a number of the Caribbean systems of belief, voodoo has mixed African and European origins. All have a common theme in their appeals to spirits to intervene in life on earth. Spirits, or Iwas, are summoned, in drumming and dance, to "mount" a follower, who then falls into a trance, taking on the spirit's characteristics, dancing and speaking in tongues or making predictions. The

A voodoo ceremony, by Gérard Valcin

ZOMBIES

There is "evidence" in Haiti of people turned into zombies ("undead" souls) while still alive. A poison is believed to reduce their metabolic rate so that they appear dead. After burial, they are supposedly exhumed, revived and then used as slaves.

worship of spirits was originally brought by slaves from Africa and merged with Caribbean beliefs and Catholic saints. In Haitian voodoo the snake god Damballa, who makes his followers dance in a writhing motion, is equivalent to St Patrick, often pictured with snakes at his feet; Ogun, the god of war, whose followers appear to be brandishing swords, is associated with St James and Erzulie is equated with the Virgin Mary. Like the angels of the Christian pantheon, Iwas can be benevolent or vengeful. They come to advise, but they must also be appeased. If times are hard it is because the Iwa is displeased. *Rada* Iwas, such as Erzulie, are known for their wisdom and benevolence; *petro* Iwas, like Tijan Petro, for their power.

Voodoo ceremonies are conducted according to a calendar, which includes important Catholic events; for example, devotees celebrate the appearance of the Virgin Mary at the Ville Bonheur waterfall near Mirebalais on 16 July each year. Here followers, particularly those with problems of love, come to wash themselves in the *Saut d'eau* (waterfall) in order to receive the blessing of Erzulie and the Virgin Mary. The usual setting for a ceremony is a village temple with a mud floor, a *houmfo* and the ceremony proceeds under the direction of a *houngan* (priest) or a *mambo* (priestess). After recitations from the Catholic liturgy, the drums strike up with the special rhythms of the lwa to be invoked. An initiate then traces on the ground the lwa's *véver*, a complex pattern of lines laid out with cornmeal. Eventually a dancer is mounted by an lwa and exhibits his or her characteristics, either making predictions to the community, giving advice or making demands. The lwa will be presented with its favourite food or drink and eventually there may be an animal sacrifice. Followers who have been mounted apparently remember nothing after the event.

It is almost impossible for visitors to Haiti to attend a genuine voodoo ceremony, but occasional shows are held with commentaries; contact Le Péristyle de Mariani, on the outskirts of Port-au-Prince.

Obeah Another feature shared by all the Caribbean beliefs is the use of obeah, or magic, known as *myal* in the British Caribbean and *wango* in Haiti. Obeah men (*bocors* in Haiti) act as advisers and intervene in human affairs through the use of incantations and spells. These may be used to heal a sick person, to ensnare a lover or to settle a score; they may also rid a person of a vengeful duppy (ghost). Spells are set with herbal concoctions and other ingredients, such as blood, sweat, eggshells and broken bottles. Obeah was outlawed in Jamaica as early as 1760, but it is still practiced widely, though secretly, in rural areas all over the Caribbean region.

THE DRUMS OF VOODOO
The driving force behind every voodoo ceremony is the drumming, which engenders a trance and summons a particular lwa. There are three drums of different sizes, each one carved of mahogany; and each lwa has its own particular drum rhythms.

181

OTHER RELIGIONS
Besides the revivalist sects of pocomania and Revival Zion, Jamaica has many spirit-based religions. Kumina is a religion with less European influence than most – probably because it arrived relatively recently, brought by free Africans who came willingly to Jamaica after emancipation in 1838. Kumina appeals to its own zombies, the spirits of ancestors, as well as to the gods of the Congo, its followers' original homeland. Convince is a faith that appeals to the African *bongo* gods and to the spirits of the maroon leaders (see panel, page 147), as does Kromanti. There are similar sects in Trinidad (the Shouters) and in St Lucia (the Kele).

A ritual mask, which is worn by men taken over by female spirits

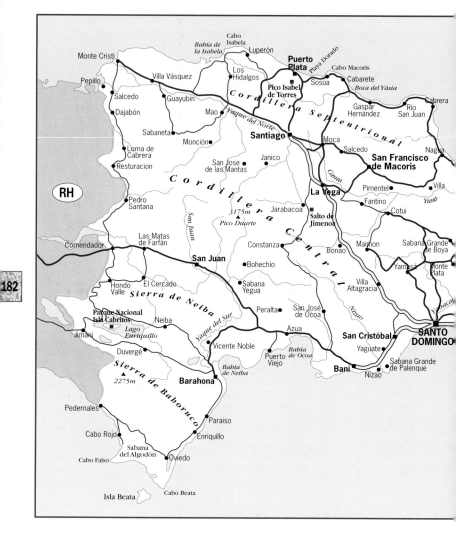

The Dominican Republic

The country Columbus called "the fairest land under heaven" is home to the oldest European settlement in the western hemisphere, but the Dominican Republic has two modern faces. Its glorious beaches, fascinating colonial heritage and mountain-top "resorts" contrast sharply with the grinding poverty of many of its islanders. With its 5,310km shoreline, the Dominican Republic has one of the largest tourist industries in the Caribbean. Most of its hotels are mid-range beach-front resorts, scattered in complexes along the northern and eastern shores, but other options include the luxury Casa de Campo – where polo ponies can be rented – or a hotel in Santo Domingo's historic city centre. The island also has quiet, isolated resort towns, such as Cabarete and Las Terrenas, where you can relax in guesthouses under the palm trees, or

Map labels:
Bahía Escocesa
Cabo Cabrón
Las Terrenas
Las Galeras
Sánchez
Samaná
Bahía de Samaná
Sabana de la Mar
Parque Nacional Los Haitises
Las Cañitas
El Valle
Cordillera Oriental
Batey Papgayo
Bayaguana
Hato Mayor
El Seibo
El Macao
Ramón Santana
Los Llanos
Saco
Higüey
Cabo Engaño
Punta Cana
Careta
Boca Chica
San Pedro de Macoris
La Romana
Altos de Chavón
San Rafael del Yuma
Isla Catalina
Bayahibe
Bahía La Altagracia
Bahía de Yuma
El Algibe
Isla Saona
Canal de la Mona

0 20 40 60 km
0 20 40 miles

QUISQUEYA
Quisqueya was the name used by the indigenous Taino for their island when Columbus arrived in 1492. It is still used as a poetic name for Hispaniola, but principally survives as the name of a locally brewed beer. (Presidente is a lighter and slightly more bitter but tastier local beer.)

183

SANTERIA
Just as the Haitians have voodoo (see page 179) and the British Islands have obeah, so the Latin islands observe santeria, which is a mix of African animist beliefs and Catholic doctrine. There are the same drum-driven ceremonies, animal sacrifices and posses- sions, as well as witchcraft practitioners, who use local plants and other small objects to make their concoctions.

windsurf till you drop. The Dominican Republic is one of the cheaper and better value package tour destinations in the Caribbean and it can be easily reached from the USA and Canada, both by scheduled and charter flights. Cruise ships from the USA stop at Puerto Plata. There are charter

Carvings set up for sale at a Dominican Republic market stall

"Mexican night" at a local restaurant

flights from Europe, although if you are travelling independently you may have to go via Miami or via Spain. Despite the million or so annual visitors to the island, the tourist industry is surprisingly

unobtrusive once you have left the fringe of hotels that run along the coast. In contrast to many of the islands in the Caribbean, which are visibly affected by the industry, the Dominican Republic is large enough to allow independent travel and to maintain a lively local Latin culture. In September 1998 Hurricane Georges hammered the southeastern half of the country causing widespread destruction. However, the tourist infrastructure was swiftly repaired, illustrating its vital importance to the local economy.

One of the best places in the Caribbean to immerse yourself in history is the colonial city in Santo Domingo, the oldest city in the Americas, which enjoyed its heyday in the 16th century when conquistadors came here to plan their voyages to the American mainland. Nowadays you can relax in the bars and restaurants of the 12-block Colonial Zone surrounded by the architectural glories of the Spanish era. This is a Latin American island, full of surprises. Merengue music is heard everywhere; if you get on a bus, you might find the passengers singing along. Islanders gather on the plazas in the late evening to take in the cooler air; and they love to dance, so the clubs are always popular meeting places.

LA ISABELLA

Santo Domingo was not the first of the "New World" towns. La Isabella, named after the Spanish queen, was settled by 1,000 willing adventurers in 1493 on Columbus' second voyage. The site is near Luperon on the north coast, but there are only archeological remains now. The colonists moved to Santo Domingo's present site in 1498 because La Isabella, set among malarial swamps, was unhealthy and riches beckoned after gold was found nearer Hispaniola's southern shore.

184

The Dominican Republic occupies the eastern two-thirds of the island of Hispaniola – a contraction of *La Isla Española*, as Columbus called it when he landed in 1492 (Haiti claims the western third of the island, ceded to French rule by the Spaniards in 1697). At 48,600sq km, it is the second largest country in the Caribbean after Cuba; geographically, it is the most extreme. Topping the massive Cordillera Central, Pico Duarte (3,176m) is the tallest mountain in the West Indies and in the southwest, Lago Enriquillo is a lake set in the lowest point of land, 35m below sea level. It encircles arid, thorny islands that serve as a protected sanctuary to exotic birds and reptiles, such as the flamingo, the iguana and the indigenous caimen (a kind of crocodile).

In the north there are rampantly fertile mountains with crashing rivers; in the south, on the Barahona peninsula, there is desert. The greater part of the country has seemingly endless stretches of bright green hillsides and cane fields, spiked with magnificent royal palm trees.

ISLAND LIFE The 7.5 million or so Dominicans are of mixed African and European blood, with a strong Amerindian influence, dating from the early days of colonial settlement and recognisable in many Dominicans' distinctive straight, dark hair. This is a desperately poor nation; its poverty is particularly evident in the countryside and on the outskirts of the main towns, where many people live in makeshift shanty flats. The limited public services break down on a regular basis (big hotels have their own power plants). Since there is no social safety

DOMINICAN DISHES
Comida Criolla, or Créole food, as local dishes are known, includes a wide range of meats: beef, farmed by *campesinos* (cowboys) in the southeast, pork, goat (*chivo*) and chicken. These are served in rather heavy but tasty dishes such as stew, *sancocho*, which is made with a variety of meats and *mondongo*, made with tripe. Seafood and fish are popular, as are many tropical vegetables, including plantains and cassava.

185

Fruit-sellers lay out their wares on the roadside in a Dominican Republic market

Windsurfers at the luxury resort of Casa de Campo

FRESH FRUIT MILK SHAKES

Dominicans use their fruit to the best advantage in freshly prepared drinks. *Jugo* is plain squeezed fruit juice served with ice, but the best drinks are *bastidas*, squeezed fruits whisked up with milk and ice. Flavours include *piña* (pineapple), *china* (orange), *lechola* (pawpaw) and *guanabana* (soursop).

MERENGUE

The national rhythm of the Dominican Republic is the merengue, a strongly Latin and impossibly quick beat. You will hear it played by local string bands and in the clubs, where dancers exercise their elastic legs, racing across the dance floor in a close embrace. There is a merengue festival in Santo Domingo each year, in the third week of July, when bands and dancers fill the streets.

net, life can be extremely hard for the islanders, some of whom endeavour to escape to the USA. This journey is a notoriously dangerous one, however, often undertaken in inadequate, leaking boats.

The Dominican Republic throws the contrasts of Caribbean tourism into the sharpest relief. With so many prosperous tourists passing through, opportunists have inevitably come to regard them as walking dispensers of dollars and outside the tourist complexes you will probably be hassled for money. There is considerable prostitution – "sex tourism" has now become an established trade in some places – and unsurprisingly there is an increasing incidence of AIDS.

The Dominican Republic has a troubled political tradition, which has hit ordinary Dominicans hard. Throughout the 19th century, control of the island lurched from one ruling power to another, as Spanish, Haitians, Americans and Dominican independence fighters battled for supremacy. Independence finally came in 1844, but the country soon fell into the hands of despots and slid into bankruptcy.

The USA sent troops to administer the country between 1916 and 1924, to a mixed reception from islanders, who longed for stability but resented military rule. In 1930 General Rafael Leonidas Trujillo, the Dominican army's commander, established a ruthless dictatorship. He ruled the country for the next 30 years, treating it as his own personal estate, organising the "disappearance" of countless opponents and rifling through the treasury.

Trujillo was assassinated in 1961 and there followed a series of coups, civil war and military intervention by the US. Elections were held in 1966, and after a rocky start, the political scene has remained on a fairly stable, pro-US footing for 30 years.

The official language of the country is Spanish with English spoken in tourist areas.

►►► Altos de Chavón

Altos de Chavón is near the eastern town of La Romana, attached to the Dominican Republic's premier resort, the huge and luxurious Casa de Campo. The "Heights of Chavón", standing high above the Chavón river, is a pretty replica of a medieval Spanish hilltop town. The village has a slightly unreal feel, for the 30 or so coral-rock houses are so obviously imitations. But many parts of the village are festooned with colourful bougainvillea blooms, there are quaint cobbled streets and artful wrought-iron balconies, which all in all makes this a pleasant and satisfying place to spend an afternoon or evening. It is partly an artists' colony, so shopping here for crafts and art in the galleries and workshops is a treat.

As well as the history and archaeology museum, there are good restaurants and bars. The attractive church of St Stanislaus can be visited and there is a 5,000-seat amphitheatre where concerts are staged. Visiting performers have included Julio Iglesias and Frank Sinatra, who sang for the inaugural concert. There are also fabulous views of the Chavón river valley, particularly when it is lit up at night. Buses connect Altos de Chavón with Casa de Campo.

►► Cordillera Central

The Cordillera Central is the Dominican Republic's highest and most beautiful mountain range, running through the centre of the country from the northwest down towards the capital. It contains the highest mountain in the Caribbean, the Pico Duarte (3,176m). To hike to the summit takes three days from the town of La Ciénaga. Make sure you take a guide and all the food you need for the trip. Although the lower mountains are covered in royal palm trees, the pine-clad heights are tall enough to have frost; the steep, fertile valleys (where un-Caribbean fruits such as strawberries and apples prosper) are cut by cold waters from the mountains above. The towns of Constanza and Jarabacoa are cool hillside retreats, popular with visitors from the capital who regard them as an escape from the heat below. Look for the waterfalls of Aguas Blancas 18km from Constanza and the 30m Jimenoa Falls near Jarabacoa.

NEW COMMUNITIES
As well as the community of German and Austrian Jewish refugees who were granted sanctuary in Sosúa on the north coast in the 1930s (see page 188), Trujillo invited a community of Japanese farmers in the 1950s, offering them land in return for passing on their farming skills. Some of their descendants still live and work around Constanza.

187

Tourist hotels and tropical greenery: the north coast resort of Sosúa

BEACHES

There are fine beaches on the Amber Coast. The resorts are clustered around protected bays, where palm-backed sand shelves gently into the sea and these are the best places to go for watersports. Sosúa gets very crowded, but further on there are long strips of deserted sand, battered by the Atlantic waves and winds. Cabarete is renowned for windsurfing and also has a fine beach.

AMBER

Amber is the national gem of the Dominican Republic, which has some of the world's largest amber reserves and a large mining area in the Cordillera Septentrional. Strictly speaking amber is not a stone, but is the sap from trees, which has solidified over millions of years. The youngest is the lightest in colour and can be almost translucent; it is graded by colour, through rich yellow to red. The most valuable are pieces with prehistoric insects or leaves preserved within them. Be wary of pieces offered to you on the streets; these may be plastic.

►► Puerto Plata and the Amber Coast

The Amber Coast, on the north shore, has the greatest concentration of Dominican tourism. Here, several hotel complexes cater to package tourists who fly into the international airport near Puerto Plata, but the seaside villages of Sosúa and Cabarete, with excellent beaches, have bars and guesthouses that are ideal for independent travellers. Puerto Plata itself has a strong Dominican life. Attractive old Créole houses still stand in the town and the squares, with shady trees and benches, come alive in the late afternoons with old gents and salesmen selling lottery tickets. There are just a couple of hotels on the rocky seafront, but the town has a number of good restaurants and bars (see pages 282). The **Amber Museum►►** (tel: 586 2848. *Open* Mon–Sat 9–5. *Admission: inexpensive*), in a grand town house with classical balustrades and columns, has exhibits explaining the origin and mining process of the gem. A cable car takes passengers 800m to the top of Mount Isabel de Torres, just south of the town; its running times are unpredictable, but hotels will usually arrange seats for visitors. A statue of Christ dominates the magnificent view of the coast and the Cordillera Septentrional.

Playa Dorado is a purpose-built resort, a collection of hotels to the east of the town. It is set on a superb beach, where there are watersports and a good beach bar, but this is private and reserved for hotel guests. The resort town of **Sosúa►►** is split into two parts, set on either side of the lively Sosúa beach: Los Charramícos is the westerly, more Dominican half; El Batey has a stronger European influence, a legacy of the wave of Austrian and German Jewish refugees who came here fleeing the Holocaust (several restaurants still serve Austrian and German food). Here you will also find some of the best local restaurants and small hotels.

One of the best resorts on the island, **Cabarete►►►** is a lazy seaside town with palm-thatch garden bars and beachside restaurants, patronised by windsurfers; the Windsurfing World Championships are occasionally held here. Beyond Cabarete, the beaches continue, on and off, for several kilometres along the north coast.

Restaurant in Puerto Plata

The Dominican Republic's landscape is graced by thousands of royal palm trees, soaring up to 50m from the ground and exploding into bushy palm fronds. Dominicans who travel away from home will often say that they miss the royal palm most of all.

Around 2,600 species of palm trees and shrubs grow in the tropics and subtropics, varying in height from 15cm to 60m. Palm trees do not have branches, but their fronds, which can be up to 9m in length, emerge in sequence at the top of each stem, pointing vertically at first and gradually leaning to the side as younger fronds push them aside.

The coconut palm As well as being the quintessential Caribbean palm, the coconut is the most useful and versatile. Almost all of its parts can be used: the fronds in thatch and the trunk in building; in the past, the husk of the coconut was used to weave ropes and mats; coconut flesh is eaten and copra (dried coconut flesh) can be used to make oil for washing or burning. Coconut milk, a popular drink, has even been used as an intravenous fluid. In all the Caribbean islands, you will find vendors

THE PALMCHAT
Native to Hispaniola, the palmchat is the national bird of the Dominican Republic. It has a greenish-brown coat and a white breast with dark streaking and lives and feeds in flocks. Its communal nest has separate compartments for up to 30 pairs and is built on the trunk of the royal palm.

189

who will slice the top off a coconut (usually with a machete) to allow you to drink the liquid inside.

The royal palm This most stately and magnificent of palms grows throughout the Caribbean and is Cuba's national tree. It can stand up to 50m high, with a smooth trunk as much as 1m thick, and a bushy crown of fronds. The heart of the royal palm is used in salads and its fruit is used for animal feed.

Other palms The cabbage palm is similar in appearance to the royal palm, although it grows only to about 40m. Known as the *palma cana* in Spanish, the latania palm, with fan-like fronds, is used for weaving, particularly in St Barts. The ornamental golden palm is a bright green bush that appears in many Caribbean gardens, and the fishtail palm bears fruit that can be distilled into alcohol.

Picture-postcard views – palms and perfect water in the Dominican Republic

PALM AVENUES
Royal palms and cabbage palms are often planted to form beautiful avenues. Some of the best are the Allée Dumanoir, on Basse-Terre in Guadeloupe and the driveway that leads to Codrington College in Barbados (see page 220).

Dawn at Las Terrenas, Samaná peninsula

BEACHES
On the northern side of the Samaná peninsula strips of golden sand stretch either side of Las Terrenas, and hotels rent out water sports equipment. On Samaná Bay itself you can arrange to visit Cayo Levantado, an offshore island, or make your way up to Las Galeras, a small beach resort in the northeast.

LARIMAR
The Dominican Republic has a unique variety of turquoise, known locally as Larimar. This hard, light-blue stone, sold as jewellery throughout the country, is mined in the Bahoruco mountains on the southwestern Barahona peninsula.

▶▶▶ Samaná

In the isolated northeast, the lush Samaná peninsula is somewhat off the beaten track, but it is worth making the effort to get there to spend some time in the town of Las Terrenas, the island's best resort. Set on the northern shore of the peninsula across a ridge of mountains, Las Terrenas has golden sand swept by low-hanging palms. There is an easy-going feel to the place, with its string of thatched restaurants, candle-lit at night, and its few excellent hotels and guesthouses. It makes an ideal backdrop to an afternoon spent listening to a Dominican string band (guitar, soul-comb, cheese-grater and sit-on beat-box).

Set on the huge Samaná Bay (named Golfo de las Flechas, or Gulf of Arrows, by Columbus after the local Carib Indians showered him with arrows), the town of Samaná itself is not very attractive, although it has a few guesthouses and a collection of good restaurants on the waterfront. You can arrange to see the **whales**▶▶▶ that collect offshore early in the year (from January to March); try your hand at deep-sea fishing; visit the offshore island of Cayo Levantado, where there is a good beach and some facilities; and escape to the **Los Haïtises National Park**▶▶, where among the limestone caves and mangroves you can see terns, jacanas and ibises. At Las Galeras, in the northeast, there is a good beach with a couple of quiet hotels.

▶ Santiago

You may only mean to pass through Santiago, which is the country's second city, but it makes a good traveller's stop. It is a working city set on the cliffs above the Yaque river in the Cibao Valley, one of the country's most fertile regions. It is worth noting that the hustlers are not as active here as they are in the tourist resorts, so the chance to "escape" may appeal. At the **Museo Tomás Morel del Arte Folklorico**▶▶ you can see exhibits of local arts and crafts and also the carnival masks worn at religious festivals.

Sugar was such a valuable commodity during the 17th and 18th centuries that it became known as "white gold". Empires were built on the sugar trade; whole islands were planted with sugar cane, and navies were sent to capture and defend them. Meanwhile, the planters grew rich and their African slaves lived and laboured in miserable subjection.

Sugar cane (*Saccharum officinarum*) is an overgrown grass. It grows to about 3.5m, can be a green or deep purple colour, and takes 18 months to mature, blooming with a tall, white, wispy ear. Cane fields are sometimes burned to rid the canes of their corn-like leaves, creating enormous columns of smoke that are visible for some distance.

Cane-cutting is gruelling work. In colonial times, teams of cutters would work in lines, led by singers and drummers and swinging their machetes in time to the music. Once the cane was cut, other gangs carted it off to the mill. The cane-cutting season lasted for about six months, ending in July; the annual Barbados carnival, Cropover, and the zafra in Cuba, are survivors of the end-of-season celebrations.

The River Antoine Rum Distillery's sugar mill, Grenada

Technology has advanced from mule-driven mills to wind-driven equipment and finally steam-driven crushing machinery, but sugar production has remained basically unchanged for 350 years. Canes are cut to length and passed repeatedly through metal rollers, so that the juice runs away and the pulp, or bagasse, emerges dry. Bagasse burns well and is used to fire the engines that drive the rollers. The cane juice is clarified in the boiling house in huge copper boiling pans (which are also heated with bagasse). As it cools, the sugar crystallises into granules. Nowadays the sugar is passed through a centrifuge, separating the crystals from the molasses, which is itself used as animal feed and for distilling rum.

In the mid-19th century, the successful development of sugar beet in Europe as a viable alternative to cane sugar began to threaten the West Indian trade, and now only a few islands cultivate sugar crops in any quantity. The biggest in the Caribbean are Cuba and the Dominican Republic, while Jamaica runs in at a fairly distant third place.

SUGAR LOAF
Sugar loaf mountains can be found all over the English-speaking world. They take their name from their steep-sided shape, which resembles the "loaf" of early sugar manufacture. Wet processed sugar would be placed in a mould like an inverted pyramid and allowed to drain, so that the brown molasses would seep to the bottom and white sugar crystals would be left at the top. When the mold was broken, a pyramid-shaped "loaf" of sugar was revealed.

Other Caribbean states

FRANCIS DRAKE

Francis Drake was something of a scourge around Santo Domingo. He first came to the Caribbean in 1565, on a voyage with Sir John Hawkins selling African slaves to the Spaniards and later returned to pursue the more profitable action of attacking and ransoming their settlements. Drake captured Santo Domingo in 1586, setting up his headquarters in the cathedral and ransacking it for any loot he could lay his hands on. After gaining fame in Britain for his defeat of the Spanish Armada in 1588, Drake eventually died of dysentery off Porto Bello in Panama, in 1595.

COLUMBUS'S LIGHTHOUSE

The Faro a Colón has been dogged by bad luck since its construction was first suggested a century ago. It was eventually built to designs submitted to a competition in 1929 by a British architect, J Gleave. The project was adopted by Trujillo in the 1930s and then abandoned because it was so expensive. In 1987 the lighthouse became the personal project of President Balaguer, who spent vast amounts of his poor country's reserves building it. It is the butt of many sarcastic jokes among Dominicans; when the lighthouse is lit, it drains electricity from the rest of the city. More imposing than attractive, it contains six museums and (it is said) the explorer's remains (tel: 591 1492. *Open* Tue–Sun 10–5. *Admission: inexpensive*).

▶▶▶ Santo Domingo

Santo Domingo, the island's capital and largest city, is the oldest surviving European settlement in the Americas. Its heart is the colonial city, on the bank of the Ozama river on the island's southern shore, but La Capital, as it is known, has expanded enormously over the centuries and now has around 2 million inhabitants. It has all the problems of fast-growing cities in poor countries: congestion, inadequate electricity and water supplies, and grinding poverty. But there is also a compelling Latin vibrancy here – best seen on the **Avenida del Puerto**▶▶▶, as crowds gather for their evening promenade.

Hidden by its ancient walls above the Avenida del Puerto, the **colonial city of Santo Domingo**▶▶▶ is a calm enclave, with coral-rock alleyways and shady courtyards. Its most impressive building is the **Alcazar de Colón**▶▶▶ (tel: 687 5361. *Open* Mon, Wed–Fri 9–5, Sat 9–1. *Admission: inexpensive*), just inside the city walls. Built in 1514 for Columbus's son Diego as his vice-regal palace, the solid stone house is fronted by a double row of arches; its interior has been restored in suitable period style. Ranged before it are the viceroy's administrative buildings, the **Atarazana**▶▶. Dating from 1507, these once contained the colonial armoury and customs houses; they now house a collection of craft shops and art galleries, restaurants and a couple of bars. The city's oldest surviving building is the Casa del Cordón (1503), which is now a bank, and can be found across the street from the post office; look for the Franciscan order's cord motif, which is carved above the door.

From the Alcazar the city walls lead to **Calle de las Damas**▶▶, named after colonial ladies who would promenade here. Set in the former colonial offices, the **Museo de las Casas Reales**▶▶ (tel: 682 4202. *Open* Tue–Sat 9–4:45, Sun 10–1. *Admission: inexpensive*) displays exhibits from early Spanish colonial times, including suits of armour and wall maps. The imposing **Panteon Nacional**▶ (*Open* Mon–Sat 10–5. *Admission free*), guards an eternal flame that commemorates Duarte, Sánchez and Mella, the national heroes who formed the under-

ground independence movement La Trinitaria during the Haitian occupation in the 1830s and eventually won independence for the Republic in 1844. Further along the street are the cool, quiet palace courtyard of the **Casa de Bastidas▶▶** and the **Fortaleza Ozama▶**, a fortress whose cannons have now been set in peaceful gardens.

The Plaza de Toledo alley leads into the Parque Colón, Columbus Square, where a statue of the explorer overlooks benches and trees. On the southern side of the square is the **Catedral Santa María la Menor, Primada de America▶▶**, the oldest cathedral in the Americas. Completed in 1523, the cathedral, with its pointed battlements, was said to be the burial place of Columbus until his remains were moved to the Faro a Colón in honour of the quincentennial celebrations in 1992 – although there are rival claims from Cuba and Spain. The cathedral is guarded but you can usually go in to visit, where you will see a bishop's throne made of mahogany.

From the Parque Colón, El Conde, one of the city's busiest shopping streets, leads up to the **Parque Independencia▶▶**, the chaotic hub of the modern city. All distances in the country are measured from here. Behind the old city gates are the imposing memorial and sunken mausoleum dedicated to Duarte, Mella and Sánchez. Leading off the square, the Avenida Mella is another shopping street, where you will find the Mercado Modelo, the lively market. To the south is the **Malecon▶▶**, the palm-lined seafront boulevard where Dominicans like to take the evening air.

Inland, the landscaped expanses of the **Plaza de la Cultura▶** house the National Theatre, the National Library and Modern Art Gallery and two museums. Despite its rather dull appearance, it is worth visiting the Museum of the Dominican Man, where exhibits trace the history of Caribbean Indians and their customs. Visually more impressive is the **Palacio Nacional▶**, a baroque palace built by the dictator Trujillo on Calle Dr Delgado.

On the city's northwestern outskirts, the **Jardín Botánico Nacional▶▶** (tel: 687 6211. *Open* Tue–Sun 9–5. *Admission: inexpensive*) has an orchid house and an aquatic plant house of flowering lilies. In the eastern suburbs, the **Faro a Colón▶▶** is a 30m lighthouse built in the shape of a cross as a monument to Columbus (see panel opposite).

BOCA CHICA

Boca Chica is a lively tourist town about 32km east of Santo Domingo. Popular with Dominicans, it gets busy at weekends; there are a number of small guesthouses and flats here and many restaurants and bars near the beachfront.

EL CONUCO

This lively Santo Domingo restaurant on Calle Casimiro de Moya, decorated with palm thatch and gravel, is based on the theme of *conuco* (the country). Ancient farming tools are hung on the walls among old wives' sayings carved on wood. Meals are local country fare – mainly tripe and stews, but there are less daunting options (such as Créole-flavoured chicken and plantains in batter) and the waiters, dressed up as *campesinos* (cowboys), in boots, jeans and bandanas, have been known to dart off in the middle of taking an order and start dancing.

Alcazar de Colón

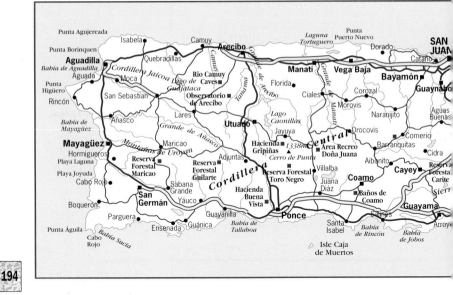

Puerto Rico

With good communications and plenty of hotels, you'll find Puerto Rico easy and attractive to explore. San Juan can claim to be the best preserved Spanish colonial city in the Caribbean and has a lively cultural and artistic life; the southwest has the best beaches and quieter accommodation. As a semi-autonomous commonwealth territory of the USA, Puerto Rico is well known to American travellers. It is easy to reach – flights from Miami, New York and several other US cities land at San Juan's Luis Muñoz Marin airport, as do flights from Canada, and European airlines connect at New York. It also has a large, well-organised tourist industry; the beaches around San Juan are as developed as those in Miami and Old San Juan, seven beautifully restored blocks of 18th-century colonial buildings, has become one of the Caribbean's foremost cruise ship destinations. But there is far more to Puerto Rico than the tourist circuit. As well as a vibrant culture, the island offers endless exploration in its rain forests, caves, mountains and

Billboards are everywhere on the streets of Puerto Rico

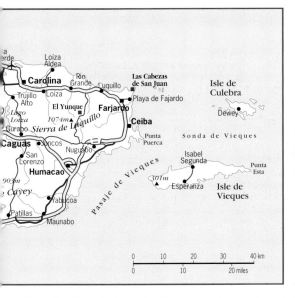

PUERTO RICAN EATING
San Juan serves food from all over the world, but do not miss out on the local dishes. Many are based on rice, including *arroz con pollo* (spiced chicken and rice) and *asopao*, like a paella. Seafood is often spiced with traditional flavourings: *sofrito* (onion, garlic and pepper) and *adobo* (lemon, garlic, salt and spices). Side dishes include *mofongo* (spiced and battered plantain) and *yuca frita* (spiced cassava with cloves and parsley).

hidden beaches, the best of which are on the southwest coast and the two sleepy offshore islands of Vieques and Culebra. The entire island can be circumnavigated on a highway that touches the coast at several resorts and passes through secondary towns such as Arecibo, Aguadilla, Mayagüez and Ponce, each of which has an airport. A highway crosses the eastern part of the island from San Juan to Ponce on the south coast and many secondary roads run into the interior.

The most easterly of the Greater Antilles, Puerto Rico lies 1,600km southeast of Miami and is almost rectangular in shape – 177km in length and about 60km from north to south with a range of mountains running

TREE FROGS
The call of the coquí, a favourite Puerto Rican variety of tree frog, is almost synonymous with the tropical night. About 3cm long and with over-large eyes, tree frogs can be heard in every Carib-bean island (each species has a slightly different call) and they are particularly noisy at night and just after it has rained.

through the centre of the island from east to west. The range marks a distinct division of climate: on the north side there is rain forest and the rain in the northwest has created amazing karst cave systems (see page 200); in the south, the land is mainly dry and cactus-covered.

HISTORY Although it was visited by Columbus during his second voyage to the Americas in 1493, Puerto Rico was not settled by Europeans until 1508, when an expedition from Santo Domingo was led by Juan Ponce de Léon, who became the island's first Governor. Having first exploited and then defeated the native Tainos Indians, Ponce de Léon died in Cuba on a search for the Fountain of Youth. His bones were brought to San Juan and eventually laid in San Juan Cathedral.

For the next 300 years, Puerto Rico's settlers suffered constant invasion – from Caribs, pirates and raiding European armies. After decades of neglect by its mother country, the colony was revived by a Spanish envoy in the 18th century and trade from its sugar exports began to pick up. A new constitution was granted in 1812 and an independence movement started to emerge, only to be ruthlessly put down by a succession of Spanish military governors. An uprising in 1868 that led to the first declaration of a republic was soon put down by the

A fire engine and filigree ironwork in the restored Ponce fire station

THE US CONNECTION
Puerto Ricans have formed large communities on the American main-land, particularly in New York, where they are known as Nuyoricans. The island has special Treasury laws, according to which the islanders do not pay Federal taxes and therefore are not represented in Congress.

Spanish, but in 1897 autonomy was finally granted. Before the new government could fulfil its role, the USA, at war with Spain, invaded the island and seven months later Puerto Rico was ceded to the Americans. US citizenship was granted to islanders in 1917, but senior government appointments remained in American hands. Initially there was a movement towards independence – a 1937 rally ended in 19 deaths after police shot at the protestors. In 1952 the island became a Commonwealth of the USA and recent political debate has revolved around the question of whether Puerto Rico should become the 51st State of the Union. One of the obvious benefits of the American connection is Puerto Rico's prosperity, in comparison with nearby islands.

The 17th-century Cathedral of Our Lady of Guadeloupe on the main square in Ponce

THE *GUAYABERA*

Predictably, American fashions have come to Puerto Rico in a big way, but the traditional dress for men on the island is the *guayabera*. Shaped rather like a jacket or an extended shirt, this is worn as the outer garment over an undershirt or T-shirt. Most are made of cotton and are worn during the day, but there is a more formal version for evening wear, made with pineapple fibre. The *guayabera* is usually embellished with patterned embroidery, running in stripes down the chest.

197

Puerto Rico took a big wallop from Hurricane Georges in September 1998, but the US connection turned the disaster into an economic boom, with $3.5 billion in aid pouring in to repair the 50,000 houses destroyed or severely damaged. The tourist industry was largely unaffected and all hotel damage was quickly repaired.

ISLAND LIFE American and Latin American culture live side by side in Puerto Rico and often meet in an incongruous mix. Both English and Spanish are widely used – Spanish is the official language of Parliament; high-rise, air-conditioned office buildings tower over traditional Caribbean markets; cable TV, fast-food and American cars are all a way of life, but so are roadside stalls and, away from the larger towns, a simple, rural existence. Like most West Indians, the 3.9 million Puerto Ricans constitute a racial mix and include Africans, Spaniards, Italians and Lebanese. They are strongly Catholic and their most important festivals, the *fiestas patronales* (Saints' Days celebrations) combine a devout faith with the compulsion to dance – particularly to the salsa, a racing beat led by brass and African drums. Held by each individual town, the *fiestas* have costume balls, parades, picnics and fairs; perhaps the most exuberant of them all is the Festival of the Innocents, on 28 December, in which the whole town of Hatillo on the north coast becomes a costumed brawl. Music festivals are held throughout the year featuring different styles of island music, such as the *danza*, the *plena* and the *seis*.

Puerto Rico has a strong culinary tradition. Many dishes are based on rice, but plantains are also used as a staple in *mofongo* and *piñon* (see panel, page 195). Daytime snacks can often be bought at the roadside fruit stalls – try *alcapurria* and *bacalao* (crab and codfish batter balls) or *empañadas* and *picadillos* (meat- or cheese-filled sandwiches).

The most popular island pastimes are baseball and cock-fighting (see page 209).

Festival of the Innocents at Hatillo, on the north coast near Arecibo

*Hacienda Gripiñas –
colonial-style hotels on
an old coffee plantation
high in the Cordillera
Central*

ARECIBO OBSERVATORY
The Arecibo Observatory is
an impressive sight: a
bright white dish, 396m
across, neatly cupped in a
karst sinkhole. It listens
to waves across the
spectrum and bounces
them back to the massive
recording gear that hangs
198m above the dish
itself (there is a two-
storey building up there,
too). The information is
then relayed to the offices
before being sent to
Cornell University for
analysis (tel: 878 2612.
Open Wed–Fri noon–4,
Sat–Sun and holidays
9–4. *Admission:
inexpensive*).

▶▶▶ Cordillera Central

The Cordillera Central, the major mountain range in
Puerto Rico's interior, runs parallel to the coast, splayed
east and west on either side of the island's highest peak,
Cerro de Punta. Running through them is the **ruta
panoramica▶▶▶**, a scenic road stretching over 193km
from coast to coast, taking in forest reserves and waterfalls. It's a long trip (two or three days), particularly if you
stop off to explore, but there are charming mountain
hotels *en route* and good roadside cafés and the journey
reveals a little-known side of Puerto Rico.

The *ruta panoramica* sets off from Maunabo, in the southeast of the island, beyond the tourist resort of Palmas del
Mar. From here it rises into the Cayey mountains and the
Carite Forest Reserve▶, a cool environment with rain
forest and dwarf forest inhabited by 50 species of bird and
then Cayey itself, where it crosses the main San Juan to
Ponce road. It then continues to Aibonito and
Barranquitas, two modern towns in steep-sided valleys.
Close by is the **San Cristobal Canyon▶▶**, an
impressive cleft over 198m deep, where there is
a 30m waterfall. To the south, Coamo is an old
colonial town, founded in 1579; the medicinal
springs to its south were used by the indigenous Indians and later by Ponce de Léon. In the
19th century, they became fashionable as baths;
restored as a modern *parador* (a government-
run inn/hotel; tel 825 2239), they still retain a
period dining room.

Ascending steadily, with magnificent views,
the route continues to Doña Juana Recreational
Centre, where there are 60m falls and on to the
Toro Negro Forest Reserve, a magnificent area
of undeveloped forest where there are trails to
the island's highest point, Cerro de Punta
(1,338m). Just a few kilometres from here is one
of the island's most charming retreats, the
Hacienda Gripiñas▶▶▶ (tel: 828 1717). This
parador, set in the wooden estate house of a former coffee plantation, overlooks the valley and
represents the best of old colonial Puerto Rico.

Although the *ruta panoramica* itself continues
westwards, it is worth making a detour to the
north at the town of Utuado. Beyond another
attractive *parador*, lost in greenery on the shores

of Lago Caonillas, the **Caguana Indian Ceremonial Park**▶▶ (tel: 894 7325. *Open* Wed–Sun 9–4:30. *Admission free*) is set in a valley surrounded by massive peaks. It has a small museum and about 10 *bateyes* – sport and ceremonial grounds used by the indigenous Amerindians. Surrounded by carved stones, they are believed to date from the 9th century but may be even older.

Just to the north of the park, in karst country (see page 200), is the largest radio telescope in the world, the **Arecibo Observatory**▶▶. This 8-hectare dish, owned by Cornell University, fills a whole valley and made the first discovery of quasars. Not far off is the **Río Camuy Cave Park**▶▶ (tel: 898 3100. *Open* Wed–Sun 8–3:45. *Admission: moderate*), a cave system where an introductory lecture is followed by a trolleybus ride and walks through the caves. Thousands of years of dripping rainwater have created impressive stalactites and stalagmites in caverns 50m high. The hillside town of Lares, situated on the southern boundary of karst country, was the setting for a rebellion against Spanish authorities in 1868, revered in Puerto Rican history as the *Gito de Lares* (the Cry of Lares).

Rejoining the *ruta panoramica* itself at Adjuntas, you climb into higher hills, with superb views. The road passes through the Guilarte Forest Reserve (where there are walking trails) and near the Maricao Forest Reserve, with a fish farm and a viewing tower overlooking the entire west coast. Nearby there is another charming parador, the Hacienda Juanita.

From here, the route descends to sea level, arriving at the coast at Mayagüez, the island's third largest town. The **Mayagüez Zoo**▶▶ (tel: 834 8110. *Open* Wed–Sun 9–4. *Admission: moderate*) exhibits animals in open compounds; and a wide range of tropical plants are on view at the **Tropical Agricultural Research Station**▶ (tel: 831 3435. *Open* Mon–Fri 7–4. *Admission: moderate*).

Tourist bus logo

199

Sun and cloud alternate all day in the lush Cordillera Central forest

The Caribbean archipelago runs southeast from the Tropic of Cancer, near the tip of Florida, down to the coast of South America and has an impressive variety of terrain. The islands lie on the join of the Atlantic and Caribbean tectonic plates, where massive ructions have produced a string of volcanoes in the Eastern Caribbean. At the same time, the warm tropical sea has given rise to coral reefs, which have gradually clustered the islands with limestone deposits as they age and die.

CAVE VISITS
All coral-based islands have caves, carved out by rain over the centuries. The best organised cave tours include the Río Camuy park (see page 199) in Puerto Rico and Harrison's Cave (see page 218) in Barbados. Both tours have introductory explanations and a trip on a trolleybus to view the stalactites and stalagmites. The Cueva del Indio in the Viñales region of Cuba are also worth visiting, as is Anguilla's Fountain Cave, thought to have been an Arawak religious site.

NAMES AND USES
In the British Caribbean old limestone shelves (dead coral reefs) on the seafront are known as "ironshore" and in the Spanish Caribbean as "black teeth". Many early Caribbean buildings were constructed with the bright, pitted coral rock, quarried on the islands.

Over the millennia corals have created whole islands. When a hard coral dies it leaves a limestone skeleton, on which the next generation of corals can fix itself. Eventually a reef is formed and, as the level of the sea rises and falls, the growing reef can be left exposed as land. Wave action breaks down the dead reefs, carving natural bridges, blowholes and coastal caves, as well as creating bright, white sand. The islands that form a line from Anguilla through Antigua to Grande-Terre in Guadeloupe are all coral limestone, as are the Caymans, encrusted around a string of old volcanoes that died off 100 million years ago.

In the Greater Antilles, age-old coral lime-stone has been pushed up into the mountains by seismic activity. There it has been eroded into areas of cone and tower karst mountains, named after a region of shaggy-topped lime-stone outcrops in the former Yugoslavia. Karst peaks are distinctive, steep-sided mountains between 100 and 200m tall (they once had natural roofs suspended between them, but these were eroded by heavy rain and collapsed long ago). From above they look like shaggy egg cartons; beneath them, the rocky earth is laced with sink-holes, caverns and underground rivers. In Jamaica karst mountains are known as "cockpits" (steep-banked pits for cock fights). Karst peaks can also be seen around Viñales in Cuba (where they are called *mogotes*), in the Dominican Republic's Los Haïtises National Park and in the northwest of Puerto Rico.

200

▶▶▶ Ponce and surrounds

Isolated from San Juan by the central mountain range, Ponce has a radically different feel from the island's capital; the area is hotter and has less rain, so its pace of life is more leisurely. The 200,000 Ponceños are renowned for their independence and for their pride in a heritage that dates from the 17th century, when Ponce de Léon's great-grandson founded the city.

Ponce's tree-lined central plaza and a number of streets surrounding it have recently been restored. Most striking is the striped red and black fire station, the **Parque de Bombas**▶▶ (tel: 284 4141. *Open* Wed–Mon 9:30–6. *Admission free*) built in 1882. Constructed to a Spanish-influenced Puerto Rican design, the Cathedral of Our Lady of Guadeloupe dates from 1670 and the Casa Armstrong Poventud, a turn-of-the-century townhouse, has been well restored with period furniture and now houses a tourist office. The **Ponce Museum of Art**▶▶ (tel: 848 0505. *Open* daily 10–5. *Admission: inexpensive*) has an excellent collection of European and Latin American art.

One of the best views of the city is from El Vigia, the enormous cross on the hill, where an earlier version was designed to guide ships to land. Also on the hill, **Castillo Serallés**▶▶ (tel: 259 1774. *Open* Tue–Sun 9:30–5. *Admission: inexpensive*) is the extravagant former family home of the distillers of local rum Don Q. Weekend ferries leave the Playa de Ponce for the small and popular off-shore island Caja de Muertos (named after the coffin it resembles), which has excellent beaches and coral reefs.

The **Tibes Indian Ceremonial Center**▶▶ (tel: 840 2255. *Open* Tue–Sun 9–4. *Admission: inexpensive*) is set in forested parkland behind the town. On an Amerindian village site, thatched houses and *bateyes* have been re-created and a museum displays finds from the area. On Route 10, in the hills above the town, is the **Hacienda Buena Vista**▶▶ (tel: 722 5882. *Open* Wed–Sun for tours by appointment. *Admission: inexpensive*), a restored late 19th-century coffee estate, which is worth a visit. There is a small museum and original machinery, driven by water. You will also see the bags and painted stencils that were used to export the product a century ago.

ARAWAK CEREMONIES
It takes a stretch of the imagination to re-create in your mind the excitement surrounding the games and dancing of the ceremonial parks when Arawak Indians were celebrating. Games were played with shuttlecocks and heavy balls, which had to be kept aloft using a huge belt around the waist. Festivals would continue for two or three days and the participants would spend a lot of time under the influence of a hallucinogenic drug. Having purged himself by vomiting, the chief would make predictions. As well as the Tibes Ceremonial Center, the park at Caguana, near Utuado, set in a lovely forested valley, deserves a visit.

201

Red and black stripes on the Parque de Bombas

In his book The Old Man and the Sea, *Ernest Hemingway tells of a poor fisherman in Cuba and his fight to hook an enormous blue marlin. In another of his novels,* Islands in the Stream, *a boy and a marlin are engaged in a desperate struggle. Big-game fishing suited Hemingway's macho image and he was one of the sport's most passionate practitioners, relishing the rich sealife of the Caribbean waters.*

BIG AND BEAUTIFUL

One of the most beautiful fish in these waters is the sleek sailfish, with a silver belly, a blue back and a large, blue dorsal fin that looks like a sail. It can grow to about 3m in length and weigh 90kg. Other smaller fish include wahoo, a grey-blue fish with a crescent tail, which grows to nearly 2m and can weigh up to 54kg and, about the same size, the tarpon, slim with silvery scales. The dorado (so-called because of its golden colour) or mahi-mahi has red fins and grows to about 1m in length.

Barracuda

Big-game fishing was made possible by the invention of the motorised boat at the end of the 19th century and fishermen soon gathered along the coasts of the Gulf Stream (Cuba, the Florida Keys and Bimini in the Bahamas), where the biggest fish live. Today it is possible to fish off most of the Caribbean islands and the sport is particularly popular off Cuba, Jamaica, the Dominican Republic and the Cayman Islands.

Deep-sea fishing boats have tall upper decks, or tuna towers, from which their pilots can look out and trail a number of lines from different rods. This is a strenuous, physical sport and once a fish has been hooked, the fisherman will strap himself into a "fighting chair". Some species are immensely strong, weighing over 450kg, and the fight can last for several hours: line is played out in order to prevent it from snapping, allowing the fish to dive and move around. The unfortunate catch is then slowly hauled in; most fish are killed in the process (though catch-and-release fishing is increasingly popular).

The Caribbean's principal big game fish are the blue and the white marlin. Both have spears extending from their noses and long dorsal fins. The blue marlin can grow up to 680kg. Other fish include tuna: yellowfin, albacore and skipjack (the most important commercial fish, which is trawled and processed in Puerto Rico) and the blue-fin tuna, which can grow to 4m and weigh 770kg.

202

▶▶ San Germán and the Southwest

Puerto Ricans take their holidays in the southwest of the island. Here, the country is hotter than elsewhere and there are good beaches in the area; consequently, a number of small local tourist towns have collected along the coast and come alive in the summer.

The main road from Ponce to Mayagüez cuts inland and passes the town of **San Germán**▶▶▶, the second on the island to be founded by the Spaniards (in 1573). It remained prominent until the 19th century, despite threats from pirates and now has a university and attractive old townhouses. Dating from 1606, the **Porta Coeli Church**▶▶ (tel: 892 5845. *Open* Wed–Sun 9–4:45. *Admission free*) has been restored and contains a museum of religious art and colonial paintings from 18th and 19th centuries.

A golden sunset over the hot southwest coast of Puerto Rico, where locals go to relax

On the coast directly south of San Germán is the town of **Parguera**▶▶, which has a more hedonistic, seaside feel. Local seafood restaurants, cabins on stilts and small villas overlook the mangroves on the coast and the beach (not one of the best) is some way out of town. A more worthwhile local attraction is the nearby phosphorescent lake (see panel, page 210).

Perhaps the best town in the area is **Boquerón**▶▶, a small seafront resort on the southwest coast. Backed with huge palm trees, its beach is one of the island's best and gets very lively at weekends. Watersports equipment is for hire and there are several cafés. Other, more isolated beaches can be enjoyed on the island's southwestern tip near the lighthouse and the old lagoons where the islanders used to harvest salt. There is also a small forest reserve here with mangroves.

To the north along the coastline are more resort towns, with *paradores* and restaurants lining the seafront at Playa Joyuda and Playa Laguna. This west-facing coast is excellent for sunset-watching and offshore there are a number of small islands that are rarely visited, including Desecheo and Mona, a deserted nature reserve with soaring cliffs, which can only be reached by taking a charter plane or fishing boat.

PUERTO RICAN PARADORES
The *paradores* of Puerto Rico are hotels dotted around the island, which are judged to be of a certain standard and style by the tourist board (from whom a list can be requested). They are usually small and while they are neither fancy nor chic, they often have great local character and are generally in superb settings. Puerto Ricans themselves use *paradores*, so you are highly likely to meet islanders there. The *mesons gastronomicos* are restaurants chosen according to similar criterion specialising in local cuisine.

*Pavement cafés in
Old San Juan*

*The battlements of the
Castillo de San Felipe
del Morro*

▶▶▶ San Juan (Old City)

Approached from the sea, Old San Juan looks like a massive fortress. The city is enclosed by over 9km of walls, 15m high and 6m thick, and a ring of stone sentry boxes, or *garitas*. Its formidable appearance was a necessity during the turbulent days when there was continual threat of invasion; both Francis Drake and Jack Hawkins led attacks on the city in the 16th century.

Parts of San Juan date from its foundation in 1520, but most of the colonial city has been restored to its 18th-century appearance. The streets are laid with blue cobblestones shipped from Spain as ballast and the wrought-iron streetlamps, balconies and shuttered windows all add to the rather self-conscious sense of history. Admittedly this is a tourist showpiece and it can be overrun by visitors from the cruise ships; but Old San Juan is also a city with genuine character and life.

As well as walking around the city, there is a wealth of museums and galleries to explore, including the Museo Pablo Casals on Calle San Sebastián, where the cellist's instruments are on display; the Museo de San Juan, Calle Norzagaray, which showcases Puerto Rican art, music and festivals; and the Casa del Libro, in an 18th-century house at the southern end of Calle del Cristo, with displays about printing and a library of antiquarian books. A few steps away, the Centro Nacional de Artes Populares y Artesanías is a great place to pick up souvenirs from a varied and colourful selection of locally produced arts and crafts. At this end of town, Calle Fortaleza and Calle San Francisco are the twin poles of the main shopping district, and late in the evening Calle de San Sebastián comes alive with promenaders taking the air.

OLD SAN JUAN

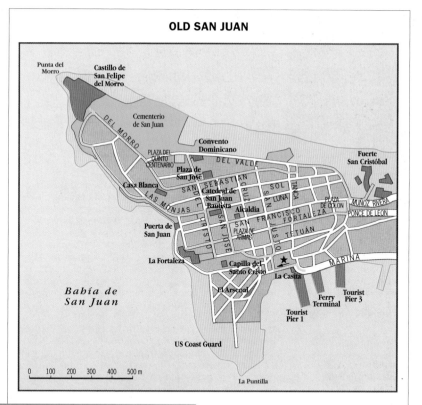

Punta del Morro

Castillo de San Felipe del Morro

Cementerio de San Juan

DEL MORRO

PLAZA DEL QUINTO CENTENARIO

Convento Dominicano

Fuerte San Cristóbal

DEL VALLE

Casa Blanca

Plaza de San José

SAN SEBASTIAN

LAS MONJAS

Catedral de San Juan Bautista

Alcaldía

SOL

LUNA

TANCA

PLAZA DE COLON

MUÑOZ RIVERA

PONCE DE LEON

SAN FRANCISCO

FORTALEZA

Puerta de San Juan

SAN JOSE

SAN JUSTO

PLAZA DE ARMAS

TETUÁN

La Fortaleza

Capilla del Santo Cristo

La Casita

MARINA

El Arsenal

Ferry Terminal

Tourist Pier 3

Bahía de San Juan

Tourist Pier 1

US Coast Guard

0 100 200 300 400 500 m

La Puntilla

Walk

Old San Juan

Start at La Casita, a colonial building housing the tourist office on the inner harbour. Walk uphill, following the city wall to Calle San José. The Plaza de Armas is the city's main square and site of the Alcaldía (City Hall). Calle Fortaleza leads to **La Fortaleza**►► (hourly tours Mon–Fri 9–3:30. *Admission free*), used as the Governor's Mansion since its construction in 1520 and renovated in 1846.

At the foot of Calle del Cristo, lined with shops and restaurants, is the tiny **Capilla del Santo Cristo**►, a chapel marking the spot where a horseman plunged over the walls during a race around the city. Heading north, you reach the Catedral de San Juan, built

in 1540 and altered in the 19th century; Ponce de Léon's bones are entombed there. A stepped alley leads downhill to one of the city gates and beyond the walls, parkland leads to the vast **Castillo de San Felipe del Morro**►►►, San Juan's main defence. Started in 1540, it took over 240 years to complete; its walls rise 42m and it has six levels of tunnels and dungeons (*Open* daily 9–5. *Admission: inexpensive*).

The route back to town brings you to the **Casa Blanca**►►. Built in 1521, this was the ancestral home of the Ponce de Léon family and now contains a museum of colonial life. On nearby **Plaza de San José**►► was the family chapel. From the **Convento Dominicano**►, with its charming inner courtyard and the Plaza del Quinto Centenario, follow the cobbled streets to the city's other defence, **Fuerte San Cristóbal**►► (*Open* daily 9–5. *Admission: inexpensive*) a 17th-century labyrinth of tunnels. Take Calle Fortaleza to return to the dock.

One of the most seductive aspects of the Caribbean landscape is its luxuriant greenery. Some islands are so fertile it is said that you could plant a pencil and expect it to take root. Hundreds of plants grow here, including flowering trees, tropical fruit trees, curious crops and creepers and the infinite variety of flowers that adorns West Indian gardens.

BOTANICAL GARDENS
The Caribbean has many excellent botanical gardens: Hope Gardens, Kingston and Castleton in the Blue Mountains in Jamaica; the Jardin Botanico Nacional in Santo Domingo, capital of the Dominican Republic; the Rio Piedras Gardens in the south of San Juan, Puerto Rico; the Jardin de Balata in Martinique; the Botanical Gardens of St Vincent; the Flower Forest and Andromeda Gardens on Barbados; the Queen Elizabeth Botanic Park on Grand Cayman; the Emperor Valley Gardens in Port of Spain, Trinidad; and the JR O'Neal Botanic Gardens in Road Town, Tortola, BVI.

The evergreen croton

Beaches and swamps Palm trees on the seashore, overhanging the sandy beaches, are a travel brochure cliché nowadays, but they are not the only coastal trees by far – manchineel (see panel opposite), sea grape (with bunches of edible, bitter grapes) and sea almond trees (bearing inedible fruit) all grow near the sea. Around the swamps and coastal lagoons are the mangroves, hardy trees that have adapted to salt water and muddy ground, where they drop a tangle of buttress and aerial roots in order to support themselves. Flowering lilies can often be seen on fresh inland water.

Dry land The drier Caribbean islands, which include low-lying areas such as the Caymans, the Dutch Leewards and the outer chain of the former British Leewards, are generally covered in green scrub, which turns to yellow as it is bleached by the sun. On Aruba and Curaçao, where this scrubland is known as *cunucu*, the cactus-like aloe vera produces oil that is used extensively in cosmetics, and the century plant throws out a 10m flowering stem about once every 10 years. In this poor soil the divi-divi tree grows stunted, with branches that bend over in the winds, looking like a head of windblown hair. Numerous cacti cover the arid land and are cultivated to make living fences in many settlements.

Grasses and flowers On the more fertile islands, grassland known as savannah is grazed by cattle and gardens situated close to sea level grow an enormous variety of flowers. The best known are bougainvillea, which bloom in spiny fingers of purple, pink and orange, and hibiscus, with around 200 different delicate and brightly coloured blooms, each of which lasts only one day. Other species to look out for include white flowering frangipani, many different-coloured ixora, allamanda and plumbago, which has purple blooms; and the more exotic garden flowers including heliconia (known as "lobster claw" because of its strange shape), red hot cat tail, a fluffy, dangling bright red bloom and the bird of paradise (*strelitzia*), with a bird-like form. The ubiquitous anthurium, with its plastic-looking leaf and furry stigma, is used to adorn dinner tables in houses all over the Caribbean islands.

Flowering trees The Caribbean's many dazzling flowering trees include the yellow and pink pouis, African tulip trees and the immortelle, which is planted to give shade to cocoa beans and makes whole valleys flame in January. The flamboyant, or poinciana, blooms red in June and July and the ackee produces red pods, whose yellow flesh can be eaten.

Other food-bearing trees include the breadfruit and the spiky breadnut; fruit trees are a valuable source of income for many islands (see page 143). The calabash fruit cannot be eaten, but its hard shell was used as a container in years gone by; and the cannon ball tree, despite its delicate flowers, grows fruit like lumps of wood. *Lignum vitae*, or the tree of life, has wood so hard and heavy that it sinks in water; mahogany tree pods release sycamore-like whirling seeds. Beware of the sharp spines on the trunk of the sandbox, so-called because its pods were used to hold sand for ink blotters. The Traveller's Tree (see panel) is so called because rain

THE TRAVELLER'S TREE
The Traveller's Tree, also known as the compass tree because it grows pointing east and west, is sometimes (and incorrectly) called a palm tree. Its leaves grow like a fan, splaying sideways as each new leaf is superseded by another in the middle. Occasionally, a spiky, inedible fruit pokes out and reveals its strange, blue, wax-like material.

207

Roadside flora in Dominica

collects in the cupped spaces between the leaves, giving travellers a ready supply of drinking water.

Higher up the slopes of the larger islands, there is a change in the vegetation and the forests begin. Countless varieties of ferns swirl into an impenetrable, tangled mass; vines clamber up the trunks and drop their lianas into the soil; and "air-plants", orchids and bromeliads thrive on the upper branches and telephone wires. At the highest altitudes, you will find small and stunted "dwarf forest".

FORBIDDEN FRUIT
The manchineel is a bushy evergreen whose small fruits are extremely poisonous; one of Columbus's sailors tried his luck and the fruit quickly became known as the "apple of death".

Skyscraper hotels tower above the beach at Isla Verde, San Juan

SAN JUAN SNACKS
Like other Caribbean islanders, the Puerto Ricans adore roadside snacks and there is a grand variety of tasty fillers at *kioskos* in San Juan and around the countryside. *Chicharron* is popular, although perhaps an acquired taste – spiced fried pork rind. *Bacalao* is frittered codfish and *alca-purrias* are also fritters, either meat or local fish, fried and served on a banana leaf. *Empañadas* are strangely flattened sandwiches and *picadillas* are meat patties.

► San Juan (New City)

Beyond the historic walls of colonial San Juan there is a real working city with a population of over one million, and urban development has sprawled along the coast and around the lagoons. Hotels and apartment houses crowd the coastline, while further inland there is a mixture of swanky commercial buildings and poor shanties that highlight the contrasts of Puerto Rican life.

To the east of Columbus Square, which marks the edge of the colonial city, is **El Capitolio► ►**, the seat of the Puerto Rican Senate and House of Representatives. Built in the 1920s, it imitates that of the White House in Washington; in the rotunda, visitors can see a copy of the Puerto Rican constitution, which was originally drawn up in 1954.

Further along the coast is **Condado► ►**, one of the town's main tourist strips. Huge hotels, interspersed with shops and conference centres, stand right on the seafront and behind them are streets full of restaurants and bars. This line of tall buildings extends along the coast solidly for the ten or so kilometres to **Isla Verde► ►**, the other main tourist area, which is crammed with yet more luxury hotels and an interesting variety of restaurants and bars overlooking a large, popular beach.

Inland are the working areas of the capital. Hato Rey is the commercial heart of San Juan, which is one of the biggest financial markets in the Caribbean. A more traditional Caribbean market operates in Río Piedras, with tropical fruits and vegetables for sale. To the south, the **Río Piedras Botanical Gardens►** (tel: 763 4408. *Open* daily 8–4:30. *Admission free*) provide a green and welcome retreat from the hustle of the city and its endless traffic. A ferry ride across the bay from Old San Juan takes you to Catano, where the **Bacardí Rum Distillery and Museum► ►** provides tours for visitors (tel: 788 1500. *Open* Mon–Sat 8:30–4:30. *Admission free*).

As tourists have flooded into their resorts and towns, many Caribbean islands have gained reputations for their gambling centres. But beyond the roulette tables, there is a popular tradition of West Indian gambling and bar games, from domino contests to local wrestling matches or even cock fights.

Caribbean casinos have all the usual games that a keen gambler would expect to find: *vingt et un*, roulette, craps and slot machines. If casino gambling is an important factor in your holiday choice, the following islands should be on your list: Aruba, which has a choice of glitzy gaming rooms with cabaret shows; Aruba's diminutive neighbour, Bonaire, will be able to offer a little low-key gambling; the Dominican Republic has casinos in all the main resorts; Guadeloupe and Martinique; Puerto Rico with a host of casinos in Condado and Isla Verde and at hotels around the island; Antigua and St Kitts in the Leeward Islands; St Croix, in the USVI, is a relative newcomer and the Dutch side of Sint Maarten, where gamblers will find a strip of casinos in Philipsburg.

GAMBLING TRAVELLERS
Cuba was one of the biggest gambling islands, attracting thousands of US visitors to its gaming houses, until 1959, when casinos and all other trappings of capitalism were outlawed by the Cuban revolutionaries. Since then Puerto Rico (and the Bahamas, which are also close to the States) have taken over as the favourite gambling destinations for American visitors.

209

Enjoying a game of dominoes outside a local bar

Cock-fighting On the French- and Spanish-speaking Caribbean islands, cock-fighting is a major spectator sport. It is a brutal event – the cocks are occasionally killed – staged in a cockpit with steeply banked seats. Cocks are prepared for weeks in advance for a fight, with special diets and grooming. On the day of the fight owners bring their birds into the ring, showing them off to the crowd and brandishing them at one another as the bets are placed. As the fight begins, two cocks lunge at each other, pecking and slashing with their claws, while the audience erupts into screams and shouts of encouragement.

In the French Caribbean, a variation on the bloodsport theme is occasionally introduced, when snakes are pitted against one another in a contest to the death. Raising fighting cocks was a traditional Caribbean method of becoming rich in times past.

DOMINOES
Played in just about every bar throughout the Caribbean, dominoes are even enjoyed by Fidel Castro, the President of Cuba. The pieces are usually laid on the playing board with a grand flourish and a loud slap; in Barbados they are referred to as "cards", and are even "shuffled" in preparation for the game.

*Casa del Frances,
Vieques, built as a
plantation house*

LUMINOUS LAKE
The phosphorescent lake
at Mosquito Bay, Vieques,
has an eerie beauty. At
night it glows where
paddles cut the water;
fish leave streaks as they
dart away and in a storm
the whole surface is set
alight. The cause is bio-
luminescence; tiny
creatures emitting light
when agitated.

Puerto Rican licence plate

▶▶ Vieques and Culebra

If you look east from Fajardo, on Puerto Rico's east coast,
you will see that the sea is sprinkled with islands and cays
as far as the horizon, culminating in the Virgin Islands.
About 9km from the mainland, Vieques is the largest of
the Puerto Rican islands; not far beyond it is Culebra, surrounded by a collection of little satellites. These islands
are dry and low, with rolling hills and some of the best
beaches in Puerto Rico. The wildlife is different from that
on the mainland – you might see red-billed tropicbirds
and turtles, which lay their eggs on the beach – and
Culebra is partly given over to a wildlife refuge.

Vieques A 45-minute ferry ride from the mainland brings
you to Vieques' northern shore and its main town, Isabel
Segunda, where the majority of the island's 8,000 inhabitants live. The central square is quiet and pleasant and
there is a tourist information office there. A restored 19th-
century **fort▶** stands on the hill above the town. In
Esperanza▶▶, on the southern coast, bars and restaurants are strung along the shorefront, a stone's throw
from the island's best beaches. Look for the **Casa del
Frances▶▶**, a stylish old plantation house.
Much of the island belongs to the US Navy
and is used for naval exercises (to the resentment of many islanders), but at other times
visitors are allowed on to the area's beaches
– including Red Beach and Blue Beach.
During World War II, Vieques was the fall-
back base for the British Navy should Britain
fall in the German invasion.

Culebra This tranquil island sits among a
small crowd of tiny coral outcrops 40km east
of the mainland. Only 2,000 islanders live on

Culebra, many in the only town of Dewey, better known as Pueblo, where there is a small information office. Parts of the island were designated a National Wildlife Refuge by President Theodore Roosevelt in 1909, primarily to protect migratory birds. Culebra's beaches and coral reefs are superb and the snorkelling is wonderful.

►►► El Yunque Caribbean National Forest
The most accessible area of Puerto Rico from the capital is the northeast, with its rich variety of mountains, mangroves and beaches. Perhaps the most popular tour is to El Yunque, an area of rain forest that, because of its position in the far northeast of the island, enjoys the best of the water-laden Atlantic winds (which bring about 450 billion litres of rain every year).

El Yunque is approached by Route 3 from town or by following the coast road out of Isla Verde and then heading into the mountains, rampant with tropical foliage, on Route 191. In this 11,000-hectare national park, 240 species of tree grow in three different varieties of forest (rain forest, montane forest and stunted dwarf forest, near the 915m peaks). Trails have been cut into the forest, with explanatory signposts and lookout platforms. The **El Portal Tropical Forest Center►►** (tel: 888 1810 or 766 5335. *Open* daily 9–5. *Admission: inexpensive*) dispenses information about the plants, animals and about 60 or so species of bird, including the endangered Puerto Rican parrot. **Guided Forest Adventure Tours►►** (*Open* Thu–Mon 10–3. *Admission: moderate*) can be arranged through hotel travel desks. As this is rain forest, there are frequent tropical showers, so it is advisable to take a waterproof coat.

On the far northeastern tip of the island there is another nature reserve at **Las Cabezas de San Juan►►** (tel: 722 5882 or 860 2560. *Open* Wed–Sun for tours by appointment. *Admission: moderate*), where boardwalks lead through the mangroves past the shore and swamp birdlife. A visitor's centre is housed in the restored 19th-century El Faro (or lighthouse), from which there are superb views out towards the Virgin Islands. The route back to town on the north coast road passes Luquillo, site of one of the island's most popular public beaches and a string of excellent roadside snack outlets. At Piñones, just before the road comes into Isla Verde, is another area of protected mangrove swamps, which is the habitat of birds such as snowy egrets, pelicans and herons.

MANGROVE BIRDLIFE
Mangrove swamps harbour lots of crustaceans, providing food for herons, terns, sandpipers and stilts. The easiest to visit from San Juan are Piñones (from Boca de Cangrejos marina) and Las Cabezas de San Juan. Guanica, in the southwest, is designated a World Biosphere site by UNESCO.

211

Bar at Esperanza

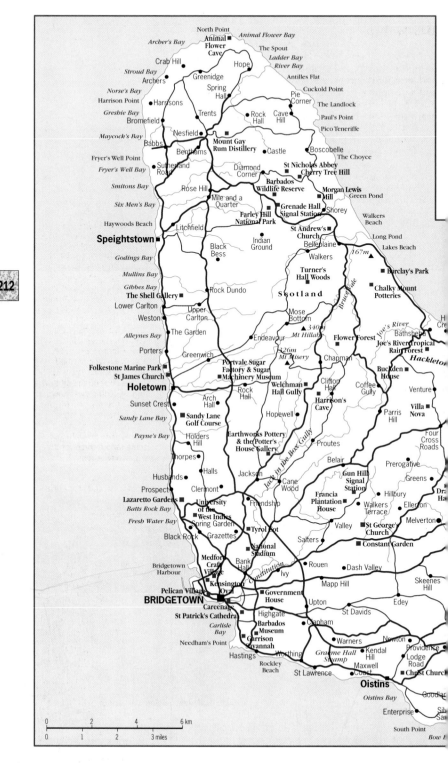

Barbados

Probably the most British of the Caribbean islands, Barbados has a gentle, undulating interior, ringed by safe and attractive beaches. It is relatively prosperous, relaxed and welcoming, and has absorbed the tourist industry gradually, without allowing it to overwhelm the life and character of the island. Popular attractions include its famous rum, its lively south coast nightlife, and its passion for cricket. Away from the low-key sophistication and luxury hotels of the west coast, Barbados's (and one of the Caribbean's) premier tourist areas, are the high-rise hotels, guesthouses and flats of the south. In contrast, the east coast is quiet and mostly undeveloped. Because the island has so many hotels and is easily reached on regular

SETTLING BY FORCE
Three centuries ago, to be "Barbadosed" was to be sent forcibly to the West Indies. Settlers were needed on the islands and the courts deported common thieves and prisoners of war there. They were set to work alongside indentured labourers, who sold their labour for five or seven years in return for their passage to the islands, on the understanding that they would be given land to plant at the end of their term. In the late 17th century, African slaves provided a large-scale labour force for the sugar plantations.

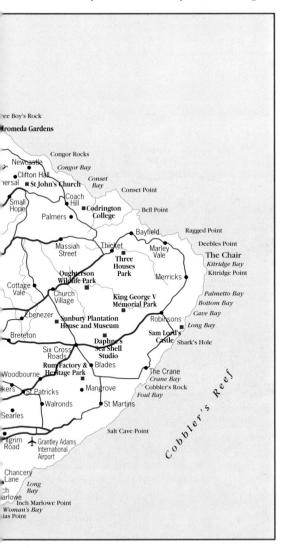

British naval hero, Lord Nelson, commemorated in Bridgetown

flights from Europe and the USA, good package deals are available to Barbados through numerous tour operators and travel agents.

Barbados is one of the best Caribbean islands for an active beach holiday. By day, watersports are easy to arrange, and there are plenty of beach bars to retire to. Divers come to enjoy the marine life of the coral reefs, and several companies offer equipment hire and scuba-diving instruction. Snorkelling is an easier alternative, and non-divers have access to underwater views from the dry comfort of the **Atlantis Submarine**▶▶ (tel: 436 8929 for reservations). Barbados has more exploring potential than other islands. The interior, although nowhere near as dramatic or lush as Jamaica or St Lucia, has pleasant scenery, with mahogany woodlands, cattle and black-bellied sheep grazing on rough meadows, traditional wooden chattel houses, and forests of sugar cane. There are also magnificent plantation houses – some open to the public, some still the homes of "high white" families of the old plantocracy, some the hub of working plantations, and one or two available for rent to visitors. By night there is a wide choice of nightclubs and many good restaurants, serving local as well as international food. Although not very cheap, several of them include magnificent coastal settings in the price.

Shaped like a pear set at a slightly tipsy angle, Barbados is made entirely of coral limestone. It measures 33km by 23km and lies in the Atlantic Ocean, 160km east of the Windward Island of St Vincent. From the sheltered western beaches, gently lapped by small waves, the land rises steadily through the cane fields and cultivated land of the central plains, culminating in the 300m escarpment of

LITTLE ENGLAND
In colonial days, the leading Barbadians were proud of their association with Britain and of being the only British Caribbean island never to be conquered by another power. They called their island, which was a highly successful colony, Little England, and having been nicknamed "Bims" by their slaves, styled themselves as inhabitants of "Bimshire", as though Barbados were a county of Britain.

214

King's Beach, on the west coast

Bajans "liming" (in discussion) on a fishing boat at Bridgetown

LITTLE BRISTOL
In the 17th century, during the early days of colonisation, Bristol was the major port on the west coast of England and many settlers on Barbados came originally from the West Country (southwest England). Speightstown's West Country residents earned it the nickname Little Bristol and their accent can still be heard in the drawled Bajan vowels.

RUM AND EXERCISE
The Sunday walk with the Barbados National Trust (a preservation body) and the Bajan rum shop are both equally hallowed institutions. On the former, a guide leads walkers through a chosen area of historic interest (perhaps a section of old railway, or an abandoned fort) for a couple of hours on Sunday mornings (tel: 426 2421; a small fee is charged). In the rum shops, customers may offer informal instruction in such essential pursuits as dominoes and talking politics.

Hackleton's Cliff in the east. North of here is the hilly Scotland district, where the island reaches its highest point, Mount Hillaby, at 340m. Powerful Atlantic waves (nicknamed "white horses") crash constantly against the dramatic eastern shoreline, carving out bizarre rock formations and steadily eroding the coast.

ISLAND LIFE The island's population of 260,000 is one of the densest in the world, a fact that is clearly visible in the urban sprawl radiating from Bridgetown along the western and, increasingly, the southern coasts. Solitude may be hard to find on Barbados, but the island is made special by its people. Bajans, mostly of African descent, are some of the friendliest West Indians; whether at the weekly Sunday **National Trust walk▶▶** (see panel) or in a local rum shop for a game of dominoes, the Bajans will give you an amiable welcome and are always ready to fill you in on all the latest island gossip.

The Barbados economy is one of the healthiest in the region and the island is busy and businesslike, with extensive investment in its tourism infrastructure. Bajans treat tourism as an important industry, and they are particularly gracious to visitors, making this an excellent island for those who wish to visit the Caribbean for the first time.

Much is made of Barbados's Englishness, the result of a long-standing colonial connection with Britain. For a time the island was even known as Little England (see panel opposite). While it is true that Barbados has visibly kept more British traits than other islands, the American influence can also clearly be seen today. Since Independence in 1966, the people have started to take pride in their Afro-Caribbean heritage, and more recently have developed their indigenous Bajan culture.

THE CAREENAGE

The Careenage takes its name from the system of tilting, or careening, the hull of a ship. (A number of waterfronts in the Windwards and nearby French islands share the same name.) A weight was attached to the ship's mast in shallow water and the ship would be tilted so that its hull and bottom were exposed, so it could be scrubbed free of barnacles and weeds.

The Careenage, Bridgetown

▶▶ Bridgetown

The capital of Barbados lies on a broad, protected bay in the southwestern corner of the island. Old colonial buildings and modern offices stand side by side in the centre of Bridgetown, but over the years the city, which has around 100,000 inhabitants, has spread steadily north and south-east along the coasts.

Bridgetown is the centre of island life, where the offices of government and big business stand above lively West Indian street markets. Its traditional heart is the Careenage, a sea inlet where, in the days of seaborne travel, lighters would bring ashore passengers from the ocean-going ships. There is not much nautical activity any more (passengers now arriving by sea will usually dock at the deep-water harbour), but yachts and fishing boats still use the inlet, and a selection of waterfront bars and cafés cater to landlubbers.

NELSON

Lord Nelson, "Preserver of the West Indies", arrived in pursuit of the French Admiral Villeneuve during the Napoleonic Wars and removed the threat of French invasion. His statue was erected on the former Trafalger Square (now renamed National Heroes Square) in 1813, but as a legacy of the colonial era, he was considered a some-what contentious figure and has been relocated after years of deliberation and pressure from proud Bajans. "Put up a Bajan man", sang the Mighty Gabby, a famous calypso star and consciousness-raiser.

On the north side of the Careenage is National Heroes Square, the hub of the city centre, flanked by two distinctive colonial public buildings, built from local coral rock in the 1870s. Crenellated and with pointed arches, they have red tin roofs and green louvered windows, which keep out the sun but allow ventilation when there is a breeze. The House of Assembly, the seat of the Barbados Parliament, which was founded in 1639, is open to visitors. British monarchs from James I to Victoria are commemorated in stained-glass windows in the Parliament chamber.

At the centre of National Heroes Square is a small fountain, its bowls supported on the tails of brightly painted dolphins, which was erected in 1865 to mark the arrival of piped water – obviously a significant event in a hot town. From the square leads one of the town's most important commercial streets, Broad Street, where Bridgetown's major shops, department stores and duty free emporiums are housed in old colonial buildings. North of here is Swan Street, a typically Caribbean (weekday) street market where vendors stand by their colourful stalls selling anything from oranges to fluorescent shoe laces or mirror shades.

Selling fruit in the capital

BAJAN DISHES
Whatever it has taken from the British in other respects, Barbados owes little to them in the way of food. Bajan fare depends more on local ingredients, including fish and vegetables such as yam, plantain and sweet potato, cooked according to Amerindian and African techniques. Pepperpot is a strong-tasting Amerindian stew made with meat and vegetables and served with traditional Caribbean rice and peas, cooked in coconut milk or with pumpkin fritters. Locally caught fish and chicken are usually curried and served in Créole sauces of pepper, tomato and onion.

St Michael's Cathedral, a few blocks east of the square, was built in 1789 and provides a haven from the town's hubbub. The restored Synagogue, originally built in the 17th century, is off Magazine Lane near the law courts; in the yard is a gravestone dedicated to Benjamin Messiah, who was renowned as a circumciser, apparently performing with "Great Applause and Dexterity".

Cheapside Market, at the northwest end of Lower Broad Street, is set in a traditional tin market building and sells mainly local food and vegetables. In the Rasta Mall goods for sale include rastafarian herbal concoctions and leather pendants from Africa. Near by, Pelican Village sells more formal arts and crafts.

In the northeastern area of the city, you will find the **Tyrol Cot Heritage Village▶▶** (tel: 424 2074. *Open* Mon–Fri 9–5. *Admission: moderate*) in the grounds of the former home of the Bajan political family, the Adams. The 1850s house is open for tours and there are artisan workshops set in traditional Bajan "chattel houses".

A few kilometres to the south of the Careenage is the Garrison Savannah, the military district of the colonial era. The old Georgian barrack buildings are still visible, some restored, others in decay, but the 120-hectare Savannah itself is now used mainly for sports events, including horse-racing and local cricket matches. The **Barbados Museum▶▶** (tel: 427 0201. *Open* Mon–Sat 9–5. Sun 2–6. *Admission: moderate*), at the corner of the Savannah, is situated in the island's former prison. The museum displays aspects of life in Barbados during Amerindian and colonial times, including the ill-fated Barbados Railway (see panel). Rooms here have been fitted using period furniture and a gallery of maps and prints is set in the old cells.

THE BARBADOS RAILWAY
During the 19th century the British built railways throughout their empire and despite its small size, even Barbados had one built in the 1880s. The line ran east from Bridgetown through the central sugar cane lands before descending to the Atlantic coast at Bathsheba and continuing to Belleplaine. It was used by workers coming into town in the week and was usually packed for church outings at the weekends. Having suffered financial problems from the start, it finally folded in 1937.

Relaxing on one of the Caribbean's famous beaches

▶ ▶ ▶ Caribbean (West) Coast

The beach that stretches up the west coast of Barbados is one of the finest in the Caribbean. Nicknamed the Platinum Coast, its golden sand is washed by calm seas, and behind a fringe of coconut palms and casuarina trees are superb hotels such as the Sandy Lane and the Coral Reef Club, long-renowned and now-renovated havens of luxury, which have given Barbados its name for tropical refinement. Interspersed among them are private villas, restaurants and cheaper hotels.

The roads north out of Bridgetown lead to the Spring Garden Highway, which comes alive each year on the first Monday in August with colourful dancing parades during the **Crop Over Festival▶ ▶ ▶**. North of the town centre is the Kensington Oval, the Barbados cricket stadium – the Bajans' fervour for the game makes attending a cricket match a rousing experience. On the coast nearby are the **Mountgay Visitor Centre▶ ▶** (tel: 425 8757. *Open* Mon–Fri 9–4) and the **Malibu Visitor Centre▶ ▶** (tel: 425 9393), where tours include a look at the vats and the distilling process and a taste of the rum. The history of the sugar-refining process is traced at the **Portvale Sugar Factory▶** (near Holetown), which is on view between February and May.

Holetown was the site of the first European settlement on Barbados in 1627, colonised after it was claimed for the British by Captain John Powell in 1625. The small but stately St James Parish Church is notable for its English style of architecture, but Holetown today mainly consists of open spaces and an excellent string of restaurants and bars. The **Folkestone Marine Park▶** has a small marine museum and a snorkelling trail through the offshore corals and inland lies **Harrison's Cave▶ ▶** (see page 220), with a network of illuminated underground caverns.

Back on the coast, **Speightstown▶**, 11km north of the capital, seems a sleepy town but has some good bars; beyond it, the countryside opens out to reveal cane fields, small settlements and deserted beaches. At the island's northern tip, you can visit Animal Flower Cave, named after the sea anemones or "animal flowers" that live there.

WEST COAST BEACHES
Calm and west-facing, the Platinum Coast is an almost continuous strip of beautiful sands, ideal for early morning walks or for sunset-watching. Though the beaches are never really crowded, you cannot expect to be alone here because there are so many hotels set along the coast. There are few divisions between the beaches and in some places you can wade through the shallows to the next beach. All beaches are public and provide a right of way and hotels have watersports facilities – non-residents can usually negotiate their use. Paynes Bay, with its easy access and choice of watersports deals, is a good option.

Sport is a unifying feature of an area made diverse by its geography. Within the former British Caribbean islands, cricket is something of an obsession: islanders will drop everything to listen to the commentary of an international match in which the West Indies team is playing. In the Spanish Caribbean the most popular sport is baseball and life comes to a halt if an important game is being played.

Cricket The West Indies have had a world-class cricket team for years – a remarkable achievement for an area with so small a pool of players to choose from. Players for the team are drawn from all the British Caribbean islands, but the main centres are the islands where there are international-class (Test Match) grounds: Jamaica, Antigua, Barbados, Trinidad and Guyana. Barbados has an impressive record, having won the inter-island competition (now called the Busta Cup) more often than any other team.

Cricket is played on the beaches and in back streets, with a tennis ball and sticks for stumps; tourists are often asked to join in. Success at cricket is a route to fame and wealth, so it is fiercely contested: the best players attain national hero status. Famous names include Viv Richards (Antigua), Clive Lloyd (Guyana), Gary Sobers (Barbados) and Brian Lara (Trinidad).

OTHER SPORT
By means of cable TV, the Caribbean is steadily being influenced by sport from America. Basketball is very popular, as is football, although the latter is restricted to the small screen and is not played on the islands. The major participant sport in the French Caribbean is American football, but the most popular spectator sport is cock-fighting (see page 209), also followed on the Spanish islands, but virtually unknown in the British Caribbean.

219

Baseball This is the national sport in Cuba, the Dominican Republic and Puerto Rico and has been played on the US Virgin Islands since the Americans arrived. Just as many West Indian cricketers go to the UK to play, so the Dominicans and Puerto Ricans, as well as several Cuban defectors, have graduated to the American pro leagues and some have achieved considerable fame and fortune. In the streets the children play a toned-down version of baseball, not unlike New York's stickball, in which they are not allowed to run.

The diamond at Charlotte Amalie, St Thomas

Other Caribbean states

The fishing village of Bathsheba on the wild and weather-beaten Atlantic coast

▶▶ Central Barbados

Inland from the capital, the land rises steadily through the Bridgetown suburbs into open country and cane fields, towards the cliffs that tower above the Atlantic coast. **Francia Plantation**▶▶ (tel: 429 0474. *Open* Mon–Fri 10–4. *Admission: inexpensive*) gives a vivid idea of the privileged lifestyle of the old Barbados planters. Standing on high ground in attractive gardens, Francia is furnished with antique furniture and decorated with maps and prints of old Barbados. Another plantation house worth visiting is **Sunbury Plantation House**▶▶ (tel: 423 6270. *Open* daily 9:30–4:30. *Admission: inexpensive)*, which has been restored. In the gardens, there are cannon and a collection of old horse-drawn carriages. It is worth taking a quick look at **Codrington College**▶, an imposing, early 18th century religious seminary and school (buildings not open to visitors), approached along an avenue of splendid royal palm trees. **Harrison's Cave**▶▶ (tel: 438 6640. *Open* daily 9–6, last tour 4 PM. *Admission: moderate*) is an extensive series of pale-gold limestone caverns off Highway 2, complete with exquisitely formed stalactites and stalagmites, subterranean streams and a 12m waterfall.

The steep, somewhat remote east coast of Barbados is an unexpected find. From the top of Hackleton's Cliff, the site of **St John's Parish Church**▶, there is a marvellous view over small country villages and down to the east coast, where Atlantic waves roll in against huge sculpted rocks. The sea here is rough and unpredictable – signs on the beaches warn of dangerous currents and advise people not to swim.

Andromeda Gardens▶▶ (tel: 433 9261. *Open* daily 9–5. *Admission: moderate)*, near Bathsheba, are set out on the hillside, made beautiful by fiery blooms and flowering trees from the tropical world, including frangipani, orchids and the Traveller's Tree (see panel, page 207). Bathsheba and Cattlewash are now fishing villages, but attractive seafront villas remain from when colonials would come here to escape from the Bridgetown heat. The Round House (tel: 433 9678) makes a good lunch stop with terrific views over the Soup Bowl, which is a favourite surfing spot.

An old rhyme describes the rum punch drunk by planters in colonial days: "One of sour, two of sweet, three of strong and four of weak." The sour is lime, the sweet is cane juice, the strong is rum and the weak is water (more likely to be fruit juice nowadays). Mix these ingredients, sprinkle with grated nutmeg and you have a genuine Caribbean rum punch.

Practically every Caribbean island distills its own rum, but the main producers are Cuba and Puerto Rico, where rums are traditionally light in colour, and Barbados and Jamaica, where they are darker and fuller in flavour. On the French islands some of the finer rums are aged to be drunk like a brandy after dinner. Most islands also produce a white rum for local consumption. St Croix produces both light and dark Cruzan rum.

Rum is a by-product of sugar, distilled from the fermented juice of sugar cane or a mix of cane-juice and molasses. Visits can often be arranged to rum distilleries, full of gurgling vats and stills and the heady, sweet smell of fermentation. All distillations of rum result in a clear liquid; darker rums gain their colour from the addition of caramel during the ageing process, and from the oak barrels in which the rum is stored. Barrels of rum were used as currency in colonial times, when rum first became an important export.

Perhaps the most famous rum manufacturer is Bacardí, which was based in Cuba before its revolution but now works mainly from Puerto Rico, where there is a huge factory outside San Juan. In Jamaica the biggest name is Appleton, producing gold rums of different ages and a strong white rum known as John Crow Batty (crow's backside). The Appleton factory can be reached from Montego Bay. From Barbados come Mountgay and Cockspur, as well as white rums such as Alleynes, and from Haiti the renowned Barbaucourt. The French islands have a long tradition of high-quality "rhum agricole" that includes Rhum St James and Trois Rivières of Martinique (both of which can be visited). Caribbean rum is used as filling in expensive chocolates and as the basis of a number of liqueurs such as Malibu.

RUM HISTORY
Rum first appeared in Barbados in about 1650, when it was known as "kill-devil" and "rumbul-lion". Pirates would drink an explosive mixture of rum and gunpowder. British sailors were entitled to a daily measure of rum from the 18th century until 1970.

221

Exotic liqueurs are produced all around the islands: Camerhogne is Grenada's mixture of rum, spices and fruit

Camerhogne
Spice
750ml LIQUEUR
OLD NAME FOR GRENADA IS THE ISLE OF SPICE
THIS PLEASANT-TASTING LIQUEUR IS AN EXQUISITE BLEND
OF LOCAL RUM WITH NATURAL SPICES AND TROPICAL FRUITS
A PRODUCT OF THE GRENADA SUGAR FACTORY LTD.
26% ALC/VOL

The Morgan Lewis Mill: one of the last of over 500 windmills that once turned on the island

SCOTTISH ORIGINS
As Barbados was once known as Little England, it is somehow fitting that there should be a hilly district to the north called Scotland. The parish is even named after St Andrew. Many Scotsmen were banished to the east of the island, including Scotland, during an early episode of racial and religious segregation in the mid-17th century, and a few of their descendants still live there, in poor white communities. These settlers became known as Redlegs, supposedly because they did not tan under their kilts.

EUROPEAN INFLUENCES
St Nicholas Abbey was built to European designs and included fireplaces; the settlers had not yet realised that even on winter nights they did not need a fire for warmth. Its curved gables help to date it to about 1650 (following the maxim "curly early, straighter later"). Competing in age with St Nicholas Abbey is Drax Hall, a privately owned 1650s stone building off Highway 4, with a wood-panelled interior and mastic-wood staircase (open only once a year).

►► Scotland

Scotland is a hilly district in northeast Barbados; a series of peaks, including Mount Hillaby, the island's highest, overlook the Atlantic coast. This remote district makes an interesting half-day drive, through isolated settlements.
  The Flower Forest►► (tel: 433 8152. *Open* daily 9–5. *Admission: moderate*), just off Highway 2, has marked paths lined with trees such as mango and breadfruit, with their green cannonball-sized fruits and a fine show of tropical blooms such as hibiscus and poinsettia. **Turner's Hall Woods►** are the last remaining area of the natural woodland that covered Barbados until it was cleared for sugar plantations. Here you can see trees native to the island – fustic, West Indian locust and sand-box trees – as well as birds and monkeys such as the Lesser Antillean bullfinch and the black Carib grackles.
  In the days when it was carpeted with sugar cane, Barbados had about 500 windmills, whose sails turned constantly in the Trade Winds, driving the millstones that crushed the sugar cane to release its juice. The **Morgan Lewis Mill►** is the last surviving example and although it does not actually turn, the old crushing gear is on view. The **Grenade Hall Signal Station►►** (tel: 422 8826. *Open* daily 10–5. *Admission: inexpensive*) is a restored link in the military communications chain. Close by, the **Barbados Wildlife Reserve►►** (tel: 422 8826. *Open* daily 10–5. *Admission: expensive*) is a free-range reserve with paths laid out in a mahogany wood and where agouti (see page 24), spectacled cayman (which looks like an alligator) and iguana roam.
  St Nicholas Abbey►► (tel: 422 8725. *Open* Mon–Fri 10–3:30. *Admission: inexpensive*), in northern Scotland, is not actually an abbey, but a plantation house that is still working. An absorbing home movie shows shots of Barbados in the 1930s, with sugar workers, turning windmills and "mauby ladies" serving the bitter mauby drink from vats that they carried on their heads.

▶ South Coast

The south coast of Barbados has a completely different feel from the better known, more sedate west coast. It attracts a younger, livelier crowd and lays a greater emphasis on activity outside the hotels, which are smaller and less expensive (package tourists often end up in this area and there are also guesthouses here). Visitors tend to spend their days sunning themselves and windsurfing on the beaches; in the evenings they pour into the restaurants and bars, moving on to the clubs in St Lawrence Gap and Bridgetown, where dancing and live music continue until the early hours. There are places to explore in the southeast, where isolated coves include Foul Bay, Harrismith Beach and Bottom Bay, but most life centres around the "gaps", the small roads that lead down to the coast off Highway 7.

Highway 7 leads from Bridgetown past the Garrison Savannah and through the seemingly never-ending urbanised sprawl of Hastings, St Lawrence and Worthing. Further east, the Crane Beach Hotel sits on a hilltop overlooking the Atlantic. **St Lawrence Gap▶▶** is a popular and busy area, with watersports facilities on the beaches around the small bay and the main centre for nightlife nearby with plenty of restaurants and bars where local bands play to packed crowds. There is usually a friendly atmosphere, but tourists have occasionally been robbed here and you should be careful.

Beyond Maxwell, known for its windsurfing, is Barbados's fourth town, Oistins, a fishing community where the daily catch is sold on the waterfront. Recently, the fish market has gained a reputation as a lively place to eat out for simple dishes (especially fish) in the early evenings – worth a detour to join in. Continue east and there is another windsurfing centre at Silver Sands Beach.

At the **Heritage Park and Four Square Rum Distillery▶** (tel: 420 1977. *Open* daily 9–5. *Admission: moderate*), visitors can observe sugar and rum manufacturing, as well as contemporary Bajan artists at work in the foundry, and pick up crafts and local produce in the shops.

LATE-NIGHT SNACKS
Baxter's Road was long a favourite with Bajans and tourists alike in search of late-night snacks of battered kingfish and a Banks beer. But allegiance seems to have switched to the fish market in Oistins, where 10 or 15 stalls sell simple fish and chicken meals in styrofoam boxes and on paper plates. In the early evening, you'll find music and a friendly crowd here.

SAM LORD
Sam Lord's Castle (tel: 423 7350. *Open* daily 10–4. *Admission: inexpensive*), in Long Bay in the southeast, is now a large hotel, but it has a grim history. It was built in 1820 by Sam Lord, a scoundrel who imprisoned his wife (she eventually escaped) and made a fortune by defrauding and, some say, murdering rich victims. He is also said to have made a pretty penny by plundering ships that he lured onto the rocks by hanging lanterns in the trees at night to fool sailors into thinking they had spotted a harbour. He would then bring his haul along an underground passage to the castle. The tale may be fanciful – the underground passage is fictitious – but Sam Lord and his crooked ways were real enough.

Watching the world from a rum shop in Bridgetown

BIRD-WATCHING

With fruit-filled feeders just a couple of metres away, the veranda at the Asa Wright Nature Centre, one of the largest and finest in the whole Caribbean, provides people who are not normally bird-watchers with an excellent view of Trinidad's spectacular birdlife. It is said that you can see 25 species before breakfast: honey creepers, hummingbirds, *cro pendulas* and toucans, among others (tel: 667 4655).

Trinidad and Tobago

This two-island nation presents a vivid contrast between bustling, cosmopolitan Trinidad and peaceful, rural Tobago. Trinidad is loud, lively and full of ethnic and cultural diversity; Tobago tends to be less developed and much more traditionally Caribbean, with its delightful beaches and rolling countryside. Trinidad's Port of Spain attracts hundreds of thousands of spectators each year to its spectacular and exhilarating carnival, while Tobago is a better option for those looking for a quieter dose of sand and sun.

This southernmost nation of the Caribbean lies off the coast of South America. Trinidad was still joined to the continent 10,000 years ago and in some places its mountains (the Southern, Northern, and Central ranges), fertile plains, and mangrove swamps are separated from Venezuela by only 11km of water. Its spectacular flora and fauna are similar to the mainland's; there are hundreds of species of butterflies and birds (more than can be found on any other Caribbean

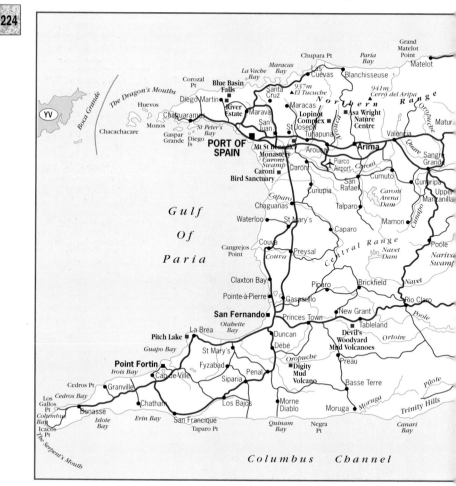

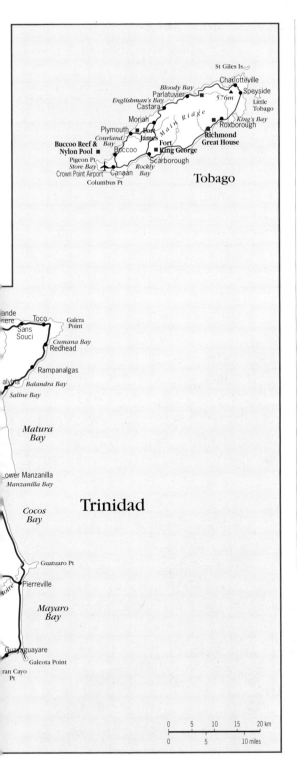

St Giles Is
Charlotteville
Bloody Bay
Parlatuvier
Englishman's Bay
Castara
576m
Speyside
Little Tobago
Moriah
King's Bay
Plymouth
Roxborough
Fort
Courland Bay
James
Buccoo Reef &
Nylon Pool
Buccoo
Fort
King George
Richmond
Great House
Pigeon Pt
Store Bay
Crown Point Airport
Canaan
Rocky
Bay
Scarborough

Tobago

ande
riere
Toco
Galera
Point
Sans
Souci
Cumana Bay
Redhead

Rampanalgas

alyha
Balandra Bay

Saline Bay

Matura
Bay

ower Manzanilla
Manzanilla Bay

Cocos
Bay

Trinidad

Guatuaro Pt

Pierreville

Mayaro
Bay

Guayaguayare
Galeota Point
ran Cayo
Pt

| 0 | 5 | 10 | 15 | 20 km |

| 0 | 5 | | 10 miles |

225

FESTIVALS
Divali is celebrated in Trinidad during October or November and honours Lakshmi, the Hindu goddess of light. During the festival, followers go from one open house to the next, drinking and feasting, and hundreds of coconut oil lamps are lit in small clay pots, illuminating whole valleys. Phagwa is celebrated in the streets in March with huge paper floats and red food dye, which is thrown over spectators, and the Muslim festival of Hosay (dates vary) commemorates the martyrdom of Hussein and features a parade of his tomb, accompanied by dancers and drummers. At the end of the year, you will hear traditional Christmas "parang" songs.

island), including 17 varieties of hummingbird and the scarlet ibis – the national bird – which can be seen flying in to roost in the Caroni Swamp (situated just south of Port of Spain) during the evening.

Tobago broke off from the continent in an earlier geological age and lies some 34km northeast of Trinidad. Its spine of volcanic mountains, the Main Ridge, is mantled with rain forest, which descends to a plain in the southwest. Much of the coastline is gouged with steep-sided bays and the underwater slopes are clad with corals, but in the gentler western end of the island there are some fine white sand beaches that are well worth seeking out.

HISTORY Christopher Columbus landed on Trinidad in 1498, during his third voyage to the Americas, and named it in honour of the Holy Trinity. During the 16th century, the island was used as a Spanish staging post in the search for the elusive El Dorado, the Golden One, whose kingdom was thought to be on the mainland near here. Tobago was probably not seen by Columbus, but after Europeans had settled there in the mid-17th century, fierce battles followed for its possession, and the island changed hands more times than any other island in the Caribbean before it was eventually taken into British ownership in 1814.

Trinidad and Tobago were politically linked in 1888 and remained a British colony until 1962, so they retain similarities to other English-speaking islands in the area – but theirs is a far more complex heritage. Spanish place names are common in Trinidad and there are strong traces of French Créole, a legacy of the Royalist settlers who fled from the French colonies in the wake of the 1789 Revolution.

The islanders joke that when the British took over, Trinidad became a Caribbean island with a French population, which was governed by the British according to laws laid down by Spain.

ISLAND LIFE The British added new strains to Trinidad's already potent mix of peoples, shipping in African slaves to work the sugar plantations and, later, after emancipation, turning to East Indian, Chinese and Middle Eastern immigrants, who worked as indentured labourers. The result is that Trinidad has a cosmopolitan population, of which nearly half is made up of descendants of Indian immigrants. Hindi, some French and French Créole are spoken as well as English; parish churches stand side by side with Hindu temples and Islamic minarets; Indian and Chinese restaurants operate alongside tropical fruit stalls; and Hindu and Muslim festivals such as Divali and Hosay are celebrated as well as the Caribbean Carnival.

Tobago was also a plantation island and most of its population is of African descent, but for the traveller and the tourist, the two islands offer radically different experiences. Trinidad has a vibrant cultural life – theatres, a concert hall and festivals – while Tobago is altogether quieter (Trinidadians tend to go there for a rest), with secluded sandy coves. It has been developed somewhat in recent years, with new hotels and guesthouses springing up along the northwest coast.

Trinidad is the place to experience hectic Caribbean bustle. Port of Spain is a lively and busy city, and music, heard everywhere, is an essential part of life. A visit to a calypso evening, or a "Tent" at Carnival time, is an essential Trinidadian experience (even though the language and repartee are hard to follow); the songs, which deal with island gossip and current affairs, are performed with great gusto by popular calypsonians, especially in the days leading up to the ultimate Trinidadian experience – **Carnival**▶▶▶ (see pages 234–235). After a week of steel bands (which were invented here) and calypso shows, Carnival culminates on Mardi Gras with a two-day pageant around the streets of Port of Spain, with hundreds of thousands of costumed revellers and onlookers dancing in the streets.

The simple life in Buccoo, Tobago

BAMBOO CANNON
Loud explosions resounding through a Trinidadian valley (or elsewhere in the Caribbean) may indicate that someone has been given a bamboo cannon, a popular child's toy that is still used at Caribbean festivities. The cannon is made by hollowing out a length of bamboo, leaving only the bottom section untouched. A small hole is then cut about 15cm from the end and kerosene is poured inside and warmed so that it turns into gas, which is lit with touch-paper, causing a heart-stopping bang.

Trinidad

Miguel Street is fictitious, created by Trinidadian writer VS Naipaul in his novel of the same name, but it does have all the characters and life of a typical West Indian town. It could be almost anywhere in the Caribbean, but Naipaul, perhaps the Caribbean's best-known writer, was born in Trinidad and set his story in the island's capital.

Port of Spain is a large, active, modern city of about 300,000 people, lying on the Gulf of Paria in the north-west. In style it's a typical Caribbean mix, with modern high-rises and traditional Créole wooden houses over-looking the bustling streets, where vendors sell wares from their carefully arranged stalls.

The heart of the town is Brian Lara Promenade; a wide avenue a couple of blocks in from the waterfront. At right angles to the square is one of the city's main shopping areas, Frederick Street. A walk up this street brings you to Woodford Square, named after Governor Woodford, who had the town rebuilt in 1813 following its destruction by fire five years earlier. On the square's western side is the **Red House**▶▶, Trinidad's parliament building, a massive Victorian pile whose two chambers can be visited, and diagonally opposite is the Anglican Cathedral of the Holy Trinity. The centre of the square, tree-shaded and surrounded by iron railings, is a local gathering place. This was the spot where Dr Eric Williams, the leader of Trinidad for many years before and after Independence, held his political rallies.

Further along Frederick Street is the **National Museum and Art Gallery**▶▶ (tel: 623 5941. *Open* Tue–Sat 10–6. *Admission free*), where displays of Trinidad historical and cultural life include the latest Carnival costumes and archive photographs dating back to the 1960s. There is also an exhibition of the paintings by the 19th-century Trinidadian artist Michel Cazabon.

TRINIDADIAN DISHES
Trinidad's food is as varied as its racial heritage and includes Indian, Chinese and French as well as Caribbean cuisine. Probably the finest local fare can be bought at Veni Mange, at 67A Ariapita Avenue, where two sisters prepare meals for lunch only. The breakfast sheds on the waterfront in down-town Port of Spain sell rice and peas or callaloo soup at good prices and street stalls sell snacks such as *rotis* (chapati envelopes filled with chicken, beef, shrimp, or potato stew) or doubles (unleavened bread doubled over with a filling of split peas). Phulouri are batter balls served with a mango sauce.

King George III's cypher on a cannon that once protected Trinidad from rival European powers

![a beer is a Caribbean... (Carib Beer advertisement mural)]

229

Carib Beer, a Caribbean-wide Trinidadian export

Just north of Frederick Street, Port of Spain's vast central park, the 80-hectare **Savannah▶▶**, officially called Queen's Park Savannah, is where Trinidadians go to walk, jog, play cricket, hockey and football and buy their chilled coconuts and evening snacks. Look out for the spectacularly extravagant houses known as the "Magnificent Seven" on the park's western side.

North of the Savannah is the **Botanic Gardens▶▶**. Among the plants on display are the red blossoms of the Trinidad national flower, the chaconia, a wild poinsettia that takes its name from the last Spanish governor. If you are lucky you might see some toucans flying home to roost in the evening. Local animals such as the jaguar-like, buff-brown ocelot are kept in the **Emperor Valley Zoo▶▶** (tel: 622 3530. *Open* daily 9:30–6. *Admission: inexpensive*), next door to the Presidential House.

OUTSIDE PORT OF SPAIN Beyond **Fort George▶**, an old defensive bastion with a line of cannons covering the approaches to Port of Spain, the Western Main Road passes through some of the city's most prosperous suburbs and continues to the northwestern Chaguaramas peninsula. At the head of the Diego Martin Valley is a museum with an original waterwheel devoted to the sugar era, at the **River Estate▶▶**.

During World War II the Chaguaramas peninsula was an American base and in the 1950s it was hoped that it would house the parliament building for the ill-fated Federation of the West Indies, in which the islands of the British Caribbean would come together in one political unit. A golf course is laid out near by and the Anchorage is a popular bathing area, although the beach is not very attractive.

For the intrepid explorer, there are caves and colonial military ruins on Gaspard Grande Island, in the channel and at the end of the peninsula is the Dragons' Mouths, the short channel that separates Trinidad from the Venezuelan coast.

VIEWS OF THE PAST
CLR James and Eric Williams were two Trinidadian historians who between them overturned the conventional colonial view of British Caribbean history. James, who lived in London until his death in 1989, was a Marxist historian, best known for his account of the Haitian Revolution, *The Black Jacobins*. Williams, whose works include *From Columbus to Castro* and *A History of the Peoples of Trinidad and Tobago*, was Prime Minister of Trinidad for many years until his death in 1981.

When Europeans first arrived in the Caribbean, turtles provided a reliable source of food because they could be kept alive on their backs on board ship. Today, numbers have dwindled drastically and some species of turtle are endangered. Their eggs (highly prized by some as an aphrodisiac) are often stolen and the turtles themselves are particularly vulnerable since they lay their eggs on the beach.

HELPING HAND
St Croix in the USVI is one of the few places turtle numbers are improving. Numbers of leatherback turtles seen at Sandy Point and Green Cay are on the increase. On nightly patrols from July through to October, biologists from the Buck Island Reef Hawksbill Turtle Research Program are out under the stars recording and analysing the nesting patterns of hawksbill, green and leatherback turtles. Their efforts have contributed significantly to the understanding and survival of the species.

HE OR SHE?
The sex of a turtle, like that of alligators and crocodiles, is determined by the temperature of the nest; the warmer the weather, the more females are hatched. The earlier hatchlings tend to be male (at the beginning of the year) and the later ones females, when the temperatures warm up.

Sea-turtles are marine reptiles with hard shells and flippers, which have remained basically unchanged for 250 million years. Five species of turtle live in the Caribbean: the loggerhead, the hawksbill, the ridley, the green turtle (once the most common, but now endangered) and, largest of all, the leatherback (also endangered), which can dive to 1,500m, weigh up to 700kg and live to 150 years old. Caribbean leatherbacks have been known to cross the Atlantic and swim as far north as Newfoundland.

The most fascinating part of a turtle's life-cycle is the way the young are hatched. The female leatherback nests

between April and June, arriving at night (often returning to the beach from which she originally came) and crawling laboriously up onto the sand to a point above the high water mark. For two hours she digs a hole with her hind flippers, to a depth of about 45cm and lays up to 200 eggs, each the size of a billiard ball. Then she covers them with sand and crawls back into the sea. The process is repeated perhaps 10 times during the season.

Over the next eight weeks the eggs incubate and eventually the 10cm hatchlings dig their way to the surface and set off for the sea, running the gauntlet of predators; apart from humans, herons and crabs lie in wait and mongooses dig them out of their nests. There is safety only in numbers. Several Caribbean hotels can arrange special trips to watch turtles nesting and at the turtle farm on Grand Cayman, in the Cayman Islands, visitors can see turtles at different stages of development.

The beaches nearest to Port of Spain are on the north coast, over the mountains of the Northern Range, which tower above the city. The best route and the most spectacular drive, is through the Maraval Valley. Popular **Maracas Bay►►**, half a kilometre wide, is flanked by massive headlands, thrown off by El Tucuche, Trinidad's highest peak. It's a traditional Trinidadian day out – part of the experience is to sample a "shark and bake", a battered fish sandwich from one of the stalls. Here, the water is occasionally rough; it is calmer at Las Cuevas, a few kilometres beyond, where there are also beach facilities. From the north coast fishing village of Blanchisseuse, a road heads southwards across the Northern Range, another long, twisting and visually stunning drive.

The Eastern Main Road leads from just behind the waterfront in downtown Port of Spain towards St Joseph, the original Spanish capital of the island. It then passes between the Northern Range and the northern edge of the **Caroni Swamp►►►** (tel: 645 1305. *Admission free*), which harbours about half of the island's bird species, including the scarlet ibis, which flies in during the evening. It is said that up to 10,000 ibises can be roosting here at a time and tours (with a guide) start at around 4:30 PM. Angostura Bitters is produced in a factory in St Joseph which is open to visitors (see panel) and high above the town is the **Mount St Benedict Monastery►**, a peaceful spot with a fine view over the central plain.

A few kilometres up the Arouca river the **Lopinot Complex►►** is an old cocoa estate cut into the huge valley early in the 19th century by the Comte de Lopinot, a refugee from turbulent Saint Domingue (Haiti). The cottage-like original estate house survives, and Trinidadians picnic under the giant Saaman trees at weekends. Early in the year the immortelle trees that were planted to shade the cocoa plants burst into a blaze of orange blooms. Several Native American descendants live in this area, where many locals speak French patois.

Whitehall, one of the "Magnificent Seven" houses that overlook the Savannah

ANGOSTURA BITTERS
Trinidad is the home of the world-famous aromatic Angostura Bitters, used in cooking and cocktails. The business was started by the Venezuelan Siegert family in the 19th century and the recipe is a secret, but involves a mixture of roots, barks, dried leaves and spices with alcohol, boiled to give the dark bitters. The Angostura factory (tel: 623 1841), on the main road to St Joseph, is open to visitors.

Other Caribbean states

V S NAIPAUL
Vidiadhar Surajprasad
Naipaul was born of a
Brahmin family in Trinidad
in 1932 and educated at
Queen's Royal College,
Port of Spain and
University College,
Oxford. Many of his novels
express pessimistic and
critical views of his native
culture. *A House for
Mr Biswas* (1961),
whose hero is based
on Naipaul's father,
describes the collapse of
the Caribbean way of life
and his earliest books,
The Mystic Masseur
(1957), *The Suffrage of
Elvira* (1958) and *Miguel
Street* (1959) all satirise
life and politics in
Trinidad.

Maracas Bay, Trinidad

In the Arima Valley is another delightful retreat, the **Asa Wright Nature Centre**▶▶ (tel: 667 4655. *Open* daily 9–5, guided walks available. *Admission: moderate*), a balconied estate house (with rooms for rent; see page 277) looking out onto a vast, green valley. Here you can hear the strange "boing, boing" call of bellbirds and see the colourful flash of a toucan or an *oro pendula* in flight. Another excellent bird-watching spot is the Hollis Reservoir just north of Valencia (for more details contact one of the bird-watching organisations listed in **Travel Facts**).

Beyond Valencia, southeast of the nature centre, the strip of urban development gives way to forested and cultivated land. The road forks here and heads south towards the Atlantic coast at Manzanilla or north via Balandra to Toco, where there are good beaches.

To reach the south of the country from Port of Spain, turn right on the Uriah Butler Highway, just out of town, which skirts the Caroni Swamp and then heads out into the cane fields. The first major town is Chaguanas; VS Naipaul lived here and the house described in *A House for Mr Biswas* stands on Main Street. The road continues to San Fernando, Trinidad's second city, where it passes the Pointe-à-Pierre oil refinery, a reminder that oil was once the island's chief export, funding its development during the boom years.

Trinidadians refer to the wilder country beyond San Fernando as the Deep South. At the town of La Brea, about 16km along the coast, is the **Pitch Lake**▶▶, a 40-hectare cauldron of natural asphalt, fed by tar from beneath and forever turning; occasionally branches, ancient artefacts and even bones are pushed up to the surface. It is worked as a mine and the pitch has been used in roads all over the world.

Tobago

With few large hotels and no crowds, this little island (only 32km by 9km) still has a tranquil charm. Tourism has developed around the southwestern tip of the island, where the best beaches are to be found, but elsewhere there are deserted coves set in the sinuous coastline and quiet West Indian villages.

Most people arrive on Tobago at Crown Point Airport, on the far southwestern tip of the island. From here it is a short walk to most of the guesthouses and small hotels and to **Store Bay**▶▶, one of the island's liveliest beaches, where breakfast sheds have been set up selling such local dishes as "bakes" (like Johnny Cakes), served with salt fish buljol. Just north of Store Bay is the most popular beach, **Pigeon Point**▶▶, where there are palm-thatched bars and watersports. An entry charge can be avoided by walking in below the high-water mark (where the sand is not private).

Continued on page 236.

A steel band performer making music on Tobago

SENSITIVE SOUVENIRS
Vendors at Caribbean beaches sell all sorts of trinkets and jewellery made from local materials. There is some good work made with calabash shells in Trinidad and Tobago and from other local beads. Beware of buying jewellery made from turtle-shell or coral, because they may well have been obtained illegally.

Trinidad's annual carnival is the Caribbean's largest, liveliest and most flamboyant party. For two days before Lent, hundreds of thousands of revellers flood onto the streets of Port of Spain, clad in bright Lycra, sequins and feathered headdresses and dance in "bands" of a thousand or more, all shuffling and strutting in rhythm. Mas, as it is familiarly known, has been adopted by other islands all over the Caribbean, but the Trinidadians still claim to do it better than anyone else.

Mas has its roots in Catholic pre-Lenten festivities of two centuries ago, in which the Trinidadian French Créoles would visit one another's houses for masked balls. After emancipation in the 1830s, ex-slaves adopted the masquerade, turning it into a drum-driven street party. Suppressed by the authorities many times, it has grown since World War II into a massive, exuberant celebration.

Carnival begins to warm up soon after Christmas, when the calypsonians (see page 238) release their songs and the steel band preliminaries are held. "Mas Camps" are busily sewing the costumes to be worn by the carnival players – including the huge King and Queen costumes – which can be designed up to a year in advance and depict themes as varied as birdlife and pirates.

The real action begins during the weekend before the beginning of Lent. On the Friday night, a competition is held to select the winning King and Queen of the Bands – magnificent centrepiece figures that can be up to 10m tall and are lavishly constructed.

These pirates – in carnival mood – sport sunglasses and wristwatches

On Saturday the children take their turn in Kiddies Carnival and in the evening Panorama, the finals of the steel band competition (see pages 80–81), features the last eight steel bands, many 60-players strong, competing for the year's top title.

The Calypso Competition finals are held on Sunday night, with calypsonians vying for the year's most prestigious singing title, the Calypso Monarch. During the evening the winners of the King and Queen of the Band competitions put in an appearance.

On Monday the dancing begins and the revellers are out on the streets by 3 AM for jouvert (from the French Créole *jour ouvert*, but pronounced "jouvay"), with music provided exclusively by steel bands. Leading the parade are impish "djab-djabs" (from the French *diable*) and "moko-jumbies" who walk on stilts. Many dancers cover themselves in axle grease and mud (snazzily dressed onlookers are liable to be hugged). Jouvert comes to an end at about 9 AM and is followed at midday by more formal music and dancing by the Carnival Bands.

Tuesday, Mardi Gras, is the day of the main procession, or road march and judging day for the Carnival Bands. They assemble early in the morning and begin their strut around the streets, passing the four main judging areas – Brian Lara Promenade, Adam Smith Square in Woodbrook, Park Street and the Queen's Park Savannah. Each band, which may have as many as 3,000 players, is divided into sections, with players dressed in different costumes. At the rear of each band are the King and Queen. Music is provided by trucks interspersed among the sections and the noise is deafening. In the full heat of the Trinidadian sun, dancing is exhausting work and the players usually employ someone to wheel a portable bar around. By dusk the procession is finished, with dancing until the official finish at midnight.

Although many Caribbean carnivals are held on Mardi Gras and run along similar lines, some islands stage them at New Year or in the summer, to celebrate the end of the cane-cutting season. In Barbados, Cropover is on the first Monday in August and in Cuba, the Zafra celebrations are at the end of July. Perhaps the most enjoyable feature of Caribbean carnivals is that, unlike those of Rio or New Orleans, anyone can join in and dance.

CARNIVAL DANCES
Dances go in and out of vogue year by year, but the traditional step is the "chip", in which players drag their feet and swing their knees and hips, occasionally throwing their arms up in the air. Winding and grinding are dances in which players move their hips with their legs wide apart, sometimes alone, sometimes pushing up against another dancer (or in a conga). Groins and backsides feature prominently in the dance and partners perform in all imaginable combinations (back to back, back to front, etc).

235

Other Caribbean states

PELICAN PERILS

Pelicans can often be seen throughout the Caribbean islands sitting on a rock or a convenient offshore post, diving for fish – hurtling arrow-like down at the water but barely entering it. In time, this battering damages their eyes and many of them gradually go blind. Unable to fish well, eventually they die.

Drinks-shack and vegetable stall, Tobago

Continued from page 233.

Offshore are two Tobagonian landmarks: **Buccoo Reef►►**, although sadly overrun, still impresses with colourful coral and fish, which visitors can observe through a glass-bottomed boat and the **Nylon Pool►►**, a waist-deep area of warm water with a silky, sand bottom. On the other side of the bay is the village of **Buccoo►►**, where fishing boats with brightly painted diamond patterns lie on the sands. The Hendrix Bar is the scene of a weekly celebration known as **Sunday School►►**.

Past Mount Irvine Bay, the site of Tobago's 18-hole golf course and Stonehaven Bay (both good beaches), is Courland Bay. The name Courland has a strange origin: it comes from a peninsula in what is now Latvia, from which a number of settlements of Tobago were attempted in the 17th century. There is a monument to their memory in **Plymouth►**, Tobago's second town, where there are just a couple of streets and Fort James, on the point overlooking the bay. **Back Bay►►**, on the other side of Plymouth, is an attractive stretch of sand.

Beyond Plymouth, the road winds its way into Tobago's countryside, through hillside villages such as Les Coteaux and Moriah, before descending to the coast and a series of sandy, palm-backed bays: **Castara**▶▶, **Englishman's Bay**▶▶▶ and **Parlatuvier**▶▶. From Bloody Bay the main road leads up into the **Tobago Forest Reserve**▶▶, a rain forest with walking trails, before descending to the island's south coast at Roxborough.

Scarborough▶ is the capital of Tobago, a quiet and undistinguished town set over the hills above Rockly Bay on the south coast. At the top of the hill is the town's old defence, **Fort King George**▶, which is well preserved with its cannon covering the approaches to the town. Next door is the **Tobago Museum**▶▶ (tel: 639 3970. *Open* Mon–Fri 9–5. *Admission: inexpensive*), with displays of island history and Ameridian and colonial artefacts; and on the other side of town are the **Botanical Gardens**▶ (tel: 639 3970. *Open* Mon–Fri 9–5. *Admission: inexpensive*).

The road to the eastern end of the island winds its way along the palm-backed south coast, in and out of huge bays and through small Tobagonian settlements. A 15-minute walk from Roxborough, near the junction of the inland and coastal roads, is the **Argyle Waterfall**▶▶, a three-stepped cascade where you can take a swim after the walk. There is another waterfall at **King's Bay**▶, to the east of Roxborough.

After climbing an impossibly steep hill the road reaches Speyside and then Charlotteville (lying at the island's eastern tip), two quiet Tobagonian towns in the island's best scuba-diving area. On the Atlantic coast, Speyside overlooks the island seabird sanctuary of **Little Tobago**▶▶, and boat trips leave from the dock.

Beaching the boat in Tobago after fishing on the high seas

THE FRIGATEBIRD
The magnificent frigatebird, or Man-o'-War bird, nests on Tobago's northeastern cliffs. With its dark plumage, scissor-shaped tail and a wingspan of over 1m, this is an impressive but aggressive bird, which attacks other species for their food. It swoops from above or behind, shaking the victim until it disgorges its meal. Tours of Tobago's wildlife are arranged by David Rooks (tel: 639 4276).

Calypso is a flamboyant and witty singing tradition that originated in Trinidad. Styles range from rap to serenade and lyrics touch on life, the universe, politics and more. Some have a socially conscious edge; some are comical and gossipy, others are just plain "slack" (raunchy). But all calypsos entertain and they jam the airwaves as Carnival approaches.

CALYPSO STARS

Most calypsonians adopt singing names as colourful as their lyrics and dress. It's all part of the theatre that defines calypso. The most popular prefixes are "The Mighty" and "Lord". The two biggest names in the world of calypso are The Mighty Sparrow (alias Slinger Francisco), who first won the Calypso Monarch title in 1956 and has been crowned a total of eight times, and fellow Trinidadian, Lord Kitchener (Aldwyn Roberts), known for composing steel band songs and who won the Roadmarch title 11 times before his death in 2000. Singing Sandra, the 1999 Calypso Monarch, is one of only two women to win the title. Other names include Atilla the Hun, Lord Executor, Lord Invader, Watchman (a policeman) and The Mighty Chalkdust (a schoolteacher).

Calypso is a legacy of Trinidad's dual African and French heritage. The first known calypsonian or "shantwell" was Gros Jean, who sang for a French planter 200 years ago. Since the beginning of this century calypsos have been sung in English, the language of Trinidad, and as their popularity has increased, other English-speaking Caribbean islands have adopted the tradition.

Calypsos are the major musical force behind Carnival, at the beginning of Lent each year (see pages 234–235). There are three main calypso competitions. The Roadmarch competition judges the year's best dancing tune in the parties (fêtes) and in the Carnival parade. The title is won by the calypsonian whose song is played most as the Carnival bands cross the judging stages.

In Ex-tempo, two calypsonians compete in quickfire singing, alternating verse by verse. A topic written on a piece of paper is handed to the singers, who are given 30 seconds to prepare a calypso. Teasing the opponent is more important than rhyme or meter and the winner is usually the person who gets the biggest laugh.

The most coveted and fiercely contested title is the Calypso Monarch (changed from Calypso King when women entered the field). Calypsonians release their songs in January, so that they become well known on the radio. Then they perform in calypso "tents", acting the songs out in an attempt to be selected for the next round. Calypso Monarch finals are held on the Sunday before

Lent – a cross between a variety show and a comedy evening. Calypsonians perform to huge audiences, making digs at the other singers and adding topical comments to their songs to provoke a response from the crowd.

Travel Facts

Arriving and departing

The best way of reaching the Caribbean is with an experienced tour operator; they command the best air fares and hotel rates. Their brochures are available in most travel agencies. For top of the range companies in the UK contact: Caribbean Connection (tel: 01244 355 300), Caribtours (tel: 020 7751 0660), Elegant Resorts of the Caribbean (tel: 01244 897999) and Harlequin Worldwide (tel: 01708 850300). Slightly less expensive are: BA Holidays (tel: 0870 2424245), Kuoni (tel: 01306 740888) and Thomas Cook (tel: 01733 417000). Less expensive still are Airtours (tel: 0870 2412567), Thomson Holidays (tel: 0870 5502555) and Virgin Holidays (tel: 01293 744209). For villa operators contact Caribbean Expressions (tel: 020 7431 2131) Caribbean Chapters (tel: 020 7722 0722) and the Owners' Syndicate (tel: 020 7801 9801). Some companies specialise in smaller hotels, which market themselves in groups such as Caribinns (tel: 01242 604030), Valley Vacations (tel: 01706 212333), Thomas Cook (as above). You can travel independently on a seat-only ticket on a charter airplane; ask your travel agent for the best prices. Scheduled flights are more expensive but more flexible. Airlines with regular scheduled services from Europe to the Caribbean, some via the US, include Continental Airlines, US Air, Air Jamaica, BWIA, Delta, American Airlines and Air France. In addition there are charter flights to more popular destinations, mainly during the winter season (Dec–Apr). British Airways (tel: 0345 222111) also act as sales agents for LIAT, one of the major airlines linking the Caribbean islands. You can buy three types of LIAT Air Pass which enable island hopping: the Caribbean Explorer (valid up to 21 days, maximum three stopovers), the Eastern Caribbean Air Pass (21 days, minimum three stopovers, maximum six) and the Super Caribbean Explorer (linking the Caribbean with Guyana and Venezuela, maximum stay 30 days, unlimited stopovers). BWIA (tel: 020 8570 5552) operates a far-island (international passengers only) and a 10-island Air Pass for 30 days.

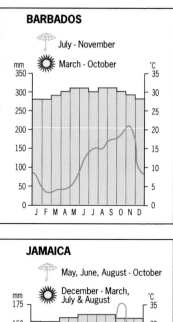

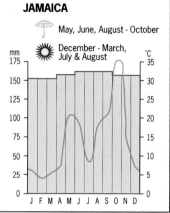

Departure tax is payable from most islands; this varies and there may be exemptions for children. Don't forget to have enough currency to cover this.

For general information, contact the Caribbean Tourism Organisation, 42 Westminster Palace Gardens, London SW1P 1RR (tel: 020 7222 4335) and through individual tourist offices.

Camping and student/youth travel

In general camping is discouraged, particularly on beaches. Few islands have designated campsites and there are very few youth hostels.

The Caribbean is not known for budget accommodation, but there are some cheap guesthouses and dive lodges on many islands, which rarely feature in tourist brochures. Most tourist offices have lists.

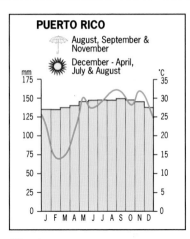

PUERTO RICO

☂ August, September & November

☀ December - April, July & August

Climate
Temperatures average 27–29°C but are lower at higher altitudes. October and November are the wettest months (June in Trinidad and Tobago); December to May is the driest period.

Crime
Attacks and thefts are rare; the most likely hassle is from persistent sales-men on the beach. Some islands are hustle-free, but be wary in large towns and cities. There is much poverty, which brings with it the temptation to petty theft. Keep doors locked, take care of your valuables and mind where you walk after dark. Don't take too much money out with you and don't display wealth by wearing expensive jewellery or producing wads of cash.

Most hotels and some hotel rooms, have safes. Report losses first to the hotel or apartment manager, then to the police and tourist board.

Dialling codes
Numbers include the international dialling code from the UK. Anguilla 001 264, Antigua and Barbuda 001 268, Barbados 001 246, Dominica 001 767, Cayman 001 345, Grenada 001 473, Jamaica 001 876, Dominican Republic 001 809, Puerto Rico 001 787, Montserrat 001 664, St Kitts & Nevis 001 869, St Lucia 001 758, St Vincent and the Grenadines 001 784, Trinidad and Tobago 001 868, British Virgin Islands 001 284 and US Virgin Islands 001 340.

Netherland Antilles (Bonaire, Curaçao, Saba, Sint Maarten and Sint Eustatius) 00 599, Aruba 00 297, Guadeloupe, St Barts and Saint-Martin 00 590, Martinique 00 596 , Cuba 00 53 and Haiti 00 509.

Travellers with disabilities
The Caribbean is not particularly well-equipped for travellers with disabilities. Many hotels are built on hillsides, making wheelchair access difficult. The Jamaica Tourist Board produces a list of hotels with an "H" to denote facilities for the "handicapped"; Trinidad and Tobago use a "D" for disabled, but check what the facilities are before booking. Individual island tourist boards can find out about specific properties that may be suitable.

Emergency telephone numbers
These telephone numbers are being standardised. Check them on arrival.
Anguilla Police and ambulance: 911
Antigua and Barbuda Police and ambulance 999 or 911
Aruba Police: 100; ambulance: 115
Barbados Police: 211; ambulance: 511
Bonaire Police 717 8000; ambulance: 717 8900
Curaçao Police: 114; ambulance: 112
Cayman Islands Police: 911; ambulance: 555 or 911
Dominica Police and ambulance: 999
Dominican Republic Police and ambulance: 911
Grenada Police: 911; ambulance: 434
Guadeloupe Police: 17 or 97 90 03; ambulance: 97 78 44
Jamaica Police: 119; ambulance: 110
Martinique Police: 17; ambulance: 15
Montserrat Accident and Emergency: 491 2802
Puerto Rico Police and ambulance: 911
Saba Police: 416 3237; ambulance: 416 3288
St Barts Police: 27 66 66; ambulance: 18
St Eustatius Police: 111; ambulance: 140
St Kitts and Nevis Police and ambulance: 911
St Lucia Police and ambulance: 911
Saint-Martin Police: 17 or 87 50 10; ambulance: 87 86 25 or 87 72 00
Sint Maarten Police: 111; ambulance: 130

241

St Vincent and the Grenadines Police and ambulance: 999
Trinidad and Tobago Police: 999; ambulance: 990
Virgin Islands (British) Police and ambulance: 999 or 911
Virgin Islands (US) Police and ambulance: 911

Health

Immunisation against yellow fever may be required if you arrive from an infected area. Otherwise immunisation is not generally required, but typhoid, polio and tetanus injections are often recommended, as well as hepatitis A for those staying outside tourist areas. Consult your GP. Health insurance should be taken out before you travel; if you are on regular medication take supplies with you, though there are plenty of chemists for over-the-counter products. Tapwater is not always safe to drink, so check on arrival.

Money

On islands where the official currency is the Eastern Caribbean dollar (EC$), the exchange rate is fixed to the US$: **Anguilla**; **Antigua**; **Dominica**; **Grenada**; **Montserrat**; **St Kitts and Nevis**; **St Lucia**; **St Vincent and the Grenadines**.

Other currencies: **Aruba** Aruban florin (Af); **Barbados** Barbados dollar (BDS$); **Bonaire** and **Curaçao** Netherlands Antilles florin/guilder (NAf); **Cuba** pesos ($); **Cayman Islands** Caymanian dollar (CI$); **Dominican Republic** Dominican peso (RD$); **Guadeloupe** French franc (FF); **Haiti** gourde; **Jamaica** Jamaican dollar (J$); **Martinique** French franc (FF); **Puerto Rico** US dollar; **Saba** Netherlands Antilles florin/guilder (NAf); **St Barts** French franc (FF); **Sint Eustatius** Netherlands Antilles florin/guilder (NAf); **Saint-Martin** French franc (FF); **Sint Maarten** Netherlands Antilles guilder or florin (NAf); **Trinidad and Tobago** Trinidad and Tobago dollar (TT$); **Virgin Islands** (British and US) US dollar. US$ are accepted on most islands.

Public toilets

There are not many of these available in the Caribbean, though some islands have basic facilities, which are usually at a rustic beach bar. It is a good idea to use toilets at hotels and restaurants.

Travel insurance

Your travel insurance should cover accident, health, baggage and possessions, cancellation and so on. If you are taken ill or have an accident, you will almost always be expected to pay and health care is not cheap. If you are going to be sailing, diving, windsurfing or similar, you should make sure your policy covers you – read the small print.

THE WINDWARD ISLANDS

Dominica (area code 767)

Car hire and driving

A local driving licence is required, obtainable from airports, the Vehicle Licensing Office, High Street, Roseau and some hire companies (Mon–Fri). You must be 25–65 and have a valid driving licence and at least two years' driving experience.

Hire companies include **Best Deal Rent-a-Car** (tel: 449 9204) **Garraway Rent-a-Car** (tel: 448 2891) **Island Car Rental** (tel: 448 0738) **Valley Rent-a-Car** (Roseau 448 3233; Portsmouth 447 2996).

Driving is on the left. The main roads are good; others are hazardous, with potholes, hairpin bends and a distinct lack of road signs. The speed limit is 32kph (20mph) in populated areas. Petrol is paid for in cash. Seatbelts are recommended. Drink-drive laws are enforced. Get an Ordnance Survey map from the Tourism Office in Roseau.

Getting around

By air: There are no direct flights to Dominica from the US or Europe; the main international airport gateways are Antigua, Barbados, St Lucia and Sint-Maarten, and the neighbouring French islands of Guadeloupe and Martinique. Dominica has two airports: the most convenient for the south of the island is Canefield, just outside Roseau; the other, Melville Hall, is in the north 62km (an hour's journey time) from the capital. Local carrier **LIAT** serves both; **American**

Eagle from Puerto Rico flies into Melville Hall, as does **American Airlines** from Antigua and **Air Guadeloupe**.

By boat: Highspeed catamarans operated by **Express des Iles** link Dominica with Guadeloupe, Martinique and St Lucia. For information and reservations, contact **Whitchurch Travel Agency** (tel: 488 2181). Dominica also has cruise ship berths on the Roseau waterfront and in Cabrits National Park, Portsmouth.

By road: Taxis, minibuses and hire vehicles have licence plates with H as the last letter. Taxi rates are fixed and quoted in EC$ and US$: make sure you know which is being quoted. They are displayed at the airport and tourist office. In Roseau, try **Mally's Taxi Service** (tel: 448 3114) and **Izoe 24 hour Taxi/Tour Service Taxi** (tel: 449 8545). Few taxis work after 6 PM, except by prior arrangement.

Buses are cheaper; flag them down on the road by the airport.

Sightseeing and activities

Tours, including hiking and photo safaris, are offered by: **Antours Dominica** (tel: 448 6460), **Dominica Tours** (tel: 448 2638), **Ken's Hinterland Adventure Tours** (tel: 448 4850), **Mally's Tour & Taxi Service** (tel: 448 3114), **Nature Island Destinations** (tel: 449 6233), **Paradise Tours** (tel: 448 5999), **Rainbow Rover Tours** (tel: 448 8650), **Whitchurch Travel Agency** (tel: 448 2181). You need an experienced guide for tours in the Morne Trois Pitons National Park. Dominica is excellent for scuba-diving. Arrange trips to view corals and whale-watching (Oct–May) through **Dive Dominica** (tel: 448 2188), the **Anchorage Dive Centre** (tel: 448 2638) and **Dive Castaways** (tel: 449 6844). Book sailing at dive shops.

Tourist information

The Dominica Division of Tourism, National Development Council, PO Box 293, Roseau, Commonwealth of Dominica (tel: 448 2045) has information books at the airport. In the UK, contact the Office of the High Commission, 1 Collingham Gardens, London SW5 0HW (tel: 020 7370 5195).

Grenada (area code 473)

Car hire and driving

A local driving permit can be bought from most hire companies or the Fire Station on the Carenage; show your UK or international driver's licence. Hire companies include: **Avis** (tel: 440 3936); **Budget Car Rentals** (tel: 444 2277); **David's Car Rentals** (tel: 444 3399); **Jerry's Auto Service** (tel: 440 1730); **Thomas & Son** (tel: 444 4384); **Thrift Rent-a-Car** (tel: 444 4984); **Y&R Car Rentals** (tel: 444 4448). Carriacou: **John Gabriel** (tel: 443 7454). Driving is on the left. Seatbelts are not compulsory but recommended. Petrol has to be paid for in cash.

Getting around

By air: Point Salines International Airport receives daily **American Eagle** flights from Puerto Rico, regular **BWIA** international services from New York, Miami and Toronto, and London via Trinidad. **BA** and **JMC Airlines** offer twice-weekly flights from the UK. Local inter-island carriers include **LIAT**, **EC Express** and **Caribbean Star**.

By boat: Ferries operate daily from St George's to Carriacou and then to Petite Martinique daily except Saturday. See list of local tour operators for yacht charter companies.

By road: Hire vehicles have a licence plate with the letter H. Taxi rates are set by the government and quoted in US dollars, but you can pay in either currency. Buses leave from Market Square, St George's and can be flagged down elsewhere. Minibuses ply shorter routes. From Carriacou, buses link Hillsborough with Windwardside and Tyrrel Bay. Motorcycles and bicycles can often be rented from hotels or car-hire firms.

Sightseeing and activities

Taxis can be rented as sightseeing guides. Contact local tour operators for excursions around Grenada, trips to Carriacou, Petite Martinique and the Grenadines, hiking tours, boat trips, car hire and taxi service.
St George's: **Adventure Jeep Tour** (tel: 444 5337); **Fun Tours** (tel: 444 3167); **Sunsation Tours** (tel: 444 1594);

243

Henry's Safari Tours (tel: 444 5313); **Carib Tours** (tel: 444 4363); **Sunshine Tours** (tel: 444 2831). Sports and watersports operators include: **(scuba) Dive Grenada** (tel: 444 1092) and **Eco Dive** (tel: 444 7777); horse-riding: **The Horseman** (tel: 440 5368); hiking: **Henry's Safari Tours** (tel: 444 5313) and **Telfor Hiking Tours** (tel: 442 6200); dolphin and whale-watching excursions (Dec–Apr) can be arranged with **Starwind Enterprise** (tel: 440 3678); deep sea fishing: **Captain Peters** (tel: 440 1349) and **Evans Chartering Service** (tel: 444 4422); yacht charter companies: **Footloose Yacht Charters** (tel: 440 7949); **The Moorings** (tel: 444 4439); **Starwind Enterprises** (tel: 440 3678). Carriacou: tours can be arranged through **Martin Bullen Tours** (tel: 443 7204); scuba-diving through **Carriacou Silver Diving** (tel: 443 7882) and **Tanki** (tel: 443 8406).

Tourist information
Grenada Board of Tourism, The cruise ship dock, St George's (tel: 440 2001); on Carriacou (tel: 443 7948). Grenada Hotel Association, Ross Point Inn, Lagoon Road, St George's (tel: 444 1353). In the UK: Grenada Board of Tourism, 1 Battersea Church Road, London SW11 3LY (tel: 020 7771 7016).

St Lucia (area code 758)

Car hire and driving
A St Lucia temporary driver's licence must be purchased at the airport, the police station in Castries or the car-hire office. Take your current driver's licence. Companies include **Avis** (tel: 452 2202), **Budget** (tel: 452 0233), **Cool Breeze Jeep-Car Rental** (tel: 454 7898), **St Lucia Yacht Car Rental** (tel: 452 5057). Some companies insist on a minimum number of years' driving experience. Driving is on the left. The speed limit is 48kph (30mph). There are penalties for drink-driving and illegal parking. Pay for petrol with cash.

Getting around
By air: St Lucia has two airports: Hewanorra International Airport in the far south of the island (road transfers to the hotels in the north take at least 90 minutes); and George Charles Airport (better known as Vigie) in the capital, Castries. Hewanorra is served by **Air Jamaica** and **BWIA** from the US; **Air Canada**, **British Airways**, **Virgin Atlantic** and **BWIA** from the UK; as well as several charter operators from North America and Europe. **American Eagle** flights from Puerto Rico fly in and out of Castries and inter-island travellers will find local carriers **LIAT**, **BWIA**, **EC Express** and **Helenair**, who also fly into the capital, offer plenty of options for exploring the region.

By boat: A hydrofoil ferry service, **Caribbean Express**, operates between St Lucia and Martinique, Guadeloupe and Dominica. A few hotels have their own boats; for day sailings contact **Brig Unicorn** through your hotel, or **Endless Summer** (tel: 450 8651). Yacht charter companies include: **Destination St Lucia**, Rodeny Bay Marina (tel: 453 8531); **The Moorings**, Marigot Bay (tel: 451 4357).

By road: The north is well served by buses and private minibuses, until about 10 PM (later on Fri). The last bus from Soufrière to Castries leaves at noon. Taxis or minibuses are easily available and can organise tours: **Vigie Taxi** (tel: 452 1599), **St Lucia Taxi** (tel: 452 2492), **AA Taxi** (tel: 459 0001).

Sightseeing and activities
Tours are usually organised through the hotel or tour company rep. Local tour operators include: **Barefoot Holidays** (tel: 450 0507), **Barnards Travel** (tel: 452 2214), **Carib Travel Agency** (tel: 452 3176), **Cox & Co.** (tel: 452 2211), **Pitons Travel Agency** (tel: 450 1486), **Spice Travel** (tel: 452 0865), **St Lucia International Travel** (tel: 452 1293), **Sunlink Tours** (tel: 452 8283). For local cultural tours, contact **St Lucia Heritage Tourism** (tel: 451 6058). For deep sea fishing contact **Captain Mike's** (tel: 452 7044). Dive operators include: **Buddies Scuba**, Rodney Bay (tel: 450 8406) and **Scuba St Lucia**, Anse Chastenet (tel: 459 7755). Windsurfing: contact **Island Windsurfing**, Vieux Fort (tel: 454 7400). For horse-riding: **Trim's Riding Stables** (tel: 452 8273) and **Morne Carbaril Estate**, Soufrière (tel: 459 7340).

Tourist information

St Lucia Tourist Board, Pointe Seraphine, PO Box 221, Castries (tel: 452 7577). There are offices in Jeremie Street, Castries, Soufrière, and in both the airports. In the UK: St Lucia Tourist Board, 421a Finchley Road, London NW3 6HJ (tel: 020 7431 3675).

St Vincent and the Grenadines (area code 784)

Car hire and driving

Take your normal or international licence to the airport, the police station in Bay Street, or the Licensing Authority in Halifax Street to purchase a local licence. The minimum age is 17, but some companies may insist on you being older. Hire companies on St Vincent include: **Avis** (tel: 456 4389); **Ben's Auto Rental** (tel: 456 2907); **David's Auto Clinic** (tel: 456 4026); **Kim's Rentals** (tel: 456 1884); **Unico** (tel: 456 5744). Drive on the left. Seatbelt laws exist and speed limits are 32kph (20mph), 24kph (15mph) for buses and lorries. Pay for petrol with cash.

Getting around

By air: St Vincent and the Grenadines are not served by direct flights from the UK or US. The islands can be reached by air via six main gateways – Barbados, Grenada, Martinique, St Lucia, Puerto Rico and Trinidad – with connections to St Vincent, Bequia, Canouan, Mustique and Union Island. International services to the gateway destinations are provided by **Air Canada**, **Air France**, **Air Jamaica**, **American Airlines**, **British Airways** and **BWIA**, while inter-island operators include **Air Martinique**, **American Eagle**, **Caribbean Star Airlines**, **Mustique Airways** and **St Vincent Grenadines Air**. The longest connecting flight is from Puerto Rico (2.5 hours); the shortest from St Lucia (20 mins).
By boat: Ferries leave St Vincent every day to Bequia and three times a week to the Grenadines (Canouan, Mayreau and Union): they depart from the dock in Kingstown harbour and arrive at Port Elizabeth in Bequia 70–90 minutes later. *MV Admiral I* and *II* (tel: 458 3348) and the *Gem Star* (tel:

458 3472) all serve Bequia. The *MV Barracuda* (tel: 456 5180) mail boat travels south on Mon and Thu at 10:30 AM, stopping at Bequia, Canouan, Mayreau and Union Island, returning Tue and Fri. Yacht charter companies include on St Vincent: **Barefoot Yacht Charters**, Blue Lagoon (tel: 456 9526); **Sunsail Worldwide Sailing Ltd.** (tel: 458 4641). Bequia: **Frangipani Yacht Service** (tel: 458 3255); Union: **Anchorage Yacht Club** (tel: 458 8221). Day sails and boat trips to inaccessible beaches can be arranged by **Baleine Tours** (tel: 457 4089); **Fantasea Tours** (tel: 457 4477) and **Passion Day Charters** (tel: 458 3884). Based in Bequia, the traditional schooner **Friendship Rose** (tel: 458 3373) takes day trips to the southern Grenadines. Union Island, contact **Captain Yannis** (tel: 458 8513) or the **Anchorage Yacht Club** (tel: 458 8221). Scuba-diving: **Dive St Vincent** (tel: 457 4928); **Dive Bequia** (tel: 458 3504); **Anchorage Dive Club Union** (tel: 458 8221); **Grenadines Dive Union** (tel: 458 8138).
By road: The roads of St Vincent and Bequia are rough and winding, but most areas are accessible by bus and taxi. Rates are fixed and a list is available at the Department of Tourism offices or at the airport. To prearrange a taxi tour, ask in your hotel or contact the **Taxi Drivers' Association** (tel: 457 1807); or **Sam Taxi Tours and Yacht Agency** (456 4338; Bequia: 458 3686).

Minibuses depart from Market Square in Kingstown. Hail them anywhere along the route (indicated on the windshield). Smaller islands have taxi-vans and pick-up trucks with benches in the back. Water taxis are available from docks.

Bicycles can be rented from **Sailor's Tours**, Kingston, St Vincent (tel: 457 1712) and from **Lighthouse Villas**, Lower Bay, Bequia (tel: 458 3084).

Sightseeing

Tours and trips can be organised through **Archipelago Tours**, Kingston (tel: 456 1686); **Barefoot Holidays**, Blue Lagoon (tel: 456 9526); **Corea & Co**, Halifax Street, Kingstown (tel: 456 1201); **Emerald Travel & Tours**, Halifax St (tel: 457 1996). Visitors with

245

a particular interest in eco tours should contact **HazECO Tours** (tel: 457 8634) or **Petit Byhaut** (tel: 457 7008). On Bequia: **Grenadine Travel Co.**, Port Elizabeth (tel: 458 3795). On Union: **Wind and Sea**, Clifton (tel: 458 8678).

Tourist information
St Vincent and the Grenadines Department of Tourism, PO Box 834, St Vincent (tel: 457 1502). A tourist information office is situated in Bay Street, Kingstown; also at ET Joshua Airport. Bequia's Tourism Bureau is on the main dock, Port Elizabeth (tel: 458 3286); Union Island Tourist Information (tel: 458 8350). In the UK: St Vincent and the Grenadines Tourist Office, 10 Kensington Court, London W8 5DL (tel: 020 7937 6570).

246

THE LEEWARD ISLANDS

Anguilla (area code 264)

Car hire and driving
You need a valid driver's licence for a temporary licence, on sale at hire companies or at the police station in The Valley. The minimum age for car hire can be 18, 21 or 25. Rental companies include **Carib Rent a Car** (tel: 497 6020) and **Island Car Rentals** (tel: 497 2723). Drive on the left. The speed limit is 48kph (30mph). Seatbelts are recommended. Smaller petrol stations prefer cash.

Getting around
By air: The nearest international airport gateways to Anguilla are Sint Maarten, Antigua, St Kitts, St Thomas (USVI) and San Juan in Puerto Rico. Wallblake Airport is served by local couiers including **Winair**, **Air Anguilla**, **LIAT** and **American Eagle**.
By boat: Ferries between Blowing Point and Marigot, Saint-Martin, leave every 30 minutes from 7:30; also day trips to St Barts. Ferry information (tel: 497 6665). Book boat trips with **Island Yacht Charter Co. Ltd.** (tel: 497 3743), who offer a choice of full- or half-day charters, excursions to St Barts, snorkelling and fishing trips. Scuba-diving: **The Dive Shop** (tel: 497 2020) and **Anguillan Divers** (tel: 497 4750).

By road: Use taxis or hire cars. Taxi rates are set by the government. For larger groups, hire and taxi companies have minibuses. Cycles (not motorbikes) can be hired through travel agents (see below).

Sightseeing
Tours are organised through your hotel, villa manager, or travel agent. Taxi drivers will also arrange tours (fees are negotiable). Local tour operators include **Malliouhana Travel & Tours**, Box 237, The Valley (tel: 497 2431 or 497 2348).

Tourist information
Anguilla Tourist Office, PO Box 1388, The Valley (tel: 497 2759). In the UK: Anguilla Tourist Office, PO Box 2119, Woodford Green, 1G8 0GZ (tel: 020 8505 8973).

Antigua and Barbuda
(area code 268)

Car hire and driving
You need to purchase a provisional licence, issued on presentation of a valid driver's licence. You have to be 18 to drive and some companies set a minimum age for renting a car (21 or 25) and include "extras" in their quotes. Companies include **Budget** (tel: 462 3009), **National** (tel: 462 2113), **Capital** (tel: 462 0863), **Matthew's Car Rental** (tel: 462 9532) and **Avis** (tel: 462 2840).

It is virtually impossible to hire a car during Carnival, so if you're going to need one then, book ahead. To hire a car in Barbuda, arrange it before leaving Antigua. Driving is on the left; the speed limit is 64kph (40mph). Seatbelts are recommended; and there are no drink-driving laws. Petrol usually has to be paid for in cash.

Getting around
By air: Services from North America (via San Juan and other cities) are operated by **American Airlines**, **Air Canada** and **BWIA; British Airways** and **Virgin Atlantic,** as well as various charter companies, fly direct from the UK. Antigua is a hub for local island transport: **LIAT** has the greatest number of services. Other operators include **Caribbean Star**, **Air**

Guadeloupe and **Air St Kitts-Nevis**. Small charter planes are available through **Carib Aviation**. **LIAT** has several flights a day to Barbuda.
By boat: There are no ferries between Antigua and Barbuda, but several local operators make the four-hour boat trip, or visit on a day sail excursion with swimming and snorkelling. Try **Kokomo Cat** (tel: 462 7245), **Treasure Island Cruises** (tel: 461 8675), or *The Jolly Roger* "pirate" ship (tel: 462 2064). Watersports operators include: **Kelly's Watersports Antigua** (tel: 462 8693) and **Sea Sports** (tel: 462 3355); for windsurfing: **Windsurfing Antigua** (tel: 462 9463) and scuba-diving: **Dive Antigua** (tel: 462 3483) and, in English Harbour, **Dockyard Divers** (tel: 460 1178). To charter a yacht, contact: **Nicholson Yacht Charters** (tel: 4460 1530), **Sunsail** (tel: 463 6224) or **Sun Yacht Charters** (tel: 460 2615).
By road: Taxi rates are displayed at the airport and drivers should carry a rate card. Check whether they are quoting the fare in US or EC dollars. All taxi drivers double as guides and hotels may have a team who also take tours. Alternatively contact **Capital Car Rental** (tel: 462 0863). A private bus system runs in the south and east, with no timetables and few stops; this is the cheapest way around (ask in your hotel for the nearest stop). There are no buses in Dickenson Bay or Barbuda: it is best to rent a jeep.
  Bicycles can be hired from **Sun Cycles** in Antigua (tel: 461 0324).

Sightseeing
Local tour operators will also fix island and inter-island excursions. Try **Antours** (tel: 462 4788), **Alexander Parrish** (tel: 462 0638) and **Kiskidee** (tel: 462 4801).

Tourist information
The Antigua and Barbuda Department of Tourism, PO Box 363, Nevis Street, St John's (tel: 462 0480). Also at the airport. Try also Antigua Hotels Association, St Mary's Street, St John's (tel: 462 0374). In the UK: Antigua and Barbuda Tourist Office, Antigua House, 15 Thayer Street, London W1M 5LD (tel: 020 7486 7073).

Montserrat (area code 664)
Because of the volcanic activity, most car hire companies, watersports operators and travel agents have ceased trading for the time being.

Car hire and driving
There are no hire companies at the airport, but it is normally possible to arrange delivery to meet your flight. Present a valid driver's licence to purchase a temporary Montserrat driving permit from Police Headquarters in Salem (tel: 491 2555). Car-hire companies: **Be-Peep's** (tel: 491 3787); **Grant Enterprises R Trading** (tel: 491 9654); **Neville Bradshaw Agencies** (tel: 491 5270). Drive on the left; the speed limit is 48kph (30mph). Small petrol stations prefer cash.

Getting around
By air: Antigua is the international gateway airport for Montserrat, and there are regular helicopter services to the island (daily except Wed and Sun; see panel on page 79). **Caribbean Helicopters**, Jolly Harbour, Antigua (tel: 460 5900) offer Montserrat volcano viewing tours.
By boat: For ferry services from Antigua, see panel on page 79. On the island, boat trips and sport fishing excursions can be arranged through **Bruce Farara** (tel: 491 8802) and **Danny Sweeney** (tel: 491 5645).
By road: There are just a few minibuses, so hire cars and private taxis are preferable. Taxi fares between principal destinations are set by the government; check whether the fare quoted is in US or EC dollars.

Nevis (area code 869)

Car hire and driving
Driving is on the left. Watch out for potholes and livestock on the roads. A local temporary driving licence must be bought from the traffic department, at the police station in Charlestown. Hire companies will pick you up from the airport or your hotel and help with arrangements. Most insist on a minimum age of 25. Companies include: **Nevis Car Rental** (tel: 469 9837); **Nisbet Rentals** (tel: 469 9837); **Noel's Car Rental** (tel: 469 5199); **Stanley's Services**

247

(tel: 469 2597); **Striker's Car Rental** (tel: 469 2654) and **TDC Rentals** (tel: 469 5690).

Getting around
By air: International visitors can make connections for Nevis from the airport gateways of St Kitts, Antigua, Sint Maarten and San Juan, Puerto Rico. Newcastle Airport is well served by local carriers including **LIAT**, **Winair**, **Carib Aviation** and **Nevis Express**.
By boat: Several companies offer inter-island ferry services between Nevis and St Kitts. There are up to eight sailings in each direction daily with a 40–60 minute crossing. For schedules see the latest edition of the free *St Kitts & Nevis Visitor* magazine. To charter a sea taxi from Oualie Beach to Turtle Beach on St Kitts contact **Nevis Watersports** (tel: 469 9060). For a day's catamaran tour, with snorkelling, contact **Leeward Island Charters** (tel: 465 7474).
By road: Private minibuses operate a round-island bus service in both directions from Charlestown, leaving from the main square. Taxis have set rates, usually in EC dollars. Payment can be made in either currency; add 25 per cent between 11 PM and 6 AM. Taxi numbers include **City Taxi** (tel: 469 5621).

Sightseeing and activities
Taxis provide half-day island tours, or contact **All Seasons Streamline Tours** (tel: 469 1138). For walking tours to the rain forest, contact **Top to Bottom** (tel: 469 9080) and for a walking tour of the plantations try **Eco-Tours** (tel: 469 2091). Horse-riding is available through **Hermitage Inn** (tel: 469 3477). **The Four Seasons Resort** has a golf course (tel: 469 1111). Watersports are available on Pinney's Beach and at Oualie Beach. Contact **Nevis Watersports** (tel: 469 9060), **Windsurfing Nevis** (tel: 469 9682), or **Scuba Safaris** (tel: 469 9518).

Tourist information
Local information is available from the Nevis Office of Tourism, Main Street, Charlestown (tel: 469 1042), near the waterfront ferry dock and at the airport. In the UK: 10 Kensington Court, London W8 5DL (tel: 020 7376 0881).

St Kitts (area code 869)

Car hire and driving
Purchase local driving licences from the traffic department at the fire station in Basseterre (tel: 465 2241). Regulations and prices as for Nevis. Rental companies: **Avis** (tel: 465 6507), **Caines Rent-a-Car** (tel: 465 2366), **Cool Profile Ltd.** (tel: 465 2648), **Courtesy Rent a Car** (tel: 465 0189), **Delisle Walwyn** (tel: 465 8449), **TDCThrifty Rentals Ltd.** (tel: 465 2991), **Tropical Car Rental** (tel: 465 4167).

Getting around
By air: Robert Llewelyn Bradshaw Airport in St Kitts is accessible via charter flights from Europe and North America. For scheduled airline services change in Antigua or Sint Maarten, or link with **American Eagle** from San Juan, Puerto Rico. Within the Caribbean, St Kitts is well served by local carriers (see Nevis above).
By boat: There are daily ferry services between St Kitts and Nevis (see the latest edition of *St Kitts and Nevis Visitor* magazine) and you can also charter a sea taxi from Turtle Beach on the south peninsula for the 10 minute crossing to Nevis. **Leeward Island Charters** (tel: 465 7474) offer day sail cruises to Nevis aboard sleek 20m catamarans with time for snorkelling and lunch, as well as deep sea fishing expeditions. Day sails are also available from **Blue Water Safaris** (tel: 466 6740).
By road: On St Kitts, privately run minibuses make regular unscheduled trips along the main coastal roads, starting at the ferry terminal on the waterfront in Basseterre. Taxis have set rates listed in *St Kitts and Nevis Visitor* magazine. Add 25 per cent to the rates between 11 PM and 6 AM. Try **St Kitts Taxi Association** (tel: 465 4253) and the **Circus Taxi Stand** (tel: 465 3006).

Sightseeing and activities
Island tours can be arranged through taxi drivers and tour companies: **Kantours** (tel: 465 2098), **TDC Flamboyant Tours** (tel: 465 6170) and **Tropical Tours** (tel: 465 4167). An island tour takes 3–4 hours. For half- or full-day walking tours to the rain

248

forest, contact **Greg's Safaris** (tel: 465 4121); for walks into the crater of Mount Liamuiga, **Kriss Tours** (tel: 465 4042). Horse-riding is available through **Trinity Stables** in Frigate Bay (tel: 465 9603). There is a golf course in Frigate Bay (tel: 465 1290). For windsurfing, jet skis and snorkelling, contact **Mr X Watersports** (tel: 465 0673), which you will find next to the Monkey Bar on Frigate Bay. Scuba operators include **Pro Divers** (tel: 465 3223) at Turtle Beach and **Dive St Kitts** (tel: 465 1189) at Bird Rock.

Tourist information
The St Kitts Tourism Authority office is in the Pelican Mall (PO Box 132), Bay Road, Basseterre (tel: 465 4040). Tourist information can also be found at the airport. In the UK: 10 Kensington Court, London W8 5DL (tel: 020 7376 0881).

THE VIRGIN ISLANDS

British Virgin Islands
(area code 284)

Car hire and driving
A temporary BVI licence must be purchased from hire companies, issued on presentation of a current foreign licence. The minimum age for renting a car is 25. Cars can be hired in Tortola, from: **Alphonso Car Rentals** (tel: 494 8746); **Avis** (tel: 494 3322); **Dollar** (tel: 494 6093); **Hertz** (tel: 494 6228); **National** (tel: 494 3194). In Virgin Gorda, **L & S Jeep Rental** (tel: 495 5297). Driving is on the left and the speed limit is 64kph (40mph) but 32kph (20mph) in residential areas. Most cars are left-hand drive. Petrol stations take credit cards. Seatbelts are compulsory. You can usually share someone else's taxi in Virgin Gorda for a contribution.

Getting around
By air: There are airports on Tortola and Virgin Gorda, and connections from Europe are via Antigua or San Juan, from the US via San Juan or St Thomas (and then by ferry). Tortola is linked to the USVI by **American Eagle**, **LIAT** and **Winair** amongst others, and all three also fly down to the Eastern Caribbean.

Clair Aero Services (tel: 495 2271) fly from Tortola to Anegada four days a week. A small plane can also be chartered through **Fly BVI** (tel: 495 1747).
By boat: There are daily passenger launches between Tortola, Virgin Gorda, Jost Van Dyke, St Thomas and St John. Ferries from Tortola to St Thomas and St John are operated by **Native Son** (tel: 495 4617), **Smith's Ferry Services** (tel: 495 4495), **Inter Island Boat Services** (tel: 495 4166); from Tortola to Peter Island: **Peter Island Ferry** (tel: 495 2000); from Tortola to Virgin Gorda: **Speedy's** (tel: 495 5240), **Smith's Ferry Services** (see above) and **North Sound Express** (tel: 495 2138). From Virgin Gorda to St Thomas, **Speedy's** (see above) and **Native Son** (see above). From Tortola to Jost Van Dyke: **Jost Van Dyke Ferry Service** (tel: 494 2997). Bareboats can be hired for cruises, local boats for special tours. Contact: **The Moorings**, Road Town (tel: 494 2331), **Sunsail**, West End (tel: 495 4740), **North Sound Yacht Vacations**, Road Town (tel: 494 0096). Day sailing can be arranged through **White Squall II** (tel: 494 2564), **Kuralu** (tel: 495 4381) and the **Catamaran Ppalu** (tel: 494 2872). In Virgin Gorda contact **Spice Charters** (tel: 495 7044) or **Spirit of Anegada Day Sails** (tel: 496 6825).

Sightseeing and activities
Guided tours are offered by the **BVI Taxi Association** (tel: 494 2322) and **Travel Plan Tours** (tel: 494 2872). On Virgin Gorda contact **Mahogany Taxi Service** (tel: 495 5469), which organises tours for a minimum of two people. Scuba-diving companies include **Underwater Safaris** (tel: 494 3235) and **Baskin in the Sun** (tel: 494 2858), both in Tortola. In Virgin Gorda try **Dive BVI** (tel: 495 5513). For windsurfing off Tortola contact **Boardsailing BVI** (tel: 495 2447).

Tourist information
BVI Tourist Board, 134 Road Town, Tortola (tel: 494 3134) and in Virgin Gorda Yacht Harbour (tel: 495 5181). In the UK: BVI Tourist Board, 54 Baker Street, London W1M 1DJ (tel: 020 7240 4259).

US Virgin Islands
(area code 340)

St Croix

Car hire and driving
The minimum age is 18; 25 with some companies. A full driver's licence will suffice. Companies include: **Budget** (tel: 778 9636), **Charlie's** (tel: 773 1678), **Hertz** (tel: 778 1402), **Horizon** (tel: 779 3900), **Olympic** (tel: 773 8000), **Thrifty** (tel: 773 7200). Drive on the left. The speed limit is 88kph (55mph). Drink-driving and seatbelt laws are strictly enforced. Petrol is cheap; credit cards are accepted.

Getting around
By air: International carriers serving the USVI are **American**, **Continental**, **Delta**, **Northwest**, **TWA**, **United** and **US Air**. Local carriers include **Air Sunshine**, **American Eagle**, **Cape Air** and **LIAT**. Seabourne Aviation (tel: 773 6442) operate a daily seaplane service linking Christiansted with St Thomas. The first flight is 6:45 AM from St Croix (Sun 8:15 AM) and the last is at 4:15 PM.
By boat: For day sails and Buck Island tours, contact **Bilinda Charters** (tel: 773 1641); **Teroro II** (tel: 773 3161); and **Diva** (tel: 778 4675). For windsurfing tuition and rentals, wave runners, sea kayaking and parasailing contact **St Croix Watersports** (tel: 773 7060). For scuba-diving try **VI Divers** (tel: 773 6045) and **Dive Experience** (tel: 773 3307) in Christiansted and **Scubawest** (tel: 772 3701) in Frederiksted.
By road: Taxi vans can be called from your hotel or found at the airport and, when cruise ships are in, at the pier in Frederiksted. The **St Croix Taxi Association** (tel: 778 1088) runs taxi vans on the main roads from Christiansted to Frederiksted; also try **Cruzan Taxi Association** (tel: 773 6388); **Caribbean Taxi and Tours** (tel: 773 9799).

Sightseeing and activities
Island bus tours are offered by **St Croix Transit Tours** (tel: 772 3333) and **Safari Bus Tours** (tel: 773 6700). Horse-riding tours are run by **Paul and Jill's Equestrian Stable** (tel: 772 2880).

For guided hikes in the scenic East End or Annaly Bay, contact **Caribbean Adventure Tours** (tel: 773 4599). For cycling contact **St Croix Bike and Tours** (tel: 772 2343) in Frederiksted. For springtime whale-watching excursions (Feb–Mar), contact the **Environmental Association of St Thomas-St John (EAST)** (tel: 776 8338).

Tourist information
The US Virgin Islands Division of Tourism has an office at 41a Queen Cross Street (Box 4538), Christiansted, St Croix 00822 (tel: 773 0495) and at Strand Street, Frederiksted (tel: 772 0357). St Croix Hotel and Tourism Association, PO Box 24238 (tel: 773 7117 or 800/497 7030). In the UK: Molasses House, Clove Hitch Quay, Plantation Wharf, London SW11 3TN (tel: 020 7978 5262).

St Thomas and St John

Car hire and driving
You need a valid driver's licence and the minimum age for drivers is 18; in general hire companies prefer you to be at least 25. On St Thomas: **Avis** (tel: 774 1468); **Budget** (tel: 776 5774); **E-Z Car** (tel: 775 6255); **Dependable** (tel: 774 2253); **Discount** (tel: 776 4858); **Tri-Island** (tel: 776 2879). On St John: **C & C Rental** (tel: 693 8164); **Hertz** (tel: 693 7580); **St John Car Rental** (tel: 776 6103). Driving is on the left. Wearing a seatbelt is compulsory and the drink-driving laws are enforced. The speed limit is 56kph (35mph). Credit cards are accepted; pay before filling up with petrol.

Getting around
By air: From Europe the best connections are made via Antigua or San Juan, Puerto Rico. Services from the USA include **American Airlines**, **Continental**, **Delta**, **United**, **US Airways** and many charter airlines. Some of these airlines also make the link to St Croix, as does **American Eagle** or the seaplane service (tel: 777 1227). Links to the rest of the Caribbean are made by **Air Sunshine**, **Cape Air** and **LIAT**. For helicopter travel, contact **Air Centre Helicopters** (tel: 775 7335).

By boat: There are two ferry routes between the islands: Charlotte Amalie to Cruz Bay (six a day) and Red Hook to Cruz Bay (daily, every hour: 6:30 AM, 7:30 AM, 8 AM–midnight). For more details, contact **Transportation Services** (tel: 776 6282).

Ferries link St Thomas and the British Virgin Islands (Tortola, Virgin Gorda and Jost Van Dyke); proof of citizenship is required to embark here. For ferries from Red Hook (St Thomas) to Jost Van Dyke, stopping *en route* at Cruz Bay (St John) take an hour contact **Inter Island Boat Services** (tel: 776 6597). Ferries from Charlotte Amalie (St Thomas) to Tortola take 45 minutes to the West End or an hour-and-a-half to Road Town; contact **Native Son** (tel: 774 8685) or **Smith's Ferry** (tel: 775 7292). There are ferries from Red Hook (St Thomas) to West End (Tortola), 30 minutes (contact Native Son or Smith's Ferry) and from Cruz Bay (St John) to West End (Tortola), 30 minutes (contact Inter Island). Ferries also leave from Charlotte Amalie and Red Hook for Virgin Gorda. For direct Red Hook-Virgin Gorda services, contact Transportation Services or Inter Island; for Charlotte Amalie-Tortola-Virgin Gorda, contact Smith's Ferry.

Yachts can be chartered with or without a crew, usually through a broker. Check that the vessel is a member of the VI Charter Yacht League (tel: 774 3944), the local professional association of crewed charter boats. A full list of brokers is available from the tourist office.

Powerboats with or without captains can be rented from numerous companies. Contact **Nauti Nymph** (tel: 775 5066) or **See and Ski** (tel: 775 6265). You can also book day sailings, submarine rides or short fishing excursions with **Fantasy** (tel: 775 5652), **Sundance** (tel: 779 1722) or **Winifred** (tel: 775 7898). **Atlantis Submarine** (tel: 776 5650) is based in Havensight Mall. Scuba operators include **Aqua Action Dive Center** (tel: 775 6285) or **Chris Sawyer** (tel: 777 7804) In St John, day sailings with **Catamaran Adventure** (tel: 771 6950) For scuba-diving contact **Low Key Watersports** (tel: 693 8999).

By road: On St Thomas, taxis are usually found at the ferry, airport, shopping and resort areas, opposite Emancipation Park and along the waterfront in Charlotte Amalie. In St John they tend to cluster around Cruz Bay Dock, but can be hailed anywhere. Taxi fares are fixed and prices are published at the airport and hotels. St Thomas taxis are usually estates or minivans that take five or six passengers to drop off at their stops; on St John open safari buses serve as taxis. Public buses on St Thomas are irregular, although there is a country bus service between Red Hook and Charlotte Amalie. An hourly bus service begins at 5.30 AM from town and the last one leaves Red Hook around 8:30 PM. Open-air safari buses operated by the VI Taxi Commission run between Charlotte Amalie–Red Hook and Charlotte Amalie–Havensight Mall. The service is available Mon–Fri 12:15–5:15 PM (every 15 min).

Sightseeing

St Thomas: tours are mainly conducted in minivans or safari buses. The **Virgin Islands Taxi Association City-Island Tour** (tel: 774 4550) offers a variety of island tours; **Tropic Tours** (tel: 774 1855) runs half-day tours, which includes shopping and sightseeing, by bus.

St John: the **St John National Park Visitor Centre**, Cruz Bay (tel: 776 6201) does guided tours on and offshore; a **St John Taxi Services Inc** (tel: 693 7530) island tour covers Cruz Bay, Annaberg Plantation and the north coast beaches.

Tourist information

The USVI Division of Tourism can be contacted at PO Box 6400, Charlotte Amalie (tel: 774 8784) and at PO Box 200, Cruz Bay, St John (tel: 776 6450). There are two visitor centres in Charlotte Amalie, one opposite Emancipation Park and the other at Havensight Mall. The National Park Service has visitor centres at the ferry areas on St Thomas (Red Hook) and St John (Cruz Bay). In the UK: Molasses House, Clove Hitch Quay, Plantation Wharf, London SW11 3TN (tel: 020 7978 5262).

251

FRENCH ANTILLES

Guadeloupe (area code 590)

Car hire and driving

Normal driver's licences are valid for up to 20 days, after which an international one is needed. The minimum driving age is usually 18. Cars can be rented at the airport from: **Avis** (tel: 21 13 54), **Budget** (tel: 21 13 48), **Hertz** (tel: 21 13 46), **Jumbo Car** (tel: 91 55 66), **Europcar** (tel: 21 13 52), **Karukéra Car** (tel: 21 13 79), **Citer** (tel: 83 22 88), **Pop's Car** (tel: 83 39 73), **Pro Rent** (tel: 26 73 44), **Soltour** (tel: 21 13 77). Car-hire companies have desks at the airport, hotels and in Pointe-à-Pitre and Basse-Terre. Drive on the right. Seatbelt and drink-driving laws are enforced. Most petrol stations take credit cards.

Getting around

By air: Pôle Caraïbes international airport outside Pointe-à-Pitre is the main airport gateway to Guadeloupe. It is served by **Air Canada**, **Air France**, **American Airlines** and **Air Guadeloupe** from North America, and by **Air France**, **Air Liberté**, **AOM** and **Corsair** from Europe. There are numerous local airlines providing inter-island services including **Air Guadeloupe**, **Air Martinique** and **Air Saint-Martin/St Barth** for the other French islands and a few other stops, plus the Caribbean-wide services of **LIAT**. Sightseeing flights are offered by **Alpha Aviation** (tel: 88 70 10) and helicopter tours by **Azur Aéro Services** (tel: 94 86 77).

By boat: A number of operators serve the offshore islands. For daily services to Marie-Galante (Grand Bourg) from Pointe-à-Pitre, contact **Brudey Frères** (tel: 91 60 87) or take the fast catamaran service provided by **Express des Iles** (tel: 83 12 45). **TMC Archipel** (tel: 83 19 89) ferry passengers to Marie-Galante's second town, St Louis, aboard a high-speed catamaran daily. For Les Saintes, both **Brudey Frères** and **Express des Iles** provide a daily service to Terre-de-Haut from Pointe-à-Pitre; while **Companie Deher** makes daily crossings to Terre-de-Haut from Trois-Rivières on the east coast of Basse-Terre.

As well as trips to the out islands, Express des Iles also link Pointe-à-Pitre with Martinique, Dominica and St Lucia. All times and prices are subject to change, so it is wise to check before travelling. There are, however, no ferries to St Barts or Saint-Martin. Safe anchorages and marinas, for ferries and yachts in Grande-Terre, are at Marina du Bas-du-Fort, Gosier and Marina de St-François (in the heart of town); or Marina de Rivière Sens, Basse-Terre.

Numerous companies around the Bas-du-Fort marina rent out bareboat or crewed yachts and motorboats, including **Star Voyages Antilles** (tel: 90 86 26), **Sun Sail** (tel: 90 82 80) and **Tropical Yacht Services** (tel: 90 84 52).

By road: Taxi fares are set by the government and prices are posted at the airport, taxi stands and major hotels. Taxi stands in Pointe-à-Pitre are on boulevard Faidherbe et Chanzy, rue Achille René Boisneuf and rue Alexandre Isaac in front of the tourist office (tel: 82 21 21). In Basse-Terre **Cours Nolivos Taxi** (tel: 81 79 70) offers tours at set fares to various points; the tourist office or your hotel can arrange for an English-speaking driver.

A public bus service operates around the island, 5 AM–6 PM, stopping at *arrêtbus* signs, or wherever you hail it. Pay when you get off. The three bus stations in Pointe-à-Pitre, La Darse, Mortenol and Bergevin, serve different parts of the island. Fares are posted at the station.

Scooter rentals are widely available in the main towns and coastal resorts. They are certainly the best way to get around the out islands for day trippers who want to explore rather than lie on the beach. Push bikes are also popular and several companies offer mountain bike tours (see below) as well as rentals. Just remember that Grande-Terre is rather flat, while Basse-Terre is mountainous.

Sightseeing and activities

Ask the tourist office for English-speaking guides. Pick-ups at the hotel, lunch and guide services are usually included in the price. Local tour operators include **Navitour** (tel:

83 49 50) and **Nouvelles Frontières** (tel: 83 91 42). Sea excursions, particularly to the mangrove reserve, can be organised by companies around Bas-du-Fort Marina, or contact the **King Papyrus** *bateau-mouche* (tel: 90 92 98), which departs from the Marina Pointe-à-Pitre for trips to the Réserve Naturelle du Grand Cul de Sac Marin marine preserve, an important feeding ground for waterfowl. Day sails can be arranged through **Les Heures Saines** (tel: 98 86 63), who also offer whale-watching excursions aboard their catamaran based at Rocher de Malendure, Pigeon-Bouillante on the west coast of Basse-Terre. This is in the Réserve Cousteau, a must for divers, and **Heures Saines**' dive operation (tel: 98 86 63) organises both day and night dives. Other dive operators include **Aux Aquanautes Antillais** (tel: 98 87 30), **Blue Dive** (tel: 85 53 09) and **C.I.P. Bouillante** (tel: 98 81 72).

Hiking in the national park and up the Soufrière volcano can be arranged through **Vert Intense** (tel: 55 40 47). There are various adventure tour operators offering mountain biking, hiking, sea kayaking and canyoning experiences: these include **Parfum d'Aventure** (tel: 88 47 62), **Points Bleu Soleil** (Basse-Terre tel: 99 30 33 and Grande-Terre tel: 22 87 77), or **Vert Intense** (see above). Watersports are equally well catered for with (amongst others) jet ski excursions arranged by **Aventures des Iles** (tel: 85 02 77); windsurfing with the **Karukera Surf Club** (tel: 23 10 93); and waterskiing with **A.G.S.N.** (tel: 26 17 47).

Tourist information
Office Départemental du Tourisme de la Guadeloupe, 5 square de la Banque, 97110 Pointe-à-Pitre Cédex (Guadeloupe) (tel: 89 46 89). Office du Tourisme de Basse-Terre, Maison du Port, 97100 Basse-Terre (tel: 81 61 54); Office du Tourisme de St-François, Avenue de l'Europe, 97118 St-François (tel: 88 48 74) and in Bouillante (tel: 98 73 48). There is also a tourist information booth at the airport. In the UK: French Government Tourist Office, 178 Piccadilly, London W1V 0AL (tel: 020 7499 6911).

CONVERSION CHARTS

FROM	TO	MULTIPLY BY
Inches	Centimetres	2.54
Centimetres	Inches	0.3937
Feet	Metres	0.3048
Metres	Feet	3.2810
Yards	Metres	0.9144
Metres	Yards	1.0940
Miles	Kilometres	1.6090
Kilometres	Miles	0.6214
Acres	Hectares	0.4047
Hectares	Acres	2.4710
Gallons	Litres	4.5460
Litres	Gallons	0.2200
Ounces	Grams	28.35
Grams	Ounces	0.0353
Pounds	Grams	453.6
Grams	Pounds	0.0022
Pounds	Kilograms	0.4536
Kilograms	Pounds	2.205
Tons	Tonnes	1.0160
Tonnes	Tons	0.9842

MEN'S SUITS							
UK	36	38	40	42	44	46	48
Rest of Europe	46	48	50	52	54	56	58
US	36	38	40	42	44	46	48

DRESS SIZES						
UK	8	10	12	14	16	18
France	36	38	40	42	44	46
Italy	38	40	42	44	46	48
Rest of Europe	34	36	38	40	42	44
US	6	8	10	12	14	16

MEN'S SHIRTS						
UK	14	14.5	15	15.5	16 16.5	17
Rest of Europe	36	37	38	39/40	41 42	43
US	14	14.5	15	15.5	16 16.5	17

MEN'S SHOES						
UK	7	7.5	8.5	9.5	10.5	11
Rest of Europe	41	42	43	44	45	46
US	8	8.5	9.5	10.5	11.5	12

WOMEN'S SHOES						
UK	4.5	5	5.5	6	6.5	7
Rest of Europe	38	38	39	39	40	41
US	6	6.5	7	7.5	8	8.5

253

Martinique (area code 596)

Car hire and driving
Drivers must be at least 21 and hold a driver's licence; after 20 days you'll need an International Driver's Permit. Companies include **Avis** (airport tel: 42 11 00); **Budget** (airport tel: 42 16 79, Fort-de-France tel: 70 22 75); **Europcar** (airport tel: 42 42 42); **Hertz** (tel: 42 16 90); **Jumbo/Thrifty** (airport tel: 42 16 99, Pointe du Bout tel: 66 11 55, Ste-Anne tel: 76 80 82); **National/Citer** (tel: 72 40 13); **Pop's Car** (tel: 42 16 84); and **Euradom** (airport tel: 42 17 05). The speed limits are 100kph (62mph) on the highway and 50kph (31mph) in town. Seatbelts are mandatory; drink-driving is strictly penalised.

Getting around
By air: From Europe, **Air France** and **AOM** fly transatlantic from France into Lamentin Airport outside Fort-de-France. From the US, **Air France** fly several times a week from Miami, and there are more frequent connections from San Juan, Puerto Rico. Local carriers include **American Eagle** (out of Puerto Rico offering numerous connections with flights to and from the US mainland), **Air Guadeloupe**, **Air Martinique** and **LIAT**. Sightseeing flights are offered by **Alizés Air Services**, Ste-Anne (tel: 25 26 98).
By boat: A fast power-catamaran service links Martinique with Guadeloupe and the Windward Islands of Dominica and St Lucia. It is operated by **Express des Iles**, Terminal Inter-Iles, quai Ouest, Fort-de-France (tel: 63 12 11). Reservations can be made through local travel agents. Though inexpensive, the crossings can be pretty rough, so consider the short plane hop as a viable alternative. Local ferries ply Fort-de-France bay taking passengers from quai Desnambuc on the central waterfront across to the beaches of Pointe de Bout, Anse Mitan and Anse à l'Ane. There are frequent crossings throughout the day, but check the time of evening services.
By road: Taxis can be found mainly at the airport, at taxi ranks in Fort-de-France and at major hotels. For **Radio Taxis** call 63 63 62. Fares are regulated by the government (a list is available

254

from the airport) and are expensive, especially if you arrive at night, when a 40 per cent surcharge is added. Private taxis can be found at the Savane, along boulevard General de Gaulle and place Clemenceau in Fort-de-France. You can also travel by bus or shared taxi: the main terminal to catch either of these is at Pointe-Simon, on the sea front in Fort-de-France, otherwise try around boulevard General de Gaulle. Buses are run privately, from 5 AM to 8 PM, and leave when they're full. Shout *arrêt* to stop one. There is also an inter-urban bus network. Shared taxis (*taxi collectif* or *taxicos*) start early and run until 6 PM with regular fixed routes. Most start at Pointe-Simon and serve all the *communes*.

Motorscooters and bicycles can be rented from agencies in all the main tourist resorts. **VTT Tilt**, Pointe du Bart (tel: 66 01 01) offers 18-speed mountain bikes (*vélo tout terrain*), as do **Blue Monday**, Diamant (tel: 76 18 80) and excursion specialists **Sud Loisirs** (tel: 76 81 82). The **Parc Naturel Regional de la Martinique** (tel: 73 19 30) has designated cycle routes off the beaten track and organises bike and walking tours in and around beauty spots.

Sightseeing and activities
The following local agents will find you guided tours by car or bus, trips on sailing boats and cruise ships, excursions in glass-bottomed boats, trips to Dominica, St Lucia and the Grenadines: **Caribtours** (tel: 50 93 52), **Madinina Tours** (tel: 70 65 25). **Azimut** (tel: 70 07 00) offers a guided tour of Fort-de-France. For hiking, contact the **Bureau de la Randonnée** (tel: 78 30 77), or **Aventures Tropicales** (tel: 64 58 49), who also organise adventurous pursuits from jeep safaris and mountain biking excursions to canyonning. Scuba operators include: **Planète Bleue**, Pointe du Bout (tel: 66 08 79) and **Sub Diamond Rock** (tel: 76 25 80). Windsurfing equipment can be rented from the east coast centres of **Club Nautique du Vauclin** (tel: 74 50 83) and the **Club Nautique du Marin** (tel: 74 92 48). General watersports operators include **Alizé Fun** in St Anne (tel: 74 71 58). Charter sailing

boats can be hired through **The Moorings** (tel: 74 75 39) and **Star Voyage** (tel: 66 00 72).

Tourist information
Office Départemental du Tourisme de la Martinique, rue Ernest Deproge, Bord de Mer, BP 520 97200 Fort-de-France Cédex (tel: 63 79 60). There are information offices on the waterfront in the town and at the airport. In the US contact: Maison de la France, 670 North Michigan Avenue, Chicago, IL 60611 (tel: 312/751 7800). In the UK: French Government Tourist Office, 178 Piccadilly, London W1V 0AL (tel: 020 7399 3500).

St Barthélemy (area code 590)

Car hire and driving
Cars can be hired at the airport: in peak season there may be a three-day minimum. Some hotels have their own car fleets and many offer 24-hour emergency road service. **Avis** (tel: 27 71 43); **Budget** (tel: 27 66 30); and **Europcar** (tel: 27 73 33). There are two petrol stations, one near the airport (credit card-operated self-service pumps, open 24 hours, closed Sun), the other in Lorient (closed Thu, Sat afternoon and Sun).

Getting around
By air: St Barts' tiny airport at St Jean can only handle small planes, so the main international gateway to the island is Juliana Airport on neighbouring Sint Maarten. **Air Caraïbes** shuttles back and forth between St Barts and Sint Maarten and, together with **Saint-Barth Commuter**, offers services to French Saint-Martin. **Winair** makes a twice-weekly flight to Anguilla; and **Air St Thomas** links the island to St Thomas, USVI. Helicopter tours can be arranged with **Caribbean Helicopters Ltd.**, Antigua (tel: 264/460 5900). **By boat:** St Barts is linked to the neighbouring island of Sint Maarten/Saint Martin by regular high speed ferry services. For information contact **The Edge** (tel: 599/544 2640), which plies the route between Philipsburg and Gustavia; while **Voyager** (tel: 27 54 10) serves Baie Nettlé and Philipsburg from

Gustavia. **Marine Service** (tel: 27 70 34) runs day trips around St Barts and cruises to Saint-Martin, Anguilla, Saba and the Virgin Islands on its four-cabin catamaran; also rents out powerboats; **Océan Must** (tel: 27 62 25) operates day sails around St Barts and to neighbouring islands. **By road:** There are taxi stands at the airport and in Gustavia on rue de la République. Cabs are unmetered, so you may be charged more if you stop on the way. Minibuses and taxis do island tours. Radio cabs can be called on 27 66 31 or 27 75 81. Fares are 50 per cent higher after 8 PM. Motorcycles can be hired near the airport and in Gustavia (helmet compulsory). Try **St Barth Moto Bike** (tel: 27 67 89) and **Barth'loc** (tel: 27 52 81).

255

Sightseeing and activities
Tours can be arranged through your hotel, the tourist office or taxi operators including **Hugo Cagan** (tel: 27 70 79) and **Florian Laplace** (tel: 27 63 58). Local operators include **St Barth Tours and Travel** (tel: 27 60 33). Scuba-diving: **West Indies Dive** (tel: 27 70 34) and **Odyssée Caraïbe** (tel: 27 55 94). **Wind Wave Power** (tel: 27 82 57) offers watersports equipment rentals on Grand Cul de Sac beach.

Tourist information
The Office du Tourisme de Saint Barthélemy, Quai du Général de Gaulle, Gustavia (tel: 27 87 27). For UK see Guadelope.

Saint-Martin/Sint Maarten (area code French side, 590 plus six digits; Dutch side, 599 plus seven digits)

Car hire and driving
Your own driver's licence is sufficient to hire a car on both sides: you must be at least 25. Cars can be hired at Juliana Airport. Companies include: **Avis** (tel: 87 50 60 or 545 2316); **Budget** (tel: 87 21 91 or 545 4030); **Cannegie Car Rental** (tel: 542 2397); **Continental** (tel: 87 77 64); **Esperance** (tel: 87 51 09); **National/Europcar** (tel: 27 32 80 or 544 2168); **Sandy G Car Rental** (tel: 87 88 25). Motorbikes and scooters are also widely available.

Driving is on the right and road signs are international. Speed limits are 80kph (50mph) outside the towns, 30kph (19mph) in towns; drink-driving carries fines, as do illegal parking, speeding and running traffic lights; seatbelts should be worn and petrol is paid for in cash.

Getting around
By air: Sint Maarten/Saint-Martin is is well served by international and local carriers. Juliana Airport on the Dutch side receives international air traffic including **American Airlines**, **Continental Airlines**, **TWA** and **US Air** flights from North America, and **Air France** and **KLM** flights from Europe. **Air Guadeloupe**, **Air Martinique**, **Air St Barthélemy** and **Air St Martin** fly into Grand Case Airport on the French side as well as Juliana; **ALM**, the local Dutch carrier, operates out of Juliana. Other local carriers include **BWIA** and **LIAT**. **Heli-Inter Caraïbes** (tel: 87 35 88) run sightseeing excursions and act as taxis or as emergency services.

By boat: There are anchorages around the island and a flourishing yachting scene. For trips to the neighbouring French island of St Barts, contact **The Edge**, Philipsburg (tel: 544 2640), or **Voyager** (Baie Nettlé tel: 87 10 68, Philipsburg tel: 542 4096). There are services every day, though the operator varies. The Edge and Voyager also make regular trips to Saba, and ferries to Anguilla depart half-hourly throughout the day from the Marigot waterfront. You will need a form of identification with a photograph and there is a departure tax.

Companies chartering boats, with or without a skipper, include: **The Moorings** (tel: 87 32 54), in Oyster Pond, and **Sunsail** (tel: 27 42 85). Day trips by sail or motorboat to nearby islands or coves, including Anguilla, are organised from the Dutch side aboard *Blue Beard* (tel: 545 2898) and *Sualiga* (tel: 542 2167). From the French side, sailing excursions are organised through **Saint Martin Evasion** (tel: 87 13 60), **Rising Sun Tours** (tel: 87 14 22) and through the marinas at Port La Royale (tel: 87 20 43), the Capitainerie de Oyster Pond (tel: 87 33 47) and Port Lonvilliers (tel: 87 31 94). General

watersports operators offering equipment rentals include **Blue Ocean International** in Baie Nettlé (tel: 87 89 73), **Kakao Watersports** in Baie Orientale (tel: 27 02 98) and nearby **Kontiki Watersports** (tel: 87 46 89). Scuba-diving: **Ocean Explorers** (tel: 544 4357) and **Scuba Fun** in Anse Marcel (tel: 87 36 13).

By road: Taxi rates across the island are fixed and standardised – you can get a list from the tourist offices and rates are posted at the airport. Call: 87 56 54 (Marigot); 545 4317 (Juliana Airport); and 542 2359 (Philipsburg). Authorised taxis display stickers of the Sint Maarten Taxi Association. Buses run between 7 AM and 7 PM from Philipsburg through Cole Bay to Marigot.

Sightseeing
For sightseeing, contact **Island Reps Tours** (tel: 545 2392), **Rising Sun Tours** (tel: 544 2855 or 87 14 22), **St Maarten Sightseeing** (tel: 545 3921) and **Dutch Tours** (tel: 542 3316).

Tourist information
Dutch side: Sint Maarten Tourist Bureau, W G Buncamper Road 33, Philipsburg, Sint Maarten (tel: 542 2337). In Europe, contact Marilyn M Pieters, Nocturnestraat 9, 2553 SK Den Haag, Netherlands (tel: 31 70 40 42 101). French side: Office du Tourisme de Saint-Martin, Port de Marigot, 97150 Saint-Martin (tel: 29 05 73), on the waterfront in Marigot. In the UK contact the Maison de la France, 178 Piccadilly, London W1V 0AL (tel: 020 7399 3500).

NETHERLANDS ANTILLES

Aruba (area code 297)

Car hire and driving
You need a valid national or international licence; age range policies may vary with different companies. All companies include unlimited mileage, but not insurance. Try **Airways** (tel: 821845); **Avis** (tel: 828787; airport 825496); **Budget** (tel: 828600; airport 825423); **Dollar** (tel: 822783; airport 825651); **Five Star** (tel: 827600); **Hertz** (tel: 824400; airport 824886); **Localisa Rent-A-Car**

256

(tel: 837490); **Marco's Car Rental** (tel: 865889); **Safari** (tel: 839670); **Thrifty** (tel: 835335); **Toyota Rent-a-Car** (tel: 834832; airport 834902). Main roads are in good condition, but most attractions are down dirt roads: four-wheel drive vehicles are recommended. Drive on the right. Road signs are international. Speed limit in towns is 40kph (25mph), 60kph (37mph) out of town.

Getting around
By air: Aruba is well-served by carriers from North America. Those offering direct flights from a variety of US destinations include **American Airlines**, **Continental**, **Delta**, **TWA** and **US Airways**; **Air Canada** also flies direct; and there are a number of charter flights. The local Dutch airline, **Air ALM**, flies to Aruba from Miami via Curaçao, in addition to offering various inter-island routes. There are numerous air services to destinations throughout South America. From Europe, **Martinair** (a subsidiary of KLM) provides a twice-weekly service from Amsterdam.
By boat: Based in Oranjestad's Seaport Village Marina, **Atlantis Submarine** (tel: 836090) transfers passagers by catamaran out to the Barcadera Reef and their mini-submarine. The sub dives to a depth of 45m and the excursion lasts for around 50 minutes. They also operate the semi-submersible *Seaworld Explorer*, which visits a reef area and the site of a World War II German shipwreck.

Sailing cruises around the island, or moonlight, catamaran or dinner cruises, with stops for swimming and snorkelling, can be arranged through **Aruba Watersports Center** (tel: 866613), **De Palm Tours** (tel: 824400), **Discovery Tours** (tel: 875875), **Rainbow Runner** (tel: 864259), **Red Sail Sports** (tel: 861603), **Pelican Watersports** (tel: 872302) and **Wave Dancers** (tel: 825520).

The tourist office has a list of boats available for day or half-day charter for deep-sea fishing.
By road: Taxi rates are fixed – make sure you agree on the price before setting off; prices go up in the evening and overnight. Taxis can be flagged down, or call 822116 (main dispatch office, Oranjestad). Taxi drivers should all have Tourism Guide Certificates and speak English.

Buses run between Oranjestad and the southeast of the island and to the beach hotels and between Oranjestad and the airport. Oranjestad bus station is on Zoutmanstraat. There are also jitney cars that operate like shared taxis. A jitney or bus from Oranjestad to San Nicolas will drop you off at the airport. Buses stick to their timetables – which are available from the tourist offices – and run one or two an hour.

To rent motorcycles, scooters and mopeds, contact **Donata Car & Cycle** (tel: 834343); **Ron's Motorcycle Rental** (tel: 862090); **George's** (tel: 825975); **Semver Cycle Rental** (tel: 866851).

Sightseeing and activities
The major local operator, **De Palm Tours** (tel: 824400), has offices in most hotels offering a three-hour tour of Aruba's highlights and a day-tour to Curaçao and to Caracas, Venezuela. For a two-and-a-half-hour guided adventure tour of the North Coast and Arikok National Park, contact **Four Wheelin't in Aruba** (tel: 860239).

Other operators include: **ECO Destination Management** (tel: 872921); **Friendly Tours** (tel: 823230); **Kremer Touristic Services** (tel: 879039); **Watapana Tours** (tel: 835191). The rugged North Coast region and Arikok National Park make for a great horse-riding safari; stables offering rides include **Rancho Diamari** (tel: 860239) and **Rancho Notorious** (tel: 860508). There is excellent windsurfing off Aruba; check out **Roger's Windsurf Place** (tel: 861918) or **Sailboard Vacations** (tel: 862527) amongst others. Scuba-diving operators include **Aruba Watersports Center** (tel: 866613); **Dive Aruba** (tel: 825216); **Pro–Dive** (tel: 822520).

Tourist information
Aruba Tourism Authority, L G Smith Blvd. 172, Box 1019, Oranjestad (tel: 823777) for brochures and guides. There are also tourist offices at the harbour in Oranjestad and at the airport. In the UK, contact Saltmarsh Partnership, The Copperfields, 25 Copperfield Street, London SE1 0EN.

257

Bonaire (area code 599)

Car hire and driving

A national or international licence is required and most of the 10 or so companies stipulate a minimum age. Try **ABC** (tel: 717 8980); **Avanti Car Rental** (tel: 717 5661); **Avis** (tel: 717 5795); **Budget** (tel: 717 8300); **Flamingo Car Rentals** (tel: 717 8888); **Everts Car Rental** (tel: 717 8099); **Total** (tel: 717 8313); **Island Car Rental** (tel: 717 2100); **Sunray Car Rental** (tel: 717 5230); **Trupial Car Rental** (tel: 717 8487).

Driving is on the right. The speed limit in built-up areas is 32kph (20mph) and outside towns 60kph (37mph) unless otherwise specified. There are no traffic lights and the main roads are good, but there are 32km of unpaved roads that get very muddy during the rainy season. Roads are apt to become one-way halfway along. Beware of potholes, lizards and herds of goats. There are very few watering holes: on island trips take food and drink supplies.

There are petrol stations in Rincon, Kralendijk and Antrejol, open Mon–Sat 7 AM–9 PM; Kralendijk is also open Sunday.

Getting around

By air: Air ALM provides daily services into Bonaire's Flamingo Airport from Miami via Curaçao, and twice-weekly direct flights from Atlanta, as well as inter-island services to regional transport hubs such as Aruba and Trinidad. **Air Aruba** offers connecting services to Bonaire from its US routes. From Europe, the only direct flight is **KLM**'s weekly service from Amsterdam. **By boat:** More people come to Bonaire to dive than to sail or putter around in boats (ask hotels about their diving packages). Klein Bonaire is reached by diving boats: hitch a lift if you do not plan to dive and don't miss the return. Snorkelling, picnicking and sunset cruises are offered by the Siamese junk *Samur* (tel: 717 5592), the *Woodwind* (tel: 717 8285) and the *Sea Witch* (tel: 717 5433). **By road:** Taxis are not metered, but prices are fixed and should be agreed with the driver beforehand. Taxis can

be ordered through hotels or from a central dispatch office (tel: 717 8100); they do not tout for fares. Any taxi will take you on an island tour. Motorbike and scooter rentals are widely available.

Sightseeing and activities

Ask in the tourist office about visits to the two flamingo nesting sites. **Bonaire Tours** (tel: 717 8778) and **BarankaTours** (tel: 717 2200) offer bus tours of the island. For a more active cycling or snorkelling tour, contact **Discover Bonaire** (tel: 717 5252). Scuba-diving operators are in the hotels: **Captain Don's Habitat** (tel: 717 8290) and **Sand Dollar Dive and Photo** (tel: 717 5433). For windsurfing and kayaking: **Jibe City** (tel: 717 5233).

Tourist information

Bonaire Tourism Corporation, Kaya Grandi #2, Kralendijk (tel: 717 8322 or 717 8649). In the US: Bonaire Tourist Office, 10 Rockefeller Plaza, Suite 900, NY, NY 10020 (tel: 212/956 5912). Visitors from Europe can contact Bonaire Tourist Office Europe, PO Box 472, NL-2000 AL Haarlem, The Netherlands (tel: 00 31 23 54 30 704).

Curaçao (area code 599)

Car hire and driving

Your own driver's licence must be presented. Many of the car-hire companies have airport offices, letting you compare prices: **Budget** (tel: 868 3466); **Caribe Rentals** (tel: 461 3089); **Hertz** (tel: 868 1182); **National Interrent** (tel: 869 4433 or airport 868 3489); **Rent a Yellow** (tel: 767 3777); **Ruiz Rent a Car** (tel: 737 3184); **24 Hours Car Rental** (tel: 461 7376). The north coast is worth seeing by car but much of it is down dusty lanes.

Driving is on the right and international signs are used. The speed limit in built-up areas is 40kph (25mph) and out of town 60kph (37mph) unless specified. Traffic from the right has right of way.

Getting around

By air: Curaçao's busiest air carrier is **Air ALM** (a local subsidiary of KLM), which provides a regular direct service from Miami offering convenient connections with **BA** flights from the UK and numerous US domestic and international carriers. ALM also offers inter-island services between Aruba, Bonaire and Sint-Maarten, and services to Caracas, Venezuela. **American Airlines** links Curaçao to Puerto Rico. Both ALM and KLM fly transatlantic from the Netherlands.

By boat: There are three dive trips a week aboard the ***Sailing Ship Bounty*** (tel: 560 1887), a lovely gaff-rigged schooner, while **Waterworld Curaçao** (tel: 465 6042) offers a variety of boat trips including snorkelling and sunset sails, or contact **Miss Ann** (tel: 767 1579) for details of excursions, boat and surfboard rentals and water-skiing. For deep sea fishing trips, try **Jerry de Vries** (tel: 560 5793), or **War Eagle** (tel: 560 2081).

By road: Taxis have TX on their licences. Fares are fixed and should be agreed upon first. Meters are soon to be installed. There are taxi stands at the airport and hotels and Plaza Jojo Correa, downtown Willemstad. Fares go up by 25 per cent after 11 PM and there may be a charge for excess baggage. For the central taxi office call 869 0752. Tipping is not obligatory. Some hotels provide free transport to and from the city centre.

Yellow public buses (known locally as convoys) or private vans or cars with BUS on their licence plates, take 6–14 passengers and are a cheap way of getting around. There are regular bus routes between major sights, leaving from Punda Bus Terminal (market place) or Otrabanda Bus Terminal, Rif Fort.

Sightseeing and activities
For tours beyond Willemstad, try **Casper Tours** (tel: 465 3010); **Taber Tours** (tel: 737 6637); **Kunuku Tours** (tel: 666 2514); **ABC Tours** (tel: 767 2141). Hourly tours of the Hato Caves are given by local guides, for reservations and information call 868 0379. Christoffelpark (tel: 864 0363) offers bird-watching and guided jeep trips – take the Westpunt bus from Otrobanda bus terminal, every two hours from 7 AM. The big hotels have scuba-diving operators, or you can

try **All West Diving** (tel: 864 0102), **Underwater Curaçao** (tel: 461 8131) and **Masterdive Inc** (tel: 465 4312).

Tourist information
The Curaçao Tourism Development Board has a booth at the airport (tel: 868 6789) and the head office on Pietermaai 19, PO Box 3266, Willemstad (tel: 461 6000). There are also various visitor information kiosks, one at the Cruise Terminal in Otrabanda, and another at Wilhelminaplein in Punda. For information in the UK, contact the Curaçao Tourist Board, 421a Finchley Road, London NW3 6HT (tel: 020 7431 4045).

Saba (area code 599)

Car hire and driving
Cars can be hired (produce your own driver's licence), including a full tank of petrol and unlimited mileage, from **Caralfan Rent-A-Car** (tel: 416 2575), **Johnson's Rent A Car** (tel: 416 2469), or **Scout's Place** (tel: 416 2205).

Driving is on the right, along the island's only road, The Road. In the event of a breakdown, call the only petrol station (Fort Bay) on 416 3272.

Getting around
By air: All access to Saba is via Sint-Maarten/Saint Martin. Local carrier **Winair** makes the short flight several times a day from Sint Maarten's Juliana International Airport.

By boat: Sea crossings (1hr) to Saba are offered by **The Edge** from Pelican Marina, Sint Maarten (Wed, Fri, Sun), **Voyager** from Bobby's Marina, Sint Maarten (Thu) and **Marigot**, Saint-Martin (Tue). For scuba-diving, contact **Saba Deep** (tel: 416 3347), **Saba Divers** (tel: 416 2740) and **Sea Saba** (tel: 416 2246), all of whom have boats that are available for round-island trips, deep-sea fishing, trips to nearby islands or other parts of Saba.

By road: There are about 10 taxi drivers on Saba and they all do guided tours. They can also arrange diving or nature walks; some have guesthouses. It is also safe to hitch-hike: wait for a lift by the wall opposite the Anglican Church in The Bottom, or the wall opposite Saba Deep in Fort Bay. There are no buses.

Hiking: Saba has 18 nature trails through the rain forest and up Mount Scenery. For a botanical tour, try **James Johnson** (tel: 416 2630).

Tourist information
Saba Tourist Office, PO Box 5271, Windwardside (tel: 416 2231).

St Eustatius (area code 599)

Car hire and driving
You will need a valid driver's licence from your own country, or an international driver's licence. Local rental agencies include **ABC Rental** (tel: 318 2595); **Browns Car Rental** (tel: 318 2266); and **Lady Ama's Services** (tel: 318 2712). Cars are reliable, but the roads are not: watch out for potholes. Driving is on the right, but some roads are very narrow and liable to be frequented by cows, goats and sheep. Road signs are in Dutch and English.

Getting around
By air: Winair is the only airline serving Statia with flights from Sint Maarten several times a day, Saba (10 minutes) and to St Kitts.
By road: Taxi drivers will give a tour of the island, which takes about an hour. More information from the Historical Foundation Museum, Simon Doncker House, Oranjestad (tel: 318 2288). Most places are within walking distance: the Historical Foundation has a brochure detailing a 90 minute walking tour of the Upper and Lower Towns. Taxi drivers include Josser Daniel (tel: 318 2358) and Blondell Berkel (tel: 318 2406).

Hiking: There are 12 nature trails – leaflets available from the tourist office. Or take a two-hour guided trek into tropical rain forest on the Quill volcano, organised through the tourist office. Scuba-diving can be arranged through **Dive Statia** (tel: 318 2435) and **Scubaqua** (tel: 318 2160).

Tourist information
There are two tourist offices: at the airport (tel: 318 2620) and the main St Eustatius Tourist Bureau, at the entrance to Fort Oranje, 3 Fort Oranjestraat, Oranjestad, St Eustatius, Netherlands Antilles (tel: 318 2433).

OTHER CARIBBEAN STATES

Jamaica (area code 876)

Car hire and driving
Most major international companies are represented and there are many local ones; a list of the Jamaica U-Drive Association members is obtainable from Jamaica Tourist Board, address below. A valid driver's licence is required and you must be at least 24. A sales tax of 15 per cent is added on top; accident and health insurance and collision damage waiver optional. Some petrol stations are closed on Sundays and petrol paid for with cash. The speed limit is 48kph (30mph) in towns and 80kph (50mph) on highways. Drive on the left.

In Montego Bay: **Chen's Rent-A-Car** (tel: 952 2398), **Jamaica Car Rentals** (tel: 952 5586). Negril: **Vernon's Car Rentals** (tel: 957 4354). Ocho Rios: **Caribbean Car Rentals** (tel: 974 2123) Port Antonio: **Eastern Rentals** (tel: 993 3624). Kingston: **Island Car Rentals** (tel: 926 8861), **Galaxy Car Rentals** (tel: 925 4176).

Car hire firms can be contacted on the following US toll free numbers: **Avis** (tel: 800/331 1212); **Bargain Rent-a-Car** (tel: 800/348 5398); **Island Car Rentals** (tel: 800/892 4581); **Dayless** (tel: 800/729 5377).

Getting around
By air: Jamaica is a major Caribbean gateway with an abundance of scheduled flights and charter services from destinations throughout North America, as well as South America and Europe. The majority of services land in Montego Bay, and some continue to Kingston. From North America, **Air Jamaica** offers regular flights from New York, Atlanta, Philadelphia, Baltimore, Los Angeles and three Florida airports, as well as Nassau, Bahamas. **American Airlines**, **Northwest**, **TWA**, **US Airways** and **Air Canada** also provide scheduled services. Air Jamaica and **British Airways** fly transatlantic direct. Local carriers offer inter-island services: Jamaica is linked to the Eastern Caribbean by **BWIA**; Grand Cayman by **Cayman Airways**; Havana, Cuba by **Cubana**; and Curaçao by **ALM**.

Helitours (tel: 974 2265) run sightseeing trips, with pick-ups at most local airports. Helicopters can be chartered.

By boat: Ask at your hotel or nearest tourist information centre about private charters for deep-sea fishing, scuba-diving and sailing.

By road: Buses are by far the cheapest way of getting around. They run all over the island and can be flagged down at bus stops and in between. Bicycles and motorbikes can be rented at most resorts. Taxis are in all resort areas but are not often metered; prices between destinations are fixed, so ask the price for the journey beforehand or be prepared to bargain with the driver. Look out for red PPV plates (Public Passenger Vehicle).

Sightseeing and activities

The Tourist Board visitor guide, *One Love*, lists main excursions and attractions. Your hotel will be able to organise any tour, which may be in a taxi, with driver-guide, or minibus: the cost will include admission prices.

Local tour operators will organise your own island tour and inter-island travel: In Montego Bay: **Blue Danube** (tel: 952 0886); **Forsythe's Jamaica** (tel: 952 0394); **Glamour Tours** (tel: 979 8207); **Jamaica Tours** (tel: 953 3132); **Sunholiday Travel & Tour** (tel: 952 5629). In Negril: **Caribic Vacations** (tel: 953 9874). In Port Antonio: **Valley Hikes** (tel: 993 3881) for walks and eco-tours. In Ocho Rios: **Blue Mountain Tours** (tel: 974 7075) for guided downhill bike tours with visits to coffee farms and a waterfall swim; **Tourwise** (tel: 952 4943); **Holiday Services** (tel: 974 2948). In Kingston, contact **Tour Marks** (tel: 929 5078). Scuba operators are based in all main towns. In Montego Bay, try **Poseidon Divers** (tel: 952 3624), in Negril, **Dolphin Divers** (tel: 957 4944) and **Negril Scuba Center** (tel: 957 9641); in Ocho Rios, try **Reef Divers** (tel: 973 4400); in Port Antonio, **Lady G'diver** (tel: 993 8988).

Tourist information

Jamaica Tourist Board, PO Box 360, 64 Knutsford Boulevard, Kingston (tel: 929 9200); and Montego Bay; Negril; Ocho Rios; Port Antonio. In the US: 801 2nd Avenue (20th floor), New York, NY 10017 (tel: 212/856 9727), as well as Chicago, Los Angeles, Miami and Ontario, Canada. In the UK: Jamaica Tourist Board, 1-2 Prince Consort Road, London SW7 2BZ (tel: 020 7224 0505).

Cayman Islands (area code 345)

Car hire and driving

A valid driver's licence and a Cayman driving permit must be shown. Different companies specify different minimum ages for hiring cars. The main companies are: **Ace/Hertz** (tel: 949 2280); **Andy's Rent-a-Car** (tel: 949 8111); **Budget** (tel: 949 5605); **CICO-Avis** (tel: 949 2468); **Coconut Car Rentals** (tel: 949 4377); **Economy Car Rental** (tel: 949 9550); **Just Jeeps** (tel: 949 7263); **Thrifty** (tel: 949 6640). Petrol is sold in imperial (160oz) gallons. Rental firms can be contacted on their US freephone numbers: **Ace/Hertz** (tel: 800/654 3131) and **Coconut** (tel: 800/941 4562).

Driving is on the left and some hire vehicles have left-hand drive; drink-driving laws are strictly observed; seatbelts are recommended.

Getting around

By air: Grand Cayman's Owen Roberts International Airport is the main port of entry to the islands. From North America, **American Airlines, Continental, Delta, Northwest** and **US Air** all offer direct services from a variety of departure points, and there are frequent daily services from Miami to Grand Cayman with American Airlines and **Cayman Airways**. Cayman Airways also serves several other US and Caribbean destinations, and there are a number of charter flights from the US and Canada. **British Airways** flies twice-weekly from the UK via Nassau, Bahamas. The local carrier **Island Air** flies between Grand Cayman and the sister islands of Cayman Brac and Little Cayman four times a day (journey time about 45 mins). There are also Cayman Airways flights to Cayman Brac.

By boat: On Grand Cayman boat excursions can be arranged through **Red Sail Sports** (tel: 945 5965) and

Soto's Cruises Ltd (tel: 945 4576). Diving can be organised through: **Fisheye** (tel: 945 4209); **Aquanauts** (tel: 945 1990), **Sunset Divers** (tel: 949 7111), **Divers Down** (tel: 945 1611) and **Ocean Frontiers** (tel: 947 7500). Cayman Brac: **Brac Aquatics** (tel: 948 1429). Little Cayman: **Paradise Divers** (tel: 948 0001).

By road: There is a limited public bus system in operation on Grand Cayman but there are plenty of cars, scooters, bicycles and taxis to hire. Taxi rates are determined by the government and published in CI$, so always ask the driver how much the trip will cost before you start. Private bus services run between West Bay and George Town at irregular intervals. Buses can be flagged down along the route. On Cayman Brac, jeeps, cars, scooters and bicycles can be rented from **B&S Motor Ventures, Cycle & Car Rentals** (tel: 948 1646).

Sightseeing and activities

There are numerous local travel agents (see below) that offer land and water-based excursions and tours; all such activities can be booked on arrival in Grand Cayman.

Local tour operators are mostly in Grand Cayman: **EVCO Tours** (tel: 947 8418); **Majestic Tours** (tel: 949 7773); **Reid's Premier Tours** (tel: 945 3345); **Tropicana Tours** (tel: 949 0944); **Vernon's Sightseeing Tours** (tel: 949 1509). In the smaller islands, go through the hotels.

Tourist information

Department of Tourism, The Pavilion, Cricket Square, George Town (tel: 949 0623). In the UK, contact the Cayman Islands Department of Tourism, 6 Arlington St, London SW1A 1RE (tel: 020 7491 7771).

Cuba (area code 537)

Car hire and driving

Hiring a car is definitely the best way of seeing Cuba, but it is expensive. Your own national driving licence is sufficient to hire a car; you must also present your passport. Car rentals are available from Cuba's two main rental operators in Havana:

Cubacar (tel: 33 2277 or 33 7233) and **Havanautos** (tel: 23 9815 or 23 9657). Other Havana-based local agencies include **Rent a Car Transtur** (tel: 24 5532 or 24 7644), **Via Rent a Car** (tel: 33 9780), **Micar** (tel: 33 6725) and **Rex** (tel: 33 9160), which also offers a limousine service. Cuba is subject to intermittent petrol shortages, so if you see an open petrol station, fill your tank. In Havana almost anyone with a car, whether an official taxi or not, will pick up tourists and take them to their destination for dollars. Roads connecting all the country's major regions and towns are in decent condition.

Getting around

Internal travel is cheap but frustrating to arrange. Buses, trains and planes are often overbooked, so you may have to wait days for a seat; journeys are delayed and departure times changed. Reconfirm everything (especially flights). If travelling by bus or train and prepared to pay in dollars, ask around to see if there is a way to avoid the interminable queues.

By air: Cuba is connected to Europe by scheduled flights with **Cubana Airlines**, **Aeroflot**, **Air France**, **Air Jamaica**, **British Airways** and **Iberia** as well as charter services; Cubana and BA fly direct from the UK. There are no direct flights from the US, but **Air Canada** flies to Cuba. Local inter-island connections are possible via the Dominican Republic, Grand Cayman and Jamaica amongst others. In addition to Havana's José Martí International Airport, international flights also serve Camagüey, Cayo Largo del Sur, Holguín, Santiago de Cuba and Varadero. Domestic flights link a number of other towns and resort areas.

Airports are not always near their towns, so allow for taxi and bus fares. Flights fill very quickly, so book in person, with **Cubatur** or at the Havana offices of **Cubana Airlines** (tel: 33 4949) or **Aerocaribbean** (tel: 79 7524), conveniently situated amongst the other airline offices on Calle 23 in Vedado. Pay in US dollars; or try to book from home well in advance.

By boat: There is a ferry from Surgideno de Batanano, south of Havana, to Isla de Juventud; boats go to the 1,200 offshore cays of the Archipelago de Camagüey; for example, from Santa Lucia to Cayo Sabinal. Yacht tours and boat trips from Cayo Largo to Cayo Avalos or Cayo Rosario (snorkelling, picnic) can be booked through Hemingway Marina at Varadero. Boats equipped for fishing and deep-sea trips leave from Playa del Este, Varadero, Playa Santa Lucia, Guardalavaca, Santiago de Uba and Isla de Juventud.

By road: Within the cities buses (*guaguas*) run on fixed routes; exact change needed. These are crowded and unreliable, but run through the night. Destinations are sometimes on the windscreen.

There are two kinds of taxis: *peso* taxis (black and white checks on their front doors) – are not supposed to take tourists but they will if you give them a dollar fare. Hail them even if they appear to be taken: the driver will split the fare (negotiate as you get in). The *peso* taxi base is by the bus terminal in Havana. In the main resort areas of Havana, Varadero and Santiago, dollar or turistaxis operate.

In Havana, companies include **Taxis OK** (tel: 24 1446) and **Taxis Transtur** (tel: 33 5539) or book through a hotel. Newer taxis should set their meters at No 1 in the day and No 2 at night; older taxis have no meters and have fixed rates in or around Havana; agree the rate beforehand.

Around the island: *guaguas* run between towns within a province: they are crowded but unbeatable for a taste of local life. However, in the present difficulties they are almost impossible to catch. Long-distance buses run all over the island (Havana to Baracoa in the east) and are usually large, quite comfortable coaches. Book ahead, a day in advance for buses and trains.

Shared taxis (*colectivos*) supplement the local buses, leaving the inter-municipal bus station once they are full; you just have to find one going where you want to go. They are roughly twice the bus fare.

By train: Fares are cheap but journeys slow; be at the station 30 minutes before departure to confirm your seat and have your ticket stamped. Trains leave from Avenida de Belgica y

Arsenal, Old Havana to larger cities; trains for Pinar del Río leave from the West (Occidente) station.

Sightseeing Organised bus tours: day trips to Trinidad or Pinar del Río can be booked through Cubatur offices in hotels, or negotiate to share a *colectivo*. Cubatur has information desks in tourist hotels, with tickets for organised excursions (head office: Calle F, No 157, e/9na y Calzada, Vedado, La Habana 4; tel: 33 4155). They can also help with booking hotels and advise on transportation. **Havanatur**, Edificio Sierra Maestra, Av. 1ra, e/Calle O y 2, Miramar, Havana (tel: 24 7541) also in hotels, has some English-speaking guides.

Cubatur offers day trips from Havana to Soroa, Viñales, Trinidad, Varadero, Cienfuegos and Guama; also a *Vuelta a Cuba*, seven-day trip round the island by bus and air and excursions to Cayo Largo. Departure can depend on a minimum number of people signing up for a tour. Check whether the trip is on and what actual departure time will be. Others worth trying are **Gaviota Tours** in Havana and Varadero (tel: 66 6777) and **Viajes Horizontes**, Vedado (tel: 33 4042). **Cubamar**, Vedado (tel: 66 2523) offers specialised nature-based tourism.

Tourist information
Cubatur (see above) is the government agency that organises most travel within Cuba. You might also try Havanatur (as above). In the UK, contact the Cuban Tourist Office, 154 Shaftsbury Avenue, London WC2H 8JT (tel: 020 7240 6655).

Health Cuba has a large number of well-trained doctors as part of the most preventive advanced health-care system in Latin America, but there are serious shortages of medical equipment and all medicines. Visitors can refill prescriptions and obtain basics such as aspirin or ibuprofen at tourist-only pharmacies in major cities. Bring your own basic medicines and prescriptions. Never drink the tap water. Aside from potential *turista* symptoms, some travellers have been known to pick up type A hepatitis.

Money Although Cubans are paid in virtually worthless pesos, the US dollar is king in the Cuban economy for tourists and locals alike. Prices have risen astronomically in recent years, and Cuba is no longer a bargain as the government has become greedy. Credit cards from American banks are not accepted. Virtually every item that you wish to purchase, from taxi rides to hotels, is charged in US dollars, so take as much cash as you need, and are comfortable carrying.

Crime Police are ubiquitous in Havana and their presence has dramatically reduced street crime fed by increasing tourism and economic desperation. However, petty thievery is pervasive, and occasional muggings still occur in Havana, Varadero and other touristed areas. Hustling and prostitution are common among both sexes. Note, however, that Cubans are no longer allowed in tourist hotels and that in certain cities, government authorities now effectively prohibit sexual relations between foreigners and Cubans unless married.

Dominican Republic
(area code 809)

Car hire and driving
Your own driver's licence or an international licence allows you to drive in the Dominican Republic for 90 days. The minimum age for hiring a car is 25.

The following companies all have offices in Santo Domingo: **Avis** (tel: 535 7191); **Budget** (tel: 562 6812); **Dollar** (tel: 546 6801); **Nelly** (tel: 544 1800); **Hertz** (tel: 221 5333); **Honda Rent-a-Car** (tel: 567 1015); **National** (tel: 562 1444). Car hire is expensive because of high tariffs on vehicles; credit cards are accepted and a large deposit taken, usually twice the weekly hire fee.

Driving is on the right, but local drivers can be erratic; watch out also for motorcyclists in towns. Tolls of a few cents are levied on all principal roads out of the capital. Speed limits are, unless otherwise specified, 80kph (50mph) on highways, 60kph (37mph) in suburban areas; 40kph (25mph) in

cities. Petrol stations are few and far between in country areas and generally close at about 6 PM. Avoid night driving as narrow mountain roads are dark and treacherous. Cars driven by tourists are often stopped by police at the entrance to and exit from towns – this is nothing to worry about.

Getting around
By air: There are several international airport gateways into the Dominican Republic. The busiest is Las Américas International Airport outside Santo Domingo, but holidaymakers heading for the north coast resorts of Cabarete, Playa Dorada, Puerto Plata and Sosúa will find plenty of flights making directly for Gregorio Luperón International Airport. There are also airports at Barahona, Punta Cana, Santiago and the new Romana International at Casa de Campo. More than 60 charter flight operators from the US and Europe serve the Dominican Republic. European operators include **Air France**, **AOM** and **Iberia** and there are scheduled flights from North America. There are also good inter-island connections to major regional transport hubs such as **American Eagle's** frequent daily services to San Juan, Puerto Rico; while **ALM** flies to Sint Maarten and Curaçao. For domestic flights, contact **Air Santo Domingo** (tel: 683 8020).
By boat: Leisure craft take you on trips to offshore islands, such as Cayo Levantado, from the dock at Samana and from Los Cacaos.
By road: Taxis are unmetered. Although fares are government-regulated, they are negotiable assuming you and the driver speak the same language. Fares to destinations outside the city are posted in major hotels and at the airport.

Telephone-dispatched taxi services are another option: this is a 24-hour service with rates agreed over the telephone, depending on distances covered.

Publicos, blue-and-white or blue-and-red cars that run regular routes stopping to let passengers on and off, are much cheaper and prices are fixed between cities. However, the cars can often be overcrowded and uncomfortable.

Private buses – *conchos* or *colectivos* – are the colourful way to get around. Most leave from around Parque Independencia in Santo Domingo; exact change required.

Private air-conditioned buses make regular trips from Santo Domingo to a number of regions. To reserve a seat call **Metro Buses** (tel: 566 7126 in Santo Domingo, 586 6062 in Puerto Plata, 587 4711 in Santiago) or **Caribe Tours** (tel: 221 4422), whose prices tend to be cheaper.

Motoconchos (motorbike taxis) are found on the streets of Puerto Plata, Sosúa and Jarabacoa: flag them down on the road and negotiate the fare.

Motorcycles can be hired around Puerto Plata and Playa Dorada; you must ensure that you use the lock, as there is no insurance on theft. Bicycles can be rented from many of the hotels on the north coast. Ask at reception.

Sightseeing and activities

Prieto Tours (tel: 685 0102) offers half-day bus tours of Santo Domingo, beach tours, tours to Cibao Valley and the Amber Coast and others. **Turinter** (tel: 686 4020) does a full-day tour of Samana and speciality tours (museums, shopping, fishing). **Apolo Tours** (tel: 586 1802) offers a full-day tour covering Playa Grande, Santiago and Sosúa. **Go Dominican Tours** (tel: 586 5969) offer a combination of tours, jeep safaris and activities from rafting to horse-riding. The safaris head up into the hills to visit coffee plantations and flower farms. Try **Iguana Mama** (tel: 571 0908) for mountain biking excursions and hiking.

Sosúa is a good scuba-diving centre. Dive trips and equipment rentals can be arranged through dive shops in main resorts.

Tourist information

The main office of the Ministry of Tourism is at the corner of Avenida México and Avenida 30 de Marzo, PO Box 497, Santo Domingo (tel: 221 4660). There is also an office in the Zona Colonial, at main airports and regional tourist areas such as Cabarete, Pueto Plata and Sosúa. In the US, contact the Dominican Republic Tourist Office, 136 E 57th Street, Suite 803, New York, NY 10022 (tel:

212/588 1012), also in Chicago and Miami. In the UK, 18-20 Hand Court, High Holborn, London WC1V 6RZ (tel: 020 7242 7778).

Puerto Rico (area code 787)

Car hire and driving

Your national driver's licence is preferred by companies to an international licence. There are several rental agencies including **Avis** (tel: 253 5926), **Hertz** (tel: 791 0840), **National** (tel: 791 1805) and **Budget** (tel: 791 0600).

Driving is on the right, with a maximum speed on the expressway 88kph (55mph). Take a phrasebook if you are going off the beaten track.

Getting around

By air: Puerto Rico is a major Caribbean transportation hub served by direct flights from all over North America; carriers include **Air Canada**, **American Airlines**, **Continental**, **TWA**, **United** and **US Airways**. **British Airways** fly direct from the UK. Puerto Rico-based **American Eagle** serves 21 Caribbean destinations from its base in Puerto Rico from the neighbouring USVI right down to Tobago. Other local operators include **Air Jamaica**, **Air St Thomas** and **ALM** (for the Dutch Antilles). There are also domestic flights to main towns such as Arecibo, Mayagüez and Ponce, and the offshore islands of Culebra and Vieques are accessible by small plane from San Juan and Fajardo.

By boat: Regular ferry services cross San Juan Bay from Old San Juan to the suburb of Cataño, and they can make a cheap and interesting sightseeing opportunity.

For the out islands off the east coast, passenger ferries run by the **Fajardo Port Authority** (tel: 863 4560) shuttle between Fajardo Beach and Vieques three times a day, taking 45 minutes. From Fajardo to Culebra there are two ferries daily. Tickets on both routes are inexpensive. For information about ferries from Mayagüez, on the west coast, to the Dominican Republic, tel: 832 4800.

Sportfishing charters can be arranged through **Captain Mike's Sport Fishing Center** (tel: 721 7335)

265

and **Dorado Marine Center** (tel: 796 4645) both in San Juan Bay Marina, or **Tropical Fishing Charters**, El Conquistador Marina, Fajardo (tel: 863 6594).

By road: All taxis are metered but can be hired unmetered for sightseeing. In San Juan, white-coloured taxis *turísticos* with a logo on the door serve the main tourist areas, and offer fixed rate fares between the airport or cruise ship piers and tourist destinations such as Old San Juan, Condado and Isla Verde. There are additional charges for more than two pieces of luggage, waiting times and night journeys between 10 PM and 6 AM.

Another option is the **Airport Limousine Service** (tel: 791 4745), providing a shared shuttle van service from the airport to hotels in Condado, Isla Verde and Old San Juan.

Metropolitan Bus Authority services are a cheap and easy way to get from Isla Verde and Condado into Old San Juan. Buses A5 and B21 run every 20 minutes or so on this route; bus stops are marked "Parada". Open-air trolleys also rattle around Old San Juan covering a central route up to Plaza de Armas and a northern route to El Morro. The service is free and passengers can get on and off at any stop.

Shared taxis (*publicos*) have yellow licence plates with P or PD at the end and operate all over the island, stopping in each town's main plaza. They take up to 17 passengers and their routes and fares are fixed by the Public Service Commission. Main terminals are at the airport and Plaza Colón in Old San Juan.

Sightseeing and activities

For scuba-diving contact **Caribbean School of Aquatics** (tel: 728 6606) and **Caribe Aquatic Adventures** (tel: 724 1882). In the southwest, contact **Parguera Divers Training Centre** (tel: 899 4015). Tours of San Juan, the Bacardí Rum plant, the beaches and the rain forest can be arranged via: **Rico SunTours** (tel: 722 2080); **United Tour Guides** (tel: 723 5578); **Cordero Caribbean Tours** (tel: 786 9114). Some eco-based tour operators include **Tropix Wellness Outings** (tel: 268 2173) and **Encantos Ecotours** (tel: 272 0005).

Tourist information

Puerto Rico Tourism Company, PO Box 902-3906, San Juan 00902-3906 (tel: 721 2400 or 800/866 7827) offers a wealth of assistance in the form of maps, contact lists and brochures including the comprehensive *Qué Pasa* visitors guide. There are tourist information offices at the airport (tel: 791 1014), at La Casita, near Pier 1, Old San Juan (tel: 722 1709) and also in Ponce at 2911 Los Cabos Avenue (tel: 843 0465). Town halls throughout the country will have information desks. In the UK call 0800 898920.

Barbados (area code 246)

Car hire and driving

A visitor's driver's licence must be purchased from car-hire companies; drivers must have held a full licence for at least two years and be over 24. Car-hire companies are in every district (the tourist board has the complete list), including: **Corbins Car Rentals** (tel: 427 9531); **Coconut Car Rentals** (tel: 437 0297); **National** (tel: 422 0603); **P&S Car Rentals** (tel: 424 2052); **Stoutes Car Rentals** (tel: 435 4456); **Sunny Isle Car** (tel: 435 7498).

Motorscooters and bicycles are also a good way to get around. Driving is on the left and speed limits are 48kph (30mph) in towns and 80kph (50mph) on the highway. Seatbelts are not mandatory and there are no drink-driving laws as such. Petrol generally has to be paid for in cash.

Getting around

By air: Barbados is a major regional transportation hub with excellent connections to North America and the UK. **Air Canada**, **Air Jamaica**, **American Airlines** and **BWIA** all fly direct from North America, while **American Eagle** provides frequent onward connecting services from Puerto Rico. From the UK, there are scheduled flights with **British Airways** and **Virgin Atlantic**, plus a wide range of charter flights. The neighbouring Windward Islands and the Grenadines are easily accessed through local operators including **Air Martinique**, **Caribbean Star**, **LIAT**, **Mustique Airways** and **TIA**.

Helicopter tours are offered by **Bajan Helicopters** (tel: 431 0069). **By road:** Bright yellow minibuses with blue stripes, run by the Barbados Transport Board, provide a regular service around the island, with destinations usually displayed at the bottom left-hand corner of the windshield. There are two terminals in Bridgetown, plus Speightstown Terminal in the north providing a service to Bridgetown along the west coast, to eastern areas and a bypass service from Speightstown to the south coast. A number of privately owned maxi-taxis (minibuses) and route taxis also operate (not colour-coded). These can be picked up at normal bus stops. Taxi fares between principal destinations are set in Bds. dollars – check first.

Sightseeing and activities
Tours can be organised through hotels or through companies such as: **Bajan Tours** (tel: 437 9389) and **LE Williams Tour Co** (tel: 427 1043). For a four-wheel-drive tour to remote areas, contact **Adventureland 4x4 Tours** (tel: 429 3687) or **Island Safari** (tel: 429 5337). **VIP Tour Services** (tel: 432 2901), which runs private air-conditioned cars with driver/guides. **The Barbados National Trust** (tel: 426 2421) organises interesting guided Sunday walks. For visits to the Grenadines, St Lucia, Grenada, Tobago and Angel Falls by sea and air contact **St James Travel & Tours** (tel: 432 0774) or **Chantours** (tel: 432 5591).

Scuba-diving operators include: **Blue Reef Watersports** (tel: 422 4444), **Hightide Watersports** (tel: 432 0931), or **Dive Boat Safari** (tel:427 4350). For windsurfing contact **Club Mistral** (tel: 426 4000) on the south coast. Boat trip options include the *Jolly Roger* party boat (tel: 427 7245); catamaran cruises with **Cool Runnings** (tel: 436 0911); and **Tiami** (tel: 427 7245); or ocean kayaking with **Ocean Adventures** (tel: 436 2088).

Tourist information
Barbados Tourism Authority, PO Box 242, Harbour Road, Bridgetown, Barbados (tel: 427 2623). In the US: 800 2nd Avenue, New York, NY 10017 (tel: 212/986 6516); also Los Angeles and Miami. In the UK: 263 Tottenham Court Road, London W1P 7LA (tel: 020 7636 9448).

Trinidad and Tobago (area code 868)

Car hire and driving
To hire a car you must have a valid driver's licence and be at least 21. For a comprehensive list of car-hire companies in Port of Spain, Piarco Airport, San Fernando and the south of Trinidad and Tobago, ask for the *Discover Trinidad and Tobago* booklet from the tourist office. Beware: in Trinidad it can sometimes take an entire morning for a satisfactory hire car to be delivered. **Singh's Auto Rentals** (tel: 625 4247); **Thrifty** (tel: 669 0602); **Econo Car Rentals Ltd** (tel: 622 8074); **Johnney's Car Rental** (tel: 674 0463). On Tobago it is more economical to rent a jeep than take a taxi, although there are some great taxi driver/guides. Tobago car rental: **Auto Rentals** (tel: 639 0644); **Rattan's Car Rental** (tel: 639 8271); **Sunflower Tours** (tel: 429 8941); **Tobago Travel** (tel: 639 8778).

Driving is on the left. There is a front-seatbelt law and drink-driving laws are strictly enforced (fining or detention). Speed limits are 80kph (50mph) on the highways, 40–60kph (25–37mph) on minor roads and 30kph (18mph) in residential areas.

Getting around
By air: The national airline, **BWIA**, flies direct from New York and Miami to Trinidad's Piarco Airport outside Port of Spain, and to Tobago's Crown Point Airport. **American Airlines** has a Trinidad flight out of Miami, and **American Eagle** provides connections from Puerto Rico to Tobago. BWIA also flies direct to Trinidad from the UK; **British Airways** flies to Tobago and there are regular charter services. **Air Caribbean** and **LIAT** make the 15-minute hop between Trinidad and Tobago up to ten times a day; LIAT's inter-island services link the islands to the rest of the Eastern Caribbean and Puerto Rico. Charter aircraft in Trinidad through **Trinidad & Tobago Sightseeing Tours** (tel: 628 1051).

267

By boat: A car ferry service from Port of Spain to Tobago (Scarborough) leaves daily, taking between 5–6 hours, with food and drink on board; you can return by plane . You can rent a cabin for evening sail. Reservations can be made through the tourist board (see below); buy tickets at ferry offices in Port of Spain (tel: 625 3055) and Scarborough (tel: 639 2416).

For scuba-diving and snorkelling, try **Tobago Dive Experience** (tel: 639 7034); **Aquamarine Dive Ltd**, Speyside (tel: 660 4341); **Man Friday Diving**, Charlotteville (tel: 660 4676). For trips to Buccoo Reef, day sails and general watersports, contact the hotels or **Kalina Cats** (tel: 639 6305) and **Ron's** (tel: 660 4941).

By road: There are two types of taxis: hire and route, identifiable by their H licence plates. Rental taxis are private, carrying you where you want. They do not have meters and although their rates are theoretically fixed, they tend to be negotiable (especially during Carnival). An official list of rates for some routes, quoted in TT dollars (although most taxi drivers accept US dollars), is posted at the airport or obtainable from the Tourist Board. Drivers also do tours: prices depend on how many passengers there are, how far you wish to travel and how long you want the driver to wait for you: take the official rate as the basis for all your negotiations.

Less expensive are route taxis, which operate like buses on certain routes, picking up as many passengers as they can fit in their vehicles. They tend to start and finish their journey around Brian Lara Promenade, Port of Spain and come in two forms: cars taking four or five passengers – flag one down and ask where it is going – and maxi-taxis. These are colour-coded minibuses that seat 11 or 25 and ply particular routes according to their colour. Yellow taxis operate around Port of Spain, red in eastern Trinidad, green for south Trinidad, black for Princes Town, brown for San Fernando and blue in Tobago. Both kinds of taxi will sound their horns as they go, to let you know if they still have some room on board. Public buses run by the Public Transport Service

Corporation (PTSC) are either very old (blue) or new and air-conditioned (red, white and black). They follow special bus lanes from Port of Spain to San Fernando, to Arima and to Chaguanas. Check with your hotel reception or the tourist board for rates and pick-up points for all modes of transport.

Sightseeing and activities
In Trinidad, tours of the Caroni Bird Sanctuary are run by naturalists **Winston Nanan** (tel: 645 1305, 658 0308) and **David Ramsahai** (tel: 663 4767). General tour companies in Port of Spain include: **Bacchus Taxi and Car Rentals** (tel: 622 5588); **Hub Travel**, Hilton Hotel (tel: 624 3111); **Legacy Tours** (tel: 623 0150); **St Christopher Taxi Service**, Hilton Hotel (tel: 624 3560); **Travel Centre** (tel: 623 5096, 623 8785); **Trinidad & Tobago Tours** (tel: 628 1051); **Southeast Eco-Tours** (tel: 644 1012); **Pax Nature Tours** (tel: 662 4084); **Naipaul's Tours & Travel** (tel: 623 5516); **Bibi's Tours & Travel** (tel: 679 4584). For operators outside Port of Spain, investigate the *Discover Trinidad & Tobago* booklet from tourist offices.

In Tobago, David Rooks of **Nature Tours** (tel: 639 4276) offers guided walks and trips to offshore bird colonies. Other companies in the sightseeing business include **Ansyl Tours** (tel: 639 4125) and **Tobago Travel** (tel: 639 8778).

Tourist information
Tourism and Industrial Development Co (TIDCO), 10-14 Phillips Street, Port of Spain (tel: 623 1932). Tobago NIB Mall, Scarborough (tel: 639 2125). TIDCO is also at Piarco Airport (tel: 669 5196) and Crown Point Airport (tel: 639 0509). Trinidad and Tobago Hotel and Tourism Association, Unit B, 36 Scott Bushe Rd, Port of Spain (tel: 624 3928). In the US: Trinidad and Tobago Tourism Office, 350 5th Avenue, Suite 6316, New York, NY 10118 (tel: 800/748 4224 or the Tourism Hotline 888/595-4TNT). In the UK: Mitre House, 66 Abbey Road, Bush Hill Park, Enfield, Middlesex EN1 2QE (tel: 020 8350 1009).

Hotels and Restaurants

HOTELS

Styles and standards of Caribbean hotels vary enormously, as shown by the differences in price. There are very sophisticated beach clubs where individual cottages have ocean views, but most hotel rooms are in large resort complexes. In every recommendation except the very cheapest, rooms have their own bathrooms. A number of villas and short-term apartments are mentioned below. For independent travellers there are a few guesthouses and local business hotels on each island. Most hotels are on the beach; if not, this is indicated. Most also have swimming pools.

There is no standardised system of classification in the Caribbean, but all hotels booked through tour operators and travel agents will be registered with the tourist board on the island and checked by the operators.

Prices, highest from December to April, are reduced by 20–25 per cent during the rest of the year. Each island has a different system, with supplementary room taxes. A service charge of 10–15 per cent is often levied.

Hotels are divided into four price categories, based on the rate for a double room in high season:

Inexpensive (£): (a double room for less than US$75)
Moderate (££): (a double room for between US$75 and $200)
Expensive (£££): (a double room for between US$200 and $400)
Very expensive (££££): (expect to pay more than US$400)

Dialling codes Most Caribbean islands have a three-digit country code. However, if you are calling from Europe, this may be prefixed by 1, the country code for the US. Check before dialling.

THE WINDWARD ISLANDS

Dominica (767)
Hotels on Dominica levy a 15 per cent goverment tax on all bills.

Evergreen Hotel (££)
Castle Comfort tel: 448 3288
Pool and pleasant waterfront setting; dive packages. Small and welcoming.
The Garraway Hotel (££)
Roseau tel: 449 8800
Modern high-rise building well positioned on the waterfront in town. Very comfortable rooms with a good restaurant, and good service.
Papillote Wilderness Retreat (£)
tel: 448 2287
Ten rooms set in a grand tropical garden fed by the Trafalgar Falls. Good walking.
Picard Beach Cottage Resort (££)
Portsmouth tel: 445 5131
Eight beach cabins, comfortable Caribbean style, right on a good black sand beach.

Grenada (473)
Hotels on Grenada and Carriacou levy an 8 per cent government tax on all bills.

Caribbee Country House (£££)
Carriacou tel: 443 7380
Charming old colonial-style inn set on a hillside a short walk from the extremely fine cove, Anse la Roche. Intimate and friendly; home-cooked Caribbean cuisine.
Coyaba (££)
Grand Anse tel: 444 4129
Friendly beach resort with comfortable rooms in large buildings and neat tropical garden. Entertainment in the bar and thatch-roof restaurant; good sports facilities.
La Sagesse Nature Center (£–££)
tel: 444 6458
Romantic hideaway in a 1920s beachfront estate house with nine simple but stylish rooms, plus two veranda cottages (one offering real Robinson Crusoe budget rooms).
Spice Island Inn (££££)
tel: 444 4258
High luxury on Grand Anse beach. The 66 rooms are large and air-conditioned, and some Whirlpool Suites stand directly behind the palms and sand. Entertainment in the beachfront restaurant and bar.

The Grenadines (784)
Hotels charge 7 per cent government tax.

Cotton House Hotel (££££)
Mustique tel: 456 4777
Set in the ancient stone estate building of a former cotton plantation; sumptuous beds and furnishings. Pool and fantastic views to go with superb food.
Dennis's Hideaway (£–££)
Mayreau tel: 458 8594
Six rooms with a restaurant and bar nearby; modern but made special by Dennis himself, who plays the guitar and sings.
Frangipani (££)
Bequia tel: 458 3255
Set in an old family vacation villa on the Port Elizabeth waterfront. Antique gentility and personable West Indian style.
Friendship Bay Hotel (£££)
Friendship Bay tel: 458 3222
Appealing complex on the south side of the island. Passable beach; excellent beach bar; some watersports.

St Lucia (758)
All hotels on St Lucia levy an 8 per cent government room charge.

Anse Chastanet (£££–££££)
Soufrière tel: 459 7000
Forty-eight rooms and villas scattered on the hillside and on the grey sands of secluded Chastanet bay; good diving and seclusion.
Candyo Inn (£–££)
tel: 452 0712
Small, friendly inn within a short walk of Reduit Beach. Self-contained apartments.

270

Ladera Resort (£££–££££)
tel: 459 7323
A magnificent setting on the shoulder of one of the Pitons. Antique furniture rooms open to the view and the noise of tree-frogs.
Marigot Beach Club (££–£££)
Marigot Bay tel: 451 4974
In the wonderful setting of a narrow, steep-sided inlet festooned with palms. Villas and cottages: charming and laid-back.
Royal St. Lucian (££££)
Reduit Beach tel: 452 9999
A grand and luxurious hotel, with central atrium and wings, commanding the beach. Every modern convenience in the huge rooms.

St Vincent (784)

All hotels on St Vincent levy a 7 per cent government room tax.

Petit Byahaut (£££)
tel: 457 7008
Just four units (one a room-size tent) above the secluded beach of Petit Byahaut bay, which can be reached only by boat. Stylishly rustic, but has hot running water.
Umbrella Beach Hotel (£)
tel: 458 4651
Set in lively strip of restaurants and bars at Villa. Small and simple.
Young Island (££££)
tel: 458 4826
A Caribbean gem – cottages scattered around the tropical garden of Young Island, 180m off St Vincent's southern coast. Facilities include pool, bar, restaurant and sports.

THE LEEWARD ISLANDS

Anguilla (264)

Hotels on Anguilla add a government tax of 10 per cent.

Cap Juluca (££££)
Maunday's Bay tel: 497 6666
A line of bright, white Moorish domes rising out of the Anguillian scrub along the superb sandy stretch of this peerless. High luxury with sunken baths and richly coloured Oriental rugs.
Harbour Villas (££)
Island Harbour tel: 497 4393
Self-catering apartments in the fishing village of Island Harbour, in the northeast of the island. Plenty to do nearby, but you may want to hire a car.
Malliouhana (£££–££££)
Mead's Bay tel: 497 6111
On a cliff overlooking the sweeping beach below, Malliouhana has a mix of styles; terracotta tiles, slender columns and arches, touched with colourful Haitian prints. Smoothly run hotel, with every luxury and a very elegant dining room.
La Sirena (££)
Mead's Bay tel: 497 6827
A small and friendly hotel perched above the beach. Affordable rates on an island of heavyweights. Some entertainment.

Antigua (268)

Hotels on Antigua add a government tax of 8.5 per cent; 7 per cent for restaurants.

Admiral's Inn (££)
English Harbour tel: 460 1027
Within the historic walls of Nelson's Dockyard; rooms quite simple. A lively crowd of sailors collects at the bar.
Catamaran Hotel (£–££)
tel: 460 1036
Well-priced hotel with kitchenettes not far from the activity of English Harbour in the south.
Copper and Lumber Store (££–£££)
Englsih Harbour tel: 460 1058
A small hotel set in the grounds of Nelson's Dockyard; functional brick walls beautified with tropical plants and urgent naval air transformed into a retreat of historic laziness.
Curtain Bluff (££££)
Morris Bay tel: 462 8400
Once again the height of Antiguan elegance since its renovation. Main house on the bluff, between two excellent beaches. Lavish in the dining room and wine cellar.
Hawksbill Beach Resort (£££–££££)
Five Islands tel: 462 0301
Very comfortable beach-front resort south of St Johns. Cottages ranged above a series of bays; plenty of watersports.

Montserrat (664)

Hotels on Montserrat add a government tax of 7 per cent.

Erindell Villa Guesthouse (£)
Woodlands tel: 491 3655
Comfy, well-equipped rooms with private entrances set in tropical gardens. Family atmosphere with food service available, a large pool and laundry.
Vue Point Hotel (££)
tel: 491 5210
Twelve newly refurbished self-catering cottages overlooking Old Road Bay. Pool, tennis and popular beach bar down below.

Nevis (869)

Hotels on Nevis add a government tax of 7 per cent.

Four Seasons (££££)
Pinney's Beach tel: 469 1111
A reliable beach holiday spot. Elegantly decorated and luxurious rooms. "Olde Worlde" decor and tropical profusion in the garden.
Hermitage (£££)
Fig Tree Parish tel: 469 3477
A gem of the Caribbean, set in one of its most ancient wooden houses. Romantic, pretty rooms in cottages embellished with ginger-bread pointing around a lawned garden with palms, each with a hammock and view.
Oualie Beach Hotel (££)
Oualie Beach tel: 469 9735
West Indian gingerbread cottages providing 34 rooms in the north of the island, overlooking St Kitts. Low-key but fun.

Hotels and Restaurants

St Kitts (869)

Hotels on St Kitts add a government tax of 7 per cent.

Rawlins Plantation (£££)
Mount Pleasant tel: 465 6221
The closest you can come to the lavish grandeur of plantation life. Ten luxurious rooms scattered around the estate grounds; fine West Indian cuisine and rum punch with a view from the impressive 18th-century great house.

Timothy Beach Resort (££)
South of Basseterre tel: 465 8597
Good value suites on the fine strip of sand in Frigate Bay. Beach hotel, but pretty quiet.

THE VIRGIN ISLANDS

British Virgin Islands (284)
Hotels in the BVI add a government tax of 7 per cent to all bills.

Anegada, Cooper Island and Jost van Dyke

Anegada Reef Hotel (£££)
Anegada tel: 495 8002
Just 20 simple, stylish beachfront and garden rooms (full-board). Excellent diving and fishing.

Cooper Island Beach Club (££)
tel: 495 9084
Comfortable rooms in pretty cottages on the friendly, active Cooper Island.

Sandcastle (££)
Jost van Dyke tel: 495 9888
Four beach cottages and two rooms, gardens and bar a stone's throw from White Bay.

Tortola

Cane Garden Bay Beach Hotel (£–££)
tel: 495 4639
A lively hangout on Tortola's busiest beach. Rooms air-conditioned and simple, but plenty of activity all around.

Long Bay Beach Resort (£££)
tel: 495 4252
Delightful rooms and villas, some on stilts above the beach, others nestled in tropical gardens. Quiet but classy.

Virgin Gorda

Bitter End Yacht Club (£££–££££)
North Sound tel: 494 2745
Lively resort for watersports fans – sailing school, windsurfing, short hops to nearby beach bars. Some entertainment, but also hideaway hillside cabins of high luxury.

Little Dix Bay (££££)
tel: 495 5555
Low-key high luxury. Cottages in spacious and neatly tended grounds, looking onto an excellent strip of sand.

Olde Yard Inn (££)
The Valley tel: 495 5544
Quiet retreat with the beach a short drive/ride away. Attractive open-terrace restaurant.

US Virgin Islands (340)

St Croix
Hotels in the USVI add a government tax of 8 per cent.

Buccaneer Hotel (£££–££££)
tel: 773 2100
Luxurious beach and golf resort ranged across grassy slopes leading down to the sea. Spacious and attractive rooms with private balconies or terraces, plus fine dining.

Cormorant Beach Club (£££)
tel: 778 8920
Low-key beach hotel – very attractive rooms with terraces or balconies overlooking the palms and sea. Quiet and refined with an excellent restaurant.

Hilty House (££)
tel: 773 2594
Four delightful rooms in the main house, where the shell of an old rum factory has been converted into an open living area leading onto the pool deck. Also two garden cottages.

St John

Caneel Bay (£££–££££)
tel: 776 6111
A very elegant resort where rooms are set in beautifully tended gardens around a great house. Watersports on the resort's seven beaches, otherwise reliable relaxation.

Gallows Point Resort (££)
tel: 776 6434
Elegant suites with all modern comforts. Just a short walk from downtown Cruz Bay.

Maho Bay Camps (££)
Maho Bay tel: 776 6504
An eco-conscious place with simple tented units on a wooded hillside above the bay and more luxurious showcase eco-friendly studios.

St Thomas

Bolongo Bay Beach Club (£££)
tel: 775 1800
Lively sporting resort – watersports, scuba, tennis – on a charming sandy bay on the south of the island. Sport activities by day, entertainment by night.

Hotel 1829 (££–£££)
Charlotte Amalie tel: 776 1829
A lovely town house hotel with a quiet, sophisticated air. Dinner is usually served to a piano accompaniment.

Ritz-Carlton (££££)
Great Bay tel: 775 3333
The most luxurious in St Thomas: a large suite-hotel set around a bay on the east coast. Watersports (excellent windsurfing) and gourmet dining.

Sapphire Beach Resort and Marina (£££)
Sapphire Beach tel: 775 6100
Recently renovated and expanded resort hotel right on the beach with good snorkelling and watersports. All comforts are available; there is a lively beach party each Sunday.

THE FRENCH ANTILLES

Guadeloupe (590)

Some hotels on Guadeloupe add a room tax of a few dollars.

Auberge de la Vieille Tour (£££)
Gosier tel: 84 23 23
Large but genteel resort, rooms ranged on the hillside around an old windmill tower. Dining room above the private hotel beach.

Auberge des Petits Saints aux Anarcadiers (££)
Terre de Haut, Les Saintes tel: 99 50 99
A charming art and antique-filled Créole home in town. Fine French cuisine.

Les Flamboyants (£–££)
Gosier tel: 84 14 11
On a hilltop just outside town, an old family villa with neat and simple rooms. A walk from the beach; pool and kitchen. Breakfast only.

Le Hamak (£££–££££)
St-François tel: 88 59 99
Rarified relaxation in private bungalows, tucked away in a beautiful profuse Guadeloupean garden on the seafront. As the name suggests, each bungalow has its own hammock.

Martinique (596)

Some hotels on Martinique add a room tax of a few dollars.

Auberge de l'Anse Mitan (£–££)
Anse Mitan tel: 66 01 02
A friendly hotel, still with some old West Indian charm; tucked away at the end of the beach, but not far from the action of the town.

La Bonne Auberge (£)
Trois-Ilets tel: 66 01 55
Small and friendly hotel, with simple rooms set in modern buildings in the heart of the tourist town of Trois-Ilets. Nice tropical dining room.

Habitation Lagrange (£££–££££)
Le Marigot tel: 53 60 60
Set in a superb restored plantation house in the banana groves in the northeast. No beach but elegant relaxation and fine cuisine.

Hotel Diamant les Bains (££)
Diamant tel: 76 40 14
Quiet and very friendly hotel; 24 rooms overlooking a pretty garden; views of Diamond Rock. An ideal retreat.

Saint-Barthélemy (590)

Some hotels on St Barts add a room tax of a few dollars.

Hôtel la Banane (£££)
Lorient tel: 27 68 25
Amusing crowd in the bar; rooms decorated with traditional Caribbean flourishes. Building lost in a tropical garden that overhangs a pool.

Les Ilets Fleuris (££)
Hauts de Lorient tel: 27 64 22
One-bedroom cottages with kitchens and views perched on one of St Barts' numerous hilltops. The affordable rates include car rental, and the beach is 5 minutes away.

Manapany Cottages (£££–££££)
Anse des Cayes tel: 27 66 55
The finest luxury; 52 rooms in sumptuous suites and cottages, near a good beach.

Saint-Martin (590)

Some hotels on Saint-Martin add a room tax to your bill.

Captain Oliver's (£££)
Oyster Pond tel: 87 43 706
Small hotel on Oyster Pond lagoon, from where many of the guests take to the seas to sail and dive. Short water-taxi ride to the beach.

Esmeralda Resort (£££–££££)
Baie Orientale tel: 87 36 36
Right on the beach, this resort has adopted traditional gingerbread style and added to its luxurious cottages, each of which has its own pool. Sport and restaurants.

Hévéa Hotel (££)
Grand Case tel: 87 56 85
In the centre of town, this small Créole hotel-restaurant has an easy charm.

La Samanna (££££)
Baie Longue tel: 87 64 00
Very chic and stylish, standing above the excellent sand of Long Beach. Built in a curious mix of styles, with vast rooms, fine views, extreme luxury, and extreme prices.

THE NETHERLANDS ANTILLES

Aruba (297)

Hotels on Aruba add a government tax of 5 per cent to all bills.

Amsterdam Manor Beach Resort (££)
Eagle Beach tel: 871492
Attractive Dutch-style complex with 72 self-catering units ranging from studios to two-bedroom apartments set around quiet courtyards. Restaurant and mini-mart.

Divi Aruba Beach Resort (£££–££££)
tel: 823300
A low-rise hotel in the land of high-rises with an excellent beachfront setting. There are also attractive gardens.

Bonaire (599)

Hotels on Bonaire add a government tax of 5 per cent to all bills.

Captain Don's Habitat (££–£££)
Kralendijk tel: 717 8290
Has grown from a small diving resort to a very comfortable and laid-back hotel, now with cottages and villas as well as rooms.

Carib Inn (££)
Kralendijk tel: 717 8819
Excellent choice for relative comfort and price. Nine simple rooms, good diving. No restaurant, but kitchenettes.

Harbour Village Hotel (£££)
Playa Lechi tel: 717 7500
The most comfortable hotel on Bonaire, with plush and brightly painted suites in villas dotted around a sandy garden and pool.

273

Hotels and Restaurants

Curaçao (599)

Hotels on Curaçao add a government tax of 7 per cent to all bills.

Avila Beach Hotel (££–£££)
Willemstad tel: 461 4377
The most elegant and traditional of Curaçao's hotels, which has now been modernised. It is set on edge of town with a small beach and a dining room open to the breezes.
Princess Beach Resort and Casino (££)
Willemstad tel: 736 7888
This is a large resort spread out along the seafront. There are also a number of sports and gambling available.

Saba (599)

Hotels on Saba add a government tax of 5 per cent to all bills.

Cranston's Antique Inn (££)
tel: 416 3203
Set in a classic wooden Saban house in The Bottom. The creaking floorboards and some four-poster beds all add up to give the Inn local island charm.
Juliana's (££)
Windwardside tel: 416 2269
Small, cosy and informal, Juliana's is a favourite with the dive crowd. This is helped by being just outside the inexpensive price bracket. The property has both rooms and self-catering apartments, plus a pool and a restaurant.
Scout's Place (£–££)
tel: 416 2740
Intriguing spot on the hillside in Windwardside. Comfortable rooms and a lively bar.

St Eustatius (599)

Hotels on St Eustatius add a government tax of 7 per cent to all bills.

Kings Well Hotel (££)
Bay Road, Oranjebaai tel: 318 2538
Simple but spacious rooms are offered, plus a few with kitchenettes. If you don't wish to cook there is a small yet lively restaurant.
Old Gin House (££)
Lower Town tel: 318 2319
This historic hotel has reopened and is aiming to regain its status as the best on St Eustatius.

Sint Maarten (599)

Hotels on Sint Maarten add a government tax of 5 per cent to all bills.

The Horny Toad Guesthouse (££)
tel: 545 4323
Excellent setting on Simpson Bay, attentive service and friendly, fully equipped rooms.
Passangrahan Royal Inn (££)
Philipsburg tel: 542 3588
Old colonial air in the louvred foyer and a welcome oasis of peace and quiet in the shopping turmoil of Front Street. Twenty-eight rooms, restaurant and bar.

OTHER CARIBBEAN STATES

Jamaica (876)

Hotels in Jamaica add a general consumption tax of 10 per cent to all bills.

Blue Mountains

Strawberry Hill (£££)
Irishtown tel: 944 8400
A Sybaritic mountain retreat, one of numerous Caribbean properties owned by Chris Blackwell of Island Records. Handsome villa accommodation with views, discrete yet charming service, a spa and superb food, plus utter peace and quiet and deliciously (comfortably) cool evenings.

Kingston

Terra Nova Hotel (££)
New Kingston tel: 926 9334
Elegant grand old upmarket house in lawned gardens; 32 attractive rooms, pool and a good dining room.
Morgan's Harbour Hotel (££–£££)
tel: 967 8030
A pleasant, shady two-storey motel with an open-air restaurant, pool, beach and yacht marina, five minutes' walk from Port Royal and a breezy ferry ride to downtown Kingston.

Mandeville

Astra Country Inn (£–££)
tel: 962 3265
Forty rooms are set in a modern building just outside town: family-run and friendly. Tours can be arranged to the surrounding countryside.

Montego Bay

Cobaya Beach Resort and Club (£££)
Mahoe Bay tel: 953 9150
A plantation-style inn on the beachfront just east of the city. Although there are 50 rooms, the property has a more intimate character and offers a warm welcome to families. Facilities include restaurants, bars, tennis, dive shop and other watersports.
Coral Cliff Hotel (£)
tel: 952 4130
Graceful old villa near town centre. Some rooms in the modern buildings behind. Pool, beach within walking distance.
Half Moon Club (£££–££££)
tel: 953 2211
Simply the classiest in Jamaican high luxury, on a fine beach. Elegant rooms decorated in black and white; 19 pools, tennis, golf, riding, health club, and very fine dining.
Richmond Hill Hotel (££)
tel: 952 3859
On the hilltop above the Montego Bay, an elegant town house with additional rooms and suites (20 in all) in rather quaint style. Restaurant, pool and free beach/town shuttle.

Negril

Charela Inn (££)
tel: 957 4277
Despite its 49 rooms, this beach hotel has an intimate feel. Watersports are on offer, and there is a fine French restaurant.
Grand Lido (££££)
tel: 957 5010
On the fine sand of Bloody Bay, this is a top-grade all-inclusive hotel – the champagne is on demand.
Negril Cabins Resort (£–££)
tel: 957 5350
Airy wooden cottages on stilts surrounded by exuberant foliage across the road from the beach. However, basic rooms have no air-conditioning. Restaurants, bars, on-site dive shop, tennis, children's playground, baby-sitting and a shuttle into town are part of the package.

Ocho Rios

Boscobel Beach (£££–££££)
tel: 975 7330
All-inclusive resort on a fine beach, designed especially for families with children. Finger-painting instruction through to disco lessons will occupy them while you indulge in watersports and sunning.
Hibiscus Lodge Hotel (£–££)
tel: 974 2676
Simple rooms on the clifftops, near the action of town, but also only a short walk to the beach. Good food can be found in the restaurants and facilities include a garden and watersports.
Jamaica Inn (£££–££££)
tel: 974 2514
Sir Winston Churchill was a fan of this venerable establishment, and would probably still feel quite at home in the slightly formal surroundings (jackets for dinner). Generously proportioned rooms combine colonial décor with modern comforts and wonderful private verandas. Dining, pool, croquet plus a secluded beach.

Port Antonio

Dragon Bay (£–££)
tel: 993 8514
Affordable all-inclusive 1-, 2- and 3-bedroom villa accommodation in landscaped gardens. Restaurants, bars, pool, tennis, dive shop and volleyball on the beach.
Mocking Bird Hill (££)
tel: 993 7267
Small and charming hotel with just 10 rooms and an eco-friendly ethos that prefers ceiling fans to aircon and heats water by solar power. Restaurant, bar and pool, plus eco-tours.
Trident Villas and Hotel (£££–££££)
tel: 993 2602
An enclave of supreme elegance, stunningly presented main house and rooms in manicured gardens. On a ledge of coral reef, small beach, but a fine pool.

The Cayman Islands (345)

Hotels on the Cayman Islands add 6 per cent government tax to all bills.

Beach Club Colony (£££)
Grand Cayman tel: 949 8100
A low rise building set right on Seven Mile Beach with a vast number of watersports on offer. Rooms are comfortable to luxurious.
Brac Reef Beach Resort (££)
Cayman Brac tel: 948 1323
Good base for a diving holiday with a dive shop on site, an attractive beachfront position, relaxed atmosphere and 40 rooms with patio or balcony.
Hyatt Regency (£££–££££)
Grand Cayman tel: 949 1234
One of the most luxurious hotels in Cayman, just across the road from Seven Mile Beach. Modern building, but with attractive old-colonial flourishes. Restaurants, golf course, watersports on the beach.
Sunset House (££)
Grand Cayman tel: 949 7111
This unpretentious waterfront dive resort has simple rooms and a laid back atmosphere. It is a short distance south of George Town and only five minutes from a sandy beach.

275

Cuba (53)

Havana

Habana Libre Tryp (£££)
tel: 07/33 4011
Tall building at the head of La Rampa, built as the Havana Hilton back in the 1950s and renamed the Habana Libre by the young revolutionaries.
Inglaterra (££–£££)
tel: 07/62 7075
On the Parque Central, at the edge of the colonial city, the Inglaterra is a short walk away from the sights. There is a pleasant bar in the elaborate foyer and the rooms are comfortable.
Plaza (£££)
tel: 07/33 8583
A fine, colonnaded building on the Parque Central, grand breezy interior with palms and pillars. Newly decorated, comfortable rooms.

Outside Havana

Gran Hotel (££–£££)
Varadero tel: 05/66 8243
With 411 rooms and 300 metres of beach, two pools (one with a children's section), air-conditioning, all-inclusive meals and water-sports, and all the American amenities, this is a prudent option for families or budget watchers visiting Varadero.
Horizontes Villa Playa Girón (££)
Bay of Pigs tel: 05/4118
History buffs will appreciate the pool, as well as the air-conditioning and other comforts of this 292-room beachfront bungalow complex after visiting the nearby Bay of Pigs museum.

Hotels and Restaurants

Hotel Casa Granda Santiago (££–£££)
tel: 0226/86600
Built in 1914, the elegant Casa Granda has 58 fully equipped rooms right in the heart of atmospheric Santiago.
Pelícano (££–£££)
Cayo Largo tel: 05/48333
The island of Key Largo offers great beaches and the best diving in Cuba. The 300 beach-front rooms come with an all-inclusive package. Amenities include a pool, restaurants, multiple bars and plentiful watersports.
Horizontes Los Jazmines (£)
Viñales tel: 08/93205
This hotel is in an old villa standing high above the Viñales valley offering fine views.
Paradisus Varadero Beach Resort (£££)
Varadero tel: 535/66 8267
Luxury rooms in beach villas; good Caribbean beach location with non-motorised watersports, bars and clubs.

The Dominican Republic (809)

Hotels in the Dominican Republic add a government tax of 6 per cent.

Altos de Chavón and the Southeast, Cordillera Central

Barceló Bávaro Beach (£££)
Punto Cana Higuey tel: 686 5797
Behind the superb palm-fringed beach lie a clutch of popular resort hotels, of which this is one. Comfortable air-conditioned rooms, plenty of restaurants and bars, plus watersports, golf and tennis.
Casa de Campo (£££–££££)
La Romana tel: 523 3333
A top resort complex with some of the Caribbean's most chic villas and hotel rooms – polo, golf, beach sports, a choice of restaurants – all set in beautifully landscaped grounds.

Puerto Plata and the Amber Coast

Natura Cabanas (£–££)
Cabarete tel: 571 1507
Guests stay in thatched garden bungalows at this soothing beachfront spa offering aromatherapy, massage, mud baths and more, plus activities from biking to jeep safaris.
Piergiorgio Palace Hotel (££)
Sosúa tel: 571 2626
Victorian seaside inn gets an Italian makeover in this elaborate homage to Sosúa's heyday set in landscaped gardens with pools and cliffside restaurant.

Samaná

Occidental Gran Bahía (£££)
tel: 538 3111
Supremely elegant gingerbread mansion east of Samaná, opposite the fine beaches of Cajo Levantado. Old Caribbean air and comfort and high standards of service.

Hotel Tropic Banana (£)
Las Terrenas tel: 240 6110
One of the best travellers' haunts in the Caribbean, where a lively crowd gathers for music at the poolside; 30 rooms in a spacious palm garden near the beach.

Santo Domingo

Boca Chica Resort (££)
tel: 412 2001
The closest beach resort to the capital – about 30 minutes away. The Boca Chica offers an all-inclusive plan with a sophisticated ambience and elegant rooms.
Hotel Sofitel Frances (££)
Calle Las Mercedes tel: 685 9331
Small and charming hotel in an historic building arranged around a fountain courtyard, which invites you to linger with a book. Nineteen stylishly uncluttered rooms and a French restaurant.
Renaissance Jaragua (£££)
Avenida Washington tel: 221 2222
Luxury is available in this large and glitzy hotel on the Malecon. Choose from its four restaurants, a club with entertainers and a casino. Tours can also be arranged.

Puerto Rico (787)

Hotels in Puerto Rico add a government tax of 7 per cent (9 per cent in hotels with a casino).

Cordillera Central

Hacienda Gripiñas (££)
Jayuya tel: 828 1717
A *Parador* set in a charming timber-framed coffee estate house. It is not elaborate, but has a wonderful old-time Caribbean feel.
Horned Dorset Primavera (£££)
Rincón tel: 823 4030
Luxurious rooms that overlook the hotel garden or the sunset out to sea. Elegant central area with a library for afternoon tea and cocktails. Very fine cuisine.

Ponce

Hotel Melia (££)
Calle Cristina 75 tel: 842 0260
The Melia is just off the central square in Ponce. The well-priced rooms are modern and air-conditioned.

San German and the South West

Parador Boquemar (£)
Boqueron tel: 851 2158
This modern building the near beach can offer the traveller comfortable rooms, a pool and a restaurant.
Villa Parguera (££)
Lajas tel: 899 7777
Low rates for a welcoming resort hotel on the waterfront, set in a tropical garden. Pool and good local restaurant on the bay.

San Juan: New City

Casa Mathieson Inn (££)
Calle Uno 14 tel: 762 8662
These simple – yet air-conditioned – rooms
are near Isla Verde beach. The Inn also has
a restaurant.
El Prado Inn (££)
Calle Luchetti 1350 tel: 728 5925
Set in a neat family villa, between Condado
and Isla Verde; walls festooned with tropical
blooms. El Prado has 10 simple, reasonably
priced rooms and a swimming pool.
Radisson Ambassador Plaza (£££–££££)
1369 Ashford Avenue tel: 721 7300
Right on the Condado strip near to the beach,
close to shops and 10 mins from Old San
Juan. Rooms and suites; roof top pool,
children's activity programmes, casino.

San Juan: Old City

Gallery Inn (££)
tel: 722 1808
Restored town house with circular staircases,
courtyards and terraces: bohemian feel as it
incorporates an art gallery.
Hotel El Convento (£££)
Calle Cristo 100 tel: 723 9020
A magnificent old building in the colonial city –
black and white tiles, stained panelling and
tapestries hung on the walls. Once a convent,
it retains a calm and cloistered air.

Vieques

La Casa del Francés (££)
Esperanza tel: 741 3751
A charming old estate house, with
chessboard tiles and a cool courtyard.
The owner is a Hemingway-like character
who is always amusing. Swimming pool,
home-cooked food.

Barbados (246)

Hotels on Barbados add a 5 per cent
government tax to all bills.

South Coast

Bougainvillea Beach Resort (££)
Maxwell tel: 418 0990
Studios and suites in an attractive resort with
pools, restaurants, watersports and tennis. All
rooms have terrace or balcony and kitchenette.
Crane Beach Hotel (££–£££)
St Philip tel: 423 6220
In a superb setting on the cliffs, where the pool
and restaurant, above the pretty cove 30m
below, have magificent views. Eighteen rooms
in a small apartment building and in a coral
stone castle.
Sandy Beach Island Resort (£–££)
Worthing tel: 435 8000
Just down the road from St Lawrence Gap, this
bright modern hotel has rooms or 1- and 2-
bedroom self-catering suites. Pool, restaurant
and bar; watersports by arrangement.

West Coast

Cobbler's Cove (££££)
tel: 422 2291
South of Speightstown, Cobbler's Cove has 39
beautifully decorated suites set above a fine
strip of sand.
Sandridge Beach Hotel (£–££)
St Peter tel: 422 2361
This is an oasis of beachfront affordability
on the upper reaches of the Platinum Coast.
The fifty-eight units range from rooms to
studios and self-catering suites, all with
access to a number of pools, restaurants
and watersports.
Sandy Lane Hotel (££££)
St James tel: 432 1311
A legend in Caribbean elegance and hospitality,
Sandy Lane has recently undergone a complete
remodelling.

Trinidad and Tobago (868)

All hotels in Trinidad and Tobago add VAT of
15 per cent to published prices.

Trinidad

Asa Wright Nature Centre (££)
Arima tel: 667 4655
An old colonial estate house with an enormous
screened veranda: it is set in the secluded
forests of the northern range. This nature
centre makes an ideal base for bird-watching
and general relaxation.
Hilton (££)
Port of Spain tel: 624 3211
This is a busy centre for those passing
through the capital, but it is also quite well
organised for tourists. It has superb views
over the Savannah.
Hotel Normandie (£–££)
St Ann's tel: 624 1181
Quiet hotel tucked away in a valley that has
now been swallowed up by Port of Spain. Fine
French fare.

Tobago

Arnos Vale (££)
tel: 639 2881
In its own steep-sided valley festooned with
tropical blooms, the Arnos Vale has 38 rooms
and suites in a complex and in a central
estate house. There is a beach bar, a pool
and a boutique.
Old Donkey Cart House (££)
tel: 639 3551
On a hillside just outside Scarborough, with
very comfortable rooms clustering around a
pool. A wonderful choice if you are looking for
privacy and seclusion, and it is attached to an
excellent restaurant.
Plantation Beach Villas (££–£££)
tel: 639 0455
Very attractive, old colonial style villas situated
above the beach at Stonehaven Bay. Self-
catering; swimming pool and bar down below;
cooking can be arranged.

RESTAURANTS

Good food is found in many Caribbean hotels as well as the establishments listed below. The price categories relate to average local prices on each island.

Inexpensive: (£)
Moderate: (££)
Expensive: (£££)

THE WINDWARD ISLANDS

Dominica

Garraway Hotel (£££)
tel: 449 8800
Excellent fare in the hotel's Balizier Restaurant overlooking the waterfront in Roseau itself.
Guiyave (££)
Roseau tel: 448 2930
Pretty balcony setting above the street for a hearty local lunch (no dinner).
La Robe Creole (££–£££)
Roseau tel: 448 2896
Cosy historic building down near Fort Young and good Créole food featuring local specialities stylishly presented.

Grenada and Carriacou

La Belle Créole (£££)
Grande Anse tel: 444 4316
The terrace dining room of the Blue Horizons hotel: *nouvelle cuisine* with a West Indian lilt.
The Boatyard (££)
L'Anse aux Epines tel: 444 4662
Bar and restaurant in marina, simple fare, bar livens up at the weekend, some entertainment.
Callaloo by the Sea (£)
Hillsborough, Carriacou tel: 443 8004
Great lunch spot with a waterfront terrace at the south end of Main Street.
Coconuts (£££)
Grand Anse tel: 444 4644
Classic beach setting, tables inside the pretty house or just above the sand. Also known as the French restaurant; fine French-Créole cuisine.

The Grenadines

On the small Grenadine islands you will be dependent on your hotel.

Basil's Bar (££)
Mustique tel: 458 4621
In a charmed setting on stilts on a magnificent bay; the favourite haunt of island visitors and passing yachtsmen. Entertainment.
Dennis' Hideaway (££)
Mayreau tel: 458 8594
Bar and dining room on a terrace on the hillside with good local fare.
Mac's Pizzeria (££)
Bequia tel: 458 3474
Wooden deck above a tropical garden, excellent pizzas, plus seafood and Créole dishes.

St Lucia

Bang Between the Pitons (£)
tel: 459 7864
Courtyard surrounded by old wooden Créole houses between the comical pitons. Local and international fare with flair.
Café des Arts (££)
Gros Inlet tel: 452 0742
Airy wooden building that makes a pleasantly relaxed setting for this friendly café.
Dasheene (£££)
tel: 459 7323
The location – between the Pitons and high above the sea will take your breath away – as will the top-notch cuisine and the fine wine list. A must for gourmets.
Froggie Jacks (££)
Vigie Cove, Castries tel: 458 1900
Enviable waterside setting on the harbour. The chef-owner tackles Caribbean ingredients, particularly seafood, with aplomb.

St Vincent

Basil's Bar (££)
Kingstown tel: 457 2713
Downstairs from the Cobblestone Inn, set in an old stone trading warehouse; international and local fare.
French Restaurant (£££)
Villa tel: 458 4972
Authentic French restaurant with a long standing reputation and an amazing selection of lobster dishes.
Lime Restaurant & Pub (££)
Villa tel: 458 4227
Informal bar and terrace for meals and snacks overlooking Young Island on the Villa strip. Has been known to get lively.

THE LEEWARD ISLANDS

Anguilla

Blanchard's (£££)
Mead's Bay tel: 497 6100
Top quality international fare and notable wine list offered in a charming and elegant house.
Mango's (£££)
Barnes Bay tel: 6479
Above the beach on a breezy veranda, reserve a table for well prepared new American cuisine.
Ripples (££)
Sandy Ground tel: 497 3380
Busy beach bar-restaurant with both indoor and outdoor seating and menu featuring salads, grilled fish and pasta dishes.

Antigua

Admiral's Inn (££–£££)
Nelson's Dockyard tel: 460 1027
Housed in a lovely Georgian building dating from 1788, the Inn offers fresh seafood, home-made soups and other fare in a lively nautical atmosphere. The secluded dining terrace overlooks English Harbour.

Julian's (£££)
Church Street at Corn Alley, St John's
tel: 462 4766
Charming setting in old West Indian house and imaginative classic-modern cuisine.
Shirley Heights Lookout (££)
tel: 460 1785
High above English Harbour, a veranda with a view. Burgers, salads or local dishes, best known for riotous Sunday afternoon assembly.

Montserrat

In the present situation, the hotels are a good option: try **Tropical Mansions**, **Sweeneys** (tel: 491 8767), or the **Vue Pointe** (tel: 491 5210). For a good dinner reserve ahead at **Ziggy's**, Mahogany Loop (tel: 491 8282).

Nevis

Hermitage Plantation (£££)
Fig Tree Parish tel: 469 3477
Elegant, candlelit veranda in the main house of the hotel, adventurous and delightful West Indian cuisine. Reservations advised.
Nisbet Plantation (£££)
Newcastle tel: 469 9325
In the charming old colonial setting of an 18th-century great house. Victorian décor and tempting menu of Continental and Caribbean dishes. Reservations advised.
Sunshine Beach Bar & Grill (£)
Pinney's Beach tel: 469 5817
Proprietor Sunshine mixes a mean rum-based Killer Bee to wash down freshly grilled shrimp, fish, chicken and slightly more pricey lobster.

St Kitts

Golden Lemon (£££)
Dieppe Bay tel: 465 7260
Exquisite local and Continental fare in the delightfully restored historic surroundings. Fine lunchtime stop, but even better at dinner.
Rawlins Plantation (£££)
Mount Pleasant tel: 465 6221
Some of the best local food in the islands, served in the charming setting of a plantation house: a good choice for lunch.
StoneWalls (£–££)
Princes Street, Basseterre tel: 466 7454
Great bar in a tropical garden setting serving a hearty line in jerk pork and pasta dishes.

THE VIRGIN ISLANDS

The British Virgin Islands

Cooper Island Beach Club (££)
tel: 494 3721
The only bar on Cooper Island, a bright patio right above the sand where you can enjoy a grill and a salad with a passing sailing crowd.
Peter Island (£££)
tel: 495 2000
Worth the short ride from Roadtown to Peter Island for top Caribbean and international cuisine after a day out on the island.

Tortola

Brandywine Bay (£££)
East End tel: 495 2301
With a magnificent view of the Channel from the breezy terrace, enjoy the fine Italian cuisine.
Mrs Scatliffe (££)
Carrot Bay tel: 495 4556
Delectable local fare, pumpkin soup and curry goat followed by tropical fruit ice-creams.
Pusser's Store and Pub (££)
Road Town tel: 494 3897
Lively haunt, located near the ferry terminal; warmly decorated with burnished brass and panelled walls. Hearty pub grub.
Sugar Mill Restaurant (£££)
Apple Bay tel: 495 4355
In a candlelit stone building from old colonial times; extremely fine West Indian cuisine.

Virgin Gorda

Chez Bamboo (££)
The Valley tel: 495 5752
Brightly painted dining room in town serving Créole and Caribbean fare.
The Rock (£–££)
Tower Road tel: 495 5482
Bar-restaurant with a great boulder-strewn setting close to The Baths. An Italian-Caribbean-American menu; live music; cold beers; and cocktails.

The US Virgin Islands

St Croix

Blue Moon (££–£££)
Frederiksted tel: 772 2222
Deep and dark setting under the arches in an old Front Street trading building. Jazz and cajun fare: be warned – it does get busy.
Top Hat (£££)
Company Street, Christiansted tel: 773 2346
Very pleasant restaurant upstairs in an old town house. The menu is international and particularly notable for its Danish dishes.

St John

Morgan's Mango (££)
Cruz Bay tel: 693 8141
Great veranda setting opposite the National Park dock with new Caribbean and some Argentinian fare. Live music sometimes.
Paradiso Restaurant (£££)
Mongoose Junction, Cruz Bay tel: 693 8899
The décor here is worthy of a Manhattan nightclub, and the cocktail bar and quiet music add to the atmosphere. The Italian dishes are the best.

St Thomas

Café Wahoo (££)
Red Hook tel: 775 6350
Seafood and fish on a deck above the lagoon at the ferry dock; lively and fun.

279

Hotels and Restaurants

Craig and Sally's (£££)
Frenchtown tel: 777 9949
A varied and interesting Mediterranean-Asian menu with an excellent wine list.
Cuzzins's Caribbean Restaurant (££)
7 Back Street, Charlotte Amalie tel: 777 4711
Deliciously prepared local food from conch, Créole and curries to stuffed lobster served by friendly staff in an historic (and conveniently central) building.

THE FRENCH ANTILLES

Guadeloupe

Château de Feuilles (£££)
Anse Bertrand tel: 22 30 30
Worth a trip to the northern tip of Grande-Terre, where you dine on a terrace in a profuse garden. Excellent French and local fare.
Côté Jardin (£££)
Point-à-Pitre tel: 90 91 28
Elegant, air-conditioned dining with a good wine list in the lively yacht-filled marina.
Les Oiseaux (££)
Saint François tel: 88 56 92
Pleasant, veranda setting for an eclectic combination of French and Créole food.
Le Vieux Port (££)
St François tel: 88 46 60
On the waterfront, this lively and rustic setting specialises in fresh fish and lobster.

Martinique

Auberge de la Montagne Pelée (£–££)
Morne Rouge tel: 52 32 09
A useful pit stop for tours of the north of the island. Terrific views; French and Créole cooking; in particular, try the freshwater crayfish gratin.
La Savane (£)
Fort de France
A series of snackwagons with loud music where you can sit out in the crowd and eat sandwiches and simple dishes.
Le Colibri (££)
Morne des Esses tel: 69 91 95
A veranda with a fantastic view and some of the most adventurous French Créole food on the island, all prepared by Clothilde Palladino.

Saint-Barthélemy

Maya's (£££)
Public tel: 27 75 73
Popular waterfront restaurant under the palms in public. Fish and Créole are specialities.
Le Rock (££)
Saint-Jean tel: 27 72 94
The international fare served on this beach-front deck is wonderfully light, making it a great lunchtime stop.
Le Sapotillier (£££)
Gustavia tel: 27 60 28
Set in the capital of St Barts, this is a charming and elegant restaurant with excellent classical French cuisine.

Saint-Martin

Bar de la Mer
Marigot tel: 87 81 79
Cocktail bar-restaurant just off the waterfront.
Bistrot Nu (££)
Marigot tel: 87 97 09
Some of the best Créole food in the island.
Fish Pot (£££)
Grand Case tel: 87 50 88
Elegant surroundings and superb French-Caribbean cuisine plus a balcony above the bay.
Les Lolos (£)
Grand Case
Very cheap barbecued food and beer from the roadside in the middle of town. Worth stopping for lunch.
Le Tastevin (£££)
Grand Case tel: 87 55 45
On a tropical terrace above the waves. Classic French cuisine and service.

THE NETHERLANDS ANTILLES

Aruba

Charlie's Bar (£)
Zeppenferdstraat 56 tel: 845086
Bar and restaurant in the east of Aruba, hung with memorabiliia, famous for jumbo shrimp.
Gasparito (££)
Gasparito 3 tel: 867044
Delicious Dutch Antillean food in a traditional old Aruban country house, behind Palm Beach.
Papiamento (£££)
Washington 61 tel: 64544
The best cuisine in the best setting, a country house where tables are inside or by the pool: a delightful experience, but make reservations.

Bonaire

Mi Poron (£££)
Kralendijk tel: 717 5199
Home-cooked Bonaire cuisine in the courtyard of a traditional house, in the middle of town.
Rendez-vous (£–££)
Kralendijk tel: 717 8454
Charming restaurant set in a modern town house. You dine on the veranda or inside. Continental dishes, with some local cuisine.
Richard's (££–£££)
Kralendijk tel: 717 5263
Easy-going spot on a seafront terrace south of the town and one of the island's best eateries. Excellent local cuisine and seafood.

Curaçao

De Taveerne (£££)
Salinja tel: 737 0211
Intimate atmosphere in the low-lit cellar of an old estate house. The menu is continental, using the best local fish and vegetables.
Fort Waakzamheid (££)
off highway, Otrobanda tel: 462 3633
Open-air setting in an old fortress high on a hill in the west of Willemstad.

Golden Star (££)
Socratesstraat 2 tel: 465 4795
Cold and over-decorated dining room, but the
finest West Indian food in town.
Jaanchi Christiaan (£)
Westpunt tel: 864 0126
Great lunch stop in the north of the island.
Sample local seafood and possibly iguana
stew on the terrace.

Saba

Chinese Restaurant (££)
Windwardside tel: 416 62268
Modern house high on the hill with a long list of
Cantonese dishes to eat in or take out.
In Two Deep (£)
Fort Bay tel: 416 3438
Café for sandwiches and salads and a drink
after scuba-diving.
Scout's Place (££)
Windwardside tel: 416 2740
Drinks and hearty portions of wholesome
Caribbean food; some entertainment.

St Eustatius

Kings Well Bar & Restaurant (££)
Bay Road (by Smoke Alley) tel: 318 2538
Grand position on Oranjebaai with views of the
Lower Town. The menu is an eclectic German-
Continental-American hybrid featuring prime US
beef and schnitzels.
Stone Oven (£)
Faeschweg, Oranjested tel: 318 2809
Good Caribbean food in a small town house
set with neat wooden tables.

Sint Maarten

Da Livio (£££)
Front St tel: 542 2690
Delectable Italian fare on a waterfront terrace
in Philipsburg. Very popular.
Kangaroo Court Café (£–££)
tel: 542 4278
Great baked goods and fine coffee make this
pleasant courtyard café the best breakfast
spot in Philipsburg. On a side street not far
from the cruise ship dock.
Le Perroquet (£££)
Simpson Bay tel: 545 4339
In a pretty house overlooking a tropical garden,
French menu with some very exotic extras like
lion and ostrich.

OTHER CARIBBEAN STATES

Jamaica
Restaurants add a General Consumption tax of
10 per cent to all bills.

Blue Mountains

Blue Mountain Inn (£££)
Gordon Town tel: 927 1900
Old plantation house setting, very fine fare of
Créole dishes as well as international classics.

The Gap Café (£)
tel: 923 7078
Stupendous view over Kingston, good stop for
lunch or tea.

Kingston

Chelsea Jerk Centre (£)
Chelsea Avenue tel: 926 6322
Very local; pork and chicken jerked meat;
watch the hot pepper sauce.
Guilt Trip (££)
Barbican Road tel: 977 5130
Hip gathering point, with cakes by day and
international and new Jamaican cuisine
by night.
Palm Court (££–£££)
Hilton New Kingston tel: 926 5430
Elegant restaurant in a swish high-rise Hilton
popular with business visitors. The mezzanine
level dining room offers a very good and
stylishly presented continental menu.

Montego Bay

281

Marguerite's (££)
Gloucester Avenue tel: 952 4777
Terrace on the sea and under the stars, for
cocktails and light meals. Margueritaville, next
door, offers international fare in a rowdy,
sports-bar atmosphere.
Norma's on the Wharf (£££)
Reading tel: 979 2745
Stunning waterfront setting opposite the town
with very fine Continental cuisine. Reservations
will be required.
Pork Pit (£)
Gloucester Avenue tel: 952 1046
Take-away or sit at the garden benches to eat
pork, chicken, fish and spare ribs with coconut
milk or beer.

Negril

Cosmo's Seafood Restaurant (££–£££)
Manley Boulevard tel: 957 4330
Al fresco beachfront bistro with shady tables
under spreading seagrape trees. Meaty conch
chowder is a speciality, check out the catch of
the day, or splash out on delicious plain grilled
lobster.
Rick's Café (££)
West End Road tel: 957 0380
Rick's is a local institution and bastion of
Negril culture from its nightly sunset cocktail
session to cliff diving performances. The so-so
pub food is eclipsed by the atmosphere.

Ocho Rios

Almond Tree (£££)
Hibiscus Lodge Hotel tel: 974 2676
Fine setting on the cliffs with floodlit greenery;
good for local cuisine.
Double V Jerk Centre (£)
Main Street heading east tel: 974 0174
A wooden cabin in a tropical garden, good
stopover for jerk.

Hotels and Restaurants

Little Pub (£–££)
59 Main Street tel: 974 2324
Do not be put off by the sports bar, the outdoor restaurant is a great little spot. Wide-ranging menu covers seafood stir fries, Jamaican jerk, pasta, curries and generous burgers.
Parkway (££)
tel: 974 2667
Tasty local fare on a modern West Indian veranda setting.

Port Antonio

Daddy D's (£)
West St tel: 993 2116
Best local fare in a typical West Indian setting.
Huntress Marina (££)
tel: 993 3053
On the waterfront in the harbour, rustic and local fare.
Trident Hotel (£££)
tel: 993 2602
Very elegant setting of a colonial-style veranda, top local cuisine. Although living on past gourmet glories, reservations are still needed.

The Cayman Islands

Apollo 11
North Sound, Grand Cayman tel: 947 9568
Cool waterfront bar in an old shed. Live music.
Cracked Conch by the Sea (££)
West Bay, Grand Cayman tel: 945 5217
Lively bar and restaurant. Conch is served cracked (beaten tender) along with other fish.
Grand Old House (£££)
South Church Street, Grand Cayman tel: 949 9333
In a charming old colonial house; excellent Continental dishes as well as a few local ones. Make a reservation.
Pirates Point Resort (££)
Preston Bay, Little Cayman tel: 948 1010
Reservations are also required to sample Gladys Howard's delicious and stylish brand of cooking.
Ristorante Pappagallo (£££)
Spanish Cove, Grand Cayman tel: 949 1119
Huge palm-thatched, air-conditioned *cabana* set on an isolated lagoon. Northern Italian menu. Reserve a table.

Cuba

Havana

D'Giovanni (££)
Calle Tacon, Zana Colonial tel: 7/61 2183
Italian dishes in an old colonial house.
El Floridita (£££)
Calle Montserrate 557 tel: 7/33 8856
A favourite of Hemingway's, famed for its *daiquiris* (worth going just for them). Elegant if ritzy dining room, fine cuisine.
El Patio (££)
Plaza de la Catedral tel: 7/61 8504
Charming setting in the Zona Colonial. Café downstairs on the cobbles, meals upstairs.

Papa's (££)
Hemingway Marina tel: 7/22 5592
Waterfront setting and seafood specialities in the lively marina complex which is popular with visitors for its atmosphere and disco.

Outside Havana

Las Américas (£££)
Varadero
Once a private home on the waterfront, now serving international dishes; fine views.
Los Jazmines (£)
Viñales
Magnificent setting. Local Cuban cuisine.
El Mesón de Quijote (££)
Varadero
Set in open grounds far down the peninsula; Spanish menu.
1900 (££)
Calle San Basilio, Santiago de Cuba tel: 23507
Charming old townhouse; local Cuban food.

The Dominican Republic

Altos de Chavon

Casa del Río (£££)
Altos de Chavón tel: 523 3333
Fantastic setting above floodlit river with a mix of Caribbean and international dishes.
La Casita (££)
La Romana tel: 223 0568
Good Italian joint serving plenty of seafood dishes as well as pastas and risottos.

Puerto Plata and the Amber Coast

Barco's (£–££)
Malcón 6, Puerto Plata
Great people-watching from the sidewalk terrace and a mixed menu of pizzas, steaks, seafood and more.
Casa del Pescador (£££)
Carretera 5, Cabarete
Top choice for a romantic evening out. Excellent seafood is the hallmark of this candlelit dining room on the beach.
Hemingways's Café (£–££)
Playa Dorado tel: 320 2230
A modern-day shrine to Papa Hemingway with old photos and strangely named dishes such as the For Whom the Bell Tolls fajitas. Late night live music draws a young crowd.
On the Waterfront (£–££)
Calle Dr Rosen, El Batay, Sosúa tel: 571 3024
Great seafood restaurant with wonderful ocean-front deck that can also provide breakfast and a welcoming bar.

Samaná

Camilo (££)
Malcón, Samaná
Head to the waterfront for tasty local food in an attractive setting. The creamy *pollo asopao* (chicken with rice) is a good bet.

L'Hacienda
tel: 538 2383
Grilled food on a breezy veranda to Latin music and hot salsa.

Santo Domingo

El Conuco (££)
Calle Casimiro de Moya tel: 686 0129
Riotous restaurant with decorations from the *conuco* (country); with singing waiters.
Independencia (£)
just off Parque Independencia
Some of the best local food around, slightly chaotic service but a good Dominican experience all in all.
Vesuvio (££–£££)
on the Malecon tel: 221 3333
Big, very popular restaurant. Top Italian and Dominican fare.

Puerto Rico

San German and the Southwest

El Bohio (££)
Playa Joyuda tel: 851 2755
On a breezy deck above the waves. Unpretentious but the best of local fish.
Vista Bahia (££)
Cabo Rojo tel: 851 4140
Right on Playa Joyuda; steaks and seafood.

Ponce

El Ancla (£££)
Avenida Hostos 9 tel: 840 2450
Out of the city centre, an air-conditioned lounge on Ponce beach, menu consists mainly of seafood with copious local vegetables.

San Juan

Amadeus (££)
Calle San Sebastian 106 tel: 722 8635
Stylish restaurant serving nouvelle Puerto Rican cuisine, near the lively bars of Plaza San Jose.
La Casita Blanca (££)
Calle Tapia 351, Santurce tel: 726 5501
Small but very lively restaurant specialising in Puerto Rican food, and lots of it. Charming setting, amusing waiters.
La Mallorquina (££)
Calle San Justo 207 tel: 722 3261
Set in a century-old house, still with its antique furnishings. Good local food.

Barbados

Atlantis (££)
Bathsheba tel: 433 9445
The hotel itself is clearly past its prime, but the setting on the clifftops and the food, a West Indian buffet, is still superb.
Carambola (£££)
Derricks, St James tel: 432 0832
Superb setting on the cliff of the west coast, delectable Caribbean and Continental cuisine.

The Cliff (£££)
St James tel: 432 1922
Topnotch international cuisine in an extremely elegant and dramatic setting.
David's Place (££)
Main Road, Worthing tel: 435 9755
Breezy setting above pretty St Lawrence Bay; excellent Bajan food, delicious desserts.
Josef's (£££)
St Lawrence Gap tel: 435 6541
Private home turned into elegant oceanfront restaurant, the cooking is international and the quality is excellent.
Pisces (££)
St Lawrence Gap tel: 435 6564
Charming setting on a trellis-lined veranda above St Lawrence Bay. Mainly seafood and fish but with some other dishes.

Trinidad and Tobago

Trinidad

The Breakfast Shed (£)
Waterfront, Port of Spain tel: 624 3404
Refectory-style dining room with vast pots and pans bubbling away, fine local fare.
Le Chateau de Poisson (££)
Ariapita Avenue, Port of Spain tel: 622 6087
Charming gingerbread town house hung with greenery; seafood and fish is served in a variety of spices.
Moon Over Bourbon Street (££)
West Mall, Port of Spain tel: 637 3448
A delightful cocktail bar and rooftop restaurant out of town, decked out like a transatlantic liner. Some entertainment.
Rafters (££)
Warner Street, Port of Spain tel: 628 9258
Hip video bar and restaurant located in an old warehouse.
Tiki Village (££)
Kapok Hotel, Port of Spain tel: 622 6441
Popular top floor restaurant with views over the city; Polynesian and Chinese menu.
Veni Mange (££)
Ariapita Avenue, Port of Spain tel: 624 4597
Popular lunchtime (only) haunt, serving delicious West Indian cuisine – it is highly recommended.

Tobago

Black Rock Café (£££)
Black Rock tel: 639 7625
Veranda painted pink with white louvres. Créole dishes with salads and steaks.
Old Donkey Cart House (£££)
just out of Scarborough tel: 639-3551
Charming floodlit garden and pretty house, good local and international fare.
Rouselle's (££)
Scarborough tel: 639 4738
Upstairs lounge bar with tables where you can eat good local food.
Store Bay (£)
Local take-out meals, curry goat, crab and dumpling, and delicious local fruit juices.

Index

A

agriculture 14–15
Anegada 96, 97
Anguilla 69, 70–71, 246, 271
  Barnes Bay 71
  Captain's Bay 71
  eating out 278
  Fountain 71, 200
  Island Harbour 71
  Limestone Bay 71
  Little Bay 71
  Maunday's Bay 71
  Mead's Bay 71
  Rendezvous Bay 71
  Road Bay 71
  Sandy Ground 71
  Shoal Bay 71
  Shoal Bay West 71
  The Valley 71
Antigua 69, 72, 73, 76, 246–247, 271
  Betty's Hope 73
  Clarence House 76
  Devil's Bridge 73
  Dickenson Bay 73
  Dow's Hill Interpretation Centre 76, 87
  eating out 278–279
  Fig Tree Hill 76
  Harmony Hall 73
  Monks Hill Fort 76
  Nelson's Dockyard 76, 77
  Old Road 76
  St John's 73
  Shirley Heights 76
architecture
  gingerbread houses 141
  wattle and daub houses 141
Aruba 11, 124, 127, 128–129, 256–257, 273
  Andicouri 129
  Eagle Beach 129
  eating out 280
  Hooiberg 129
  Oranjestad 129
  Palm Beach 129
  San Nicolas 129

B

Barabal 55
Barbados 212–213, 266–267, 277
  Andromeda Gardens 220
  Atlantis Submarine 214
  Barbados National Trust 215
  Barbados Wildlife Reserve 116, 222
  Bridgetown 216–217
  Caribbean coast 218
  central Barbados 220
  Codrington College 220
  Crop Over Festival 218
  Drax Hall 222
  eating out 283
  Flower Forest 222
  Folkestone Marine Park 218
  food and drink 223
  Francia Plantation 220
  Grenade Hall Signal Station 222
  Gun Hill Signal Station 220
  Harrison's Cave 200, 218, 220
  Holetown 218
  Malibu Visitor Centre 218
  Morgan Lewis Mill 222
  Mountgay Visitor Centre 218
  Oistins 223
  organised tours 267
  Portvale Sugar Factory 218
  rum shops 215
  St Lawrence Gap 223
  St Nicholas Abbey 222
  Sam Lord's Castle 223
  Scotland 222
  south coast 223
  Speightstown 215, 218
  Trafalgar Square 11
  Turner's Hall Woods 222
  Tyrol Cot Heritage Village 217
Barbuda 69, 72, 76, 246–247
  frigatebird sanctuary 76
Beef Island 92
Bequia 53
boat-building 54, 70
Bolivar, Simon 135
Bonaire 124, 127, 130–131, 258, 273
  Bonaire Marine Park 130
  eating out 280
  Kralendijk 131
  Onima 131
  Pink Beach 131
  Rincon 131
  Washington Slagbaai Park 131
Bonaparte, Josephine 49, 118
Bridgetown (Barbados) 216–217
  Barbados Museum 217
  Careenage 216
  Garrison Savannah 217
  House of Assembly 216
  markets 216–217
  National Heroes Square 216
  St Michael's Cathedral 217
  Synagogue 217
buccaneers 175

C

calypso 238
camping 240
Canouan 55
Carnival 227, 234–235
Carriacou 52, 55
Castro, Fidel 167–168, 171, 173
Cayman Brac 162, 163, 165
Cayman Islands 162–165, 261–262, 275
  eating out 282
  Fort Christian 103
  Government House 102
  Virgin Islands Legislature Building 103
Charlotte Amalie (St Thomas) 102, 103
climate 241
Columbus, Christopher 28–29, 158, 193
conversion charts 253
Cooper Island 97
coral reefs 74–75, 200
Coward, Noël 159
crime and personal safety 241
cruising 20
Cuba 144–145, 166–175, 262–263, 275–276
  aquarium 74
  Bay of Pigs 171
  Cayo Largo 168
  Cayo Levisa 173
  Cienfuegos 174
  cigars 172
  Cojimar 173
  Cueva de Ambrosio 173
  eating out 282
  Guantanamo 173
  Havana 168, 170–171
  history 167–168
  La Vigia 171
  Moncada Garrison 173
  Pico Turquino 175
  Pinar del Rio Province 172, 173
  politics 18, 169
  Santiago de Cuba 175
  Sierra Maestra 175
  Trinidad 168, 174
  Varadero 173–174
  Viñales 173
  Zapata Peninsula 174
Culebra 195, 210, 211
Curaçao 11, 124, 127, 132–135, 258–259, 274
  Christoffel National Park 135
  Curaçao Liqueur Distillery 135
  Curaçao Sea Aquarium 74, 135
  eating out 280–281
  Hato Caves 135
  history 132–133
  Landhuis Brievengat 135
  Willemstad 133–134

D

disabilities, travellers with 241
Dominica 41–45, 242–243, 270
  Boiling Lake 42
  Botanical Gardens 42
  Cabrits National Park 44
  Canefield 44
  Carib Territory 43
  D'Auchamps Gardens 42
  Dominica Museum 42
  eating out 278
  Middleham Falls 44
  Morne Trois Pitons National Park 42
  Papillote Wilderness Retreat 42, 44
  Portsmouth 44
  Roseau 42
  Trafalgar Falls 42, 44
  Valley of Desolation 42
Dominican Republic 145, 182–193, 264–265, 276
  Altos de Chavón 187
  Amber Coast 188
  Amber Museum 188
  Boca Chica 193
  Cabarete 188
  Casa de Campo 187
  Cordillera Central 187
  eating out 282
  La Isabella 184
  Las Terrenas 190
  Los Haïtises National Park 190, 200
  Pico Duarte 185, 187
  Playa Dorado 188
  politics 185–186
  Puerto Plata 188
  Samaná 190
  Santiago 190
  Santo Domingo 184, 192–193
  Sosuà 188
  whale-watching 190
Drake, Francis 100, 102, 192

E

earthquakes 63
emergency telephone numbers 241

F

Fallen Jerusalem 97
fauna 116–117
  birdlife 116–117, 131, 153, 155, 189, 237
  marine life 74–75, 149, 202
  turtles 230
  zoos 116
Fédon, Julien 46
festivals 80, 108, 225
fêtes patronales 104
Fleming, Ian 159

Index

flora
African tulip tree 86
beaches and swamps 206, 211
botanical gardens 206
flowering trees 207
grasses and flowers 206
Lignum vitae tree 149
manchioneel 207
palm trees 189
poinciana 86
rain forest 111, 207
scrubland 206
Traveller's Tree 207
Flynn, Errol 160
folklore 45, 61
food and drink 22–24
bananas 14, 58, 160
coconuts 189
Créole 107
fruit drinks 59, 186
jerk 147
pepperpots 27, 52, 223
rum 22, 46, 114, 167, 221
specialities 24
spice crops 48, 51
tropical fruits 143
see also individual islands
French Antilles 104–123
Guadeloupe 11, 108–113
history 106–107
Martinique 11, 114–119
Saint-Barthélemy 120–121
Saint-Martin 122–123

G

gambling 209
Garvey, Marcus 150, 159
Gauguin, Paul 119
Ginger Island 97
Grand Cayman 162, 163, 164–165, 261–262, 275
Cayman Islands National Museum 164
Cayman Turtle Farm 165
George Town 164
Hell 165
Pedro St James Historic Site 165
Queen Elizabeth Botanic Gardens 165, 206
Seven Mile Beach 163, 164
Stingray City 165
Greene, Graham 180
Grenada 46–52, 243–244, 270
Bianca C wreck 49
Dougaldston Estate 51
eating out 278
Fédon's Camp 46
Grand Anse 49

Grand Etang National Park and Forest Reserve 51
La Sagesse Nature Centre 51
L'Anse aux Epines 51
Morne Fendue 52
Morne Rouge Bay 49
nutmeg processing plants 51
River Antoine Rum Distillery 51
St George's 47, 49
spices 48
The Grenadines 53–55, 245–246, 270
Bequia 53
Canouan 55
eating out 278
Mayreau 55
Mustique 55
Palm Island 55
Petit St Vincent 55
Tobago Cays 55
Tyrrel Bay 52
Union Island 55
Young Island 53, 65
Guadeloupe 11, 108–113, 252–253, 273
Allée du Manoir 110
Basse-Terre 108, 109, 110, 112
Basse-Terre (capital) 112
Cascade aux Ecrivisses 112
Chutes du Carbet 110
Domaine de Sévérin 112
eating out 280
Fort St-Charles 112
Grande-Terre 108–109, 110
Guadeloupe Aquarium 74
history 106–107
La Désirade 113
Maison de la Forêt 112
Maison du Bois 112
Maison du Cacao 112
Malendure 112
Morne-à-l'Eau 110
Musée du Rhum 112
offshore islands 113
Parc Archéologique des Roches Gravées 110
Parque Zoologique et Botanique 116
Pointe des Châteaux 110
Pointe-à-Pitre 109–110
Smugglers' Trail 111
Soufrière 106, 112
Trois-Rivières 110
Guana 92

H

Haiti 11, 176–181
history 178–179
Hamilton, Alexander 82
Havana (Cuba) 170–171
Casa de las Americas 171

Castillo de la Fuerza 170
Cementerio Cristobal Colon 171
Malecon 171
Memorial Museum 170
National Museum 170
Old Havana 170
Plaza de la Catedral 170
Plaza de la Revolución 171
Prado 171
Revolutionary Museum 171
health 242
health insurance 242
immunisation 242
Hemingway, Ernest 167, 171, 173, 202
Hispaniola 176, 185
history of the Caribbean
Arawaks and Caribs 12, 26–27, 43
Columbus, Christopher 28–29, 158, 193
emancipation 36–37
European settlement 12, 28–33
slave trade 33, 34
sugar industry 14, 33, 34–35
hotels 270–277
hurricanes 62–63

I

insurance 242

J

Jamaica 144, 146–161, 260–261, 263, 274–275
Appleton Rum Estate 149
Athenry Gardens 160
Bamboo Avenue 148
Belvedere Plantation 155
Berridale 160
Black River 148
Black River Safari 148
Bloody Bay 157
Blue Hole 160
Blue Mountains 148–149
Bob Marley Performing Centre 155
Boston Bay 160
Castleton 149
Catherine Hall 155
Cinchona 149
Cockpit Country 149
coffee factories 148
Coyaba River Gardens 159
Croydon in the Mountains 155
Dunn's River Falls 158
eating out 281–282
fauna 153, 155
Fern Gully 159
Firefly 159

food and drink 22, 147, 158
Frenchman's Cove 160
Good Hope 155
Great River 155
Greenwood Great House 154–155
Harmony Hall 159
Hedonism II 157
history 146–147
John Crow Mountains 160
Kingston 150
Little London 155
Long Bay 157
Mandeville 153
maroons 147
Marshall's Pen 153
Martha Brae river 155
Maya Lodge 149
Montego Bay 154–155
Moore Town 160
music 152
Negril 157
Nine Miles 156
Nonsuch Caves 160
Ocho Rios 158
Port Antonio 160
Port Royal 151
Prospect Plantation 159
Rafter's Village 155
Reach Falls 160
Rio Grande 160
Rock 155
Rockland Feeding Station 155
Rose Hall 154
Round Hill 155
St Ann's Bay 158–159
Seaford Town 155
Seville Nueva 159
Shaw Park Botanical Gardens 159
Shooter's Hill 153
Spanish Town 150
Treasure Beach 148
Tryall 155
World's End Rum Distillery 149
YS Falls 148
James, CLR 229
Jamesby 55
Jost van Dyke 96

K

Kingston (Jamaica) 150
Bob Marley Museum 150
Devon House 150
Hope Botanical Gardens 150
National Gallery of Art 150
National Heroes Park 150
New Kingston 150
Parade 150

L

La Désirade 104, 113
landscapes 10–11

285

Index

Leeward Islands 66–87
Anguilla 69, 70–71
Antigua and Barbuda 69, 72–77
history 68–69
Montserrat 69, 78–79
Nevis 69, 82–83
St Kitts (St Christopher) 84–87
Les Saintes 113
Lewis, Sir Arthur 57
Little Cayman 162, 163, 165

Marie-Galante 113
Château Murat 113
Le Trou à Diable 113
marijuana 161
markets 50
Marley, Bob 156
Martinique 11, 114–119, 254–255, 256, 273
aquarium 74
Balata 119
butterfly farm 119
Case-Pilote 119
Diamond Rock 118
eating out 280
Écomusée de la Martinique 118
Fort-de-France 115
Grande Anse des Salines 118
Habitation Clément 118
history 106–107
Jardin de Balata 119
Le Carbet 119
Le Martin 118
Les Anses-d'Arlets 118
Maison de la Banane 118
Maison de la Canne 118
Musée Gauguin 119
Musée Historique 119
Musée de la Pagerie 118
Musée Volcanique 119
Pointe du Bout 118
Rhum St James rum distillery 118
Ste-Anne 118
St-Pierre 119
Trois Rivières 118
Mayreau 55
money 242
Montego Bay (Jamaica) 154–155
Craft Market 154
Doctor's Cave Beach 154
Marine Park 154
Pork Pit 154
Sam Sharpe Square 154

Montserrat 69, 78–79, 247, 271
eating out 279
Great Alps Waterfall 79
Helicopter flights 79
Montserrat Volcano Observatory 79
Plymouth 78
Morgan, Henry 101
music
calypso 238
festivals 80
marching bands 152
reggae and soca 80, 152
salsa and merengue 80–81, 186
steel bands 81
trovas (Cuban ballads) 169
zouk and compas 81
Mustique 55

Naipaul, V.S. 228, 232
Navy Island 160
Necker Island 96, 271–272
Nelson, Lord 77, 83, 216
Netherlands Antilles 124–143
Aruba 11, 124, 127, 128–129
Bonaire 124, 127, 130–131
Curaçao 11, 124, 127, 132–135
history 125, 126
Saba 124, 127, 136–137
Sint Eustatius 124, 127, 138–139
Sint Maarten 124, 127, 140, 142
Nevis 69, 82–83, 247–248, 271
Bath Hotel and Spring 83
Charlestown 82
eating out 279
Fig Tree Church 83
Fort Charles 83
Lover's Lane Beach 83
Museum of Nevis History 82
Nelson Museum 83
Newcastle 83
Oualie Beach 83
Pinney's Beach 82–83
Norman Island 97

obeah 179
Oranjestad (Aruba) 129
Archeological Museum 129
Fort Zoutman 129
Historical Museum 129

Numismatic Museum 129
Oranjestad (Sint Eustatius) 139
Fort Oranje 139
Quills crater 139
Sint Eustatius Historical Museum 139

Palm Island 55
Palmer, Annie 154
Patterson, PJ 13
Peter Island 96, 97, 272
Petit Bateau 55
Petit Rameau 55
Petit St Vincent 55
Petit Tobac 55
Petite Martinique 52
Pigeon Island 59
pirates 100–111, 157, 177
Pissarro, Camille 103
Pointe-à-Pitre (Guadeloupe) 109–110
Aquarium 110
market 110
Musée St-John Perse 110
Musée Schoelcher 110
Place de la Victoire 109
politics 18–19
Ponce (Puerto Rico) 201
Castillo Serallés 201
El Vigia 201
Parque de Bombas 201
Ponce Museum of Art 201
Ponce de Léon, Juan 30, 196, 205
Port Royal (Jamaica) 151
Fort Charles 151
Giddy House 151
Maritime Museum 151
Port of Spain (Trinidad) 228–229
Botanic Gardens 229
Emperor Valley Zoo 116, 229
National Museum and Art Gallery 228
Red House 228
Savannah 229
Prickly Pear Cays 71
Puerto Rico 11, 145, 194–211, 203, 265–266, 276–277
Arecibo Observatory 198, 199
Bacardi Rum Distillery and Museum 208
Boquerón 203
Caguana Indian Ceremonial Park 199
Caja de Muertos 201
Carite Forest Reserve 198
Coamo 198
Cordillera Central 198–199
Culebra 195, 210, 211

Desecheo 203
Doña Juana Recreational Centre 198
eating out 283
El Yunque Caribbean National Forest 211
fauna 211
food and drink 195, 197, 208
Guilarte Forest Reserve 199
Hacienda Buena Vista 201
Hacienda Gripiñas 198
Hacienda Juanita 199
history 196–197
Isla Verde 208
Lares 199
Las Cabezas de San Juan 211
Luquillo 211
mangrove swamps 211
Maricao Forest Reserve 199
Mayagüez 199
Mayagüez Zoo 199
Mona 203
Palmas del Mar 198
paradores 203
Parguera 203
Piñones 211
Ponce 201
Rio Camuy Cave Park 199, 200
ruta panoramica 198
San Cristobal Canyon 198
San Germán 203
San Juan (New City) 194, 208
San Juan (Old City) 194, 204–205
Tibes Indian Ceremonial Centre 201
Toro Negro Forest Reserve 198
Vieques 195, 210

Rackham, Jack 157
rastafarianism 17, 161
Redonda 72
religion 16–17
restaurants 278–283
Rhone wreck 97
Rhys, Jean 41
Richards, Viv 73
river bathing 45
Rodney, Admiral 113, 139
Round Rock 97

Saba 124, 127, 136–137, 259–260, 274
The Bottom 136–137
eating out 281

Flat Point 137
Fort Bay 137
Hell's Gate 137
Ladder Bay 137
The Road 136
Saba Museum
  137
Windwardside
  137
sailing 94
**Saint-Barthélemy
  (St Barts)** 120–121,
  256, 273
eating out 280
Gustavia 121
Inter Oceans Museum
  121
Museé de Saint-Barth
  121
St-Jean 121
St Croix 91, 98, 250,
  272
Buck Island 98
Christiansted 98
Cruzian Rum Distillery
  98
eating out 279
Frederiksted 74, 98
St Croix Aquarium 74,
  98
St George Village
  Botanical Garden 98
Whim Great House
  98
St George's (Grenada)
  47, 49
Carenage 49
Grenada National
  Museum 49
Market Square 49
Yellow Poui Art Gallery
  49
St John 91, 99,
  250–251, 272
Annaberg Plantation
  99
Cruz Bay 99
eating out 279
organised tours 250
Elaine Ione Sprauve
  Library and Museum
  99
St John's (Antigua) 73
Antigua and Barbuda
  Museum 73
Redcliffe Quay 73
St John's Cathedral 73
St Kitts (St Christopher)
  84–87, 248–249,
  250, 272
Basseterre 85
Black Rocks 86
Brimstone Hill 85, 86,
  87
Caribelle Batik 86
eating out 279
Friar's Bay 86
Frigate Bay 86
Old Road Bay 86
rock carvings 86
Romney Manor 86
sugar cane factory 86
St Lucia 56–63,
  244–245, 270–271
Castries 57, 59
Rain Forest Reserve
  60

Diamond Baths 60
eating out 278
Errard Plantation 60
Marigot Bay 60
Morne Coubaril Estate
  60
Pigeon Island 59
Pitons 60
Rodney Bay 59
Soufrière 60
Saint-Martin 122–123,
  255–256, 273
eating out 280
Grand-Case 123
Marigot 122, 123
Musée de Saint Martin
  123
St Thomas 91, 102–103,
  250–251, 253, 272
Charlotte Amalie
  102–103
Coral World 74, 102
eating out 279–280
Estate St Peter
  Greathouse 102
St Vincent 64–65,
  245–246, 271
Buccament Valley 65
eating out 278
Kingstown 65
rock carvings 65
St Vincent Botanic
  Gardens 65
Salt Island 97
San Juan (Puerto Rico)
  194, 204–205, 208
Capilla del Santo Cristo
  205
Casa Blanca 205
Castillo de San Felipe
  del Morro 87, 205
Catedral de San Juan
  205
Condado 208
Convento Dominicano
  205
El Capitolio 208
Fuerte San Cristóbal
  87, 205
Hato Rey 208
La Fortaleza 205
Museo Pablo Casals
  204
Museo de San Juan
  204
New City 194, 208
Old City 194, 204–205
Rió Piedras Botanical
  Gardens 208
Sandy Island 71
Santiago (Dominican
  Republic)
Museo Tomás Morel
  del Arte Folklorico
  190
Santo Domingo
  (Dominican Republic)
  184, 192–193
Alcazar de Colón
  192
Atarazana 192
Avenida del Puerto
  192
Calle de las Damas
  192
Casa de Bastidas
  193

Catedral Santa María
  la Menor, Primada
  de America 193
eating out 193
Faro a Colón 192,
  193
Fortaleza Ozama
  193
Jardin Botanico
  Nacional 193
Malecon 193
Museo de las Casas
  Reales 192
Palacio Nacional
  193
Panteon Nacional
  192
Parque Independencia
  193
Parque Zoologico
  Nacional 116
Plaza de la Cultura
  193
shipwrecks 95, 97
Sint Eustatius 124, 127,
  138–139, 261–262,
  274
eating out 281
Fort de Windt 139
Oranjestad 139
Quill's crater 139
Sint Maarten 124, 127,
  140, 142, 255–256,
  274
eating out 281
Koolbaai (Cole Bay)
  142
Mulletbaai (Mullet Bay)
  142
Philipsburg 142
Simsonbaai (Simpson
  Bay) 142
Sint Maarten Museum
  142
zoo 142
Sir Francis Drake
  Channel 97
smuggling 54
sport and games
  Arawak games 201
  baseball 219
  big game fishing
    202
  cock-fighting 197,
    209, 219
  cricket 73, 219
  dominoes 209
  watersports 94, 95,
    97
student and youth travel
  240
Stuyvesant, Peter
  142
sugar industry 14, 33,
  34–35, 191

T

telephones 241
Terre-de-Bas 113
Terre-de-Haut 113
Tobago 224, 226, 233,
  236–237, 267–268,
  277
Argyle Waterfall 237
Back Bay 236

Botanical Gardens
  237
Buccoo 236
Buccoo Reef 236
Castara 237
Courland Bay 144,
  236
eating out 283
Englishman's Bay
  237
Fort King George
  237
history 226
Kings Bay 237
Little Tobago 237
Nylon Pool 236
Parlatuvier 237
Pigeon Point 233
Plymouth 236
Roxborough 237
Scarborough 237
Store Bay 233
Sunday School
  236
Tobago Forest Reserve
  237
Tobago Museum
  237
Tobago Cays 55
toilets 242
Tortola 92, 272
the Baths 93
Beef Island 92
Cane Garden Bay
  92
eating out 279
Long Bay 92
Long Look 92
Road Town 92
Smuggler's Cove 92
tourism 20–21
Toussaint l'Ouverture
  36, 178
Trade Winds 62
Trinidad 224, 225, 226,
  228–232, 267–268,
  277
Angostura factory
  231
Asa Wright Nature
  Centre 232
Carnival 227,
  234–235
Caroni Swamp 231
Chaguanas 232
Chaguaramas
  peninsula 229
eating out 283
fauna 117, 224
history 226
Lopinot Complex
  231
Maracas Bay 231
Maraval Valley 231
Mount St Benedict
  Monastery 231
Pitch Lake 10, 232
Pointe-à-Pierre 232
Port of Spain
  228–229
Queen's Park
  Savannah 229
St Joseph 231
San Fernando 232
Toco 232
Trinidad and Tobago
  145, 224–238

Index/Acknowledgements

V

Vieques 195, 210
  Casa del Frances 210
  Esperanza 210
  phosphorescent lake 210
Virgin Gorda 91, 93
  the Baths 93
  Biras Creek 93
  Gun Creek 93
  Spanish Town 93
Virgin Islands 88–103
  Anegada 96, 97
  British Virgin Islands (B V I) 89, 90, 91, 249, 271–2, 278
  eating out 279

history 90
Jost van Dyke 96
Necker Island 96
St Croix 91, 98
St John 91, 99
St Thomas 91, 102–3
Sir Francis Drake Channel 97
Tortola 92
travel between islands 96, 99
United States Virgin Islands (USVI) 89, 90–1, 272, 279
Virgin Gorda 91, 93, 272
  eating out 279
volcanoes 63
voodoo 17, 179, 180–1

W

Walcott, Derek 57
Willemstad (Curaçao) 133–4
  Beth Haim Cemetery 134
  Coney Island Amusement Park 134
  Curaçao Museum 134
  Floating Market 50, 133
  Fort Amsterdam 133–4
  Handelskade 133
  Jewish Museum 133
  Konigin Emmabrug 134

Mikve Israel Synagogue 133
Otrabanda 134
Punda 133
Williams, Eric 228, 229
Windward Islands 38–65
  Dominica 41–5
  Grenada 46–52
  The Grenadines 53–5
  history 40
  St Lucia 56–63
  St Vincent 64–5
  travel between 38
Wouk, Herman 98

Y

Young Island 53, 65

Picture credits

The Automobile Association would like to thank the following for their assistance in the preparation of this book:
ALLSPORT UK LTD: 219a Cricket. **BRIDGEMAN ART LIBRARY:** 178–9 *Voodoo Dance* by Jean Pierre; 178 *Voodoo ceremony around a tree* by Valcin. **S CAMPBELL:** 162 Sunrise at Brac Reef; 163 Totem pole; 164 Swimming with stingrays; 165 Straw-weaver. **MARY EVANS PICTURE LIBRARY:** 25a Raiding cattle ranches; 28–9a Columbus's fleet 1492; 28 Columbus lands San Salvador; 29 Columbus; 30–1 Drake attacks Spanish; 30 Pirates; 31 Buccaneer; 32–3a Slaves working; 32 Slaves dancing; 33 Slave in chains; 34–5 Treadmill; 35 Sugar mill; 36–7 Emancipation parade; 36 Emancipation; 37 Burke in House of Commons; 43b Spaniards and Caribs; 100b Blackbeard; 101 Spaniards loading ship. **J HENDERSON:** 9a Barbados; 10a St Vincent; 12–13 Children; 15b Oranjestad, Aruba; 16–17a Church, Trinidad; 18–9a Poster; 27 Arawak carvings; 40 Calabas Hotel; 49 St Georges; 50a Market, St Georges; 52 Maurice Bishop, St Georges; 53 Admiralty Harbour; 68 Man; 70 Boat; 76 Barbuda; 83 Nevis; 83 Old windmill; 91b Bombas, Tortola; 96 Jost van Dyke; 98 Frederiksted, St Croix; 103 Legislature, Charlotte Amalie; 112a Guadaloupe cemetery; 113a Boats; 113b Deshaires; 120 Islands; 121a Airport, St Barts; 121b Club La Dance; 124a Aruba; 124b Bolatabla, Curaçao; 125–6 Sailing ship; 125 Saba; 126 Craft stall; 128–9 Oranjestad, Aruba; 129a Windmill; 129b Jet ski; 130, 131 Salt stacks, Bonaire; 134–5 Handelsgade, Willemstad; 134a b Floating market; 135 Fisherman; 136 House; 137a Windwardside, Saba; 137b Flags; 137c sign; 138 Sint Eustatius; 139a Sign; 139b Children; 140 Car; 141a St Georges; 143c Breadfruit; 166 Car; 167 Main Square, Trinidad, Cuba; 168 Poster; 169a Santa Clara; 169b House, Cuba; 170a Old Havana; 170b Cathedral, Old Havana; 173 Cien Fuegos; 176 Tap-tap; 177 Fishermen; 180–1 Dessalines barracks; 181a Sans-Souci Palace; 181b Man; 183 Carvings; 186 Windsurfers; 187 Hotel Sousa; 189 Palm fronds; 190 Boats; 191 Sugar mill; 192 Children; 193a Columbus lighthouse; 193b Columbus Palace; 197b Festival of the Innocents; 198 Hacienda Gripinas; 210 Fire station, Ponce; 203 Sunset, Puerto Rico; 206 Croton; 210a Casa del Frances, Vieques; 211 Limers Bar, Esperanza; 215a Bridgetown Harbour; 215b Sombaero; 219b Baseball; 228 Canon, Trinidad; 234b Carnival, St Lucia; 236 Shack; 238b Calypso singer. **IMAGES COLOUR LIBRARY:** 179 Mask. **IMAGES DES ANTILLES:** 109 Course de Yoles; 155 Images des Antilles. **INTERNATIONAL PHOTOBANK:** 20a Ocho Rios market; 24 drinks; 45b Dunn's River Falls; 47, 50b St George's Saturday Market; 58b Woman and bananas; 80–1 Steel band; 155 Straw market, Montego Bay; 159 Beach, Ocho Rios; 160 Port Antonio; 206–7 Royal Poincian tree; 233 Tobago steel band. **NATURE PHOTOGRAPHERS LTD:** 74–5 Orange clown fish, Queen Angel fish (S C Bisserot); 116a Scarlet Ibis (P R Sterry); 117 Iguana (E A Janes); 230a Green turtle (D A Smith); 230b Loggerhead turtle (J Sutherland). **PARIA PUBLISHING CO LTD:** 61a The Soucouyant; 61b Mama Dio; 61c Pappa Bois. **REX FEATURES LTD:** 152a,c Shabba Ranks; 152b Shaggy; 156a,b Bob Marley. **ROYAL GEOGRAPHICAL SOCIETY:** 25 Map **SPECTRUM COLOUR LIBRARY:** 6 Bequia; 22–3a Buffet; 38 Nightlife; 81 Musician; 95a Faune Sous Marine; 111 Rainforest; 131 Kralendick Town, Bonaire; 133 Curaçao; 162 Drinks; 171 Tropicana cabaret, Havana; 184 Mexican night; 185 market; 188 Restaurant, Puerto Plata; 189 Palm-fringed beach; 200 Shell; 234–5 Carnival; 238a Nightlife. **THE MANSELL COLLECTION LTD:** 26 Indians sowing maize. **ZEFA PICTURE LIBRARY (UK) LTD:** 200a Coral.

All remaining pictures are held in the Association's own library (**AA PHOTO LIBRARY**) with contributions from: **P BAKER:** 2; 4; 7; 9b; 11; 13b; 14–5; 16b; 19; 20b; 21; 25b; 39; 41; 42; 43a; 44; 48a,b; 51; 54a,b; 55; 56; 57; 58a; 59; 62–3a; 62b; 63; 64; 65; 66; 67a; 68–9; 71; 72; 73; 77; 78a; 79; 80; 84; 85a,b; 86; 87a,b; 90; 91a; 92a,b; 93; 94a,b; 96–7; 99; 102; 105a,b; 106a,b; 107; 108; 109a,b; 110a,b; 111b,c; 112b; 114; 115a,b; 118; 119a,b; 122; 123a,b,c; 140; 141a,b; 142a,b; 143a,b; 144–5; 161a,b; 191a; 194; 194–5; 196; 197a; 199a,b; 202; 204a,b; 207; 208; 209b; 210b; 213; 214; 216; 217; 218; 220; 221a; 222; 23; 226a,b; 227; 229; 231; 232; 269a. **R HOLMES:** 100–1. **D LYONS:** 8; 60. **S & O MATHEWS:** 77. **C SAWYER** 174, 175 **A SOUTER:** 209a. **R VICTOR:** 5a,b; 10b; 12; 23b; 45a; 88; 89; 95b; 116b; 146; 149a,b; 150; 151a,b; 153; 154; 157; 158; 161c; 239a. **J WYAND:** 3; 67b; 78b; 125; 239b; 269b.

Acknowledgements

The Automobile Association would also like to thank the Sandridge Beach Hotel, Barbados, and the Ocean View Hotel, Barbados for their assistance in the making of this book

Contributors

Revision copy editor: Grapevine Publishing Services
Original copy editor: Nia Williams   Revision verifier: Justin Henderson